GEORGE W. GAWRYCH, a professor of history at Baylor University, taught for 19 years at the U.S. Army Command and General Staff College, Fort Leavenworth (Kansas), including one year as a visiting professor at the United States Military Academy. He is the author of *The Crescent and the Eagle: Ottoman Rule, Islam and the Albanians, 1874–1913* (I.B.Tauris), *The Albatross of Decisive Victory: War and Policy between Egypt and Israel in the 1967 and 1973 Arab-Israeli Wars* and co-author of *Armed Peacekeepers in Bosnia*.

The Young
ATATÜRK

From Ottoman Soldier
to Statesman of Turkey

GEORGE W. GAWRYCH

I.B.TAURIS

LONDON · NEW YORK

Published in 2013 by I.B.Tauris & Co Ltd
6 Salem Road, London W2 4BU
175 Fifth Avenue, New York NY 10010
www.ibtauris.com

Distributed in the United States and Canada
Exclusively by Palgrave Macmillan
175 Fifth Avenue, New York NY 10010

ISBN: 978 1 78076 322 4

A full CIP record for this book is available from the British Library
A full CIP record is available from the Library of Congress

Library of Congress Catalog Card Number: available

Set in Arno Pro by Tetragon, London

Printed and bound in Great Britain by T.J. International, Padstow, Cornwall

Contents

List of Images

List of Maps

List of Abbreviations

ABE   *Atatürk'ün Bütün Eserleri,* vols 1–15. İstanbul: Kaynak Yayınları, 1998–2005.

ATASE   Genelkurmay Askeri Tarih ve Stratejik Etüt Başkanlığı (General Staff Institute of Military History and Strategic Studies).

ATBD   *Askeri Tarih Belgeleri Dergisi* (Review of Military History Documents).

BCA   Başbakanlık Cumhuriyet Arşivi (Prime Ministry's Archives of the Republic).

BDFA   *British Documents on Foreign Affairs: Reports and Papers from the Foreign Office Confidential Print, Part II: From the First to the Second World War, Series B: Turkey, Iran, and the Middle East 1918–1939,* edited by Robin Bidwell. Washington, D.C.: University Publications of America, 1985.

BDH, *Kafkas Cephesi* (Caucasus Front)   T. C. Genelkurmay Başkanlığı, Harb Tarihi Dairesi. *Birinci Dünya Harbi'nde Türk Harbi: Kafkas Cephesi, 2 nci Cilt, 2 nci Kısım Kafkas Cephesi, 2 nci Ordu Harekatı: 1916–1918.* Ankara: Genelkurmay Basımevi, 1978.

BOA   Başbakanlık Osmanlı Arşivi (Prime Ministry's Ottoman Archives).

CAA   Cumhurbaşkanlık Atatürk Arşivi (Atatürk Presidential Archives).

HTVD   *Harp Tarihi Vesikaları Dergisi* (Review of War History Documents).

TBMM   Türkiye Büyük Millet Meclisi (Grand National Assembly of Turkey).

TİH	*Türk İstiklal Harbi* (Turkish War of Independence), T. C. Genelkurmay Başkanlığı (Turkish General Staff Directorate), Harb Tarihi Dairesi (War History Division).
TİH, *Ayaklanmalar* (Rebellions)	T. C. Genelkurmay Başkanlığı, Harb Tarihi Dairesi. *Türk İstiklal Harbi*, VI: *İstiklal Harbinde Ayaklanmalar (1919–1921)*. Ankara: Genelkurmay Basımevi, 1974.
TİH, *Büyük Taarruz* (Great Offensive)	T. C. Genelkurmay Başkanlığı, Harb Tarihi Dairesi. *Turk İstiklal Harbi*, II: *Batı Cephesi, 6/2: Büyük Taarruz (1–31 Ağustos 1922)*. Ankara: Genelkurmay Basimevi, 1995.
TİH, *Doğu Cepehesi* (Eastern Front)	T. C. Genelkurmay Başkanlığı, Harb Tarihi Dairesi. *Türk İstiklal Harbi*, III: *Doğu Cephesi (1919–1921)*. Ankara: Genelkurmay Basımevi, 1965.
TİH, *Güney Cepehesi* (Southern Front)	T. C. Genelkurmay Başkanlığı, Harb Tarihi Dairesi. *Türk İstiklal Harbi*, IV: *Güney Cephesi (15 Mayıs 1919–20 Ekim 1921)*. Ankara: Genelkurmay Basımevi, 1966.
TİH, *Hazırlık* (Preparation)	T. C. Genelkurmay Başkanlığı, Harb Tarihi Dairesi. *Türk İstiklal Harbi*, II: *Batı Cephesi, 6/1: Büyük Taarruza Hazırlık ve Büyük Taarruz (10 Ekim 1921 – 31 Temmuz 1922)*. Ankara: Genelkurmay Basımevi, 1967.
TİH, *İdari Faaliıyetler* (Administration)	T. C. Genelkurmay Başkanlığı, Harb Tarihi Dairesi. *Türk İstiklal Harbi*, VII: *İdari Faaliyetler (15 Mayıs 1919 – 2 Kasım 1923)*. Ankara: Genelkurmay Basımevi, 1975.
TİH, *İnönü*	T. C. Genelkurmay Başkanlığı, Harb Tarihi Dairesi. *Türk İstiklal Harbi*. II: *Batı Cephesi, 3: Birinci, İkinci İnönü, Aslıhanlar ve Dumlupınar Muhaerebleri (9 Kasım 1920 – 15 Nisan 1921)*. Ankara: Genelkurmay Basımevi, 1966.
TİH. *Kütahya*	T. C. Genelkurmay Başkanlığı, Harb Tarihi Dairesi. *Türk İstiklal Harbi*, II: *Batı Cephesi, 4:, Kütahya, Eskişehir Muhaerebleri (15 Mayıs 1921 – 25 Temmuz 1921)*. Ankara: Genelkurmay Basımevi, 1974.
TİH. *Sakarya*	T. C. Genelkurmay Başkanlığı, Harb Tarihi Dairesi. *Türk İstiklal Harbi*, II: *Batı Cephesi, 5/1, Sakarya Meydan Muharebesinden Önceki Olaylar ve Mevzi İlerisindeki Harekat (25 Temmuz – 22 Ağustos 1921)*. Ankara: Genelkurmay Basımevi, 1972.

TİH, *Sivas* T. C. Genelkurmay Başkanlığı, Harb Tarihi Dairesi. *Türk İstiklal Harbi, II: Batı Cephesi, 2: Sivas Kongresi ve Heyeti Temsiliye Devri, İstanbul'un İtilaf Devletleri tarafından resmen işgalı, Türkiye Büyük Millet Meclisi Hükğmetinin kurulması, Batı Anadolu ve Trakya cephelerinde Yunan ileri harekatı (4 Eylul 1919 – 9 Kasım 1920).* Ankara: Genelkurmay Basımevi, 1965.

TİH, *Son Safhası* (Last Phase) T. C. Genelkurmay Başkanlığı, Harb Tarihi Dairesi. *Türk İstiklal Harbi, II: Batı Cephesi, 6/4: İstiklal Harbinin Son Safhası (18 Eylul 1922 – 1 Kasım 1923).* Ankara: Genelkurmay Basımevi, 1969.

TİTE Türk İnkılap Tarihi Enstitüsü (Institute for the History of Turkish Revolution).

TSKT, *1908–1920* T. C. Genelkurmay Başkanlığı, Askeri Tarih ve Stratejik Etüt Başkanlığı. *Türk Silahlı Kuvvetleri Tarihi, III/6 (1908–1920).* Ankara: Genelkurmay Basımevi, 1996.

TSKT, *TBMM* T. C. Genelkurmay Başkanlığı, Askeri Tarih ve Stratejik Etüt Başkanlığı. *Türk Silahlı Kuvvetleri Tarihi, Türkiye Büyük Millet Meclisi Hükümeti Dönemi, IV/1 (23 Nisan 1920 – 29 Ekim 1923).* Ankara: Genelkurmay Basımevi, 1984.

Introduction

Perhaps more than the mind, logic, or judgment, what makes history is feelings/sentiments. (*Tarihi yapan akıl, mantık, muhakeme değil; belki bunlardan ziyade hissiyattır.*)

Mustafa Kemal, Adana, 15 March 1923[1]

His [Atatürk's] head burned with a thousand ideas, his inside with a thousand desires, but he never deviated from his reason. Within him lay both the idealist and the realist. He was always on fire and always so calculating. It is said that intelligence requires patience. He was never in a hurry and he did not let an opportunity escape his grasp.

Falih Rıfkı Atay[2]

MUSTAFA KEMAL ATATÜRK (1881–1938) ranks among the great leaders of the twentieth century, a product of his time and yet a man in his own right who left a record of significant achievements both as a military commander and a statesman. This study analyzes Atatürk's role as a military commander *and* as a political leader who engaged in both war-fighting and republic-building during the War of Independence (1919–22) in Turkey. In the last year of this national struggle, Atatürk formally wore two hats: political head of a provisional government and the commander in chief of the army. Among modern war leaders, Atatürk thus belongs to a small minority who successfully combined political leadership and field command in war, much like Frederick the Great and Napoleon who as heads of state also directed tactical battles. Both men, however, ruled over powerful states and waged conventional wars, whereas Atatürk faced a unique set of circumstances. He first had to establish himself as the legitimate leader over a fragmented national resistance movement while, at the same time, striving to build an effective government, rebuild a defeated army, and mobilize the people in a major war effort. To achieve victory, Atatürk employed a military strategy that evolved from essentially guerrilla warfare to a decisive campaign waged against a conventional army. The War of Independence thus became the first major modern war of liberation in the twentieth century, and Atatürk gained deserved recognition from the struggle as a gifted and talented leader.

Despite the plethora of publications about him, no one has seriously and systematically studied the military Atatürk. Furthermore, no Westerner has researched in the military archives on this topic, or, for that matter, in other archives in Turkey. In addressing this deficiency in Western scholarship, I conducted the bulk of my archival research in the Archives of the Directorate of Military History and Strategic Studies (ATASE), but also worked in the Institute of the History of the Turkish Revolution (TİTE), the Prime Ministry's Archives of the Republic (BCA), the Atatürk Presidential Archives (CAA), and the Prime Ministry's Ottoman Archives (BOA). These archives contain mainly hand-written Ottoman documents in the Arabic script, and thus are inaccessible to many researchers on Atatürk who have to rely solely on the Latin alphabet publications.

To gain insights into the development of Atatürk's intellect and character, I analyze Atatürk's own military publications, personal notebooks, official reports and correspondence, commands, letters, and speeches. These sources help decipher what and how Atatürk thought. The military dimensions of his thoughts and actions are then integrated into an analysis of leadership in the War of Independence when Atatürk balanced the interplay of policy, war, diplomacy, and strategy to succeed in the art of politics and war. Included in my research were battlefield tours of Sakarya and the Great Offensive. For a general framework for analysis, I use three terms or concepts that Atatürk frequently employed in his writings and speeches: *his*, *dimağ*, and *vicdan*. *His* translates into English as "feeling/sentiment," human emotion associated in Atatürk's mind with the "heart" (*kalb*). Emotions form an integral part of the human psyche, and, as a leader, Atatürk had to manage his own and those of others with a talent that we would commonly label today as emotional intelligence or intuitive understanding. *Dimağ*, for its part, addresses the cognitive activities of humans. In his famous two-volume dictionary *Kamus-i Türki*, or *Turkish Dictionary* published in 1899, the year Atatürk entered the War College in Istanbul, Şemseddin Sami Frasheri, the great Albanian Ottoman linguist, offers three definitions for *dimağ*: *beyin*, or simply the brain in one's head; *akıl*, or reason, the capacity to learn and understand; and *şuur*, or understanding, comprehension, intelligence.[3] As used by Atatürk, *dimağ* best translates as mind, in the sense of intellect. Atatürk substituted words like "reason" (*akıl*), "intellect" (*zihin*), and "logic" (*mantık*) for *dimağ*.

Kamus-i Türki provides several definitions for *vicdan*, including "discovering through the senses" and "feeling (*his*) in the heart or sentiment (*duygu*)." A relatively new meaning, however, came into common usage by the last quarter of the nineteenth century: "the imperceptible feeling in the heart that derives pleasure from doing good and pain from doing bad." Here, Şemseddin Sami translated *vicdan* to mean *conscience* in French.[4] The excellent *A Turkish and English*

Lexicon, edited by James A. Redhouse and published in 1890, offers four definitions for *vicdan*, the last two being "conscience" and "consciousness."[5] Atatürk
understood *vicdan* as conscience, a moral compass that enables individuals and
society to distinguish between good and evil, to guide them in their decision-
making and their actions. Atatürk spoke of both personal and a national *vicdan*
as values and virtues that drive individuals and societies to strive for noble ends.
He associated *fazilet*, or virtue, and *ahlak*, or morals with *vicdan*.

In this study, I use the Kemalist triad of sentiment (*his*), mind (*dimağ*), and
conscience (*vicdan*) as a new and systematic framework for analyzing Atatürk
as a leader. All three elements were in a continuous interplay with each other,
but not always with a discernible line distinguishing them. Studies on Atatürk,
however, emphasize the centrality of reason in his life without integrating emotions and conscience into the analysis. Yes, Atatürk prized science and rational
knowledge, but he also valued intuitive understanding and the power of emotions. Emotional intelligence was essential to be an effective leader of men, and
Atatürk devoted time to studying and discerning the human psyche. He was
thus a good listener and observer of fellow human beings. As noted in the first
quote of this introduction, Atatürk toyed with the notion that sentiment might
even be more important than reason in moving people and shaping history.
Together, sentiment, mind, and conscience helped shape Atatürk's character and
purpose-driven life, and after the War of Independence, Atatürk led the Turkish
Revolution along these three axes.

I use personal names in this study. It was not until 1934 that Atatürk required
all citizens to adopt surnames. Until then, Muslims used personal names. Before
the law, Atatürk signed his name as Mustafa Kemal or just the initials MK. When
mentioning individuals for the first time, this study identifies their full name while
placing the surname in parentheses and then continues to use the personal name.
İsmet (İnönü) thus remains İsmet through the remainder of the book. Mustafa
Kemal becomes Atatürk only in the conclusion.

A note of appreciation is necessary. I would like to thank the Fulbright Scholar
Program and Baylor University for funding my research trips to Turkey. The nine
months spent in Ankara as a Senior Fulbright Research Scholar permitted me
to conduct extensive and uninterrupted research in the archives and libraries of
Turkey. Moreover, several individuals played an important role in this study and
deserve special recognition. Colonel Dr. Ahmet Tetik and Dr. Serdar Demirtaş
enriched my understanding of Atatürk through serious conversations over tea
during my time in the military archives. I would also like to thank the following
individuals who personally facilitated my research in their particular institutions:
Dr. Ali Birinci, the Director of the Turkish Historical Society; Dr. Temuçin
Ertan, the Director of the Institute of the History of the Turkish Revolution;

Dr. Mustafa Budak, the Director of the Prime Ministry's Ottoman Archives in Istanbul; Tuncer Yılmaz, Deputy Director of the Library of the Grand National Assembly of Turkey; and officials at the Prime Ministry's Republican Archives, the Atatürk Presidential Archives, and the Anıtkabir Library. I acknowledge Donald L. Gilmore, my editor and friend, for his critical editing and polishing with great patience and steady encouragement. Daughter Teresa offered her skills and eye to prepare the photos, and together with son Andrew, provided intellectual and moral support over the course of the project. My wife Joan drew the maps in this study, as well as critically commented on all drafts. I dedicate this book to Joan, my true companion (*refika*) and a source of love, wisdom, and inspiration.

1

The Making of an Ottoman Soldier

War is a matter of vital importance to the State; the province of life and death; the road to survival or ruin. It is mandatory that it be thoroughly studied.

Sun Tzu[1]

Not being reinforced by my experience and continuous studies, my ideas on people and life are, more or less, changing from my former ones.

Mustafa Kemal, Syria, late 1906 or early 1907

MUSTAFA KEMAL ATATÜRK was a serious student of people and life who believed in the power of the mind and intuition. An avid and serious reader, he devoted himself to the study of war outside the classroom, while at the same time broadening his intellectual interests beyond the military profession into other fields. For Mustafa Kemal, theory and practical knowledge were important vehicles for developing leadership skills. As a result of his stellar performance in military schools, he graduated from the Staff College as a member of the prestigious General Staff. Quite naturally, he eagerly sought command responsibilities. It took the Revolution of July 1908, however, to release the energies of the officer corps, and Mustafa Kemal thrived in the new environment of professional opportunities.

The Road to Istanbul

Born in the winter of 1880/1881 (exact date unknown), Mustafa Kemal spent the greater part of his first fourteen years in the town of his birth, Selanik (Salonica), in Macedonia. Located 510 kilometers southwest of Istanbul, Selanik was a cultural, commercial, and economic center in the Balkans and the second most important city in the Ottoman Empire. Estimates for the early 1890s put the city's

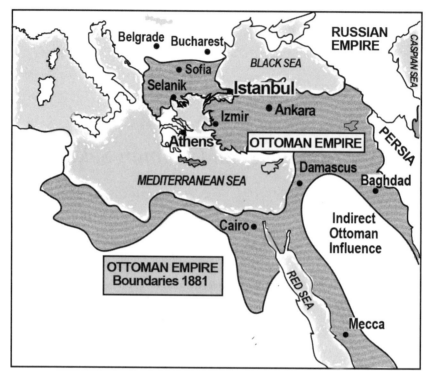

Map 1.1   *Ottoman Empire Boundaries, 1881*

population at around 150,000 inhabitants. The fifty-six mosques, five *medreses* (religious seminaries), a library, twenty-three *tekkes* (Sufi convents), sixteen churches, and twenty-one synagogues attested to the diversity of its people's backgrounds. The city claimed education and culture: three hospitals, a theater, two secondary schools, a military preparatory school, a state high school, and an agricultural school, in addition to a number of religious minority and foreign schools. All the major European countries had consulates in the city. Selanik also possessed good port facilities and railroad connections, a major marketplace, fifteen guest houses, and twenty-three factories or business establishments. Jews counted for approximately half the inhabitants. Muslims formed the second largest group, approximately 20 per cent of the population. Rums (Ottoman Greeks), Bulgarians, and Europeans constituted the remainder.[2]

Throughout his life, Mustafa Kemal carried a strong attachment to his home-town and its region. Years later while a student at the Staff College (1902–5), he would write in his personal notebook: "I am pleased, with a feeling of good fortune, to be from Selanik. If you want to know the truth better, I feel that my chest is overflowing with a feeling of pride . . . The most perfect qualities come to life in my mind."[3] Attachments to his roots and early years remained strong throughout Kemal's life. In November 1912, for example, Ali Fuad (Cebesoy) reported seeing Mustafa Kemal cry when he learned of the fall of Selanik to Greece in the Balkan Wars. At the time, he uttered a poignant question: "Will I ever see you again as a Turk?"[4] As President of the Republic, though he loved Western music, Mustafa Kemal remained wedded to Rumelian music, so much so that Falih Rıfkı (Atay), a close associate, found it a bit puzzling to witness such a strong bond to the past from one so determined to transform everything. He described Mustafa Kemal as a man whose mind had eyes looking forward but whose heart had eyes looking back at his past and all his memories.[5] Selanik's rich and diverse culture laid the seeds for Kemal's cosmopolitan mind.

Overall, the Ottoman Empire was ethnically and religiously quite hetero-geneous. Excluding areas under special administrations, such as Egypt and Lebanon, its population numbered some 17 million, with Muslims accounting for 12.5 million. On the European side, Christians outnumbered Muslims: 1.7 to 1.4 million. These figures represented a significant shrinkage in both popula-tion and territory that resulted from the Russo-Turkish War of 1877–78, when Bosnia-Herzegovina was occupied by Austria-Hungary, the Kars region by Russia, and Cyprus by Britain. Part of Bulgaria, nevertheless, became an autonomous principality, while Eastern Rumeli fell under a special administration. Adding more humiliation, the British occupied Egypt in 1882, establishing a de facto protectorate over this important province.

Mustafa Kemal had experienced a difficult childhood. His home has been aptly called "a house of mourning."[6] His father, Ali Rıza, worked as a minor civil servant, seeing service for a period as a border customs official. Zübeyde, some twenty years younger than her husband, married young and began having chil-dren at the age of fifteen. Of five to six children, depending on the account, only Mustafa Kemal and his younger sister Makbule survived to adulthood. Meanwhile, Ali Rıza ventured into business, selling timber and then salt. These enterprises failed, and Ali Rıza took to drinking, developed tuberculosis, and suffered from illness the last three years of his life.[7]

The family's life reflected the tensions between traditional and progressive forces at work in the larger Ottoman society. Based on his own account, Zübeyde, a pious Muslim, wanted her son to attend a local Muslim school and become a religious figure in his community. His given name was Mustafa or "The Chosen," an epithet of the Prophet Muhammad. In 1886–87, Mustafa began his formal education at the neighborhood religious school. This schooling lasted for only a few days. In sharp contrast to his wife, Ali Rıza desired a modern education for his son and quickly transferred him to a private school founded by Şemsi

Efendi, a champion of "new principles" that emphasized critical thinking over rote learning in education.[8]

Ali Rıza died when Mustafa was seven years old, leaving the family in a difficult financial situation. Suddenly a widow, Zübeyde sought shelter by moving the family to the farm of an uncle, one named Hüseyin Ağa, some thirty kilometers away. There a Greek Orthodox priest at a local church and an imam at a local mosque both gave Mustafa additional schooling. Then Zübeyde sent Mustafa back to Selanik to live with his paternal aunt so that he could attend a government school. Meanwhile, she married Rağıb Bey, a minor government official with four children from his previous marriage, and the couple lived in Selanik. Mustafa felt estranged in this new household and left home to stay with a relative.

In 1893, now twelve years old, Mustafa made a life-changing decision. He passed an entrance exam for the Selanik Military Preparatory School, where he enrolled against the expressed wishes of his mother.[9] Mustafa apparently had fallen under the magical spell of soldiering.

> We had a neighbor named Major Kadri Bey. His son, Ahmed, was studying at the secondary military school [in Selanik] and wore his military uniform. When I saw him, I decided also to wear such a uniform. Then I observed officers on the street. I realized that the road to reaching this rank required entering the military secondary school.[10]

Mustafa's was an era when impressionable young boys still heard stories of past Ottoman military glories and played soldier games as part of their socialization.[11] Thus the military environment provided Mustafa with steady meaning, purpose, direction, order, and discipline. Three members of his extended family—Nuri (Conker), Fuad (Bulca), and Salih (Bozok)—followed his example and enrolled in the same school, also carving out military careers for themselves. All three became Mustafa's trusted and loyal lieutenants and friends.

Mustafa's attendance at the military preparatory school in Selanik covered the period 1893–95. Throughout his life, he credited teachers as playing an important role in what he once described in a 1924 speech as "enlightening influences on the development of our souls and minds." From his Selanik days, he singled out Nakiyüddin (Yücekök), his French teacher, who during the Republic served as deputy in the Grand National Assembly of Turkey and assisted in the alphabet and religious reforms.[12] Mustafa commenced study of the French language, but mathematics became his favorite subject. His math teacher, a Captain Mustafa Efendi, reportedly gave Mustafa the second name of Kemal because of his exceptional work in the subject.[13] *Kemal* means maturity or perfection. Or, another explanation, Mustafa adopted the name on his own in honor of the famous

Ottoman poet Namık Kemal, whose influence was felt by many young people.[14] Whatever the explanation, the name change fit Mustafa well, if one understands maturity or perfection as a process in a purpose-driven life.

In 1895, Mustafa Kemal demonstrated his academic commitment to learning by graduating fourth in his class. That same year, he entered Manastır (today Bitola) Military High School. Situated 180 kilometers northwest of Selanik, Manastır had over 30,000 inhabitants and served as the capital of the province with the same name. The city also possessed a rather diverse population, with Muslims constituting approximately two-thirds of the inhabitants, with Rums, Vlachs, Bulgarians, and Jews forming much of the rest.[15] Unlike Selanik, Manastır was very much a military town, housing the headquarters of Third Army, a military hospital, two large military barracks, and a military high school. Mustafa Kemal spent almost four years, from 1895 to 1898, studying there. The curriculum emphasized mathematics, the sciences, and French.[16] Manastır exerted a major influence on Kemal's intellectual and social development. His education, both in the classroom and outside, developed in him an intellectual rigor and hunger for knowledge. Mustafa Kemal again shined as a serious, competent student. In November 1898, he graduated second in his class, a major feat given that his graduating class numbered over 700 students.

One teacher especially stood out in Manastır. Senior Captain (*Kolağası*) Mehmed Tevfik (Bilge) knew Turkish history so intimately that he instilled in Mustafa Kemal and other students a love for this subject as well as a pride in being Turks. For the rest of his life, Mustafa Kemal harbored an abiding respect for this teacher: "I owe a depth of gratitude to Tevfik Bey. He opened a new horizon for me."[17] And Atatürk never forgot the debt owed to this teacher. In 1932, during the Republic, Mehmed Tevfik became a member of the Turkish Historical Society. He published a number of books, including *Turks and Their Virtues in World History* (1928).[18] The book's subject had no doubt been emphasized in his classes.

Two fellow students in particular also exerted an important influence on Kemal's intellectual and social development. Ömer Naci, a young aspiring poet of modest talent but one filled with passion, witnessed the power of literature, poetry, and rhetoric.[19] Mustafa Kemal, like many of his peers, loved Namık Kemal, "the poet of liberty," whose ideas were suppressed by the government. Nonetheless, Mustafa Kemal was drawn to Namık Kemal, not only for his political thought, but also by the sheer beauty and power of his poetry. One teacher cautioned Mustafa Kemal that a passion for poetry would prevent him from becoming a good soldier.[20] But poetry and soldiering, Mustafa Kemal must have believed, could mix for the cultured soldier. Years later, Mustafa Kemal confided to a friend that he enjoyed having conversations with Ömer Naci, though they seldom agreed on anything.[21] The two remained good friends until Ömer Naci's death in World

War I. In this relationship, emotional bonds apparently outweighed intellectual ties. Another new friend, Ali Fethi (Okyar), for his part, broadened Kemal's mind. Born in Macedonia and fluent in French, Ali Fethi apparently introduced Mustafa Kemal to the French thought of Voltaire, Rousseau, and other political writers.[22] Mustafa Kemal, for his part, experienced difficulty mastering French. It was understood at the time that career advancement required knowledge of a European language, and French, at the time, was the *lingua franca* of the world. Mustafa Kemal thus became determined to master the language. To improve his French, he received special instruction at a local school run by Catholic lay brothers. Pursuing this extra-curricular activity demonstrated the seriousness with which Mustafa Kemal approached his education as a means for upward mobility and for enlightenment.

Then, rather suddenly, the Ottoman-Greek War of 1897 broke out and had a major impact on the impressionable students. Ottoman Greeks on the island of Crete, aided by nationalists from Greece, rose in revolt, with some of their leaders calling for union with Greece. The Athens government dispatched several battalions to the island, followed by an incursion into the Yanya region (in northwestern Greece today). On 17 April, the Ottomans declared war and, taking advantage in superiority of numbers and weapons, defeated the Greek army in quick order, moving within striking distance of Athens. Unfortunately for the empire, the European Powers intervened diplomatically and turned an Ottoman military victory into a political setback. They forced the Ottomans to return captured territory in Thessaly to the defeated Greeks and also to establish a new autonomous administration for Crete, virtually ending any meaningful control by Istanbul of the island. Streams of Muslim refugees, meanwhile, poured into Ottoman territory bringing with them word of massacres of civilian Muslims. Greece, for its part, had to pay a war indemnity. Both sides in the conflict felt humiliation, although for different reasons. The outcome of the war disturbed both students and faculty. Mustafa Kemal described how the initial confidence turned sour: "Our teachers had told us that we could occupy all of Greece. Then news of armistice talks deeply affected our enlightened officers at the school. We understood this from their faces but we couldn't ask anything. Our friend Nuri (Conker) told us that [he saw] a young officer crying and saying 'Bad, O how bad.' Still we filed out on to the streets of Manastır and shouted 'Long live our emperor.' For the first time, I did not join in on this activity."[23]

Kemal's account is credible. The Ottoman-Greek War of 1897 had accentuated the empire's weaknesses and vulnerabilities vis-à-vis the Great Powers. Once the most powerful state in Europe, the Ottoman Empire had suffered a series of demoralizing defeats and losses of territory. Moreover, these defeats in war often included civilian massacres and produced Muslim refugees, who were forced to flee their homes to relocate to the Ottoman realm. Passions consequently flared throughout the empire. In the year of the war, the poet Mehmed Emin (Yurdakul) expressed unequivocally national pride in the poem "Going to Battle," as part of his collection entitled *Poems in Turkish*. He wrote: "I am a Turk, my religion and race are great." Earlier, the word *Turk* generally meant someone boorish or uncouth, but by the end of the nineteenth century, it was gradually beginning to take on a noble meaning. Muslim Turks usually identified themselves first by religion and then their hometown or region rather than by ethnicity. Later, Mustafa Kemal claimed being influenced by this emerging Turkishness during his high school days.

Mustafa Kemal graduated from high school at the end of 1898. He had matured intellectually in Manastır. History, poetry, and literature had opened up new horizons for him. Mustafa Kemal was becoming a better-rounded individual, one with emerging broad interests, not just a focus on the military. Some of his most important learning had taken place outside the classroom. On the social side, Mustafa Kemal developed an expanded circle of friends. Now Istanbul offered him a chance to become a member of the prestigious General Staff, a prospect that would require six more years of study.

War College and Staff College

In Istanbul, Mustafa Kemal once again demonstrated the power of his mind and emotional discipline. Entering the War College (*Mekteb-i Harbiye*) on 13 March 1899 ranked 459 out of 736 students, he ended the first year twenty-ninth in his class and eleventh at the close of the second year. On 10 February 1902, he graduated eighth in a class of 549, or in the top 2 per cent, with rank of lieutenant in the infantry branch.[24] As a result of this impressive academic performance, Mustafa Kemal immediately moved on to the three-year program at the Staff College (*Mekteb-i Erkan-ı Harbiye*). In a graduating class of forty-three officers, the top thirteen graduates became General Staff officers. He graduated fifth and left the college with the rank of captain and as a member of the highly select and prestigious General Staff, based upon the Prussian model.

During the nineteenth century, the Ottoman officer corps had evolved into a more professional body. The century witnessed the emergence of a hierarchical military educational system with the establishment of the War College in 1834 and the Staff College in 1848. European military missions provided "experts" at schools and in the field, and the Ottoman war ministry actively translated manuals, books, and articles published in Europe. By the end of the nineteenth century, the Ottoman army's peacetime strength numbered around a quarter of a million officers and soldiers. In 1884, the number of *mektepli*, or the schooled officer, as opposed to the *alaylı*, or the ones who rose through the ranks, constituted about 10 per cent of the officer corps, rising to 15 per cent in 1894 and 25 per cent in 1899. Schooled meant a graduate from the War College. The officer corps overall expanded from 12,998 in 1881 to 23,269 in 1897. As part of its professionalization, the army required more schooled officers. Mustafa Kemal benefited from this expansion.

Mustafa Kemal entered the War College after a period of significant change in the curricula. Prussian military thought and culture heavily influenced the Ottoman military education system. Sultan Abdülhamid, who ascended the throne in 1876 and ruled until 1909, placed a priority on building a modern army, and he relied heavily on Germany for military expertise. Two reasons called for such a policy. First, among the major European Powers, Germany lacked direct territorial designs on Ottoman territory and thus, at least theoretically, could be more trusted than the other European Powers. Second, the Prussian army had demonstrated its military prowess in the Franco-Prussian War of 1870–71 when under the command of Helmuth von Moltke the Elder, it defeated France. Building on the military victory, Chancellor Otto von Bismarck brilliantly engineered the unification of Germany under Prussian leadership. Germany had clearly demonstrated that it possessed the best army in Europe, a model for those aspiring to reform theirs. Relations with Germany improved in the last two decades of the century.

In 1883, Colmar von der Goltz arrived in Istanbul as the head of a German military mission and stayed for thirteen years, leaving behind a generation of Ottoman officers schooled by him. His students in turn educated Mustafa Kemal and his generation. After returning to Germany in 1896, Goltz maintained an abiding interest in the Ottoman army and kept in regular communication with his former students. All the major commanders in World War I and the War of Independence graduated from the War College under Goltz's reorganization. He eventually returned to the empire and commanded the Ottoman army in Iraq during World War I, dying there from typhus in 1916. In accordance with his will, Goltz was buried within the grounds of the German Embassy in Istanbul.

Upon his arrival in Istanbul in 1883, Goltz received the command of the Inspectorate of Military Schools. The French military model hitherto had dominated the classrooms and field commands. The War College had provided three years of education and then selected the best graduates to go directly to the Staff College. Goltz revamped the curricula at both establishments, replacing the French model with the German system of the *Kriegsakademie*, with its emphasis on practical application rather than theory. The curricula saw more classes on military subjects, and regular oral and written exams became more a part of the curriculum.[25] To raise standards in the field, over 4,000 pages of German military manuals poured into the Ottoman army under his guiding hand, with the aim of ensuring complementary education in schools with appropriate field training. Several books and numerous articles by Goltz appeared in Ottoman translation during and after his tenure in the Ottoman Empire. His famous book *Das Volk in Waffen* (*The Nation in Arms*), which had appeared in Germany in 1883, was immediately translated into Ottoman and published as *Millet-i Müsellaha*, or *Armed Nation*. The Ottoman translation went through at least two reprints, showing its popularity and relevance. Mustafa Kemal referred to it in his school notes.[26] An 1891 French translation became part of Kemal's personal library.

In addition to military expertise, Goltz brought his own ideas of militarism, nationalism, and Social Darwinism to the Ottoman army, thus reflecting the military culture of industrialized warfare. In Goltz's view, war was inevitable in a Darwinian sense. Entire nations, and not just their armies, waged war, and every citizen should be obliged to perform military service. Success in battle depended upon countries being able to inculcate militaristic values in their people to create a robust nation-in-arms. In Goltz's world, officers should hold a superior place in society and the military elites should play an important role in state policies. These ideas, not unique to Goltz but popular among European militaries of the late nineteenth century, influenced the Ottoman officer corps, including Kemal's generation.[27] All this militaristic thought, however, failed to prepare an officer for war.

For a serious Ottoman officer aspiring to professionalism, *Millet-i Müsellaha* offered a systematic and critical analysis of the nature of war and of warfare in the industrial age, and rightly stands as a minor classic in military literature. The book's first sentence gives the greatest praise to Carl von Clausewitz, the great Prussian military theorist of the first half of the nineteenth century: "A military writer, who, after Clausewitz, embarks to compose *On War*, runs the risk of being compared to the poet who, after Goethe, attempts a *Faust*, or, after Shakespeare, a *Hamlet*. Anything important to be written about the nature of war can be found in the works left behind by that greatest of military thinkers ... *On War* ... constitutes the most complete work of its kind."[28] True to its opening statement, *Millet-i Müsellaha*, throughout its 568 pages, contained numerous references to Clausewitz's wisdom and insights. Goltz used Clausewitz to give his readers an appreciation of the nature of war and the demands and requirements of leadership in combat. From references to Clausewitz, Mustafa Kemal gained an appreciation of the intangibles in war.

In his analysis, Goltz championed the "basic principles of the science of war," which he regarded as "eternal," despite the changes brought about by modern, industrialized warfare with its railroads and telegraph.[29] War demanded strong and competent leadership. For Goltz, the "soul" of the Prussian army resided in the officer. Officers needed to establish authority over their soldiers in peacetime by the force of their "mind and character" through "instruction and training." They had to lead by example, demonstrating a willingness to self-sacrifice by a lack of concern for their own lives.[30] Great generalship required "excellent morals" (*ahlak-ı mükemmele*) and "exceptional intelligence and intellect" (*zeka ve dirayet-i müstesna*).[31] Knowledge was important, but leadership required both knowing and doing, and the doing was the more difficult part. Strength of will and the courage to take responsibility were essential in generalship.[32] Goltz summed up exemplary generalship as "born of zeal for action based on the union of creativity, courage, and passion and desire for honor and fame."[33] Mustafa Kemal made use of this definition to motivate others. In line with Clausewitz's thought, Goltz painted a picture of war as unpredictable in its essense. Orders rested on an insecure foundation, because there was never adequate information upon which to make solid decisions. Moreover, war fighting involved human beings, whose actions were never easily predictable.[34] War was thus presented as more an art than a science, requiring intuition, a sixth sense. In this aspect of war, Goltz resembled Clausewitz.

In addressing the relationship between policy and war, Goltz paraphrased Clausewitz, who viewed "war as the continuation of policy by other means." *Millet-i Müsellaha* stated that, "War is the continuation of policy with weapons in hand. Policy even influences the manner of the conduct of war. If this influence becomes inappropriate, then it is necessary to change the policy. A bad policy will show its bad influences on the conduct of war."[35] Policy carried a broad meaning, encompassing both foreign and domestic policies.[36] Goltz, however, sometimes differed with Clausewitz. With industrialized warfare, mass armies, and nations-in-arms, wars will be fought on such a large scale that policy will exert less influence during actual hostilities. Despite this important adjustment to Clausewitz's military theory, policy still remained paramount for Goltz in defining objectives and then in beginning, resourcing, and ending wars. "War is always the servant (*hadim*) of policy," Goltz maintained.[37] Goltz exerted an important influence on Mustafa Kemal and the schooled (*mektepli*) officers. In 1909, Mustafa Kemal paid a high tribute to Goltz on the occasion of the German general's return visit to the empire by referring to him as a "great savant and philosopher."[38]

Mustafa Kemal and his generation of officers were aware of the distinction between the art and science of war, and Clausewitz was an important military theorist in this regard. In 1899, during Kemal's first year at the War College, Ahmed Refik published a translation of Clausewitz's *Basic Principles in the Conduct of War*. The introduction contained Goltz's quote comparing *On War* to *Hamlet* or *Faust*. Ahmed Refik also contrasted Clausewitz with Antoine-Henri

Jomini, describing the latter as wedded to war as science, in sharp contrast to Clausewitz's art.[39] In *Basic Principles in the Conduct of War*, Clausewitz presented war as more of an art than a science, stressing that principles are merely guides. The basic principle of war was to possess the art of defeating the enemy in battle. Clausewitz stressed the importance of cognitive skills, with such terms as intelligence, reason, and the mind, in meeting the challenges posed by the art of war. Commanders needed to become "accustomed to making courageous decisions based on reason." Clausewitz also emphasizes the importance of moral factors in war. For him, war was geared toward three objectives: first, to destroy enemy forces; second, to capture his material sources for resistance; and third, to win public opinion. To achieve the first two goals required directing all one's power against the enemy's main or most important forces.[40] *Basic Principles in the Conduct of War*, it must be noted, represented a simplified discussion of its subject. In *On War*, his *magnum opus*, Clausewitz likened war "most closely" to a game of cards because of "the interplay of possibilities, probabilities, good luck and bad" and also compared it to commerce because of the "conflict of human interests and activities."[41] Mustafa Kemal came to appreciate Clausewitz's sophisticated understanding of war, although he saw merit in principles as a foundation.

Kemal's circle of friends and future professional contacts greatly expanded during the six years of study at the War College and the Staff College. Among the many, Ali Fuad (Cebesoy) stands out. Coming from a prominent family, he attended a prestigious French school in Istanbul where he learned French well. Ali Fuad helped Mustafa Kemal improve his French, whereas Kemal reciprocated with assistance in technical subjects.[42] Mustafa Kemal also spent three years studying German at the War College.[43] It was during this period that he apparently gained his famous love for *rakı* (anise-flavored alcoholic drink) and whiskey.

The quality of instruction at the War and Staff Colleges, as in any educational institution, varied considerably. Some instructors lacked experience to make their lesson material current and relevant. Others lacked depth of understanding with which to challenge and motivate their students. One instructor, in particular, earned the nickname General Mack, the Austrian commander whom Napoleon had soundly defeated and captured in 1805 by strategically outmaneuvering his army. This Ottoman teacher acquired the nickname by his failure to penetrate and analyze the decisions and intentions of various commanders studied in his course.[44] But there were good instructors as well. Two, in particular, stood out for Mustafa Kemal.

At the War College, Lieutenant Colonel Trabzonlu Nuri taught tactics. Students appreciated him as broadly cultured and an expert in strategy. He challenged students to expand their interests and studies outside strict military parameters: "a staff officer must equip himself with knowledge outside of soldiering. In the future, all of you will rise in responsibility as a commander." Nuri also taught guerrilla warfare. He began by asking the basic question that went to the heart of the subject: what is and what isn't a guerrilla? He noted that waging guerrilla warfare was as hard as trying to defeat it. Students performed an exercise in which a rebellion broke out near Istanbul. One part was crushed by government forces, but a second group crossed at night into Ortaköy on the European side and scattered into the surrounding hills. Nuri wanted students to consider both sides in the armed conflict. What could this group do and how could it sustain its rebellion? Then, Nuri differentiated between the role of the government and army in attempting to suppress the rebellion. He pressed students to explain the significance of a rebellion being internal versus external. This lesson raised student interest and involvement and had a lasting impression on Mustafa Kemal. Nuri had inspired students to dwell on the essence of the problem in his guerrilla lesson and nudged them to think outside their normal parameters or frames of reference. While on campaign in Libya years later, Mustafa Kemal wrote a friend that he was applying what he had learned from Nuri to his own guerrilla operations against the Italians.[45] Nuri also encouraged the young cadets to educate themselves broadly. Mustafa Kemal certainly embraced that message.

According to Ali Fuad, Mustafa Kemal had the greatest respect and love for Naci (Eldeniz) from among all his teachers at the War College, and this admiration continued until his own death.[46] Born in Manastır and a graduate of the War College in 1893, Naci, who knew both German and French, had spent two years studying in Germany. A captain, he taught training and education at the War College, which included material on morals, manners, and humanity, all subjects of great interest to Mustafa Kemal, for together they helped address the whole human being. In 1921, Naci joined Mustafa Kemal in support of the national resistance; during the Republic, he rose in rank to lieutenant general.[47] His teaching on morale and morals balanced the more technical side of war fighting taught by Trabzonlu Nuri Bey.

In his personal notes and studies after graduation from the War College, Mustafa Kemal raised some basic, profound questions. What does an officer need to know about the secrets of human nature? What is the most important means for teaching the art of soldiering? Is it possible to find two situations in war that resemble one another? Alongside these questions, Mustafa Kemal wrote "Clausewitz's word" with an exclamation mark.[48] In addition to raising essential questions about his profession, he noted that managing successful offensives in war required possessing "conviction of conscience" (*kanaat-ı vicdan*): 1) in having superiority in political ideas for achieving the objective; 2) in having forces sufficient to achieve the goal; and 3) in being superior over the enemy [in troops and/or equipment].[49] This timeless wisdom, handed down in the classroom, would serve Mustafa Kemal well in the War of Independence. Here, the centrality of policy in war stood out in his notes.

At the War College, Mustafa Kemal continued to develop intellectually outside the classroom. Newspapers served as one easily accessible source for broadening his horizons. As a first lieutenant in the War College and candidate for the General Staff, Mustafa Kemal wrote in his notebook of a "passionate attachment" to reading them. Here his notebook contained a draft of a letter to one newspaper editor. In it, Mustafa Kemal wrote that he cannot delay even a second in getting to his newspaper. He goes on to describe the editor as a source for "knowledge" (*ilim*), "culture" (*irfan*), and "spiritual power" (*feyz*) and praises his "mind." In general terms, Mustafa Kemal saw newspapers as providing "a terrain for the development of progressive ideas" (*efkar-ı terakkiperverane saha-ı inkişaf*).[50] Clearly, on one level, newspapers, despite the Hamidian government's censorship of them, did provide basic global news as well as information on important achievements and developments in other countries. But even more important, there was also easy access to uncensored foreign newspapers, especially in Istanbul. A professional, dedicated officer read newspapers as a means of staying current. Mustafa Kemal repeated the same desire for acquiring knowledge in a brief letter that he wrote on 13 April 1903 to a contemporary philosopher named Rıza Tevfik, praising him for his noble ideas, virtue, and culture.[51] These values were worthy of Kemal's emulation.

Kemal's generation of officers was influenced by General Süleyman Paşa's *World History* (1878), with its focus on the early Turkic states in Central Asia. Mustafa Kemal also admired Léon Cahun's *Introduction a l'histoire de l'Asie: Turcs et Mongols, des origins à 1405* (1896).[52] These two histories strengthened in Mustafa Kemal a pride in being a Turk with roots in Central Asia. Süleyman Paşa, who died in 1892, was in particular a very important influence. In addition to major field command, he served as Vice Director and then as Director of Military Schools, introducing into the curriculum reform based on European methods, including written exams. A reformist in both military and non-military matters, he participated in the deposition of Sultan Abdülaziz that led to the establishment of the 1876 Constitution, for which Abdülhamid eventually had him exiled to Baghdad. Süleyman Paşa wrote a number of books, including *The Feeling of the Revolution*, his account of the military coup of 1876. *World History* included original Turkish sources; *The Foundations of Composition* analyzed Turkish literary genres; and *Turkish Grammar* argued for the language of the empire being Turkish, not Ottoman. The latter two books served for a period as textbooks in military schools.[53] In Süleyman Paşa, Mustafa Kemal gained a role model: a reformist, professional, scholarly soldier with a pride in being a Turk.[54]

A major war suddenly drew Kemal's attention away from his studies and to the real world. The Japanese victory over Russia in the Russo-Japanese War of 1904–5 had a major impact on all of Europe, and the Ottoman Empire was no different. An Asian country had defeated a European power on both land and sea. The Japanese demonstrated that despite the lethality of modern weapons, such as the machine gun and long-range artillery favoring the defense, they were still able to win with the offense. Military wisdom in European armies thus tended to stress the Japanese martial traditions as the critical factor explaining Japan's military victories. "The real lesson of the Russo-Japanese War was widely seen as being that the truly important element in modern warfare was not technology but *morale*; and the morale not of the army alone, but of the nation from which it was drawn."[55] Mustafa Kemal was no different in such reasoning. His notes at the War College romanticized the Japanese people as "a warrior nation" inculcated with a willingness to die, a tradition born of 800 years of feudalism. In capturing this attitude, Mustafa Kemal used the Islamic term *şehadet*, or martyrdom.[56] In the Ottoman Empire, Islam served as a main ingredient for motivating Muslim troops in battle, and Mustafa Kemal would appeal to Islamic faith in the War of Independence.

On the political front, Mustafa Kemal and fellow students began discussing the empire's many problems. Ideas and analyses hatched from these discussions laid seeds for the Kemalist Revolution.[57] Part of Kemal's generation at the War College grew highly critical of the sultan's despotism and personalized control of the Ottoman army. During his long reign from 1876 to 1909, Abdülhamid placed great reliance on diplomacy and pan-Islamism for regime maintenance and viewed the army as a means of maintaining internal order. While modernizing its weaponry, the sultan mistrusted a modern and professional officer corps because of its exposure to Western ideas and values. He regarded the military as a potential threat to his regime. Consequently, Goltz's ideas of militarism, nationalism, Social Darwinism, and a nation-in-arms failed to resonate with him. To gain a tighter grip on the army, Abdülhamid established policies that undermined military professionalism and readiness. In 1890, he formed the Imperial General Staff at his palace as a means of micro-managing the military.[58] This arrangement ensured the palace's control over the top echelons of the army. Moreover, Abdülhamid balanced *mektepli* officers with the appointment of *alaylı*, or those who rose through the ranks, of whom some were virtually illiterate. A spy system of informants permeated the institutions of government and the military, and the sultan regularly read their reports as part of his daily briefs. Maneuvers were forbidden out of a concern that they might lead to a military coup, and small units required special permission for conducting live-fire exercises. Realistic training exercises constitute the heart of preparing an army for war, and the Ottoman army was denied this means of professionalization.

All the above constraints undermined the benefits gained from the purchase of modern weaponry, such as Mauser rifles and Krupp artillery pieces; an army derives sustenance from serious, realistic training exercises. What combat experience the Ottoman army gained in the last thirty years of Abdülhamid's reign came mainly from its role as a police force putting down rebellions and crushing guerrilla warfare or brigandage. Overall, the Hamidian system undermined professionalism and stifled creativity in the military. Consequently, senior officers directly taught by Goltz underwent a professional numbing, whereas those of Kemal's younger generation experienced frustration that resulted in varying degrees of politicization of their thought—despite the government's censorship of ideas.

Concepts of liberty, patriotism, and popular sovereignty derived from the French Revolution resonated well for impressionable students who confronted a despotic regime. Two home-grown poets also served as native sources for these revolutionary ideas for an Ottoman audience. Namık Kemal had been dead for over fifteen years, but his ideas lived on despite Hamidian censorship. He became known as the "poet of the fatherland" and "the poet of liberty." As one student and future officer noted, Namık Kemal served as "our moral nourishment," so much so that "We can say that he created a new generation."[59] Mustafa Kemal admitted to reading his poetry and books, and his classmate Ali Fuad recalled that one day Kemal announced that he wanted to memorize Namık Kemal's *Vatan Şiiri*, or *Poem of the Fatherland*.[60] This martial poem appealed to patriotic cadets with such evocative lines as these:

> *Wounds are medals on the brave's body;*
> *The grave [martyrdom] is the soldier's highest rank;*
> *The earth is the same, above and underneath;*
> *March, you brave ones, to defend the fatherland.*[61]

Tevfik Fikret, on his part, was a contemporary. Many cadets became familiar with his poem *Sis*, or *Fog*, in which he criticized the despotic regime of Abdülhamid by describing a depressing atmosphere hanging over the imperial capital. But it was *Rübab-ı Şikeste*, or *Broken Flute*, written in 1900, that contained, on its cover no less, perhaps his most famous line: "I am a poet whose thought is free, whose culture is free, whose *vicdan* (conscience) is free." Mustafa Kemal later gave special credit to Tevfik Fikret for instilling in him a revolutionary spirit.

In addition to his academic studies, clandestine reading, and nightlife, Mustafa Kemal also became involved in political activities. At the Staff College, he and several fellow classmates, including Ömer Naci, started a handwritten, clandestine paper that, among other items, pointed out the numerous deficiencies of the Hamidian regime. This activity moved to the War College, where eventually school authorities discovered the activity and put a stop to it. Later, upon graduation in 1905, Mustafa Kemal and his friend Ali Fuad were arrested for their clandestine work and placed in jail for a brief period. As punishment for his political activities, Mustafa Kemal was assigned to Fifth Army in Damascus and not granted his desire for a posting with Third Army in the Balkans.[62] The region of Macedonia had developed into a hotbed of violence in August 1903 when the Ilinden Uprising had rocked the region. Although Ottoman troops quickly suppressed the revolt, the next decade witnessed growing violence as the neighboring Balkan states of Greece, Bulgaria, and Serbia each pursued irredentist policies and competed for influence among the population. Internally, competing guerrilla bands fought not only Ottoman troops but each other. Rather than helping defend his beloved Rumeli, Mustafa Kemal found himself imbedded in the heart of Arab society.

Field Education, Politics, and the July 1908 Revolution

Service in Syria proved an eye-opener for Mustafa Kemal. Now a newly promoted captain, Mustafa Kemal assumed command of a cavalry company in the 30th Cavalry Regiment commanded by an *alaylı* officer, Major Lütfi. This assignment gave Mustafa Kemal his first combat experiences while immersing him in the Arab world. Toward the end of 1907, he wrote in his notebook that "I had begun to think for myself." He assessed, for example, his own military institution in disparaging words: "The army of the imperial state is the most unfortunate army in the world." Mustafa Kemal found himself reassessing some of his former ideas of human beings and life as he came in contact with a wide range of people, dealt with superiors and subordinates, and carried out personal studies: "Not being reinforced by my experience and continuous studies, my ideas on people and life are, more or less, changing from my former ones."[63] What led him to write such statements after only two years of service in Syria?

Mustafa Kemal saw a good part of Syria. His duties proved numerous and varied, and they brought him in contact with people from all walks of life, including local notables. On one occasion, for example, he even visited a church and met with a local priest. Extensive touring left him with the impression that every Arab household possessed a rifle, enough weapons in the hands of the civilian population to arm an entire army. The backwardness of society struck him as well. He noted areas with a school building but no teachers. He discerned much indifference and routine, mindless inertness among officials, as well as examples of corruption and bribery. The long years of Hamidian despotism had taken a toll on government and society.

But it was the workings of the Ottoman army that directly challenged the idealistic officer. Western European armies focused on preparing to fight conventional wars, the perceived threat, while leaving domestic security to police forces. The Ottoman army, on the other hand, had to function as a constabulary force as well, with duties of suppressing local unrest and feuds among its own citizens, chasing brigands, or assisting in the collection of taxes. Mustafa Kemal noted having to spend nineteen straight days in the collection of state revenues. His unit also chased brigands and helped contain a rebellion by the Druze community in the region of Havran and Quneytrah. Mustafa Kemal was especially negative about the state of the field army in Syria, an analysis driven in part by his own large ego. Officers and non-commissioned officers proved lacking in military knowledge and, more important, resisted criticism. Mustafa Kemal found his own company functioned more as an amalgam of individuals rather than a cohesive brotherhood of soldiers. To remedy this situation, he instituted education and training exercises for his men; on operations, rather than delegating to subordinates, he personally met with his officers and soldiers to ensure understanding and implementation of his orders.[64] Given the poor state of his unit, such direct supervision, rather than delegation, was most prudent.

Although busy with command duties, Mustafa Kemal regularly engaged in personal study. His journal contained material on the first Islamic battles after Muhammad's death and more extensive notes on the Waterloo campaign, with references to the actions of Napoleon, Wellington, Blücher, and Grouchy.[65] Mustafa Kemal was clearly committed to continuing his military education in the field. His intellectual interests continued to be broader than just military subjects. There are references to German poet Schiller and his play *William Tell*, as well as to the French kings Louis XIV and XV. For a brief period, Kemal read a novel by Ahmed Midhat to a fellow officer, who sometimes drifted off to sleep. Nevertheless, in a tent in Syria, far away from the physical comforts of Istanbul, Mustafa Kemal appreciated the luxury of reading without fear of discovery.[66] His reading list included *Romeo and Juliet*, *La vie américaine*, and *De l'inégalité parmi les hommes* by Rousseau.[67]

One book especially caught Kemal's interest: a seventy-nine-page translation on Benjamin Franklin. Dating his entry as November 1907, Mustafa Kemal identifies Franklin as "this great individual" and "the inventor of the lightning rod," and lists the areas of his main contributions: masonry, pottery, printing, writing, manners, and diplomacy. Most interesting, however, the notebook contains all thirteen of Franklin's virtues and includes a definition for twelve, omitting the one for humility.

1. temperance (*riyazet*) – do not eat or drink to excess
2. silence (*sükut*) – be attentive to oneself and others (a good listener and observer)
3. order (*intizam*) – let there be a time and a place for everything
4. resolve (*metanet*) – complete tasks that one has begun with steadfastness and circumspection no matter what the difficulties
5. frugality (*tasarruf*) – spend money wisely for the benefit of oneself and others
6. industry (*say*) – abstain from laziness and always be busy with necessary matters
7. sincerity (*istikamet*) – do not exaggerate or lie. Think truthfully and seriously. Say what you think
8. justice (*hakkaniyet*) – do not hurt others and help others as much as possible in one's power
9. tranquility (*sükun*) – do not be disturbed by material misfortunes but make judgments with an inner peace
10. moderation (*itidal*) – avoid extremes in everything
11. cleanliness (*nezafet*) – lack not in observing cleanliness in body, clothes, and home
12. honesty (*iffet*) – never forget "honor" (*namus*) in every matter
13. humility (*tevazu*) – [Kemal wrote nothing here, whereas Franklin had written: "Imitate Socrates and Jesus"]

A quote from Franklin ends the above list: "You cannot show anything useful to lazy citizens."[68]

For Mustafa Kemal, Franklin provided a compelling example of the best of the Enlightenment. His broad-ranging mind achieved much in science and technology, and his service as a diplomat helped advance the cause for America's independence. Moreover, Franklin was clearly devoted to developing his own personal virtues, as Mustafa Kemal also was consciously committed to his own character development. Inner attitudes and values, also, had to be reflected in proper appearance and good manners. After all, officers of well-developed character led by example. By inserting Franklin's above quote, shown at the end of the list, Mustafa Kemal demonstrated his awareness of the limitations in inspiring others to higher standards of performance, as laziness dulls passion. Perhaps Mustafa Kemal saw a general malaise in Ottoman society, which only accentuated the importance of character, and thus his interest in Franklin's thirteen virtues.

It took over a year and a half after the Staff College before Mustafa Kemal again became involved in clandestine political activity, this time in Damascus. In December 1906, he helped establish the secret Society for the Fatherland and Liberty (*Vatan ve Hürriyet Cemiyeti*).[69] The selection of the name for the

1 *Senior Captain (Kolağası) Mustafa Kemal, 1907*

secret society was telling: fatherland for patriotism and liberty for the ideals of the French Revolution, in particular from the Ottoman context, liberation from sultanic despotism. Ali Fuad founded a branch in Beirut; branches spread to Jaffe and Jerusalem. In 1907, Mustafa Kemal engineered a trip to Selanik, where he stayed for several months and apparently founded a branch of the secret society in his hometown. Members at the first meeting in Selanik included his poet friend Ömer Naci.[70] Ali Fuad claimed that by this time, 1907, Mustafa Kemal had begun discussing the need to establish a Turkish state in place of the Ottoman Empire.[71]

Back in Syria, Mustafa Kemal received a promotion to senior captain, or *kolağası*, on 20 June 1907. Then on 27 September the long-desired assignment to Third Army finally came through. Upon returning to Selanik, he discovered that his secret organization had been absorbed by the Ottoman Liberty Society, which became the Committee of Union and Progress (CUP). The CUP was seriously planning to overthrow Sultan Abdülhamid. Mustafa Kemal joined the society by February 1908. The revolutionary organization was part of a larger movement opposed to the sultan's despotism known as the Young Turks. Mustafa Kemal, for his part, used his posting in late June as inspector of the Selanik-Üsküb (Skopje) railway line to act as liaison between the CUP headquarters in Selanik and its branch in Üsküb.[72] He was clearly not among the main plotters of the revolution, but still a Young Turk.

The July Revolution began in the Balkans with a number of officers taking to the mountains and raising the standard of revolt. They called for the establishment of constitutional government. The senior army leadership was generally ill-disposed to suppress the growing revolt. Rather than face deposition, Abdülhamid restored the 1876 Constitution that had been in abeyance for thirty years. Major Enver, one year senior to Mustafa Kemal and his future rival, emerged from the rebellion as one of the "heroes of liberty." Political power gradually shifted to the CUP, but the society initially lacked a clear program of reform and comprised a loose organization in need of centralization of power. Secretive and centered in Selanik, the Central Committee used the elections and the reconstituted parliament to limit the Sultan's power while mobilizing the general populace. In time, the CUP leadership managed to build a nationally organized political party, and in February 1913, it seized power in a military coup. By 1914, the 1908 Revolution had wrought significant changes. Political power was concentrated in the CUP with its political and military wings. The political party had evolved into a powerful national organization, effective at mobilizing the people and active in the Assembly. Officers at all ranks became involved in politics.

The Second Constitutional Period (1908–20) initially saw a flowering of political and cultural discourse in the public sphere. Newspapers and journals discussed subjects ranging from Islam as a rationalist, material philosophy to women's rights. On 11 March 1913, for example, *İctihad* published "A Wakeful Dream" in which Kılıçzade Hakkı discussed a vision of the future that included princes receiving modern education, serving in the army or navy, marrying a woman of equal social status, and abandoning polygamy and concubines. In Kılıçzade Hakkı's world, Turks lived by reason and abandoned the *fez* for a national hat, and women dressed as they wished, mingled socially with men, received good education, and discarded the veil. Men, in this conception, lacked the need for the Islamic right of divorce. *Tekkes* and *zaviyes* (Sufi places of worship) were abolished, and *medreses* imparted modern education.[73] The intellectual currents of materialism, scientism, positivism, and Social Darwinism—ideas popular among the Young Turks—shaped Kemal's thoughts and *Weltanschauung*, though it is not clear when exactly and how. Mustafa Kemal came to believe in science as a panacea for transforming society. Science trumped religion, with the aim of the eventual privatization of Islam. With this belief came faith in the power of reason, logic, and the scientific method based on the superiority of Western civilization. Turkism gained strong currency, as did the notion of the army as an indispensable and noble part of the elite. Herein were clear seeds for the future Kemalist Revolution.[74] Yet Mustafa Kemal was well anchored in the military, committed to professionalism and his immediate duties, and remained somewhat distant to politics swirling within the army. During the period between the 1908 Revolution and the end of World War I, Kemal's most serious writing dealt with military matters.

At the outset, however, Mustafa Kemal had good connections to the inner circle of the CUP's military wing.[75] In December 1908, the CUP leadership tapped Mustafa Kemal with a political mission, that of going to Libya in order to gain the allegiance of the population for the Revolution. Many local Arab leaders were very suspicious of the new constitutional regime and expressed their continued loyalty to Sultan Abdülhamid. Over only two months, from December 1908 to January 1909, Mustafa Kemal managed to convince the leadership in both Bengazi and Tripoli to declare for the Constitution, offering monetary incentives and practicing the art of persuasion. This achievement required discussions with town notables, tribal şeyhs, and Sufi leaders. Mustafa Kemal even assumed a platform and addressed large crowds. The British Consul in Tripoli, J. Alvarez, described him as "an eloquent and fluent speaker" who commanded the attention of large audiences. Although tasked with gaining political support for the new constitutional regime, Mustafa Kemal also challenged the local military. At the Bengazi garrison, he implemented drills and training exercises and imposed the observance of proper dress codes and cleanliness.[76] This command style reflected not only a firm commitment to a high standard of technical competence and discipline, but also a dedication to building character through the inculcation of values and mindset, as evidenced in his interest in Franklin's Thirteen Virtues. After eliciting commitments to the 1908 Revolution, Mustafa Kemal returned to Selanik in January 1909 for an assignment on the staff of the 11th Reserve Division. Libya had provided Mustafa Kemal with invaluable experience of using authority to deal with political and religious leaders while at the same time delivering public speeches. Mustafa Kemal left Libya too quickly for a good assessment of his effectiveness as a leader, but he left good impressions.

Suddenly on 13 April 1909, a rebellion broke out in Istanbul against the CUP and the Constitution in what became known in the history books as the "Counter-Revolution." A number of military units and theology students joined in calling for Islamic Holy Law and for the return to power of Sultan Abdülhamid. Unrest surfaced in parts of Anatolia. In the Adana region in southeastern Anatolia, over 20,000 Armenians were massacred, with reports of 4,000 Muslim civilian deaths as well. Rather than permit the sultan to regain his former power, the CUP leadership and senior army commanders in Selanik decided to suppress the revolt by forming the *Hareket Ordusu*, or Operational Army, in order to move on Istanbul. Senior Captain Mustafa Kemal assumed the important duties of chief of operations. The Operational Army easily crushed the rebels, deposed the sultan, and re-established constitutional government. The new sultan, Mehmed V Reşad, essentially withdrew the sultanate from politics.[77]

The events since the July Revolution provided much fodder for discussion at the second annual congress of the CUP, held in September 1909 in Selanik. At this important gathering, Mustafa Kemal generated controversy with his bold speech. Deploring the involvement of army officers in the CUP, he argued that a professional army had to be above politics. Legal measures needed to be put in place to prevent the political participation of officers. Mustafa Kemal put forward five points: the CUP becoming a political party; the army refraining from engagement in politics; the Society cutting ties with Freemasons; the congress establishing equality within the Society; and the government disengaging from involvement in religious matters.[78] The speech seemed to argue for autonomy for the military along the German model, an army above politics.[79] His views failed to garner a majority vote, and the CUP kept officers on its rolls. Mustafa Kemal, meanwhile, focused much of his energies on military matters during this period.

In November, after the suppression of the Counter-Revolution, Mustafa Kemal was appointed to serve on the staff of Third Army, and then was transferred to the staff of V Corps in January 1911. He briefly served as deputy commander of the 38th Infantry Regiment. During the years 1909 to 1911, Third Army was a center of military reform. Despite the temptations to greater political involvement, Mustafa Kemal took "to soldiering with energy . . . He worked hard, organized staff rides and lectures, studied military history—Moltke and the campaigns of Napoleon. It was a time of new enthusiasm and quick promotion."[80] Mustafa Kemal was a perfectionist with a penchant for reform, organization, and education, along with a strong sense of duty and self-confidence. This can be seen in his activities during this two-and-a-half-year period.

Mustafa Kemal embraced his duties of training and education with boundless energy. The 1908 Revolution had removed the Hamidian shackles preventing peacetime maneuvers and live fire exercises. The military as a profession of war fighting received new life. Mustafa Kemal wholeheartedly embraced this newfound professional freedom, a freedom that was much in evidence when in August 1909 Field Marshal Colmar von der Goltz came to Selanik to participate in a military exercise. Mustafa Kemal finally met "the scholar and philosopher." But true to his self-confidence and patriotism, he resisted permitting Goltz to dictate the exercise; rather, it had to take place in accordance with Ottoman, not German, design.[81] The 1909 maneuvers involved a corps with 12,000 troops; the following year they encompassed 70,000 soldiers and two field armies.[82] Mustafa Kemal served as an umpire in the latter.

Mustafa Kemal believed in the old military adage that victory begins with the performance of the smallest parts working together. So during 1909, he took the initiative to begin translating from German into Turkish a field manual on training platoons, companies, and battalions written by General Karl Litzmann, former director of the Berlin Military Academy. To bring the manual out in quicker fashion, Mustafa Kemal decided to translate only the sections dealing with platoons, replacing German names and places with Turkish ones. *Combat Training for Platoons* appeared in February 1909, just before the Counter-Revolution of April. In his introduction of five pages, Mustafa Kemal stated his intent to follow up with translations of the sections on companies and battalions. Admitting that new field manuals normally create confusion in the military, he warned that the lack of a contemporary one, if not remedied, threatened "our existence." He further described the Ottoman army as engaged in "wrong practices that are tied to training centers by rusty chains," and he poignantly wrote that "the old manuals have to be buried in a grave." The introduction boldly encouraged corps and division commanders to take training more seriously.[83] The translation and its evocative introduction also served the purpose of spreading Kemal's name throughout the army. The commitment to professionalism in general and training in particular continued with another technical publication. In *Cumalı Military Camp: Training and Maneuvers of Cavalry Companies, Regiments and Brigades* (1909), Mustafa Kemal analyzed seven tactical problems in the exercise conducted from 19 August to 1 September of that year.

In line with his responsibilities for training and education, Mustafa Kemal traveled to France to observe the French army's maneuvers at Picardie, conducted in September 1910. The seriousness with which the French army approached the exercise left Mustafa Kemal with the impression that war between France and Germany would occur in the near future, which he filed in his report to the war ministry.[84] After his return from France, Mustafa Kemal published another section of Litzman's manual, this time *Combat Training for Companies*. It appears that he never found the time to finish the trilogy by adding a field manual for battalions. In 1911, he also published *Tactics and Maneuvers*, examining a two-day map exercise of V Corps staff. These publications and the internal reports attest to the dedication and seriousness with which Mustafa Kemal approached his duties and responsibilities within the army.

Reading and study, despite the powerful political winds swirling around him, continued to form an integral part of Kemal's military career. Mustafa Kemal, like many officers in his generation, was "profoundly attracted to Gustave Le Bon's notions of crowd psychology, in which the military held pride of place as an indispensable part of the ruling elite," and Mustafa Kemal read him carefully, probably around this time.[85] As a soldier, however, Kemal was also interested in psychology in order to understand the human being and how to motivate him in battle. Consequently, he read books on military psychology, such as *La Confiance: Essai de psychologie militaire* by Captain Constantin (1908) and *Notre armée critiquée* by Colonel Biottot (n.d.), all of which contain marks, underlining, and comments in the margins.

Cours de morale et d'education by the *École Spéciale Militaire de Saint-Cyr*, dated 1910–11, stands out in this regard. These hand-written notes, perhaps collected by Mustafa Kemal while in France, appear to contain the official wisdom of the French military. Mustafa Kemal clearly engaged the material seriously and carefully with much underlining, in some cases double underlining. For example, "The officer is always an educator who knows the physical, psychological and social dimensions of the human being."[86] Leaders needed some understanding of the human body, psychology, and sociology if they wanted to manage men effectively and humanely. *Cours de morale et d'education* discussed such subjects as the role of intelligence (*intelligence*) and the influence of feelings (*sentiment*) on thought; the influence of will (*volonté*) on intelligence; and the universality of knowledge. Biology, the nervous system, and reflexive versus conscious behavior were woven into the discussion.[87] Mustafa Kemal especially highlighted the sections dealing with the effects of fear, irresistible impulses, the fear of responsibility, the importance of officer attitudes, and group panic.[88] He appeared quite impressed with the book's stress on intelligence in the preparation for war in peacetime and the need for superiority in the physical, intellectual, and moral sphere.[89] Discipline, group honor, and the idea of patriotism caught his attention as well.[90] *Cours de morale et d'education* treated its subject in a manner that called for a comprehensive mental approach and required intuition or *coup d'œil* from officers.

Mustafa Kemal clearly strove to develop both rational and intuitive understanding of war and human beings. Writing in 1918, he noted that as a military commander "I always give much attention to military character and to psychological and morale conditions."[91] The questions Mustafa Kemal raised as a student at the Staff College continued to challenge his mind: what does an officer need to know about the secrets of human nature? What is the most important means for teaching the art of soldiering? *Cours de morale et d'education* echoed this exact intellectual and moral orientation.

Tripolitanian War (Ottoman Libya)[92]

On 29 September 1911, Italy, ambitious to develop an empire in competition with other European states, declared war on the Ottomans and invaded the two provinces of Tripoli and Bengazi in Ottoman Libya. A small Ottoman garrison of 4,000 troops proved no match for the invading Italians. Ottoman soldiers retreated into the interior of the country, where they joined forces with the Sanusi brotherhood and Arab tribes to fight the Italian occupation. The Istanbul government decided to support the struggle by sending "volunteer" officers to help conduct a robust resistance. A number of future prominent officers flocked to Libya, among them Enver. By the middle of November, the Italian expeditionary force had grown from an initial 30,000 to close to 100,000, and the Italians controlled the coastal areas.

Meanwhile, Mustafa Kemal departed Istanbul for Libya on 4 October. An Italian naval blockade argued for the safer but longer land route. In Egypt, Mustafa Kemal suffered an illness that required fifteen days of hospitalization in Alexandria. He finally reached Bengazi at the beginning of November to find the theater divided into three sectors. Enver commanded Bengazi. Mustafa Kemal was placed in charge of logistics under Brigadier General Edhem Paşa's Tobruk command. Learning to supply forces was important experience, for an army functions on its supplies. A promotion to major came on 27 November. Then on 19 December 1911, Edhem appointed Mustafa Kemal as commander for Tobruk and its surrounding area.

Kemal's previous experience in Libya helped him develop relations with the tribal leaders and the şeyhs of the Sanusi Sufi brotherhood, this time with the aim of mobilizing them as combatants against an invading European army. To help mobilize the Arabs under the Ottoman banner, Mustafa Kemal even went "native" in appearance, at times donning local tribal attire. From December 1911 until his departure in October 1912, Mustafa Kemal gained independent command experience. In February 1912, he assumed command of all Derne forces. The engagements varied in size of forces, length of combat, and intensity of fire. Most engagements were small. The Battle of Derne on 3 March, however, saw Ottoman losses at 63 killed and 168 wounded, with the Italians losing approximately 200 killed in battle. At the time, Mustafa Kemal counted eight officers, 160 regular soldiers, an artillery company, two machine guns, and 7,742 Arab tribesmen against a force of 15,000 to 16,000 Italians. Throughout the war, Ottoman forces were able to keep the Italians restricted, for the most part, to the coastal area. Frustrated with the lack of significant progress, Rome made command changes and sent reinforcements to Derne. On 11 September, the Italians launched a major attack from the town of Derne with the goal of advancing twelve kilometers. Mustafa Kemal managed with a smaller force, composed of both Turks and Arabs, regulars and irregulars, to stop their advance before the Italians reached their final objective.

Waging war in Libya presented numerous challenges to Turkish officers. The desert climate was harsh; spoken Arabic was a foreign language; and tribal customs contrasted sharply with those of urban life. On 9 December 1911, Nuri (Conker) described his early assessment of the environment to a friend thus: "Desert life isn't easy . . . I dream of the sparkling waters of Rumeli. The water here is the color of fermented millet." By April desert life appeared to have taken a major toll: "we have not been able to see a woman's face for the last three months, as they are all hidden behind heavy veils. We lead ascetic lives like the monks on Mount Athos. If we go on from here, our next stop should surely be paradise."[93]

But how did Mustafa Kemal assess his experiences while still in the midst of them?[94] Fighting with Arab tribesmen presented its own set of human and tactical problems, as seen in Kemal's report of 25 January 1912, in which he vividly described the difficulties in dealing with Arab tribesmen. Şeyhs of zaviyes (Sufi lodges) and şeyhs of tribes brought their irregular fighters to augment the meager regular Ottoman forces. Long and often "meaningless" conversations were necessary before he could get down to business with these şeyhs. In one instance, rather than issuing a command, Mustafa Kemal talked of offering a "proposal" for discussion before embarking on reaching a decision. Patience and power of persuasion seemed to be the order of business for the junior officer. Moreover, Arab tribesmen were not always dependable. In one instance, the report went on, the Arabs received money to provide a thousand "holy warriors for Islam" (mücahidler), but only 250 appeared for battle, 50 of them without weapons. Mustafa Kemal learned that şeyhs lacked the will for decisive and difficult battle, such as facing cannons and fortifications. Moreover, although the commanding officer in theory, it was difficult to motivate the Arab mücahidler directly because of the influence of their şeyhs.[95] Although critical in much of his report, Mustafa Kemal did note three years later his respect for the bravery and instinct for combat exhibited by these "African sons" and for the camaraderie established with the "Arab holy warriors for Islam."[96]

In a letter on the night of 8/9 May 1912 to his fellow officer and relative Salih (Bozok), Mustafa Kemal revealed his inner thoughts and feelings about the military profession employing the three words hissiyat (feelings), vicdan (conscience), and dimağ (mind). He began by acknowledging an emotional link. The "feelings" expressed in Salih's letter affected his own heart "with deep feelings." Despite the physical hardships and the linguistic, cultural, and social differences, he thrived in his environment. "You know [that] in soldiering I love

2 *Libya – Mustafa Kemal in foreground on the left*

its artistry more than anything." This appreciation of the art of war meant the mental and emotional challenges of dealing with the unpredictable, while relying on the mind and intuition. He claimed modest ambition. "Ah, Salih, God knows [that] until this day of my life, I have not aspired in my conscience (*vicdan*) for anything else other than being a useful member to the army." He expressed his Turkishness: his army needed to prove to the world its ability to defend the fatherland like the old Turkish army. The letter ends with admiration for "the many sons of the fatherland who sacrifice their own safety and well-being for the safety and well-being of the country and the nation."[97] Kemal's appreciation of the heroic example of sacrifice exhibited by others was a recurring theme in his writings, for he witnessed much of that in battle. His generation of officers experienced far too much combat.

How did Mustafa Kemal adapt to the tribal ethos? Appreciating the place of Islam in society, he addressed on occasions şeyhs or tribal leaders as "my religious brother" (*din kardeşim*) and called upon the warriors to fight against the "infidels."[98] He allowed the Sanusi şeyhs to use "their own methods and tactics," when appropriate, such as on the night of 21/22 December 1911, when Şeyh Muberra and his tribesmen employed their own stealth approach at night followed by a dawn assault to capture an Italian fortification atop Nadura Hill.[99] Mustafa Kemal came to admire aspects of tribal warfare, emotionally and intellectually connecting with Arab warriors. Tahsin al-Askari, an Arab officer who also served in Libya at the time, highlighted an aspect of Kemal's cultural sensitivity. Jafar al-Askari, who after World War I helped found the modern Iraqi army, quoted his brother thus:

> They [Kemal and Enver] were at complete variance with each other in their views on military tactics, organization and similar topics. Enver's constant opposition to our plans often came at the cost of heavy casualties to our undermanned units. Kemal was quite the opposite: every time he made a move, he was careful to execute it with minimum loss. He would use his forces sparingly, to maximize their usefulness. He always advised his officers to stick to this principle and avoid anything that might weaken them unnecessarily and cause loss of life.[100]

In explaining the friction between the two men, Tahsin underscored Kemal's concern for casualties. Mustafa Kemal certainly appreciated that the adversary's superiority in numbers and technology dictated husbanding one's own resources, but he also noted in the above report the reluctance of şeyhs to engage in bloody battles. He had accommodated himself to Arab-tribal culture and learned of tactics from his hosts.

In July 1912, some nine months into the conflict, Mustafa Kemal made two decisions directly addressing the intellect in war. First, on 13/14 July, he wanted his officers to have access to two military journals, *The Journal of the Army and Navy*, and the *Military Gazette*, for two distinct reasons. These publications were meant to enlighten officers as to military developments in the world while also focusing attention on the bravery of the Ottoman army.[101] Second, on 22 July, he ordered all his officers to submit an account of their combat experiences. Their reports would be important material for the eventual writing of a campaign history of the Ottoman-Italian War. He stressed the need to include: date, day, conditions, forces, orders of the commander, actions and their results, and finally to "paying attention to the psychological conditions." The psychology of troops remained a vital consideration in war. Mustafa Kemal wanted "the memoranda to remain faithul to the truth and not stray from the love of humanity (*insanlık*) or the love of truth." His officers had one month in which to submit their reports.[102] In demanding accurate accounts of the war for the future writing of a campaign history, Mustafa Kemal couched the order in terms of benefiting "humanity," thinking in universal terms.

This second assignment to Libya developed Kemal's military skills and gained for him invaluable leadership experience against a European adversary. He planned operations coordinating "coalition" forces, organized intelligence-gathering operations, held conferences and training exercises for professional development, ensured adequate logistical support, and enforced strict camp standards, including hygiene and a dress code. These measures recalled similar steps taken by him with the Bengazi garrison over three years earlier. As any good commander, Mustafa Kemal created a professional climate and environment in his command, but one that included more strictness in proper manners and behavior. Keeping soldiers busy, focused, and professional, while working to ensure proper logistical support, helps maintain morale, builds confidence, and fosters loyalty if done by personal example and with a keen instinct not to cross the line by demanding too much. From the perspective of Ottoman military culture, Mustafa Kemal was supposed to care for his troops like a father, or *baba*, at the same time knowing full well that as a commander he demanded obedience, even possibly to the point of death.

In addition to his "purely" military activities, Mustafa Kemal assumed the role of soldier-diplomat in negotiating with tribal leaders across a cultural and linguistic divide for tactical outcomes. This experience presaged the War of Independence, when diplomacy and the art of persuasion became important ingredients for final success. In Libya, Mustafa Kemal thrived in this unconventional environment, leaving him no doubt a more confident individual. Most interesting for the "official" historical record back in Istanbul, the Ottoman Parliament singled out a number of Ottoman officers for their meritorious service in Libya. Enver headed the list, but Mustafa Kemal failed to receive any mention.[103] Yet, in a report to the war ministry filed in October 1912, Enver did write a good evaluation of him, noting that Mustafa Kemal had served to the very end in an extraordinary manner despite his eye problems.[104] Actually, Mustafa Kemal was bedridden on two separate occasions, totaling some six weeks, because of a recurring eye infection.[105] Perhaps Enver blocked official recognition of an emerging rival.

National Humiliation in the Balkan Wars

The First Balkan War began on 8 October 1912 when Montenegro declared war and attacked northern Albania. Bulgaria, Serbia, and Greece soon followed suit with ultimatums demanding territorial concessions from the Ottomans but not expecting to receive them. So on 17 October, Bulgaria commenced operations into Thrace, with Serbia and Greece supporting Bulgaria's action by attacking Macedonia, with Athens also sending an army into southern Albania. On 15 October, Istanbul quickly reached an agreement with Italy, the Treaty of Ouchy, to end hostilities and the withdrawal of the Ottoman army from Libya. Ottoman officers who had volunteered to fight in Libya meanwhile scrambled to get back to Europe in order to participate in the new conflagration.

Initially, the war in the Balkans went very badly for the Ottomans. The Balkan League outnumbered the Ottoman army: 475,000 soldiers to 290,000. Ottoman forces were divided into two theaters. Çatalca Army, with 115,000 troops, guarded the Eastern Theater, while the 175,000 man Vardar Army had responsibility for the Western Theater. The first month of the war saw major reverses on the battlefield for the Ottoman Empire. Macedonia was essentially lost and the Ottoman army split in two, with 15,000 troops retreating to the region of Yanya in southern Albania while another 16,000 located in Berat in the central region. On 9 November, Ottoman forces surrendered Selanik to the Greeks without putting up armed resistance. In the Eastern Theater, the Bulgarians pushed back the Ottomans and surrounded the town of Edirne, but Çatalca Army stopped the Bulgarian advance and established a strong defensive line before Istanbul. The Ottomans also controlled the Gallipoli Peninsula. Negotiations for an armistice commenced at the end of November, creating a lull in fighting. Greece, however, refused to end hostilities until it received Yanya. Meanwhile, on 25 November, Mustafa Kemal was appointed director of operations for what became Bolayır Army Corps, located at the Gallipoli Peninsula under the command of Brigadier General Fahri Paşa. Lieutenant Colonel Fethi (Okyar), of Manastır school days, served as the chief of staff. Now, for the first time in his military career, Kemal would participate in a major

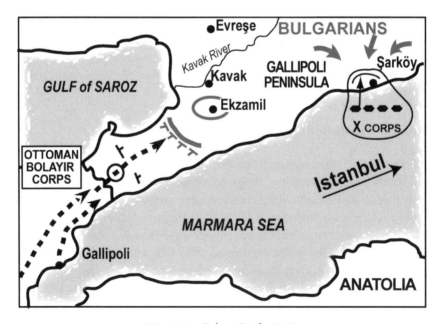

Map 1.2 *Bolayır Battle, 1913*

conflict involving two large armies pitted against each other in conventional operations.

On 23 January 1913, the CUP staged a coup and seized power, determined to resume the war to ensure the retention of Edirne. Enver personally led an assault force on the war ministry; Nazım Paşa, the war minister, was killed in the operation. Mahmud Şevket returned to the cabinet as both grand vezir and war minister. Prior to the coup, Lieutenant General Ahmed İzzet Paşa, the chief of the General Staff, had ordered the preparation of plans for a two-corps offensive to relieve the garrison in Edirne. Bolayır Corps would break out from the Gallipoli Peninsula while X Corps, part of the reserve, would conduct an amphibious landing at Şarköy and hit the Bulgarian rear. Both corps would then head for Edirne. Meanwhile, Çatalca Army would launch a supporting attack. The plan looked good on paper, and the coup failed to derail the preparations.

The execution of the plan, however, ran into problems. Weather conditions, logistics preparations, and troop movements all served to delay the combined attack until 8 February. Bolayır Corps attacked over open terrain in a frontal assault straight into the teeth of Bulgarian defenses without confirming the landing by X Corps, which turned out to be half a day late. Bolayır Corps suffered the loss of half its men in one day. Problems emerged with X Corps as well. The Bulgarians had recently fortified Şarköy, forcing the amphibious force to construct a landing site to the west of the village. Enver, who took personal charge of the bridgehead, proved unable to launch an offensive operation. Then on 10 February, just two days into the operation, Ahmed İzzet ordered X Corps to abort and withdraw from the bridgehead. Enver ended up having to use his leadership skills to extricate his force. X Corps suffered light casualties.[106] Mutual recriminations resulted from this botched operation, each corps commander and his staff blaming the other.

Undeterred by the failed operation, Fethi and Mustafa Kemal submitted on 18/19 February a new concept for another offensive to relieve the defenders in Edirne. It called for Çatalca Army to lead the main effort, with X Corps transferring to the Çatalca lines. Bolayır Corps would conduct a supportive attack. Both men presented compelling reasons for the operation. Politically, the CUP coup of 23 January 1913 was, in part, predicated on not surrendering Edirne. Therefore Ottoman public opinion, as well as national and military honor, necessitated an offensive to deliver on the promise to save this historical city. Moreover, "the liberation of Edirne would, with the encouragement of the government, result in [public] demonstrations for the continuation of the war." Here Fethi and Mustafa Kemal directly linked military operations to politics on the home front. From a military point of view, the fall of Edirne would free up Bulgarian forces to conduct a major offensive toward Istanbul. Finally, and no less importantly, Fethi and Mustafa Kemal argued from reason and logic.

31

Their plan had "resulted from scientific discussion" and had fulfilled "the duty of placing scientific reality to the fore."[107] This final wording suggested Kemal's hand: critical reasoning, the scientific method, and the power of the mind had produced an irrefutable solution.

In the meantime, X Corps had been ordered to the Gallipoli Peninsula to reinforce the battered Bolayır Corps, and its commander, Major General Hurşid Paşa, had been placed in command of both corps with Enver as his chief of staff. Fahri, Mustafa Kemal, and Fethi all became miffed at playing second fiddle to Hurşid and Enver, and all three tendered their resignations. Ahmed İzzet became livid upon receiving the plan followed by the letter of resignations. Fahri had not signed off on the plan; so no doubt it appeared that Fethi and Mustafa Kemal had acted behind his back. Ahmed İzzet expressed his disgust to Mahmud Şevket, singling out Fethi and Mustafa Kemal for unprofessional behavior. "Seriously, no army in the world has ever been run by youths devoid of official responsibility; nor has victory ever been won by an army harboring this degree of anarchy, discord and mischief." He also blamed Fahri for attacking prematurely without communicating with X Corps.[108] Ahmed İzzet viewed all this behavior as petty, unprofessional, and self-serving, if not outright insubordination. He was right to a large degree.

Rather than accept these resignations, Mahmud Şevket went with Hurşid and Enver to Bolayır Corps in order to patch up relations. After smoothing matters over, he appointed Mustafa Kemal as Bolayır Corps' chief of staff while Fethi departed for Istanbul.[109] Mustafa Kemal thus gained greater responsibility after having been so soundly criticized by Ahmed İzzet. The X Corps was transferred to the Çatalca Front as had been recommended by Fethi and Mustafa Kemal. Their sound plan redeemed them; but politics saved them. Fethi had good CUP connections. Transferring X Corps to Gallipoli would have only reinforced failure. The major offensive, however, never materialized, and Edirne eventually fell to both Bulgarian and Serbian troops. A truce followed on 16 April, with the Ottomans still in control of the Gallipoli Peninsula and a small area around Istanbul. The Treaty of London was signed on 30 May, permitting the remnants of the Ottoman Western Army in Albania to evacuate the Balkans by sea.

The victors, however, came to blows over the division of spoils. On 29/30 June 1913, Bulgaria attacked Serbia and Greece in Macedonia, setting off the Second Balkan War. Taking advantage of this strategic turn of events, Rumania, Montenegro, and the Ottoman Empire joined the fight against Bulgaria. Outnumbered and fighting on three fronts, the Bulgarian army quickly retreated from Edirne and Eastern Thrace, allowing the Ottomans to reclaim the region. In this war, Mustafa Kemal led a brigade from the Gallipoli Peninsula into Edirne. But it was Enver, however, who arrived there first and received acclaim as "the

Hero of Edirne," adding to his earlier designation as "Hero of Liberty" after the restoration of the Constitution. In this public orchestration of valor and heroism, Mustafa Kemal witnessed first-hand the value of propaganda in enhancing one's position.

Despite its poor showing in the First Balkan War, the Ottoman army managed to regain Edirne in the Second Balkan War. Both wars, however, took a huge toll. The empire lost over 80 per cent of its territory and 70 per cent of its population in Europe. Ethnic cleansing policies of the conquerors, the war on civilians, precipitated a flight of some 640,000 Muslims into the empire. Casualty figures for the Ottoman side alone ran as high as 50,000 killed in combat, with another 100,000 dying from disease. The Balkan Wars presaged the character of World War I: the heavy human carnage, the importance of field fortifications, the significance of field artillery, and the huge expenditure of ordnance. For his part, Mustafa Kemal gained limited experience in large-scale operations as a staff officer, but he directly participated in the army's poor performance and defeat. Immediately afterwards, Mustafa Kemal contemplated resigning from the army to become a deputy in the Ottoman Parliament, but Fethi convinced him otherwise.[110] After the Balkan Wars, Mustafa Kemal, true to his serious character, conducted a technical study of field fortifications and artillery.[111]

Conclusion

Mustafa Kemal possessed a passion for learning, and his intellectual interests were broad and serious, incorporating military and non-military subjects. In the field, he demonstrated a dedication to professionalism and excellence through continued serious self-study as well as in the rigor and energy with which he approached education and training exercises as a commanding or staff officer. Mustafa Kemal was clearly a serious-thinking and dedicated soldier. More important, by the eve of World War I, he had assimilated rich and diverse experiences. Eight years of field service in the Ottoman army encompassed combat on three different continents that involved conventional and guerrilla warfare, independent field command and staff work, smaller and larger forces, fighting with and against tribesmen, and engaging an occupying European army. In all of this, Mustafa Kemal showed a mental and emotional flexibility to adjust to challenging circumstances. He demonstrated competence as a junior commander in Libya. His behavior as a staff officer in the First Balkan War was problematic; but some redemption came in the Second Balkan War as chief of staff of Bolayır Corps.

Although he had developed a good network in the officer corps and had an important supporter in Fethi, Mustafa Kemal did not belong to the inner circle of the CUP. Dedicated to military professionalism, he opposed the army's involvement in politics, and he developed strained relations with Enver, the rising star in the army. His outspokenness and ambition strained relations with his superiors. What he gained from experience was most important, and his professionalism and self-confidence ensured continued advancement in the military. Unknown to him, however, a global conflagration loomed on the horizon that would give Mustafa Kemal opportunity to shine in senior command. But he had one more important assignment in peacetime before embarking to command a division in war.

2

The Great War and an Imperialist Peace

By command I mean the general's qualities of wisdom, sincerity, humanity, courage, and strictness.

Sun Tzu[1]

It is the duty of everyone in possession of conscience and honor to try to remedy the situation immediately.

Mustafa Kemal, 1914

WORLD WAR I saw Mustafa Kemal rise in rank and responsibilities to command a division, corps, army, and army group (multiple armies). He emerged from the Great War with the reputation of a fighting general worthy of admiration for his achievements on the battlefield. Senior command brought with it added concerns for strategic and operational matters in addition to tactical ones, and Mustafa Kemal matured in these areas as well. He also continued to develop his intellect through experience and by study. The Great War, nonetheless, ended in military defeat for Turkey and the severance of the Arab provinces from the Ottoman Empire. Moreover, foreign occupation and additional partition among the Entente victors, this time in Anatolia, confronted the Istanbul government and the Anatolian population. Salvaging the peace despite military defeat thus became the primary task at hand for Mustafa Kemal and his associates. They moved deliberately to prepare a national resistance with the aim of creating an independent and sovereign Turkey out of the ashes of a devastating war and defeat. For Mustafa Kemal, this transition in leadership would require more political than military acumen.

Military Attaché in Sofia

With the coup of 23 January 1913, the CUP leadership consolidated political power. By 3 January 1914, Enver had risen from lieutenant colonel to war minister and chief of the General Staff; thus he commanded the entire Ottoman army. Meanwhile, a German military mission headed by Marshal Liman von Sanders arrived in Istanbul to assist in reforming the Ottoman army. The period between the Balkan Wars and World War I witnessed a major overhaul of the military. Some 1,100 officers—including 2 marshals, 3 lieutenant generals, 30 major generals, 95 brigadier generals, and 184 colonels—were retired from the army. Such a major overhaul of command, however, created significant adjustment problems throughout the army.

During this intense period of reform, Mustafa Kemal fortunately spent his time in a foreign country and thus uninvolved in the empire's road to war. Fethi (Okyar) had resigned his military commission and accepted the position of ambassador to Bulgaria, and he convinced senior officials to assign Mustafa Kemal to Sofia as military attaché.[2] Both men went into an exile of sorts. For someone exposed to the vitality and sophistication of France and Austria-Hungary, Bulgaria appeared almost a backwater to Western civilization. Yet for Mustafa Kemal, the Bulgarians had accomplished much in a relatively short time. In 1879, Sofia, a small town of 11,000 inhabitants, had become the capital of the Principality of Bulgaria, and in the next thirty-four years had developed into an impressive, medium-sized town of over 50,000. Its tree-lined wide streets, a theater, an opera house, villas, and modern buildings, with men and women mixing in public, gave the city a Western look and feel. And a robust European diplomatic corps fueled a Western ambiance to the city's social life. Mustafa Kemal assessed the country's progress in concrete terms. While Bulgaria was the youngest of the states in the First Balkan War, its army had engaged two Ottoman theater armies and achieved impressive results. During his tenure in Sofia, Mustafa Kemal gained a first-hand appreciation of Bulgaria's non-military achievements as well, which complemented its recent military performance and had transformed Bulgarian society.

As military attaché, Mustafa Kemal matured professionally, intellectually, and culturally. He filed numerous reports, evaluating both the political and military situation in Bulgaria and in the neighboring Balkan states.[3] His assignment required political engagement, intelligence gathering, and strategic analysis of intentions and capabilities of foreign governments and armies. Mustafa Kemal's success depended on developing a social life that joined business with pleasure. He thrived in this environment as he came in direct contact with senior and junior officers as well as influential figures from Bulgarian society and the European community. The famous photograph of him dressed in a Janissary uniform en route to a party attests to the importance of this social dimension. Mustafa Kemal, meanwhile, became involved in the issue of conversion pressures exerted by the Bulgarian government on Muslim Pomaks in Bulgaria and observed Fethi as he threatened possible retaliation against Bulgarians living in Istanbul. With the outbreak of World War I, secret discussions commenced with the Bulgarian defense minister and chief of staff about the possibility of Bulgaria's entry into the conflict and other related matters.[4] Such high-stake political talks provided useful diplomatic experience for the young lieutenant colonel. Mustafa Kemal's ability to speak French well proved indispensable, and he found time for private lessons to keep improving his Gallic competency. He even worked to sharpen his German.

In 1914, while still in Sofia, Mustafa Kemal wrote his most important military work. The impetus came from his close friend Nuri (Conker), who in the winter of 1913 had participated in a conference of the 1st Infantry Division and then wrote a book entitled *Zabit ve Kumandan,* or *Officer and Commander.* He sent Kemal a copy for comment. This request nudged Mustafa Kemal into writing his own thoughts on the nature of war, combat, and leadership, issues that went into the heart and soul of the military profession. Mustafa Kemal intended to publish his commentary, also, but censors delayed its publication until late 1918, when it appeared as *Zabit ve Kumandan ile Hasbıhal,* or *Conversation with Officer and Commander.* The book, when finally published, ran thirty-two pages, including six pages of photographs, all of them of Mustafa Kemal in the Libyan campaign. Some of the discussion dealt with how he successfully fought to keep a larger Italian force bottled along the coast for a year and how his officers exercised initiative in the execution of their orders, which he claimed reflected his effective training of them.[5] When compared to the original hand-written manuscript, Mustafa Kemal removed only a few minor details for the 1918 publication. This indicated that his basic views on war had not changed despite his senior command experiences in World War I.

Conversation with Officer and Commander reveals Mustafa Kemal's essential philosophy of leadership and war. He began by complimenting Nuri's work, noting that he had read it several times until "its deep and moving meaning settled into my mind." In short, Mustafa Kemal internalized his friend's ideas and reflected on them seriously. *Officer and Commander,* it must be noted, ran 101 pages, not a quick read. Mustafa Kemal took his time to digest Nuri's ideas before evaluating them. Although not stated, he, in the meantime, wanted to publish his own ideas, which also explains his seriousness and thoughtfulness. Mustafa Kemal frequently mentioned the need for internalizing knowledge, no doubt with the aim of sharpening the mind and facilitating recall. In *Conversation,* he restated this notion: "Every officer must read these words with great attention and seriousness and must *imbed* (italics mine) their meaning into his mind."[6]

Nuri was clearly motivated by patriotism and the shame brought about by the Ottoman army's recent humiliating performance in the Balkan Wars, and Mustafa Kemal shared in this "very painful reality."[7] But Mustafa Kemal framed the compelling need for action. "It is the duty of everyone in possession of conscience (*vicdan*) and honor to try to remedy the situation immediately."[8] He also couched his analysis with "conscience and reason (*akıl*)."[9] By conscience, Kemal meant high professional and moral standards.

In discussing motivation, so essential for the military, Mustafa Kemal writes that "the means for inspiring [troops] is the power of the mind (*dimağ*) and the spirit (*ruh*) in the blood of its live members that transforms an army into a machine."[10] Thus, for him, waging war involved both mental and moral exertion, and, citing Goltz in this regard, commanders must play the critical role in fielding a good army.[11] Sacrifice becomes central to effective leadership, as noted in an Ottoman field manual, "an officer does not give any importance to his life and existence for the sake of his art." Here, Mustafa Kemal recalls the heroism and sacrifice exhibited in the Libyan campaign. Officers carry a heavy burden because they must possess knowledge and ability and show courage and valor greater than those around them.[12]

In Mustafa Kemal's view, motivating troops depended on commanders having the right attitude towards the soldiers under their command. Officers must win hearts, gain trust, and strengthen the spiritual powers of their troops. "Human beings can only be commanded and directed when their aspirations and ideas take concrete form."[13] Mustafa Kemal cited three huge historical figures who personified the hopes and dreams of their people. Moses, for one, fulfilled the desire of the Jews to be free of slavery and oppression under the yoke of the Egyptians. Jesus addressed the hopes of the poor in the form of religion based on "compassion." Finally, Napoleon embodied "the ideal of military glory" as he traversed Europe [with his army].[14] But while Mustafa Kemal presented an idealistic portrayal of officering, his examples of Moses, Jesus, and Napoleon lacked practical application to officers faced with the challenge of inspiring soldiers bereft of a sense of noble purpose when confronting death and destruction. Here was idealism at work.

But how does an army raise competent commanders and officers? Here Mustafa Kemal stresses practical experience, but not at the expense of book learning. He writes that, "The unit is the principal school from which true spiritual power can be imparted."[15] The War College provides certificates so that lieutenants become qualified to join their units in the field, but it is the commanders who must translate what they have learned into effective training of their subordinates in the art of war. Each level of command has this responsibility. A lieutenant, for example, comes under a captain who acts as the "father of the company" (*bölük babası*) and so on for battalions, regiments, etc. Commanders must lead "the sons of the nation," not as "a herd," but as "human beings," appealing to the emotions of "fame and honor" (*şan ve şeref*), a romantic and chivalrous view of leadership in war. Mustafa Kemal ends this section of his work by citing an incident while traveling on a ship when he met a young European lieutenant who was reading a military book in order to please his captain.[16] This example illustrates the importance of commanders demanding self-study from their subordinates. For the spirit of the offense, *Conversation* drew upon the Japanese defeat of the Russians on land and sea in the Russo-Japanese War of 1904–5.[17]

Six out of twenty-six pages, almost a quarter of the text, address "initiative" (*inisyativ*). Here, Mustafa Kemal discusses the nature of war. For him, war comprises unexpected and unique events. Field manuals, although valuable for presenting the basics, cannot possibly prepare officers for all occurrences. "Principles, laws, and procedures," which form the basis for the art of soldiering, must be studied and committed to memory, but they are not understood until they are put into practice. Moreover, this knowledge cannot be the main basis for an army's success, because in war events are unique. In addition, it is not the senior commanders but lieutenants who first encounter the unexpected, and they are the ones who have to make difficult decisions in a hostile environment of death and destruction. This thinking explains the wisdom behind Mustafa Kemal, as a captain, translating the two German manuals for platoons and companies. Commanders must be attuned to the reality of war for the smallest units. In making decisions in the midst of combat, Mustafa Kemal mapped out a good habit of thinking: "Officers should be slow and cautious in action, taking time to reflect in carrying out their authority. This is because units will encounter unforeseen conditions and difficulties in battle."[18] In this advice, Mustafa Kemal reflected his culture. To quote a proverb, "Haste comes from the devil," whereas German manuals were more inclined to stress "feverish haste" in decision-making.[19]

Mustafa Kemal ends his commentary in a most interesting manner. Rather than conclude with his own wisdom, he offers three pages of notes from the Libyan campaign, consisting of reports from other officers who demonstrated their heroism and sacrifice. One entry, for example, describes several soldiers wounded while others continue the fight. The last entry is especially poignant. An officer commanding 100 "Muslim fighters" continues to lead despite a bloody wound: "In order not to break the morale of my troops, I will not withdraw from the line of battle. If I die, Remzi is at my side. He will direct my forces."[20] Mustafa Kemal concluded his small booklet with these inspirational words. This example and others recalled the letter written to Salih (Bozok) in May 1912 during the

Libyan campaign when Mustafa Kemal noted how the sacrifice and heroism of fellow officers stirred his soul and encouraged him to be a better officer. Now, in 1914, these examples were recalled to inspire others to reform the army.

In *Conversation with Officer and Commander*, Mustafa Kemal reflected on the deeper meaning of war for his profession. He painted a picture of a combat environment with its share of unexpected and unforeseen events requiring a sound mind, courage, and a clear purpose from superiors. Principles of war helped only to a point, but then the officer must rely on his mind and intuition in developing a course of action and following through on it. It is also important to note Mustafa Kemal's admonition to treat soldiers as human beings, who in the midst of combat will have to take initiative and make tough decisions. Here he painted a picture of the commander as a father who cares for his soldiers as his sons, thus having empathy for those under his command. Rather than discuss the horrors of war and the carnage of the Balkan Wars, of which he had direct personal experience, Mustafa Kemal focused on officer development with high professional standards and embraced the ideals of honor, patriotism, and sacrifice as motivating factors.

In the one important section that failed to make the 1918 publication but was part of his original manuscript, Mustafa Kemal expressed strong Turkish sentiments. After invoking "Turkic" heroes Hülega, Timur and Genghiz, he called upon Turkish mothers to instill in their sons a pride in the pre-Islamic Turkic past. "Hey nation, hey Turkish woman, you who are wrapped in a 600-year-old veil but once had an open forehead for 5,000 years. Do you sing of those 5,000-year-old traditions to your sons whom you give to command as officers? Did you develop moral character in them with those songs?"[21] Here, Mustafa Kemal expressed his desire for an army based on "the inculcation of a sound Turkish national consciousness."[22] However, this section failed to appear in 1918, when Mustafa Kemal was acutely aware that appeals based on Turkism were premature given the diverse ethnic and religious nature of Muslim society in Anatolia.

A Rock at Gallipoli

The Ottoman Empire's entry in November 1914 into World War I surprised Mustafa Kemal. From Sofia, he immediately set to work to gain a senior command in the conflict. On 20 January 1915, he received notification of his assignment: command of the newly forming 19th Infantry Division. On 5 February, Mustafa Kemal joined his 57th Regiment, a unit comprising Turks, at Tekirdağ. The other two infantry regiments, the 72nd and 77th, were mainly composed of Arab soldiers. Kemal complained to corps headquarters that these Arab units lacked

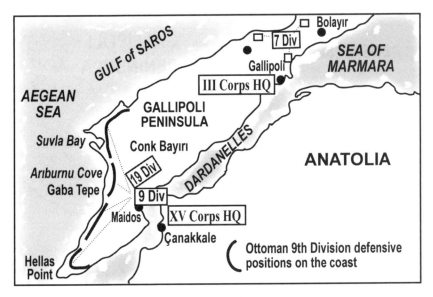

Map 2.1 *Ottoman Defensive Positions*

sufficient training and included members of the Yazidi sect, whom he described as being generally opposed to war. Corps headquarters encouraged him to make do and ordered him to deploy to Gallipoli.[23] Mustafa Kemal had two months to prepare these forces for combat, and he did to a large extent.

Gallipoli, a peninsula of some 400 square miles, guarded the entrance into the Dardanelles and the sea route to Istanbul. Between 19 and 25 February and again on 18 March, a joint British and French naval force tried and failed to punch through the Ottoman defenses, with the aim of opening a sea route to Russia through the Straits to the Black Sea. Meanwhile, the Ottoman General Staff rushed additional troops to the area. After two failed attempts by sea, Britain and France formed the Mediterranean Expeditionary Forces (MEF) under the command of General Sir Ian Hamilton, with the aim of launching a major amphibious operation to secure passage for the naval fleet. For their part, the Ottoman General Staff responded to the Allied naval attacks by forming Fifth Army, some 84,000 men, under the command of German General Liman von Sanders.

Arriving the day after his appointment, Sanders quickly inspected the defenses and found them unacceptable. Ottoman troops had deployed forward with the aim of defeating any Allied landing attempts on the beaches, but Sanders assessed the forward deployments as too thinly spread out to offer a robust defense. Instead, he ordered the establishment of light warning forces at the coastline, with larger forces stationed in the rear. Success of this defensive concept required accurate and

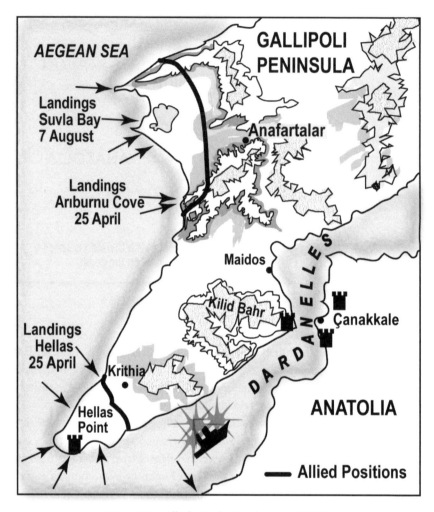

Map 2.2 *Allied Attacks March–August 1915*

timely intelligence, as well as a quick response to foil any major landings. Mustafa Kemal opposed the defensive concept and instead pushed for keeping defenses strong at the beaches, but to no avail. It is impossible to say conclusively who had the better strategy. The deployments were executed as follows. In deploying forces in depth, Sanders concentrated on three areas—the Bolayır isthmus, the southern section of the peninsula, and the Anatolian side of the entrance into the Dardanelles Straits. The Bolayır isthmus, only four and one-half kilometers in length and in the northernmost part of the Gallipoli Peninsula, received his main attention. Army headquarters was located in the town of Gallipoli. An independent cavalry brigade and the 5th Division defended the narrow isthmus. Defense of the remainder of the peninsula fell to III Corps under Brigadier General Esad (Bulkat) Paşa, Goltz Paşa's former student and erstwhile director of education at the War College during Kemal's student days there. Esad Paşa, also headquartered in the town of Gallipoli, commanded three divisions. The 7th Division deployed south of the Bolayır isthmus while the 9th covered the southern part of the peninsula, with gendarmerie watching the coast between the two divisions. Mustafa Kemal's 19th Division constituted the general reserve for III Corps. On the Anatolian side of the Dardanelles, German General Weber commanded XV Corps with its two divisions.

British General Sir Ian Hamilton's MEF initially numbered 75,000 ground troops. His plan of attack went as follows: the British 29th Division would attack Hellas Point at the southern tip of the Gallipoli Peninsula, while the French 1st Division conducted a diversionary assault at Kumkale on the Anatolian side and the Australian and New Zealand Corps (ANZAC) of two divisions of 30,050 men landed on a sandy beach between Arıburnu Cove and Gaba Tepe. After securing its landing area, the corps would move out to secure the route to Mal Tepe and thereby threaten to cut the peninsula in half. Furthermore, such a move would prevent the Ottomans from reinforcing their troops facing the 29th Division in the south. A naval feint in the Gulf of Saros in the northern section of the peninsula was designed to focus Sanders' attention there and away from the main landings. The diversion proved successful.

Mustafa Kemal gained his reputation from two major battles in the Gallipoli campaign. All three Allied landings commenced on 25 April and all three produced beachheads. Sanders, however, remained fixated on the Bolayır isthmus for the remainder of the day, and Esad Paşa joined him there.[24] Meanwhile, the British 29th Division and the ANZAC corps both landed in the sector defended by the 9th Division. At Arıburnu Cove, the 1st Australian Division was assigned the task of landing and capturing the first three ridges, the last being Gun Ridge. At 0530, word reached Colonel Halil Sami, the 9th Division commander, of landings at both Hellas Point and Arıburnu. At 0545, according to plan, he quickly ordered two battalions and a machine gun company from his 27th Regiment to the Arıburnu area, a move that helped delay the Allied advance inland. Halil Sami also requested assistance from the 19th Division. After 0900, Lieutenant Colonel Mehmed Şefik (Aker), the commander of the 27th Regiment, arrived in the area and found ANZAC forces had occupied the first two ridges and were moving up the third, so he launched counterattacks. At 0825, word reached him that Mustafa Kemal was en route with the 57th Regiment and a mountain battery.[25]

After receiving Halil Sami's request for assistance, Mustafa Kemal, for his part, tried for nearly two hours to contact either Sanders or Esad Paşa by phone.

Unable to reach either commander, he took the initiative and collected his best unit, the 57th Regiment, along with the cavalry company, an artillery battery, and a medical unit. Lacking solid intelligence but appreciating the serious threat posed by enemy forces capturing high ground and potentially cutting the peninsula in half, Mustafa Kemal chose to fight the terrain rather than the enemy.[26] He headed for the important position of Conk Bayırı without approval from his senior commanders, a bold and audacious move on his part. Committing the entire division without more information seemed reckless to him.

By mid-morning, Mustafa Kemal reached the battlefield and gained a general appreciation of the situation. The Aussies had captured the first two ridges from the shoreline, leaving the third, Gun Ridge, for contention. Esad Paşa, now apprised of the situation, left Mustafa Kemal in charge of the area, placing the 27th Regiment under his command. Mustafa Kemal occupied Conk Bayırı. By the late afternoon, he regained control of a couple of small hills, but could do no more, as his adversary had landed some 8,000 troops. By late afternoon, the ANZAC troops secured a defensible bridgehead. If Mustafa Kemal had committed his entire division at once, he might have driven the ANZACs into the sea. But employing the entire corps reserve without orders would have been a questionable proposition. Meanwhile, Hamilton had his ANZAC troops hunker down into defensive positions. His commanders, for their part, experienced problems gaining command and control over their forces, and the terrain favored the defender. By the end of the first day of battle, Kemal had helped confine the ANZACs to a small bridgehead. The following day saw little fighting.

Writing his memoirs a few years later, Sanders described Mustafa Kemal on the first day of battle thus: "[he was] by nature a commander who did not fear taking on responsibility. On 25 April he had taken upon himself to attack the enemy with his 19th division; then for the next three months on the Arıburnu front, he pushed back successfully with obstinacy and stubbornness all the enemy's violent attacks. I was able to have complete confidence in his energy."[27] That confidence did not come immediately, however, for Mustafa Kemal was a relative unknown to him. Perhaps that is why on 27 April, two days into the campaign, Sanders sent a German major to be Mustafa Kemal's chief of staff and assist him in command. Affronted by this move, Mustafa Kemal kept the German officer occupied with other activities until he finally sent him away on 15 May.[28]

During the first few days of the battle, Kemal issued an order that was later found on the body of a Turkish soldier and revealed his mindset at the time. In ordering preparations for battle the next day, he showed confidence, appealed to pride, and threatened lethal punishment:

... we must drive those now in front of us into the sea ... There is no need to scheme much to make the enemy run. I do not expect that any of us would not rather die than repeat the shameful story of the Balkan War. But if there are any such men among us, we should at once lay hand on them and set them up to the line to be shot.[29]

Professional and national honor demanded removing the shame of the Balkan Wars. But problems of coordination and stiff resistance prevented Mustafa Kemal from making any appreciable gains in territory.

Mustafa Kemal also played an important role in another critical point in the campaign, and this time Sanders confidently passed the baton of command to him. By midsummer 1915, the British and the French had increased their forces to fourteen divisions, with the aim of breaking the stalemate and reaching a decision. The new plan called for the ANZAC to break out from its bridgehead as the main effort and take Conk Bayırı and then, perhaps two days later, capture Gun Ridge. Meanwhile, IX Corps with two divisions of some 20,000 troops would land at Suvla Bay in the north. Both operations commenced during the night of 6/7 August. The IX Corps managed to secure its bridgehead but failed to exploit its success. Sanders rushed two divisions from Bolayır, some thirty kilometers distant, to Suvla Bay. When the Ottoman commander of these two divisions pleaded for more time to prepare his men for battle, Sanders fired him on 8 August at 2150 and appointed Mustafa Kemal in his stead. Conk Bayırı, meanwhile, fell to ANZAC forces on 8 August.

To meet this new threat, Sanders formed a new command, the Anafartalar Group, consisting of XVI Corps, 9th Division, and the Willmer Group, and placed it under Mustafa Kemal's command. The next morning, Mustafa Kemal pushed two more divisions into battle, gaining some ground back, and stabilized the front. Then his attention turned to retaking Conk Bayırı. On 10 August at 0430, after reconnoitering the area, Mustafa Kemal went to the main force of six battalions in order to give the signal for the attack just before daybreak. The troops launched in silence with bayonets drawn and surprised the enemy in its forward positions, capturing Conk Bayırı by 1245. Other British units withdrew as well. During the ensuing combat, Mustafa Kemal was reportedly saved from serious injury by his watch deflecting a bullet.[30] The official British history described the fall of Conk Bayırı thus: "This Turkish counter-stroke was admirably planned."[31] Attacking before daybreak in silence with bayonets provided the element of surprise, while Mustafa Kemal's presence set an example of personal courage for his troops. For his part, Sanders once again praised his Turkish commander, this time for his overall role during these critical days.[32] The front stabilized after four days of intense battle, with 17,000 Ottoman and 25,000 British casualties.

For the next several months, Mustafa Kemal commanded Anafartalar Group, a force that grew to two corps and six divisions.

Battles at Gallipoli resembled the trench warfare of the Western Front in France. Terrain restrictions and heavy troop concentrations constrained attacks to costly frontal assaults, with minuscule gains in land. Machine guns added to the lethality. A number of engagements involved gruesome bayonet fights. Despite Mustafa Kemal's exemplary leadership on several key occasions, Major İzzeddin (Çalışlar), his chief of staff during the campaign, recorded a number of failed attacks in his diary.[33] One was especially costly. On the night of 29–30 June, Mustafa Kemal launched an attack that miscalculated the enemy's intent. Rather than an engagement battle with both sides attacking each other, his forces attacked straight into defensive positions and suffered over a thousand casualties. One regiment needed reconstitution if it was to function effectively as a fighting organization. Rather than assume responsibility for the failure, however, Kemal blamed his officers for failing to take advantage of initial gains.[34] Perhaps.

How did Mustafa Kemal personally fare as a commander in this campaign? Stress was no doubt ubiquitous and palpable. On 27 August, for example, Mustafa

3   *Mustafa Kemal front row, second from left, with staff at Gallipoli*

4   *Gallipoli trench warfare*

Kemal lost patience and fired back a blunt and harsh order to the 7th Division: "I expect this news [from you]: the enemy who has entered the trenches has been destroyed and our soldiers have entered their trenches. Any news other than this is not important to me."[35] Combat stress affected his emotional state. "We are truly living a life of hell," he wrote to a female friend, Corinne Lütfü, in a letter dated 20 July 1915, the third month of the campaign. After noting the Islamic faith of his soldiers in battle, Mustafa Kemal went on to express a personal determination to resist the psychological effect of prolonged combat. "I have decided to study novels to soften the hard character that I have gained as a result of events." Along this vein, he asked Corinne for a recommendation of books to read in order to keep as much of his humanity as possible, even providing her with a contact for purchasing them in Istanbul.[36] It was an emotional recognition by him of the need to invest time and effort into maintaining his humanity and character and thereby limiting the psychological scars of war. On 11 October, three months later, Mustafa Kemal wrote his friend Salih (Bozok) that he once felt a desire to retire and withdraw from all the carnage to a corner, but he decided to continue with God's help and protection.[37] Mustafa Kemal departed Gallipoli with some calluses on his soul from the stress of combat.

In addition to books and other diversions, Mustafa Kemal derived meaning and purpose by remaining fixed on the strategic importance of defending Gallipoli for the empire. In May, after a failed night attack, he noted for his command: "All soldiers who enter battle with me must definitely understand that in order to carry out our duty of honor exactly there is no retreating one step. I remind all of you that seeking the easy road will cause . . . our entire nation to remain deprived."[38] The fall of Gallipoli would most certainly result in the abandonment of Istanbul and the relocation of the capital to Anatolia. The Ottomans had more to fight for than their adversary, who was far from home.

Although it was impossible to achieve a decisive victory in battle, or even make any significant territorial gains, Mustafa Kemal did receive several recognitions for his leadership. The Ottoman army awarded him the Silver Medal of Battle Service. On 28 December 1915, Kaiser Wilhelm II bestowed on him the prestigious Iron Cross. Even his peers recognized his leadership. Lieutenant Colonel Fahreddin Altay, Esad Paşa's chief of staff, voiced the appreciation of his comrade-in-arms when he designated the unnamed hill of Mustafa Kemal's forward headquarters in the first crucial days of the campaign as Kemalyeri, or Kemal's Place.[39] In the midst of all these recognitions, Mustafa Kemal was promoted to full colonel on 1 June. Two months later, he assumed command of Anafartalar Group.

From the onset of the campaign, Mustafa Kemal opposed entrusting the fate of the empire to German hands. Whether to defend at the beachheads or in depth emerged as an early bone of contention. On 3 May, he vented his frustrations by writing Enver, voicing his objection to German officers and arguing that the successful enemy landings vindicated his argument for defenses at the shoreline. He stressed that Sanders lacked knowledge of the Ottoman army and country and did not have the time to study the situation properly. Sanders' deployments had left the shores unguarded and thus facilitated the enemy's landings. Mustafa Kemal dismissed the mental ability of the Germans headed by Sanders, because they lacked "the hearts and consciences" to engage in the defense of the Ottoman fatherland. Here, Mustafa Kemal based his argument on patriotic sentiment, thereby calling into question German competence and commitment. He ended the letter by asking his "friend" to come to Gallipoli and assume command. Enver visited the front but chose to leave the fighting to his German general.[40]

By the end of September 1915, Mustafa Kemal became restless and sought reassignment. Despite their strained relations, Sanders proved unwilling to release him. In a letter to Enver, he counseled against granting Mustafa Kemal's request for reassignment. Evaluating his performance over the last five months, Sanders described Mustafa Kemal as "an exceptionally talented and competent officer."[41] German Colonel Hans Kannengiesser, who commanded a division and then a corps under Mustafa Kemal at the Battle of Anafartalar, also praised him thus: "a clear thinking, active, quiet man who knew what he wanted . . . He spoke accordingly but little, and was always reserved and retiring without being unfriendly. He did not appear to be very strong bodily . . . His stubborn energy gave him apparently complete control, both of his troops and of himself."[42] Kannengiesser saw Mustafa Kemal as one of those Turkish officers who acted independently and carried "a certain feeling [i.e. empathy] for the personal welfare of the troops."[43] On one occasion in the first week of the campaign, the German attended a conference held in a tent devoid of a table and chairs. The day before, 1 May, Mustafa Kemal had experienced difficulty launching a coordinated attack by all his battalions. Kannengiesser found Mustafa Kemal sitting in the middle on the ground with his legs crossed while his regimental commanders surrounded him in the same posture. The conference took place without maps as Mustafa Kemal no doubt evaluated the previous day's events and provided guidance for the future. Unfortunately, without a translator, Kannengiesser failed to understand anything.[44] Mustafa Kemal performed his duties of educating and training his officers after a battle, on this occasion employing an *a la turca* style in his capacity of father, or *baba*, of his division.

On 5 December, Mustafa Kemal gained his desired separation. Fortune would shine on this departure. On 4 November, the British War Council had decided to abandon Gallipoli, and MEF Command successfully evacuated Suvla and the ANZAC beachheads on 19–20 December and Hellas Point on 8–9 January 1916. Both evacuations succeeded virtually uncontested and with minimal casualties. Back in Istanbul, Mustafa Kemal felt fortunate for having departed Gallipoli: "My being here is a stroke of luck for me."[45] He would never have to explain why the Ottoman army allowed the adversary to withdraw his forces with such ease. Mustafa Kemal emerged from the Gallipoli campaign with a reputation within the army as a competent commander. Trench warfare in Gallipoli left casualties ranging between 200,000 and a quarter million for each side. The campaign was essentially waged at the tactical level, a brutal slugfest. As noted by Kannengiesser, "Psychological powers triumphed over physical, the spirit over the material."[46]

War on the Eastern Front, 1916–17

While on leave, Mustafa Kemal received news of his new command, XVI Corps. While forming XVI Corps in Edirne, he prepared and published a training guide for his officers: *Corps Order: Counsel for Solving Tactical Problems and for Writing Orders*. Mustafa Kemal now had a year of senior command experience behind him, and he commanded a corps with double the officers and soldiers than in the 19th Division. Writing a manual for officers made perfect sense. Brevity and clarity in prose and judicious use of wisdom characterizes this important document. *Corps Order* contains only seven pages of text, written with short and direct sentences to facilitate comprehension. The title page requires "every officer" to study its contents seriously.[47]

In the first sentence, Mustafa Kemal revealed the inner working of his intellect. "To solve a tactical problem, one must, before anything else, study the problem several times, from beginning to end, with tranquility of the mind (*sükunet-i fikir*)." This wisdom called for the officer to rein in emotions and develop an inner peace through focusing solely on the situation at hand. Such mental discipline militates against forgetting important points and would result in "the situation of both sides [in combat] settling soundly in the intellect (*zihin*)."[48] Tactical problems must be consciously internalized, and this method recalls Mustafa Kemal claiming to have read Nuri's *Officer and Commander* several times before deigning to offer criticism.

Corps Order provided templates for reaching a "definite decision" (*karar-ı kati*). Mustafa Kemal offered basic questions for consideration and then counseled that one should go with one's first instinct. Two factors in any analysis are mission and situation; terrain forms a third.[49] Relying on his own experiences in the Battles of Arıburnu and Anafartalar, Mustafa Kemal underscored that "rarely" does one have, before or even after a battle, accurate intelligence of the enemy's strengths. *Corps Order* cautioned against overconfidence, stating that the enemy had to be taken seriously, for he possessed capabilities. Then Kemal presented an awesome challenge in leadership. To fight an adversary required imagination to anticipate the enemy's actions: "mentally (*zihnen*) to pass over to the enemy's side and take on his point of view."[50] Officers must concentrate on gaining tactical successes, and they must remain firm in their decision, suggesting that he who hesitated once making a decision is lost. Toward the end, *Corps Order* set a standard for good orders: brief, clear, definitive, and "commensurate with the knowledge and capability of those who receive the order."[51] In other words, knowing your own troops is as important as knowing your enemy.

In *Corps Order*, Mustafa Kemal embraced the role of *kolordu babası*, or the father of the corps. The pamphlet provided solid military wisdom in clear and succinct language as Mustafa Kemal sought to create a command climate for fostering mature initiative in order to meet the unique situations faced in combat. Here he blended theoretical consideration of war with practical wisdom, drawing upon examples from others, field manuals, and his own career. But Mustafa Kemal also revealed insight into the inner dynamic of his own mind: study a problem carefully and seriously, do it with an interior calm, use imagination and instinct, make a decision, and then implement it without second-guessing oneself. Here was a recipe for decision-making.

Mustafa Kemal understood that being a good "father", or *baba*, required reaching out and having direct contact with troops. In Edirne on 28 February 1916, Şükrü (Tezer), a young officer, related his first encounter with Mustafa Kemal, who visited a training exercise. After a "photo op," Şükrü explained the program to him. Mustafa Kemal responded in a surprising way: he ordered Şükrü to be the judge and evaluate his soldiers, picking the winner. That day, Mustafa Kemal won Şükrü's admiration and loyalty by showing him and individual soldiers respect and attention. Şükrü found it most unusual for a corps commander to take such an interest in a mere platoon composed of ten squads of eight to ten soldiers each.[52] In observing training exercises and establishing direct contact with soldiers, Mustafa Kemal did what was expected of all good commanders: he paid due regard to small units in war, a conviction that he had shown earlier as a senior captain when he translated a German field manual for platoons and then restated it in *Conversation*. The fame and importance of senior command had not made Mustafa Kemal lose sight of small units.

Taking advantage of the successful conclusion of the Gallipoli campaign, the Ottoman General Staff formed Second Army at the beginning of 1916 under the command of Ahmed İzzet, chief of the General Staff during the Balkan Wars. On 27 March, Mustafa Kemal reached Diyarbekir, the headquarters of Second Army. At the beginning of April, news arrived of his promotion to brigadier general (*mirliva*) and with it came the honorific and prestigious title of *paşa*. By the time Mustafa Kemal assumed field command, Ottoman fortunes had suffered major reverses. The Russians had beaten back the Ottoman Third Army and captured Erzurum in February and Bitlis in March; Trebizond would fall mid-April. Kemal's XVI Corps received responsibility for the Bitlis-Muş front of one hundred kilometers over mountainous terrain. The 5th Division under Refet (Bele) covered areas south of Bitlis, and Nuri (Conker), in command of 8th Division, deployed facing Muş. Both towns were under Russian occupation. Combat strength stood at 13,741 men with 9,297 rifles, seven machine guns, and nineteen artillery pieces.[53] Baptism under fire came rather quickly.

Service on the Caucasian Front was more complex than it had been at Gallipoli. War in eastern Anatolia had dislocated many people. Muslim refugees filled the region, but there were few Christians to be found. In May 1915, the CUP government had initiated the wholesale deportation of the Armenian population, a process that resulted in the death of between 600,000 and 800,000 Armenians, a complicated subject outside the scope of this study.[54] Mustafa Kemal was not responsible for this wanton human tragedy, as he was fighting in Gallipoli during this period. During the War of Independence, however, he would resist all attempts to address the issue publically.

Unlike the peninsular campaign, the Caucasian Front offered terrain more favorable for maneuver warfare, but mountains and mountain passes constricted movement. Moreover, military operations sometimes involved coordination with irregular forces, compelling Mustafa Kemal to deal with local tribal chiefs. The theater also brought XVI Corps into direct contact with the civilian population, as various headquarters were located in towns and troops passed through populated areas. The XVI Corps headquarters, for example, was first established in Silvan, a town filled with refugees. To be effective in military operations, Mustafa Kemal found it necessary to engage local notables and senior civilian officials with the express purpose of ensuring the security and support of the population. Discussions at corps headquarters had to devote more attention to issues of communication and roads, and even included "military, political, and social subjects."[55] Thus, while familiarizing himself with his new area of responsibility, Mustafa Kemal also met with local officials and notables. Meeting with Kurds was important, for they formed a majority in the region. In the Hazro district northeast of Diyarbekir, for example, he stayed with a local Kurdish notable named Halip Bey.[56] Mustafa Kemal had to come to terms with the fact that Kurdish notables and tribesmen differed from their counterparts in Libya and that they needed to be understood on their own terms.

While the Ottoman Second Army prepared for battle, the Russians launched a major offensive on 2 July, capturing the towns of Bayburt and Erzincan from the Ottoman Third Army before the end of the month. In Mustafa Kemal's sector, the 8th Division under Nuri suffered heavy losses, causing a withdrawal. Mustafa Kemal then helped rebuild and supply the division and reinforced it with a battalion from the 5th Division so that in ten days, the 8th Division began conducting offensive operations. Then on 3 August, after over five months of preparation, Ahmed İzzet finally launched a major offensive, a move too late to help Third Army. Left to its own devices, Second Army suffered heavy losses. Only XVI Corps registered any significant gains. To encourage the 5th Division at one point, Mustafa Kemal criticized Refet's effort and then appealed to his shame and honor by noting that intelligence reports gathered by 8th Division had placed no more than two regiments in his path.[57] In the end, XVI Corps scored a double victory, capturing Muş on 7 August and Bitlis on 8 August. In

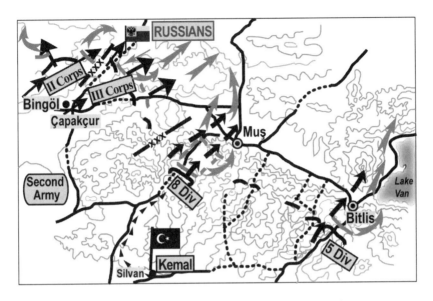

Map 2.3   *Battle of Muş and Bitlis, 2–8 August 1916*

his personal notes written over one year later, Mustafa Kemal expressed great personal satisfaction in this battle, for after conducting a successful withdrawal, he reconstituted and energized a defeated force to go on a successful offensive.[58] More than the capture of Bitlis and Muş in August, Mustafa Kemal "deserves great credit for having been able to regenerate the morale of the 8th Division" and turn it into a combat-effective force for offensive operations.[59]

But the Ottomans faced a determined foe. The Russians launched a counter-attack on 19 August, during which the 7th Division on the flank of XVI Corps sustained heavy losses to the point of collapse. Mustafa Kemal took the initiative and ordered Nuri to send forces to help its commander, helping to avert more setbacks.[60] A Russian attack at the end of September, however, forced him to abandon the town of Muş. On another occasion, he helped the 14th Division in its battle defending Çapakçur Pass. Colonel Ali Fuad found himself facing a superior Russian force with a battered division and without any reserves. Mustafa Kemal, who appreciated the strategic importance of the pass, committed forces from his XVI Corps to attack the Russian flank.[61] "The Turks had found in Kemal a young commander of first quality who did not fail to impress the power of his personality even on a most unfriendly destiny."[62] He was worthy of more responsibility.

That opportunity came on 25 November when Ahmed İzzet took leave for Istanbul and left Mustafa Kemal as the deputy commander of Second Army. This increased responsibility brought future political benefits to him: "The fighting in the east had brought together most of the officers who were to lead the Nationalist Forces in the War of Independence. On the Caucasian front in 1916, they found themselves under Kemal's command and learned to accept him as their leader."[63] For his leadership here out East, Mustafa Kemal also received the prestigious Golden Meritorious Medal in December 1916. Ahmed İzzet stayed away much too long, so Mustafa Kemal received command of Second Army. Finally, the General Staff decided to combine the Second and Third Armies, and Ahmed İzzet returned to command both.

Fighting conditions, especially in winter, were very harsh. Troops were often short on ammunition, food, weapons, and supplies. Thousands died from typhus, dysentery, and starvation. Mustafa Kemal gained the reputation of showing moral courage in addressing his difficult situation. Some men went to the gallows for corruption; others felt the brunt of physical punishment. "He was equally ruthless with the lazy and incompetent. He re-formed the regiments, reorganized the medical and the supply services, and labored unceasingly to inspire the troops with a new spirit."[64] Mustafa Kemal understood the importance of caring for the welfare of troops. On one occasion, as deputy commander of Second Army, he ordered a pullback of forces to new defensive positions, sacrificing territory for a better logistical line of supply. This repositioning occurred in anticipation of harsh weather. In ordering this move, Mustafa Kemal dismissed resistance from fellow officers, to which he replied by underscoring incidents of starvation leading to acts of cannibalism among the troops.[65] Despite bouts of illness that restricted his movement or even laid him up in bed, Mustafa Kemal toured the battlefield. His command style included regular meetings with commanders, visiting troops, and inspecting hospitals.[66]

The challenge of remaining human in the midst of the human carnage appears in Mustafa Kemal's diary, as it did earlier in his letter to Corinne Lütfü. Travel brought him in contact with dead and starving civilians of all ages and both sexes. On 9 November 1916, for example, he notes encountering a four- or five-year-old child dragging his feet about 1,000 meters behind a couple. When reproached by Mustafa Kemal for not attending to the child, the couple dismissed the child as not theirs, hence abandoning any responsibility for it. In another instance, after learning of the grave of some ten to fifteen decapitated Muslim women, he talked to three orphans, one a twelve-year-old, and gave them some money.[67] His diary includes these heart-wrenching entries, and they are written from the perspective of a war commander who is supposed to remain calm-headed with controlled emotion.

During the general inactivity of the winter months, Mustafa Kemal found time to read, reflect, write, and hold discussion sessions. At the request of the Historical Section of the Ottoman army, he filed a detailed report on the Battle of Arıburnu, using the necessary material provided to him by his chief of staff İzzeddin. It appears that İzzeddin had a major hand in drafting the document.[68] Written in January 1917, the report emphasized Mustafa Kemal's role in the campaign. In explaining the final victory in the long campaign, Mustafa Kemal gave credit at the end of his report to the courage and bravery of his commanders and soldiers and stressed the patriotic and religious motivation behind the successful defense of the doors leading to the sultanate and caliphate. İzzeddin received special mention for extraordinary service. The report ended with a list of names of officers who performed admirably.[69] This ending was similar to that in *Conversation with Officer and Commander*. The same holds true for his report on the battle of Anafartalar, but this time the material appears in an addendum with the names of division commanders and with İzzeddin receiving special mention in the last sentence.[70] İzzeddin deserved his commander's accolade. Mustafa Kemal relied heavily upon him for input and observations.[71] Such was the role of a good chief of staff. As a commander, Mustafa Kemal was committed to giving recognition to those deserving under his command. During the War of Independence, Mustafa Kemal promoted İzzeddin with corps command and assigned him an important sector for the Great Offensive. For Mustafa Kemal, loyalty and performance deserved recognition and reward.

On 21 November, after some reflection while traveling to Bitlis, Mustafa Kemal recorded several characteristics of good commanders. They know the internal conditions and morale of their units "from within," which permits them to issue commands with greater confidence. Commanders must have "friendly conversations" with subordinates and thus create a command climate in which subordinates are accustomed to expressing themselves freely. Furthermore, a good commander knows the thought processes of his subordinates: "It is useful and necessary to know how subordinates make judgments and communicate." This sound wisdom led Kemal to express the desire to write a book entitled *Moral Education and the Principles of Military Manners*. But first he believed that he had to read a book in French on the subject that would assist him in giving all officers "basic questions" for consideration. He also planned to gather the ideas of great commanders.[72] In the meantime, Mustafa Kemal remained committed to his role as *baba*, tasked with the duty of educating subordinates for the purpose of raising their level of military professionalism with such activities as training and map exercises during lulls in fighting.[73]

In addition to serious reflection on military subjects, Mustafa Kemal's notes written in eastern Anatolia in 1916 and 1917 show reading material ranging from philosophical works, to poetry, to history, to literature. The list contained *Is it Possible to Deny God?* by Şehbenderzade Filibeli Hilmi, *Éléments de philosophie* by George L. Fonsegrive, *Turkish Poetry* by Mehmed Emin (Yurdakul), *The Broken*

Lute by Tevfik Fikret, the French romance novel *Sapho: moeurs parisiennes* by Alphonse Daude, and Namık Kemal's *Ottoman History* and his *Political and Literary Articles*.[74] *The Broken Lute* contains the famous line: "I am a poet whose thought is free, whose culture is free, [and] whose conscience is free."[75] Broad self-study sustained Kemal in war.

Reading *Is it Possible to Deny God?* compelled Mustafa Kemal to write down a number of thoughts in his notebook. He identified the different types of philosophers—naturalists (*tabiiyun*), rationalists (*zihniyyun*), materialists (*maddiyun*), legalists (*hükema*), intellectuals (*mütefekkirin*), and mystics (*mutasavvıfın*)—who have grappled with the problems of the existence of the spirit, whether spirit or matter are one or separate, and an eternal versus noneternal spirit. Mustafa Kemal concluded that those who rely on knowledge and science deserve esteem and respect. He noted that the statements of medieval Muslim sages such as Imam al-Ghazali, Ibn Sina (Avicenna), and Ibn Rushd (Averroes) are "completely different" from those with vulgar opinions, but they still use "many terms with hidden meaning" (*çok rumuz*) in their explanations. Religious thinkers, he believed, endeavored to twist laws, the sciences, and philosophy to conform to their own religious interpretations.[76] Mustafa Kemal appeared a bit critical of what he regarded as religious speculations and philosophical elitism. These sages sometimes resorted to the use of symbols because they believed that the masses were unable to appreciate deeper levels of knowledge. This "elitist" approach, according to him, obfuscated solid comprehension and understanding. In any event, Mustafa Kemal clearly showed interest in philosophy in order to gain more understanding of the emotional and rational nature of human beings in particular, and the essence of things in general. Service on the Eastern Front gave Kemal time to study and reflect on the intellectual currents swirling within Ottoman society since the 1908 Revolution.

Mustafa Kemal held serious discussions on military and nonmilitary subjects with commanders and his chief of staff. A conversation on the record with a former Ottoman military attaché included a general evaluation of the requirements necessary for the position: knowledge of "European rules, diplomatic culture, and foreign languages."[77] From deeper conversations, Mustafa Kemal gained a better assessment of individuals. A long discussion on 23 May 1916 with İsmet (İnönü) on military, political, and social topics no doubt served that purpose.[78] İsmet would play an important role in the War of Independence and then serve as prime minister during most of Mustafa Kemal's fifteen years as president of the Republic. One particular discussion is especially noteworthy for the future. On 22 November 1916, Mustafa Kemal spent eight to nine hours in conversation with his chief of staff İzzeddin. Abolishing veiling and reforming social life came under scrutiny. The discussion focused on women's issues: 1) educating mothers to be capable of preparing children for life; 2) giving women their freedom; and 3) permitting them to affect "morals, ideas, and feelings" (*ahlakıyatı, efkarı, hissiyatı*).[79] Their duty as mothers encompassed developing the Kemalist triad of conscience, mind, and emotions in their children.

The day after the above conversation, İzzeddin began to read *From Superstition to Truth*, a critique of the deviation from true Islam by one M. Şemseddin. The selection of this book provides, no doubt, some indication of the tenor of the previous night's discussion. Then on 19 December, İzzeddin tackled *Is it Possible to Deny God?* which he found a rather difficult read; then a few days later, his diary entry revealed an unnamed book on psychology.[80] Prior to this flurry of reading over a six-week period, İzzeddin recorded only "lighter" reading: a novel in July "in order to pass the time" and a history book in October.[81] Now all of a sudden, he read three books, all intellectually weighty, designed to enlighten rather than entertain. In his entries for 26 and 27 December, İzzeddin briefly noted his thoughts on the body and soul, citing briefly the ideas of Aristotle and Descartes on the subject. He also underscored the importance of having principles to help understand *personality* (italics mine).[82] These entries reflected Mustafa Kemal's influence. His corps headquarters also functioned as an education center with him as its *baba*, and Mustafa Kemal continued his study and thought about the essence of life and human nature, clearly continuing and expanding on what he had begun in Syria after graduation.

When the British captured Baghdad on 11 March, Enver decided to create *Yıldırım Grubu*, or Lightning Group, a Turkish-German army group designed to recapture the lost Iraqi city. On 19 March 1917, Mustafa Kemal was assigned to participate in the *Yıldırım* plan. His Second Army had its headquarters in Diyarbekir, a provincial capital that had much more to offer intellectually and culturally than Silvan. While conducting conferences and training exercises for his officers, Mustafa Kemal used the time not only to meet regularly with senior local officials, including governors and heads of sub-provinces, but also to develop relations with other prominent figures in Diyarbekir and the surrounding area. His dining area functioned like a salon for the local who's who. Conversations covered many diverse topics. A religious official named Mehmed Tahir from an outlying district became a regular visitor and admirer.[83] Mustafa Kemal clearly used his time in Diyarbekir carefully and wisely for self-improvement and networking.

On 24 June, Enver convened a major meeting in Aleppo with senior commanders, during which he unveiled his plan for employing *Yıldırım* Group using divisions made available recently from helping the Austrians fight the Russians. On 5 July, Mustafa Kemal received command of Seventh Army as part of *Yıldırım* Army Group under Erich von Falkenhayn, who had been dismissed as Chief of the General Staff in Germany the year before for failed offensive operations.

Mustafa Kemal was not pleased with a German boss. Finally, on 20 September, he submitted a detailed report analyzing the empire's strategic situation as well as making important recommendations.

Mustafa Kemal offered harsh criticism of his own government's practices. The report recommended the empire recall all its soldiers fighting in foreign countries, adopt a defensive strategy, and focus its efforts on the Sinai front. Moreover, Ottomans should assume full control of the political and military spheres of government and not abdicate those responsibilities to the Germans. Then came a poignant analysis of the war's social effects. According to Mustafa Kemal, those beyond the government's reach were fortunate: "people who remain in their homes far from the government are, from every point of view, in a beneficial situation." The countryside was filled with "women, the destitute, or fugitives." The government had taken their material possessions despite the starvation and now faced the challenge of preventing the people's way of life from degenerating into general anarchy. Mustafa Kemal recommended solving matters in a peaceful way so as not to incur the "hatred" of the people. Embezzlement, profiteering, and bad behavior of officials were not in accordance with justice, and these practices had decayed life in every corner, in every city of the empire. The report describes the moral degeneration thus: "war can reach such conditions that compel men of honor to separate [themselves] from [their] sacred obligations. Therefore, the greatest threat that we will face in the continuance of this war is the possibility of the great structure of the sultanate one day collapsing from within."[84] This report raised the concern of the people reaching a breaking point. In fact, the empire would fight on for another year, followed by three more years of the War of Independence. Mustafa Kemal wanted a defensive strategy that served Ottoman and not German interests.

Defeat and Armistice

A major dispute with Falkenhayn led Mustafa Kemal to tender his resignation. On 11 October 1917, he traveled to Istanbul, where he took his leave. After two months in Istanbul without work, Mustafa Kemal accepted a new assignment. On 20 December, he departed for Germany on an official trip as an aide to the heir apparent Prince Vahdeddin. Naci, his beloved teacher from the War College and now aide-de-camp to Vahdeddin, joined the travelling party. In Berlin, meetings with Kaiser Wilhelm, Hindenburg, and Ludendorff brought Mustafa Kemal into the inner sanctum of the Second Reich's political and military power.

Naturally, the Kaiser and his senior military commanders painted a rosy and positive picture of Germany's strategic situation. To confirm his own suspicions,

Mustafa Kemal requested permission to visit the Western Front and see for himself. A briefing at a major field headquarters there also painted an optimistic assessment, so he went directly to young junior officers, who informed him of serious problems such as the lack of enough infantry. They also described the situation as dangerous.[85] The trip to the front left Mustafa Kemal doubtful about Germany's chances of winning the war and unimpressed with Prince Vahdeddin as a future "sultan-caliph."

Mustafa Kemal returned to Istanbul saddled with kidney problems.[86] After several months of illness and with no cure in sight, he received permission to go to Vienna for medical treatment. Before his departure, however, he managed to conduct a long interview for the press. A CUP-supported magazine published the text in a three-part series. Here Mustafa Kemal spelled out in some detail his exploits and achievements at Gallipoli. On the first day of battle, he stopped retreating soldiers and promptly ordered them to fix bayonets and dig-in against the enemy, an order that proved effective enough in helping stop the ANZAC forces. Determined not to give an inch, he revealed what became his immortal order to both the 25th and 57th Regiments: "I am not ordering you to fight; I am ordering you to die. By the time we die other forces and commanders will take our place."[87] Most interesting, Mustafa Kemal did not include this famous order in his campaign history. He was, however, determined to use the interview to gain popular recognition for his achievements, but it probably had little effect. Too many important news events drew the readership's attention.

Then on 25 May, Mustafa Kemal departed for Vienna, where after initial treatment a specialist dispatched him to a spa in Karlsbad. Convalescence provided time for reading, reflection, and socializing in a European landscape graced with visitors from the Ottoman Empire. The material included poetry, history, philosophy, French novels, and even a critique of Marx's *Le Capital*. French and German lessons revealed a continued dedication to mastering these languages for international communication.[88] Mustafa Kemal was seriously interested in political and social issues, as evidenced from his discussions in eastern Anatolia.

In a conversation with a Turkish lady, Mustafa Kemal rejected a gradualist approach toward reform and instead expressed the need for revolutionary change done quickly, and he saw himself as a model for society. Effective leaders, after all, lead by example. "After spending so many years acquiring higher education, inquiring into civilized social life and getting a taste for freedom, why should I descend to the level of the common people? Rather, I should raise them to my level. They should become like me, not I like them." These words, however, revealed arrogance, an elitist mindset of a man on a journey in life intent on bringing others along with him. In the same conversation, Mustafa Kemal addressed the role of women in society and underscored the need for reforming their place in society by providing them with modern education but without jeopardizing traditional virtues: "Let us adorn their minds with serious knowledge and science," while maintaining their chastity.[89] Illness and convalescence gave Mustafa Kemal the opportunity to reflect, study, and converse on serious matters in tranquil surroundings.

On 5 July, news reached Karlsbad of Sultan Mehmed V's death and of Vahdeddin's accession to the throne as Mehmed VI. The next day Mustafa Kemal wrote in his diary that "the greatest courage of commanders is not to fear [taking] responsibility. . . I have experienced the weight of responsibility in my soul."[90] Destiny beckoned. A new sultan offered the possibility for a new direction in policy. Continued health problems, however, kept him in Karlsbad for most of July. On 17 July, Kemal made a most interesting assessment of the last wars of the Ottoman Empire. The Ottoman army's poor performance in Libya and the subsequent disaster of the Balkan Wars had caused the collapse of the "old mentality." Surprise, insufficient time for mobilization, and the lack of good plans helped explain the latter defeat. The country needed a "truly great Turkish Army (*Türk Ordusu*)."[91] The War of Independence would give Mustafa Kemal the opportunity to build a winning tradition.

Upon receiving an order on 27 July to report to Istanbul, Mustafa Kemal reached the capital at the beginning of August, a full month after Vahdeddin's enthronement. Health problems slowed the speed of his return. He was appointed to command Seventh Army in Palestine and reached Nablus on 1 September to be part of Sanders' *Yıldırım* Group. The Eighth Army hugged the Mediterranean Sea; his Seventh occupied the center; and the Fourth held the left flank. Seventh Army, approximately 28,000 men, comprised XX Corps under Ali Fuad and III Corps under İsmet, each with two divisions. Mustafa Kemal was responsible for defending forty kilometers of a hundred-kilometer front.

British General Edmund Allenby launched a major offensive in Palestine on 19 September, nineteen days after Mustafa Kemal had arrived in Nablus. Sanders expected the main attack from the east, but instead it came on his western flank. British forces broke through the Eighth Army and therefore threatened the rear of Seventh Army, forcing Mustafa Kemal to order a withdrawal on 27 September. Some 12,000 men, less than half his original force, managed to travel a distance of fifteen kilometers to Kisve. There, Sanders wanted a defense of Damascus and placed the Eighth Army under Mustafa Kemal's command, but to no avail, as the city fell on 30 September. Its fall forced a pullback to Aleppo, where Mustafa Kemal spent twenty-four days, ten of them in bed ill, but still exercising command and maintaining a defensive line. In Aleppo, exhausted and stressed, Mustafa Kemal let his emotions and ego gain the upper hand when he blamed others in the most uncomplimentary fashion for the military setbacks. In a telegram to

Istanbul dated 7 October, he called Enver "a fool"; labeled the commander of the Eighth Army "a bewildered chicken"; summed up Cemal Paşa as essentially incompetent; and described the overall army group command under Sanders as having "lost all control from the first day of battle."[92] After more battle, including in the streets of Aleppo, Mustafa Kemal managed to extricate the forces into Anatolia by the time of the signing of the armistice, thus ending Ottoman participation in the Great War. Although the war appeared over, it proved unresolved. The struggle would enter a new phase, called the War of Independence.

Events moved quickly to end the war for the Ottoman Empire. The CUP fell from power, and on 14 October Ahmed İzzet formed a peace cabinet with Ali Fethi as interior minister and Rauf as navy minister, both friends of Mustafa Kemal. Mustafa Kemal had offered himself up as war minister,[93] but Ahmed İzzet, well aware of his independent nature, kept this important post for himself. On 19 October, the new Ottoman government entered into armistice talks. On 30 October, the Ottoman Empire signed the Mondros Armistice. The next day, Sanders handed command of *Yıldırım* Army Group, a motley force of 24,000 men, to Mustafa Kemal.

Peace came without honor. During the Great War, the Entente Powers had begun secret negotiations on how to divide the Ottoman Empire. Now, in late 1918, Britain and France led the way in imposing a total and unconditional surrender. Mondros severed the Arab provinces from the empire, with the victors gaining the right to occupy forts in the Dardanelles and the Bosporus. The Ottoman army demobilized from its current strength of 560,000 to 50,000 troops and abandoned all its garrisons outside of Anatolia. The Allies had the right to occupy any part of Anatolia if their strategic interests were threatened. The Ottoman cabinet was shocked by the severity of the conditions. Entering the Great War with a population of 22 million and an area of 1.7 million square kilometers, the Ottoman Empire now faced further truncation for the remaining 10 million inhabitants and 700,000 square kilometers.

Over the next several months, Allies fanned out throughout Anatolia, occupying important towns. An Entente force landed at Izmir on 7 November. Meanwhile, a flotilla of fifty-five Allied ships appeared before Istanbul on 13 November. A three-man High Commission, representing Britain, France and Italy, administered the capital under martial law. Over the next six months, Allied troops occupied various part of the remaining Ottoman Empire. The British concentrated on securing the Mosul region and its valuable oil fields. French troops moved into several cities in southeastern Anatolia; the Italians did the same in the southwest. Greece moved troops into Western Thrace, formerly a part of Bulgaria. It appeared that the new state of Armenia might gain the cities of Kars and Ardahan. British troops also secured Black Sea port of Samsun and

and deployed troops in the interior in Konya (southwest); the French extended their reach to the Zonguldak coal mines. By the middle of May 1919, the Entente Powers had some 50,000 troops spread throughout most of Anatolia. This activity looked quite alarming.

Toward a National Resistance

At the war's end, the new Istanbul government disbanded *Yıldırım* Group and recalled Mustafa Kemal to the capital. The signing of the Mondros Armistice sparked numerous protest demonstrations in Istanbul and throughout Anatolia. Meanwhile, patriotic commanders, including Mustafa Kemal, hid their weapons for future use. The nonviolent phase of the national resistance had begun with the signing of the armistice. Mustafa Kemal, for his part, arrived in the capital on 13 November 1918. For the next six months, he became a man of intrigue who worked secretly and discreetly, working with a clandestine circle of patriots determined to resist partition, all this done under the noses of the Allied occupiers. He was by no means alone in his efforts.

Before their flight into exile, Enver and Talat had encouraged the formation of a secret organization called *Karakol* (The Sentry) with two main aims: to protect former CUP members from prosecution and build a cadre for a possible armed struggle against foreign occupation. Over the next six months, *Karakol* prepared for a national resistance. Local CUP branches helped in the formation of Societies for the Defense of National Rights throughout Anatolia and in Thrace.[94] A few places held local congresses for creating a unity of effort and for mobilizing the population. Vice Admiral Sir S. Calthorpe, the High Commissioner in Istanbul, discerned this reality early in his tenure in a report sent to London on 29 November 1918: "the Committee of Union and Progress does not cease to exist, only it appears to have fallen into quite other hands, and to be in the process of becoming merely the nucleus round which a fairly rational Turkish national feeling is collected."[95] Mustafa Kemal would build a resistance on this organization and spirit.

Fethi (Okyar) proved an important collaborator. In the last days of the war, he founded the Ottoman Party of Liberty-Loving People whose program included defense of the Ottoman sultanate, national sovereignty in accordance with the Constitution, and rights and liberty for all peoples. Fethi also established the newspaper *Minber* (Pulpit) as the party's official organ, and its first issue on 1 November published the party's program while Mustafa Kemal was still in southeastern Anatolia. It is likely that the two men collaborated in this venture. *Minber* singled out Enver and Talat, the two top CUP leaders, for criticism. The paper discussed socialist ideas and respect for women, opposed demobilization of the army, and called for the implementation of President Woodrow Wilson's principle of self-determination.[96]

On 16 November, just three days after his arrival in Istanbul, *Minber* published an interview with Mustafa Kemal. The caption under his picture read "Kemal Paşa, one of our army's greatest commanders." The newspaper began with a short biography. Readers learned that Mustafa Kemal was detained on the day of graduation from the Staff College and then exiled to Damascus because of his "independent thinking." In providing a brief sketch of his military career, *Minber* glorified Mustafa Kemal as "the hero of the great battles of Arıburnu and Anafartalar, the savior of Istanbul from occupation." In the interview, Mustafa Kemal began by providing his qualifications for addressing political matters. His service as military attaché in Bulgaria had given him experience in both political and military matters. Then having been army group commander, Mustafa Kemal says, he had to touch upon policy matters. He presented two clear demands: freedom of the Ottoman nation and the independence of the state framed in terms of "respect and humanity." He called upon society and government officials to work together for the defense of the fatherland.[97]

For part of the interview, Mustafa Kemal presented "my deep thoughts." He briefly discussed the relationship between politics, power, and ideas. He maintained that policy (*siysaet*) must be backed by force, but force did not stem only from weapons but must embrace "spiritual matters, knowledge, morals, and science" (*manen, ilmen, ahlaken ve fennen*). A nation whose individuals lack "virtues" (*hasail*) cannot be powerful, he believed. He framed this discussion in terms of "a human being able to take his rightful place in today's human society," using the singular for one global civilization. For Mustafa Kemal, a powerful army meant having every individual, and in particular the officer and the commander, understand the requirements of civilization and science and act accordingly. He spoke of "a society with high morals (*ahlak*)."[98] This interview mixed realism and idealism.

Two days after the interview, *Minber* followed with another article on him, ending with a prophetic utterance: "it is right to expect in the future of the fatherland great service from Kemal Paşa."[99] Two other sympathetic newspapers also printed interviews with him. Moreover, Mustafa Kemal published *Conversation with Officer and Commander* in late 1918 and began work on a short history of the battles of Anafartalar.[100] As mentioned earlier in this chapter, Mustafa Kemal did not include his Turkish references when publishing *Conversation*, for he sought to appeal to all Muslims. Clearly, Mustafa Kemal used the press and the book for self-promotion with the aim of assuming a leadership role in the national resistance by portraying himself as a man of action and intellect. Moreover, going to the people and strengthening links with them formed a basic component of Kemal's strategy that continued throughout the War of Independence.

During his six months in Istanbul, Mustafa Kemal turned his home in Şişli into a center for clandestine political activity. He had become a political general. Among the main participants were Ali Fethi (Okyar), Ali Fuad (Cebesoy), Rauf (Orbay), Refet (Bele), Kazım Karabekir, and İsmet (İnönü). He was the highest ranking officer in this group. Initially, he focused on working in Istanbul to change the government. Mustafa Kemal and fellow conspirators devised a common set of objectives for defending the country from colonial occupation: an immediate stop to demobilization; an end to turning weapons and ammunition over to the Allies; the assignment of young and competent officers to troops in Anatolia; the continuance of loyal bureaucrats in their positions; and raising the people's morale.[101] This program, based on common sense, was hatched from a collective effort.

Mustafa Kemal explored the possibility of using the sultanate–caliphate as an instrument of opposition to Allied designs. He held six meetings with Vahdeddin, spanning the period from 16 November 1918 to 16 May 1919. Afterwards, Mustafa Kemal came to depict Vahdeddin as a coward and a traitor who thought only of himself and not the nation. More likely, the sultan offered lukewarm support but was constrained by the Allied occupation. Parliament presented another instrument for action. Ali Fethi had founded a political party for the purpose of influencing governmental policies through the assembly. Parliament could act as a pressure group representing the will of the people and challenging the occupation regime's policies. But on 21 December 1918, the sultan closed Parliament and then on 4 January 1919 postponed elections indefinitely. Parliament thus evaporated as an option. Arrests of some key figures at the end of January spoke for abandoning Istanbul for Anatolia. In the second half of January or the first half of February, Mustafa Kemal discussed the idea with İsmet and others, but they reached no decision.[102]

Meanwhile, the Allies expanded their occupation in Anatolia. In February, the French occupied Adana and Maraş. At the Paris peace conference, an Armenian delegation demanded an Armenia that included Van, Bitlis, Diyarbekir, Sivas, Erzurum, Maraş, Adana, and İskenderun. March saw the British occupy Urfa and Samsun, the French seize Zonguldak, and the Italians land at Fethiye on the southwest coast and move inland. April had the British troops entering the eastern city of Kars. Employing the strategy of divide and conquer, the British encouraged Kurds to think of autonomy and even helped establish the Society for the Rise of Kurdistan (*Kürdistan Teali Cemiyeti*) in Istanbul in May 1919.

Patriots in the Ottoman war ministry emerged as a center of national resistance, and these officers strove to assign patriotic officers to key command positions. In late February 1919, Ali Fuad was appointed to command of XX Corps, headquartered in Ankara. At the beginning of March, he had a final meeting with Mustafa Kemal in Şişli. In his memoirs, Ali Fuad saw his duty as gathering weapons and ammunition and preventing any demobilization of his corps. It was also very important to build a "unity between the army and the people," strengthening their "feelings of resolve, faith, and hope" and making them believe in the possibility of the country's liberation.[103] Then on 13 March Karabekir received his assignment as commander of XV Corps, and he too was determined to create bonds with the people by calling for the convening of a regional congress in Erzurum.

Now Mustafa Kemal needed an assignment in Anatolia. The Ottoman war ministry did its part once again. Mustafa Kemal was a most worthy candidate because of his impressive war record, his patriotism, his senior rank, and his relative distance from Talat, Enver, and the army's involvement in politics. The Ottoman army had been reorganized into three Inspectorates. Mustafa Kemal was tagged for the Ninth Army Inspectorate, headquartered in Erzurum. He wanted extensive powers: the authority to send commands throughout Anatolia, to command units in eastern provinces, and to give commands directly to governors in those provinces. He and the Vice Chief of the General Staff Diyarbekirli Kazım (İnanç) wrote up the job description. But neither the grand vezir nor the war minister wanted to sign such an order, lest they be held accountable for Mustafa Kemal's actions, and the chief of the General Staff Fevzi (Çakmak) claimed illness. So Diyarbekirli Kazım used a stamp and provided Mustafa Kemal with a copy.[104] Ultimately, Mustafa Kemal was appointed on 30 April with wide powers.

The Ninth Army's area of responsibility covered vulnerable and sensitive parts of the Black Sea region and eastern Anatolia. Local Ottoman Greeks appeared to be striving to create a Pontus state along the coast. In the east, the Armenian and Georgian states had designs on territory in eastern Anatolia. In his marching orders, Mustafa Kemal received an inspectorate with wide and expansive military and civil authority. He would directly command III Corps (two divisions) headquartered in Sivas and XV Corps (four divisions) in Erzurum. Any appointment or changes in regional command or in military personnel for special duties required his approval. His area of direct responsibility comprised Trabzon, Erzurum, Sivas and Van provinces and independent sub-provinces (*livas*) of Erzincan and Canik. To carry out the above duties, he had authority to communicate directly with provinces and sub-provinces. Corps commands in neighboring provinces of Diyarbekir, Bitlis, Mamüretulaziz (Elazığ), Ankara and Kastamonu were required to pay attention to his directives. His main duties were to determine reasons for unrest, collect weapons and ammunition and their placement in depots, prevent army involvement in distributing weapons to the population, and give special attention to health conditions.[105] It appears very likely that at least senior members in the war ministry knew Mustafa Kemal would use his powers to organize a national resistance, but perhaps only a few expected one that would become independent of the sultanate-caliphate.[106]

After paying his last respects to the sultan and senior officers, Mustafa Kemal set off in a boat for Samsun with fifteen officers and two clerks. Two army doctors provided medical care, as illness appeared a regular problem with Mustafa Kemal, compounded by hard work, stress, and drinking. Colonel Kazım (Dirik), a Macedonian like himself, came as chief of staff. Selecting a loyal and competent staff, it must be noted, was particularly important in May 1919. If Istanbul failed to support the national resistance as it developed in Anatolia, then Mustafa Kemal would find himself labeled by the 600-year-old Ottoman sultanate as disloyal and in rebellion. Such a situation would create a moral dilemma for some officers in determining whom they must obey. Army commanders and officers loyal and dedicated to the Nationalist resistance in Anatolia would prove critical at this juncture in the struggle.

On 6 May, Britain, France, and the United States joined together and invited Greece to occupy Izmir. British Prime Minister David Lloyd George viewed Athens as an ally in the eastern Mediterranean and thus wanted to keep Italy out of western Anatolia. The Italians, however, had been promised western Anatolia in payment for their entry in the war on the Entente side, and Italian troops had landed in Antalya in January 1919 and expanded in southwestern Anatolia to include Konya. Arnold Toynbee noted Lloyd George's designs thus: "If Turkey can be dominated by the land-power of Greece, Greece can be dominated by the sea-power of Great Britain, and so the British Government can still carry out their war-aims in the Near and Middle East without spending British money and lives."[107] For his part, Greek Prime Minister Eleftherios Venizelos envisioned the creation of two independent states: Armenia and an independent state of Constantinople and Eastern Thrace under the auspices of the League of Nations. Greece would annex western Anatolia, fulfilling part of the *Megale Idea*, or the Great Idea, i.e., a Greater Greece dream. Pontus Greeks in the Black Sea region would merge with the Greeks in Trebizond, with both areas forming a part of a larger Greek-Armenian state. Venizelos also envisioned a population exchange between Greeks and Turks in order to establish more homogeneity in each respective area, with some 450,000 Greeks expelled from Anatolia during World War I returning to their homes.[108]

Before departing for Samsun, Mustafa Kemal learned of the landing of a Greek expeditionary force in Izmir on 15 May. The War of Independence had begun in western Anatolia. The next day he left for Samsun by sea, setting foot in Anatolia on 19 May. It was the Greek action that sparked armed national resistance to foreign occupation, first in Western Anatolia and then spreading to other areas. Italy was not pleased with Greece's occupation of Izmir. The Greek occupation of Izmir went relatively smoothly, with minimal resistance. Greek troops, however, encountered determined resistance in Aydın. After occupying the town, they lost it, and then had to regain it. Two-thirds of the town was destroyed in the process, and virtually all the Muslim population fled the city. Loss of civilian life as a result of massacre and counter-massacre, forced and unforced flight, malnutrition and disease, became a tragic feature of the War of Independence. A number of Ottoman regular units dissolved in the face of a superior foe; some officers and soldiers helped constitute local militias, generally called National Forces, or *Kuvve-yi Milliye*, to wage irregular warfare against the occupiers.

Ottoman officials remained in place at first, largely because the Greeks lacked enough trained civil servants and gendarmerie to take over the local administration. This arrangement gave the appearance of Ottoman suzerainty, but reality spoke otherwise. Greeks talked of establishing a new Hellenic civilization in Anatolia. To buttress the feasibility of such a vision, the Athens government encouraged some 120,000 Greeks to migrate from Greece to western Anatolia, offering them generous monetary credit; meanwhile, between 200,000 and 320,000 Turks left during the first two years of Greek occupation.[109] Throughout the remainder of 1919 and into 1920, the Istanbul government generally discouraged its officials in Anatolia from embarking on military operations.[110] An unofficial state of war, however, quickly came into being on the new Greek-Turkish border in western Anatolia. Greece positioned six divisions in its zone, while Muslim guerrilla bands harassed their positions, and small Ottoman regular units deployed in the general area. Greeks were prohibited from chasing the guerrillas more than three kilometers beyond what became known as the Milne Line.[111] In this arrangement, the national resistance lacked a central figure of opposition to the foreign occupation.

Meanwhile, people in Istanbul immediately took to the streets to protest the Greek occupation. On 19 May, the same day as Mustafa Kemal's landing at Samsun in Anatolia, some 75,000 people gathered at Fatih Park to hear speeches. Speakers called for the rallying of "Muslims and the Turkish nation (*Türk milleti*)" or "Muslims and Turks," thus blending religion and ethnic identity. Some looked to Vahdeddin as the rallying point of these demonstrations. A few women even ascended the podium to contribute to the calls for mobilization. Meanwhile, Istanbul newspapers faithfully carried these events and speeches.[112] Halide Edip (Adıvar), already a prominent female writer and activist in the Second Constitutionalist Period, blended feminism and patriotism whenever she delivered a public address before a large crowd. She would eventually join the Nationalist cause in Anatolia and leave an important memoir with insights into Mustafa Kemal's character. While Istanbul witnessed a rise in the passion of the people, Defense of Rights Societies in Anatolia and Eastern Thrace sought to rally local populations to raise the standard of protest and demonstrate a national opposition to the Greek occupation of Izmir. Unity was required for the passions to become effective.

Conclusion

The Great War saw Mustafa Kemal grow in maturity as a senior commander, moving up the command chain from division, to corps, to army, and finally to army group. Frailty of health, no doubt compounded by combat stress, had kept him out of combat for a part of the war. Events had shown him as an ambitious individual with a large ego and a proclivity to resign when in disagreement with his superior. Despite his problematic behavior, his commanders came to regard him as worthy of receiving increased responsibilities. He produced positive results in defending at Gallipoli, in capturing Bitlis and Muş, and in withdrawing the defeated Ottoman army from Palestine and Syria, although he also suffered setbacks in military operations. His military leadership spoke of courage, confidence, initiative, and charisma with a willingness to assume greater responsibilities. Despite war, Mustafa Kemal continued to broaden his intellectual horizons in pursuit of the deeper knowledge of war, the human being, and life. Lulls in combat on the Caucasian Front and medical treatment in Istanbul and Karlsbad gave him time to study and reflect. The Ottoman Empire's defeat in war forced Enver's departure and provided an opportunity for the emergence of a new national hero. In the six months in Istanbul after the signing of the armistice, Mustafa Kemal entered the political arena, although in military uniform, embracing politics as a means to undo an unjust peace dictated by the victorious Entente Powers. Events and advice finally convinced him to head for Anatolia. Patriots in Istanbul had arranged his appointment, while other patriots in Anatolia prepared for his arrival.

3

Developing a Resistance

The history of the twentieth century suffices to remind us that there are many ways to win a war, that the various ways are not equivalent, and that the final victory does not necessarily belong to the side that dictates the conditions of peace.

Raymond Aron[1]

For the proper execution of our duty of being translators of the national conscience (*vicdan-ı milli*) for [determining] the fate of the nation and the fatherland, we cannot appear to exercise authority on any problem without linking it to the national desire.

Mustafa Kemal, 1919

MUSTAFA KEMAL no doubt felt a sense of destiny unfolding before him as he set foot in Samsun on 19 May 1919. A few days earlier, Greece had begun landing an expeditionary force in Izmir. The local Muslims responded by firing the first shots of armed resistance at them on 15 May. Organized demonstrations in Istanbul and parts of Anatolia also protested the Greek occupation of Izmir and the surrounding area. The national struggle took on a defensive posture against foreign occupation and further partition of the country. Moreover, the national aim was noble by the Wilsonian standard of self-determination, which counseled full independence and complete sovereignty. But the country lacked a recognized national leader to chart a unified course of resistance. Mustafa Kemal, to his advantage, was situated far from the European military forces in Istanbul at the time and remained freer to act on his own terms.

Drawing upon the same military wisdom that he had taught his subordinates, Mustafa Kemal appreciated the need for articulating clear and simple political objectives and holding fast to them. Moreover, success depended on him developing an appropriate means of resistance and a viable strategy. An effective national resistance required establishing central command over the remnants of the Ottoman army, gaining control of the provincial administrations, and unifying local resistance organizations. To mobilize the people and win over international opinion depended upon effective propaganda. Kemal's first seven and a half months in Anatolia proved critical for him in developing a viable national resistance centered in Anatolia.

First Steps in Anatolia

The strategic situation appeared favorable for the Entente Powers. The national resistance lacked unity and the Istanbul government was restricted in its ability to act. Mustafa Kemal, on his part, faced a complex strategic situation. Six fronts required serious attention: the Occupying Powers in Istanbul and the Dardanelles, the Greek army in the Izmir region, a nascent Armenian state and army along the eastern border of Anatolia, the British and French in southeastern Anatolia, the Italians in the southern region of Asia Minor, and the internal front, characterized by brigandage and rebellions. All was not well for the Entente Powers, however. Although anxious to partition much of what remained of the Ottoman Empire, Britain, France, and Italy lacked sufficient forces and the national will to crush a widespread armed resistance, should one develop in Anatolia. While Greece possessed the willingness to commit a large military force, Athens required financial and diplomatic support to achieve her limited but costly territorial ambitions into western Anatolia.

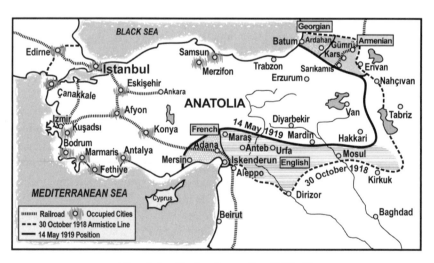

Map 3.1   *Foreign Occupation 1918–19*

Mustafa Kemal, for his part, could count on some assets. Istanbul and Anatolia, unlike the occupied areas of Iraq, Syria, and Palestine, possessed the vast majority, 90 per cent by one count, of the Ottoman officer corps. These officers had the numbers, talent, and experience conducive to forming an effective armed resistance. Moreover, the CUP had initiated preparations for a broad network of supporters that helped create Societies for the Defense of National Rights throughout Anatolia. These societies were prepared to rally the people locally in defiance of the imperialistic designs of the victors of the Great War. Most important, Mustafa Kemal had time to build a strong political and military base in Anatolia, but the unfolding of events would require sound decision-making by him.

The South Caucasus needed special attention. The collapse of tsarist Russia in 1917 had given the Ottoman Empire the opportunity to drive the Russian army out of Anatolia, and in February 1918, the Ottomans had advanced into South Caucasus. The Treaty of Brest-Litovsk on 3 March 1918 had awarded Kars, Ardahan, and Batum to the Ottomans. Meanwhile, in May 1918, Armenians, Georgians, and Azerbaijanis all declared their independence from Russia as democratic republics. The Ottomans reacted by launching an offensive into South Caucasus, advancing as far as Baku. Their defeat in World War I, however, forced the Ottomans to withdraw from South Caucasus to essentially pre-war boundaries, which negated any gains made at Brest-Litovsk. A number of Ottoman officers and soldiers, however, remained to assist the new Azeri army and to organize Muslim villagers in other key areas of South Caucasus. In Kars, local Muslims held a national congress in an attempt to create a provisional government with a parliament. Although Armenia, Georgia, and Azerbaijan sent delegates to the Paris peace conference in January 1919 in the hopes of gaining recognition of their respective independence, the Entente Powers refused to recognize these fledgling states. Meanwhile, border clashes followed the declarations of independence as each new state sought to maximize their boundaries. Internal unrest within the rebelling states added to the regional instability.

Armenia represented a clear threat. On 28 May 1919, the anniversary of the founding of the Democratic Republic of Armenia, the Erivan government proclaimed the Act of United Armenia that envisioned an enlarged state that combined the historic lands of Eastern (Russian) and Western (Turkish) Armenia. The Armenians sought to absorb the eastern provinces of Van, Bitlis, Erzurum, and Trabzon, and even land in southeastern Anatolia. Georgia, for its part, laid claims to Trabzon, placing the new republic in competition with Armenia and the Ottoman Empire. In Greece, Prime Minister Eleftherios Venizelos supported the Ottoman Greeks of Pontus, the area along the Black Sea including Trabzon province, as part of the new state of Armenia.[2]

Great Power interests enhanced the strategic value of South Caucasus and complicated matters for Mustafa Kemal. The Bolshevik regime in Moscow, in the meantime, sought to incorporate the former Russian territories in the area into a new Soviet state. Britain, on the other hand, hoped to unify anti-Bolshevik forces in South Caucasia and Russia to thwart the Bolsheviks in their expansionary aims. The Russian army under General Anton Deniken opposed all separatism, which explained, in part, why England, France, and Italy were reluctant to recognize officially all three South Caucasus states. London's main strategic interests in the region were the oil-rich area around Baku and the communication route between Iran and the Black Sea. Consequently, at the beginning of 1919, the British 27th Division, headquartered in Baku, occupied strategic locations throughout the South Caucasus, including the Baku-Batum oil pipeline and the Trans Caucasus railway. But in mid-May, however, London announced that it was withdrawing its soldiers from South Caucasus beginning on 15 June. Instead, British attention now focused on the Straits and the Black Sea. The United States, on its part, briefly toyed with the idea of an American mandate, but then assumed an "isolationist" mode.

Almost immediately upon setting foot in Samsun, Mustafa Kemal reached out to organizations throughout the country, and not just in his area of military responsibility as commander of the Ninth Army. As he wrote in his notes, success depended on inspiring everyone to the national cause.[3] On 21 May 1919, just two days after arriving in Samsun, Mustafa Kemal sent a personal message to Karabekir, the commander of XV Corps headquartered in Erzurum. He informed his comrade-in-arms that he regarded his position as Inspector of the Ninth Army as providing him an opportunity to fulfill "the ultimate duty of conscience (*en son vazife-yi vicdaniye*) owed to the nation and country."[4] After six or seven days in Samsun devoted to gathering intelligence and reaching his own assessments, Mustafa Kemal embarked with his retinue for Havza. There, he met for several hours with the local people in front of a mosque and discussed the upcoming struggle for national independence. Several individuals were brought to tears during the discussion.[5] Regular appeals to the honor, dignity, patriotism, faith, and self-interest of the people were essential to a successful national struggle.

On 29 May in a circular issued from Havza to III Corps (Sivas), XV Corps (Erzurum) and XIII (Diyarbekir) Corps, Mustafa Kemal provided the broad outline of his defensive strategy. He saw the threat coming from all directions: the Greeks in Izmir and Manisa, the Italians in Antalya and Konya, the Rum (Ottoman Greeks) people on the Black Sea, and the Armenians in the east. The Entente Powers had paralyzed the caliphate and the central government. Mustafa Kemal claimed as his aim the liberation of the nation from imprisonment. This required joining forces with trusted civil bureaucrats and mobilizing soldiers, calling them to exercise their patriotic duty. The internal and external bands of the Rum people were agitating to establish a "republic" (*cumhuriyet*) in the Black Sea region, but Mustafa Kemal felt that the local gendarmerie and soldiers there would meet their challenges "with full force." Armed [Muslim] villagers could fend for themselves in this region, while regular soldiers countered any Greek forces sent by Greece. In the event that the Entente Powers conducted military operations, fomenting local demonstrations and meetings would be the best initial response. Against possible attacks by Georgia or Armenia, Mustafa Kemal planned to use guerrillas and to augment regular forces with villagers, who would be slated to protect their own homes. The XX Corps would defend the western and southern fronts, while XIII Corps contained the Adana region and XV Corps controlled the east. Effective resistance "would require the soldiers and the people to fight united in the defense of independence."[6] On 6 June 1919, Mustafa Kemal reinforced his defensive strategy, which relied heavily on an armed population, by ordering the Erzurum governor to collect weapons from "those detrimental" to the cause of freedom while leaving the rest of the people with their firearms.[7] At this point, Mustafa Kemal envisaged a people's war.

While disseminating military instructions to those within his area of responsibility, Mustafa Kemal also received messages of support from the local population. Wilson's principle of self-determination for the Turks had struck a sympathetic chord among some protestors. On 3 June 1919, for example, a telegram arrived from the town of Safranbolu (about 200 kilometers northeast of Ankara). The Entente Powers were threatening the "Turkish nation" (*Türk milleti*) with the partition of "Turkey" (*Türkiya*). In response to this threat, the communiqué spoke of "the voice of humanity raised by President Wilson" energizing "the oppressed Turks." Drawing upon universal principles, the mayor of Safranbolu expressed the firm belief that affluence and prosperity could only come with Turkish independence, and the people of Safranbolu promised to fight to the end against the foreign occupation. The mayor signed the telegram in the name of 60,000 people.[8] Spontaneous telegrams such as this one, and other forms of similar protest, clearly revealed that elements of the population were passionately prepared to support a national resistance for independence. The telegram expressed Turkish national sentiment as well, a sentiment that remained at the national and local levels throughout the War of Independence.

Britain had taken the lead in occupying Istanbul and the Straits. Meanwhile, British officials quickly recognized Mustafa Kemal as a potential theat. On 19 May, upon learning of Kemal's departure to Samsun, General George F. Milne, the Commander in Chief of the Army of the Black Sea, immediately requested an explanation as to the duties and organization of the Ninth Army.[9] On 6 June, he demanded the Ottoman war minister to recall Mustafa Kemal to Istanbul immediately: "I consider the presence of General Kemal Pasha and his staff in the provinces as undesirable. It is unsettling to public opinion that a distinguished General and Staff should be traveling about in the country."[10] The next day, War Minister Şevket Turgut Paşa personally requested Kemal's presence in the capital.[11] Returning to Istanbul, Mustafa Kemal knew, would have clipped his wings and even might have led to his arrest; so he drew a line in the sand by waging a public relations campaign.

On 9 June 1919, Mustafa Kemal dispatched a circular to the heads of provinces and sub-provinces and to the Societies of Defense of Rights and the Anti-Annexation Societies in which he made a personal oath to embody the aspirations of the nation. The circular noted the existence of "the public demonstrations born of a national conscience (*vicdan-ı milli*)" with the goal of defending "the rights and independence of the nation (*millet*)" throughout the country. "These days of life and death (*hayat ve memat*)," he suggested, called for no compromise on independence. Then came his solemn oath: "I promise to work with all my being for our national independence."[12] The circular's message recalled Kemal's thoughts on effective leadership in *Conversation with Officer and Commander*. Leaders, in this conception, must embrace and reflect the aspirations of their people in order to gain popular support. *Conversation* cited the examples of Moses, Jesus, and Napoleon in this regard. Each historical figure made his mark on history in this way. Now in 1919, Mustafa Kemal embraced what he considered noble and sacred goals, a people striving for their independence in the face of imperialism and thereby seeking their rightful place in one human civilization. National will, however, was not singular. Not everyone willingly embraced the national struggle espoused by Mustafa Kemal.

Most Muslims understood the word *millet*, or nation, to mean the religious community of Ottoman Muslims in the empire. This community comprised various peoples, such as Turks, Kurds, Circassians, Albanians, Laz, and others. Growing numbers, though still very much a minority, understood ethnicity when, for example, they heard "Turkish nation" or "Kurdish nation," *Türk milleti* or *Kürd milleti* respectively. During the War of Independence, Mustafa Kemal relied heavily on "the vocabulary of Muslim nationalism" as the strongest common denominator.[13] The word *millet* appealed to Muslims in general. Muslim patriotism, a struggle to save the *vatan*, or fatherland and home region, worked as well. For Mustafa Kemal, final victory depended upon the mobilization of as much of the Muslim population of Anatolia as possible, to be able to wage a total war if necessary. Avoiding unnecessary religious or ethnic rifts among the various Muslim ethnic communities would serve such a war effort. Along this vein, Mustafa Kemal often identified the aims of the national struggle as including the inviolability of the Ottoman sultanate and Islamic caliphate.

From Havza, Mustafa Kemal moved on to Amasya, the headquarters of the 5th Caucasus Division, a part of III Corps under the command of Refet (Bele), and a safe haven for developing aims and strategies with his colleagues. In this opening phase of the national struggle, gaining political legitimacy was of utmost importance, and, as noted by Andrew Mango, "Kemal saw the Defense of Rights Societies primarily as instruments of popular mobilization and a source of legitimate authority . . ."[14] A national congress scheduled in Sivas was the key to this strategy. It aimed to establish a national committee to provide direction to the national resistance and to gain legitimacy for the national cause. In addition to the Defense of Rights Societies, Mustafa Kemal placed a premium on the military for mobilizing popular support. Army commanders were to serve as an important link to the people and the civil administration. The British understood this dynamic as well and pushed for more demobilization, this time of XIII Corps in Diyarbekir, a small force of fewer than 5,000 personnel. On 15 June, Mustafa Kemal wired Karabekir indicating the need to oppose such a move and informing him that he had also made such a request to the chief of the General Staff, Cevad Paşa, in Istanbul.[15]

Ali Fuad, Rauf, and Refet joined Mustafa Kemal in Amasya for the conference. Karabekir remained in Erzurum but was kept informed of the deliberations. The meetings lasted several days, with Refet joining on the last day. On 22 June, all four participants signed the Amasya Circular, addressing the people of Anatolia and the world. The Amasya Circular provided both purpose and direction for the resistance. It began with a warning: "There is a threat to the unity of the fatherland and to the independence of the nation." This brief but clear sentence also identified the political aim of the emerging resistance movement in Anatolia: territorial integrity and national independence. The Istanbul government was depicted as under Allied influence and hence incapable of representing the people's interests. Therefore, the nation had to take matters into its own hands to preserve its independence. The greatest need was for "a national committee" (*bir heyet-i milliye*) to lead the national effort and convince the world of the legitimacy of its aims. The Amasya Circular called for "a national congress" to be held in Sivas, with each *sancak* (sub-province or county) sending three delegates. In the meantime, the Defense of National Rights and the Rejection of Annexation Societies were expected to send representatives to the upcoming regional congress in Erzurum.[16] Karabekir had insisted on a regional congress to address the eastern provinces.

Mustafa Kemal appreciated that these actions would eventually lead to a break with the Istanbul government and told Ali Fuad that he did not expect to hold his military position for too much longer.[17] In such a situation, he expected that Karabekir and Ali Fuad would assume full control over military and civilian administrations in their areas of responsibility, Erzurum and Ankara respectively.[18] The sultan's government responded to the Amasya Circular on 23 June, the next day, when Interior Minister Ali Kemal ordered all provincial officials to sever communication with Mustafa Kemal. The justification for this step was simply stated. Despite "his patriotism and zeal," Mustafa Kemal had failed in the performance of his duties. Then Ali Kemal undercut the authority of his own action by admitting that he acted on the "wish and insistence" of the Extraordinary English Representative.[19]

After the Amasya Circular, Ali Fuad quickly returned to his corps headquarters in Ankara. There, on 27 June, he circulated a memorandum ordering his regional commanders to work with senior civil bureaucrats for achieving a "unity of thought." Area commanders were expected to cooperate with senior government officials, to support the Defense of National Rights and Anti-Annexation Societies, and to help establish such organizations where there were none.[20] Then on 3–4 July, Ali Fuad confronted the War Ministry, suggesting that the army could not defend the country with current force levels. Unable to have an official mobilization, the greatest need was to strengthen current National Forces units. He expressed concern over the misunderstanding generated by the government's recent decision to prohibit civil and military officials from assisting in the formation of National Forces.[21] In confronting his superiors, Ali Fuad unequivocally criticized the lack of an aggressive strategy to oppose foreign occupation.

In Amasya, Mustafa Kemal showed diplomatic prescience when he analyzed the situation of Bolshevism and Russia. Possibly as early as Havza, Soviet agents had contacted Mustafa Kemal, and he expressed to them his need for weapons, supplies, and money in a common struggle against Western imperialism.[22] Now on 23 June, in a personal letter to Karabekir, he offered a strategic analysis of the Bolshevik issue. Mustafa Kemal maintained that Bolshevism was incompatible with the religion and customs of his country, an assessment reached in part by his having studied Communist theory while on medical leave in Karlsbad (Austria). Yet Mustafa Kemal realized, nonetheless, that Turkey had common interests with Russia in confronting a common adversary, the British. Mustafa Kemal hoped to entice Moscow into providing weapons, ammunition, scientific tools, money, and human help; but at the same time, he realized that it would be foolish and dangerous to invite the Bolsheviks into the country. He also understood Western sensitivities: close relations with the Bolsheviks would pose a threat to the Entente Powers.[23]

Early in the national resistance, Mustafa Kemal appreciated the importance of Russia, a conclusion that he had gained from brainstorming sessions with fellow conspirators back in Istanbul. But at this point in the resistance, there was no reason for Moscow to take him seriously. Former Unionists in *Karakol* were initially more successful in establishing contacts with Soviet representatives.[24] It would take over a year for Mustafa Kemal to develop a good working relationship with the Soviets, developing what has been called "an unholy alliance."[25]

Erzurum Congress

Mustafa Kemal left Amasya on 26 June and arrived in Erzurum on 3 July to a waiting delegation led by Karabekir. On 7 July, he and Karabekir issued an order to all corps commanders: no eradication of military or national organizations; no relinquishing of command to anyone; and no turning in of weapons and ammunition. The circular identified the army as the servant of the national will and the guarantor of the caliphate's inviolability. It also ordered the army to prevent any interference in the actions of the Defense of National Rights and Anti-Annexationist Societies.[26] This order clearly underscored Karabekir's support of Mustafa Kemal.

On 8 July, the Istanbul government, still hoping to derail the upcoming Erzurum Congress, cancelled Kemal's official commission. Damad Ferid Paşa, pro-British and anti-Unionist, headed the government at the time. At approximately the same time, around 2250, Mustafa Kemal sent a telegram resigning his command, a difficult and unsettling decision. Colonel Kazım (Dirik), Kemal's chief of staff, compounded the anxiety when he immediately placed himself under the command of Karabekir. His action suggested that not all officers would automatically throw in their lot with Mustafa Kemal. Rauf, who witnessed Kazım's reaction, described Mustafa Kemal as turning pale. Any feelings of uncertainty and vulnerablity in him, however, were brief, for Karabekir quickly swore allegiance to Mustafa Kemal and brought along with him the officers and men of XV Corps.[27] At a crucial moment, "Kazım [Karabekir] had thrown Kemal a veritable lifeline."[28] He played a very important role at this juncture in the national struggle. The XV Corps was the largest Ottoman corps, numbering 17,860 men, in an army of some 50,000 men. In an emergency, Karabekir could mobilize a total force of as many as 50,000 with the addition of tribes and militia.[29] The XV Corps thus gave Mustafa Kemal a secure base on the eastern front, and during the next three years, Karabekir remained a reliable and dedicated front commander.

After his resignation from the army, Mustafa Kemal sent a circular addressed to the nation explaining his action. He spoke of "the danger of partition of the fatherland and the nation" and of the need to wage a "national struggle." Leaving the military gave him the freedom to work as an individual for the nation's sacred goal, and he gave his word to make whatever sacrifices were necessary. Rauf, who wrote a separate explanation of his participation in the struggle, offered a "religious" (*dindar*) motivation for his actions. Unlike Mustafa Kemal, he added "the inviolability of sultanate and caliphate" to the goals of the fatherland's liberation and the nation's independence.[30] The significance of these subtle differences would become obvious later.

The days prior to the convening of the Erzurum Congress saw numerous discussions. According to one participant, on the night of 7–8 July (on the eve of his resignation), Mustafa Kemal outlined his long-range objectives: the establishment of a republic; the elimination of the *padişah* (another title for the sultan) and the caliph; the removal of the veil; the replacement of the fez by the hat as in "civilized nations"; and the implementation of a Latin alphabet.[31] It is doubtful that Mustafa Kemal was that clear in his aims, but such topics had become items of discussion and reflection. The aim of the republic, nonetheless, became reasonable with the passage of time. Perhaps at this stage it was more sentiment. In 1918, the Muslims in Azerbaijan had established a Muslim republic, providing an example to the Islamic world.

On 19 July 1919, in a letter to Ali Fuad outlining his opposition to an American mandate, Mustafa Kemal revealed the importance of demonstrating popular support by means of a representative institution in order to gain legitimacy for the national cause. "For the proper execution of our duty of being translators of the national conscience (*vicdan-ı milli*) for [determining] the fate of the nation and the fatherland, we cannot appear to exercise authority on any problem without linking it to the national desire." He went on to clarify the importance of the upcoming congress as a means of legitimizing action. "We prefer to have our relations with foreigners be based on decisions made by congress."[32] A representative institution provided a compelling appearance of popular legitimacy.

Mustafa Kemal insisted on the Erzurum Congress opening on 23 July, the anniversary of the 1908 Revolution.[33] This decision underscored continuity with the aims of that event as well as with former Unionist members. It also suggested that Mustafa Kemal would not turn on former CUP members. Mustafa Kemal arrived at the first session dressed in a military uniform with sultan's cordon, or ornamental chord. Zeki Bey, a delegate from Gümüşhane, challenged him to remove this accessory, explaining why: "We fear arbitrary power."[34] The congress had to be a civilian affair. Karabekir, division commanders, and other officers consequently kept a distance from the sessions.[35] Mustafa Kemal, for his part, complied with Zeki's demand. But he flouted convention by wearing an atypical lamb's fur cap, or *kalpak*, instead of the traditional *fez*, recalling an earlier conversation in which he had allegedly raised the issue of changing headgear. Removing his military uniform, however, was not a guarantee against his wielding arbitrary power. Donning civilian attire, however, did underscore the political nature of the conflict and the need for civilian authority. In this sense, Zeki Bey had performed a service for Mustafa Kemal.

The congress lasted fourteen days. It opened as the Congress of the Eastern Provinces. Hoca Raif Efendi gave the first speech, which provided a religious undertone to the meetings; Mustafa Kemal delivered his on the next day. The delegates then elected Mustafa Kemal as head of the congress with thirty-eight of forty-five votes; four abstained, two voted for Rauf, and one for Trabzonlu Servet Bey. Sources vary over the actual number of delegates. By one count, fifty-seven delegates eventually participated in the proceedings: twenty-four from Erzurum, seventeen from Trabzon, eleven from Sivas, three from Bitlis, and two from Van. Mustafa Kemal and Rauf were listed as coming from Erzurum.[36]

On 30 July, during deliberations, the Ottoman war ministry ordered the arrest of Mustafa Kemal and Rauf for "activity contrary to the government's decisions" and demanded their immediate return to Istanbul. Karabekir immediately rose to Kemal's defense in a communiqué to Istanbul on the next day. Nothing had transpired, he asserted, to indicate Mustafa Kemal had violated any laws in Erzurum. Moreover, Karabekir directly criticized the government for not giving "a single note of hope to the nation," despite its facing threats from Rum brigands, designs for a greater Armenia, and the occupation of Izmir. In addition, Karabekir said, Mustafa Kemal had performed distinguished service with honor for the country.[37] By this bold letter, Karabekir demonstrated unequivocal commitment to the Nationalist agenda and support for Mustafa Kemal.

The Erzurum Congress ended on 7 August and issued a declaration informing the people of its patriotic decisions. Three threats had spurred the delegates into action: Ottoman Greek (Rum) plots, massacres perpetuated by Armenians on Muslims, and "the policy of exterminating Islam." The declaration rejected the establishment of Rum and Armenian states, opposed any special privileges for the Christian population, and promised the protection of property, life, and honor. It spoke of Ottomanism and Islam by invoking the "unity of Ottoman society" and the brotherhood of all Muslims. The delegates identified three aims embodied in the National Forces and the national will: "the integrity of the Ottoman fatherland, the assurance of our nation's independence, and the inviolability of the sultanate and caliphate." They demanded that the central government convene a "national assembly" (*milli meclis*), and that the boundaries be identified as those at the time of the signing of the armistice on 30 October 1918. The declaration, in addition, announced the creation of the Society for the Defense of Rights of Eastern Anatolia and embraced all Muslim citizens as natural members of the society. Clearly, the congress excluded Christians, viewing them as fifth columnists or "the Other." A Representative Committee, consisting of nine members, assumed the responsibility of uniting all the national organizations, from the village to the provincial levels.[38] A separate document described the fatherland as "the country of Turks and Muslims."[39] The former received a prominent position within the larger context of the Islamic community.

The Representative Committee included a Nakşbendi şeyh, Ahmed Fevzi Efendi from Erzincan, and the chief of the Kurdish Mutki tribe, Hacı Musa Bey. Although not elected by the Congress, Karabekir apparently joined the Representative Committee for a brief period.[40] Six members never showed up in Erzurum, and two never appeared after the congress. Erzurum gave Mustafa Kemal a modicum of authority and power as a civilian figure that he used to make decisions in the name of the Representative Committee. He was emerging as a national leader with a regional base.

The Erzurum Congress voiced the slogan "Either independence or death," implying no compromise and thus suggesting a total war if necessary. Rather than believing the struggle would require total mobilization, Mustafa Kemal and others saw weaknesses among the Entente Powers available for exploitation. On 14 August, for example, Mustafa Kemal, Rauf, and Karabekir evaluated the strategic situation confronting them. Britain, France, and Italy appeared to lack the ability to impose a partition of Turkey. Britain was bogged down by imperial concerns in other places, such as Egypt, Sudan, Afghanistan, and India, and possessed insufficient forces to occupy Anatolia. France was downsizing its forces in the East, and Europe was preoccupied with the threat of Bolshevism. But the Entente Powers could still pose a serious threat by establishing mandates for Kurdistan and Armenia. The Americans, meanwhile, appeared to be disposed to an independent Turkey under a mandate.[41] This assessment suggested the external threat looked bigger than it actually was. The Great Powers lacked the will and resources to impose a strict military solution on the people of Anatolia if a viable resistance could be mounted. The character of the resistance thus became the principal issue.

In Erzurum, Mustafa Kemal had embarked on a road independent of Istanbul. It thus became critical to mobilize the nation to united action. Communication emerged as a key weapon in the Nationalist struggle. "The telegraph key was metaphorically the key to the heart of the nation."[42] Mustafa Kemal, therefore, spent much time in telegraph offices communicating with his commanders and mobilizing the people, often dispatching orders but at times offering analyses and explanations to educate his target audiences. Mustafa Kemal appreciated the power of propaganda. At Erzurum, Mustafa Kemal also participated in discussions of policy issues before elected delegates, listening to their views and expressing and defending his own. Some participants voted in opposition. This dynamic experienced at Erzurum differed from the decision-making process of military commanders, who consulted subordinates but then made decisions without voting. The political process thus begun at Erzurum continued at the Sivas Congress and then through the remainder of the war with the establishment of a parliament in Anatolia. Clearly Mustafa Kemal had begun his transition to the responsibilities of a statesman.

During the Congress, British colonel Anthony Rawlinson arrived in Erzurum to evaluate the mandated demobilization. He found "no real progress" on this score. His week-long sojourn in Erzurum, however, permitted him to have a number of lengthy conversations with both Mustafa Kemal and Karabekir. Mustafa Kemal came across to Rawlinson as a soldier with wide-ranging knowledge, a man driven by a deep sense of duty and patriotism. "He has read much and travelled widely, and is thoroughly competent to give a considered opinion on all subjects of general interest either at the present day or in the history of the past." Rawlinson viewed Mustafa Kemal as "a man of great strength of character and very definite views as to the rightful position of his race in the comity of nations."[43] When publishing his memoirs in 1924, Rawlinson did have the benefit of hindsight while writing down his evaluation. By then, the war had been won.

Sivas Congress[44]

Mustafa Kemal left Erzurum on 29 August and arrived in Sivas on 2 September. The Sivas Congress, unlike the one in Erzurum, was intended to represent the entire nation. Initially only 29 delegates appeared, but this number grew to approximately 38 out of an invited list of over 200 representatives. Mustafa Kemal took care to invite delegates more aligned with his thinking than had been the case in Erzurum. Effective propaganda rectified the anemic numbers and portrayed the congress as a national one, representing all regions of the empire, unlike Erzurum with its regional membership. There was continuity between the two congresses in terms of leadership. Five members from the Representative Committee— including Rauf, Bekir Sami (Kunduk), Raif Efendi and the Nakşbendi Şeyh Ahmed Fevzi Efendi—attended the sessions. Mustafa Kemal was elected head of the congress in a secret ballot, with only three delegates voting against him.

On 5 September, the second day of proceedings, Mustafa Kemal required an oath from the participating delegates, namely: "By God, I swear that I will not follow any personal goals in the Congress other than the felicity and peace of the fatherland and the nation; I will not strive for the resurrection of the Committee of Union and Progress; and I will not serve the political goals of any political party."[45] Kara Vasıf, who headed *Karakol*, the secret organization that Enver and Talat had established before their flight into exile, attended the congress.[46] Mustafa Kemal wanted to ensure that former Unionists realigned their loyalties

5   *Sivas Congress delegates. Mustafa Kemal is center-left in the front row.*

to him, *Karakol* included. Throughout the conduct of the War of Independence, Enver remained a distant but potential rival until his death on 4 August 1922.

Mustafa Kemal used the Sivas Congress to assume responsibilities *de jure* of commanding the army in Anatolia. On 9 September, the sixth day of its meetings, the Sivas Congress created the position of General Commander of the National Forces of Western Anatolia (*Anadolu-yu Garbi Umum Kuva-yı Milliye Kumandanı*) and appointed Ali Fuad to fill the position. He would report to the Representative Committee.[47] On 9 September, Mustafa Kemal informed him of his mission: he was to take command of the militia forces on the Izmir Front with the authority to appoint "capable people of honor" and to replace any civil officials opposed to the national struggle.[48] The next day, Ali Fuad departed for his new command in Eskişehir. His task at this juncture would prove daunting.

A number of deputies pushed the issue of an American mandate. Although discussed at Erzurum, it re-emerged as a major item of discussion. At one point, twenty-five delegates signed a petition supporting the issue. Washington had been exploring the possibility for a while. President Wilson had dispatched the King-Crane Commission to investigate the situation in the Middle East. After visiting Palestine, Lebanon, and Syria, the Commission arrived in Istanbul on 31 May 1919. A number of Ottomans believed the best option for the empire was to accept an American mandate, the United States being the most disinterested Western power. A society, indeed, had been formed in Istanbul to facilitate this goal.

Halide Edip (Adıvar), a feminist and an advocate of an American mandate, convinced Mustafa Kemal to talk with an American correspondent. Louis Edgar Browne of the *Chicago Daily News* arrived in Sivas in enough time to cover the entire congress. Mustafa Kemal turned the tables on Halide Edip and won Browne over to the cause of independence. The reporter then depicted the national struggle in a positive light for his readership back home, painting it as a patriotic effort aimed at establishing an independent state. Kemal's consistency on this fundamental issue paid dividends in time. He did, however, send a letter to the United States Senate requesting it to dispatch an investigative committee to Turkey. This request made no mention of a mandate. Eventually, the U.S. Congress rejected the idea of establishing an American mandate in the Middle East. Mustafa Kemal thus won the debate in the long term, but in the short term he pretended to be friendly to the American viewpoint.

"The General Congress of Sivas," despite its meager attendance, audaciously claimed to represent the nation. On 11 September, "The Declaration of the General Congress" addressed all parts of the "Ottoman Realm" (*Memalik-i Osmaniye*) and essentially reiterated the decisions reached in Erzurum. The main goals were once again identified as the achievement of "the integrity of the Ottoman fatherland, the assurance of our nation's independence, and the inviolability of the sultanate and caliphate." Other points included the rejection of Rum and Armenian states and any special, privileged status for the Christian population; the demand for the central government to convene a national assembly; and the acceptance of the boundaries of the state as those at the time of the signing of the armistice on 30 October 1918. The Society for the Defense of Rights of Eastern Anatolia became the Society for the Defense of Rights of Anatolia and Rumeli and claimed all Muslim citizens as natural members, thereby once again excluding Christians and Jews from natural membership. This name change reflected the claim of the congress to represent the national will and hence presented a more direct challenge to the central government. Along this vein, the Sivas Congress also charged the Representative Committee, whose membership grew from nine to sixteen, with the responsibility of uniting all national organizations.[49] Refet, signer of the Amasya Circular and former commander of III Corps, joined as a new member. Mustafa Kemal viewed the Representative Committee as constituting a provisional government in the name of the people.

On 11 September, the Representative Committee issued instructions to the National Army (*Milli Ordu*) which consisted of a regular army of multiple corps and irregular forces. National Forces would be responsible for local defense and would form around mosques. Platoons would guard villages and neighborhoods. Companies would handle districts (*nahiye*) and battalions would protect the capitals of *sancaks* and provinces with regular army officers commanding these various units. The Nationalist Forces were of two kinds: stationary (*sabit*) and mobile (*seyyar*), with both responsible to local administrations and central committees.[50]

The Sivas Congress also drew up the Regulation for the Organization of the Defense of Rights Societies. Ultimate power was vested in the national will. The Representative Committee served as an executive organization and directed the relationship between the national organizations and the army. In the major towns, local Central Committees managed affairs, with military recruiter chiefs and regional commanders assisting their effort. Mobile forces assisted the regular army in combat and in security matters, whereas stationary forces protected their localities from brigand attacks and safeguarded non-Muslims. These forces served in their own areas unless a crisis demanded their dispatch to other regions. National Forces were to be organized as squads, platoons, and companies. Every individual member of the national detachments had to swear on the Quran.[51] Clearly, by this document, Mustafa Kemal intended to develop control over the National Forces and the local Defense of Rights Societies, relying on the army to play an important role in unifying the disparate groups throughout the country. On 17 October, for example, Mustafa Kemal instructed Colonel Bekir Sami, the commander of the 56th Division headquartered in Bursa, to rein in the Anti-Annexation Society in Balıkesir in western Anatolia and force it to change its name to the Society of the Defense of Rights.[52] Creating a unified national organization took time, however.

At the Congress of Sivas, Mustafa Kemal saw himself as having established the basis of a provisional government. Clearly, he had gained momentum for the national movement. Now two congresses, held in two different towns, had decided on the same agenda and the same leader. Moreover, Mustafa Kemal had three key corps in Anatolia under his authority, XX Corps in Ankara, XV Corps in Erzurum, and III Corps in Sivas. The corps commanders, meanwhile, provided a circle of protection around Mustafa Kemal. Emboldened by the Sivas Congress, Mustafa Kemal moved to strengthen his control over Anatolia.

The office of the British High Commissioner bleakly assessed the impact of the Sivas Congress on the Allied position in Turkey. The declaration by the Sivas Congress unnerved the pro-British government of Damad Ferid Paşa, who began discussing the need to display force against the Nationalists. On 29 September, the High Commissioners rejected this idea, leading Ferid Paşa to resign on 1 October. On 24 September, the people of Konya had forced their governor to flee to Istanbul; now on 3 October, local soldiers compelled the governor in Bursa to abandon his position. Istanbul's effective control appeared limited to only a few places in western Anatolia like Adapazar, Eskişehir, Kütahya, and possibly Bandırma. Moreover, the Sivas Congress had energized Istanbul's population.

"Noble-looking portraits of Mustafa Kemal and Rauf Bey adorn the local Turkish papers." According to the report, the current war minister continues to support the Nationalists, and Nationalist propaganda has taken advantage of "the unfortunate coincidence of Major Noel's presence at Malatya" [among the Kurds] during the Sivas Congress so as to inflame public opinion with assertions of British designs on Kurdistan. The report noted: "Here again the British lion has the appearance of having abandoned his imaginary project on the first display of Kemal's teeth." According to the British report, the great majority of the intelligentsia and the officer corps were "in sympathy with the nationalists," making it highly likely that the leaders of the movement would see little need to compromise on the terms for the final peace. "It would be more difficult today than it would have been eight months ago to impose on Turkey a distasteful Peace Treaty without fresh resort to force."[53] This report indicated clearly that some astute British officials detected early that the tide of events was turning in favor of the Nationalist movement. But the home front in Anatolia was far from secure in the hands of Mustafa Kemal.

A most interesting development occurred one month after the closing of the Sivas Congress. On 13 October, Velid Ebüzziya, the chief writer of the newspaper *Tasvir-i Efkar* (The Illustration of Ideas), sent Mustafa Kemal twenty-one questions. Velid supported the cause and wanted to provide better information to his readership. His fifth question asked what the main goal of the national movement was. Mustafa Kemal initially wrote down: "The main goal is to ensure the complete unity of the fatherland and the independence of the nation and the inviolability of the caliphate and sultanate." Then he crossed out the second half of his answer and left only the reference to the fatherland and the nation.[54] Mustafa Kemal saw the caliphate and sultanate as negotiable items. The newspaper, for its part, only published the reference to the fatherland and nation.[55]

By this time, Major General James Harbord, Woodrow Wilson's representative, arrived in Anatolia on a fact-finding mission concerning an independent Armenia. He had traveled 11,300 miles, including a visit to Sivas on 20 September. After his travels, Harbord filed a report and published articles on his visit in popular American magazines. In one, he described his two-and-a-half-hour meeting with Mustafa Kemal: "He talked very easily and fluently. His marshaling of his facts through the interpreter was orderly and logical, though he was apparently under considerable strain and continually drew a string of prayer beads through his rather good-looking hands, never keeping them quiet a moment."[56] After the interview, an official explained to Harbord that Mustafa Kemal had been suffering from malaria and had a fever during their meeting. Harbord left with a positive assessment of his host. "I came away with an impression of the sincere patriotism of Mustafa Kemal and his immediate associates. . . Mustafa Kemal is no cheap political adventurer. He is a military leader of proven skill."[57] Although he found his Turkish host neatly dressed in civilian clothes and sitting without any head-covering, Harbord was clearly fascinated by Kemal's record as a military leader, especially at Gallipoli. The order and discipline of the Turkish soldiers, a trademark of Kemal's command, also caught his attention. "The troops at Sivas were the best we had seen in Turkey . . . better equipped and clothed than at other stations."[58]

In his report to Washington, Harbord noted that Mustafa Kemal would accept an American mandate only if it were limited to giving advice. Mustafa Kemal wanted full sovereignty without the limitation of the mandate formula. He assured the Americans that there would be no place for Bolshevism; but neither would there be room for big capitalists. Turkey was going to chart its own path as a country of millions of artisans and workers.[59] Mustafa Kemal also kept his promise to Harbord about protecting religious minorities. On 24 September, in the name of the Representative Committee, he assured the various embassies of the national movement's commitment regarding the security of non-Muslims, as personal freedoms would be assured without regard for race or creed.[60] This promise would prove hollow.

In Sivas, Harbord met Alfred Rüstem, former Ottoman ambassador to the United States (1914). The American general remembered Rüstem as "well-known in the diplomatic and social life of our capital."[61] Rüstem had been born on the Ottoman island of Midilli as Alfred Bilinski. His father was a Polish refugee who had fled his native Poland after the failed 1848 Revolution, then entered Ottoman service as Sadreddin Nihad Paşa and married a British woman. Alfred Rüstem embarked on a career as a diplomat in the Ottoman Foreign Ministry; a native speaker of Turkish, he knew English, French, and Italian fluently. There in Sivas, he was always at Kemal's side, and the two men worked closely together for about a year.[62] Clearly, Mustafa Kemal mined Rüstem for his diplomatic expertise and experience in a circle heavily dominated by soldiers with only a sprinkling of diplomats and bureaucrats. Most senior members of the Ottoman diplomatic corps remained in Istanbul throughout the war; so Rüstem's presence was much appreciated. Then, after a sudden falling out with Mustafa Kemal, he left Ankara in September 1920 for Europe, never to return to Turkey. Eventually a reconciliation took place, and Mustafa Kemal ensured that Rüstem received a pension until his death in 1935 for services rendered for the cause.

Home Front

In developing a national liberation movement, Mustafa Kemal needed to mobilize the people around his leadership. Propaganda played an important role in affecting public opinion on the home front. On 14 September, Mustafa Kemal established an official newspaper named *İrade-i Milliye* (National Will). Its first issue was naturally devoted to coverage of the Sivas Congress, including Kemal's speech and the declaration to the nation.[63] Controlling the war narrative was important for success.

Mustafa Kemal, in the meantime, faced internal social and ethnic unrest. Normal brigandage wreaked havoc in certain areas. In a general circular of 22 August, he discussed the Rum and Armenian threats. He viewed the Rum patriarch in Istanbul and Greek prime minister Venizelos as supporting Greek guerrilla bands in the Pontus region and claimed that Greek consulates had weapons and ammunition depots ready for distribution when necessary. At the same time, the Armenians, led by their patriarch Zaven Efendi, were cooperating with the Rum (Ottoman Greeks) in places like Samsun and Trabzon. Armenian activities thus mirrored those of the Rum.[64] In this analysis, the conflict appeared as ethnically and religiously based. The Christian population was large enough to be viewed as a fifth column, and there was always the danger of Greece and Armenia cooperating against Turkey.

The Kurds represented both a tribal and an ethnic problem. After the Turks, they constituted the largest Muslim ethnic group in Anatolia, perhaps as high as 15 per cent of the population, residing mainly but not exclusively in the eastern and southeastern regions of Anatolia. Historically, the Ottoman government had found it impossible to establish central control over much of this region and managed only weak or indirect rule. Kurdish society, nonetheless, was far from homogeneous, making a strong, unified effort by Kurds a very difficult proposition. Kurds divided along tribal, Sunni-Alevi religious, and Kurmanji-Zaza linguistic lines. "Most Kurds were more interested in protecting their personal, religious, and tribal interests than in turning to Kurdish organizations to advance national aims."[65] The tribes were generally poor and illiterate, although chiefs tended to be educated and worldly wise. Kurdish *ağas*, or chieftains, and landowners, moreover, tended to support resistance to foreign provocateurs.

Kurdish national organizations were small in number and membership. Two stood out in promoting Kurdish national rights: the Kurdish Society for Assistance and Progress (*Kürd Teavün ve Terakki Cemiyeti*), founded in 1908, and the Society for the Rise of Kurdistan (*Kürdistan Teali Cemiyeti*), created in 1919. A small group of prominent Kurds had travelled to Versailles, seeking recognition of their national rights at the Peace Conference. Despite the fragmented nature of Kurdish society, there was the potential for "Young Kurds" to turn local agitation and unrest into a military struggle, however brief, for national rights and autonomy. Foreign powers, for their part, were ready to exploit Turkish-Kurdish differences for their own designs. In fact, Britain favored a separate Kurdistan as part of a post-war peace settlement. Local Ottoman officials frequently reported on British efforts to incite Kurds to rebel in areas such as Diyarbekir, Urfa, and Malatya.[66] In July and August 1919, Ottoman government authorities expressed concerns about Kurds in the Dersim region, and a *mutasarrıf* of Malatya saw danger in there being 60,000 armed Kurds inspired by Kurdish nationalism with not enough government troops in the area to suppress such a rebellion.[67]

Neither the Istanbul government nor Mustafa Kemal wanted to see the Kurds develop a separatist movement. To his credit, Mustafa Kemal had developed a good working relationship during World War I with several Kurdish tribal chiefs when he commanded XVI Corps and then Second Army. At that juncture in history, Kurds had for the most part united behind the Ottoman government against a common enemy—the invading tsarist army. Now in 1919, Mustafa Kemal employed several strategies to gain Kurdish support, or at least their acquiescence. To facilitate his design, prominent Kurds were invited to the Erzurum Congress, and three Kurds became members of the Representative Committee. Hacı Musa Bey, head of the Kurdish Mutki tribe, was one of those tribal chiefs. He had helped Mustafa Kemal retake the city of Bitlis in 1916.[68] To gain Kurdish cooperation, Mustafa Kemal played the Armenian threat card in communicating with them.[69] He understood, however, that this strategy only worked in affected areas like Van or Bitlis, i.e., the eastern and southeastern borders of Anatolia.[70] One letter to two prominent Kurdish tribal chiefs, dated 15 September, spoke of Turks and Kurds as "full brothers" working together.[71] Appeals were also made to the Islamic faith and Ottoman and Muslim patriotism. In a letter to Hacı Musa Bey on 3 December, Mustafa Kemal succinctly summarized his basic message to the Kurds throughout the war, playing up "the nobility of the Kurdish people" (*Kürd kavm-i necib*), their religious ties to the caliphate, and their inseparable brotherhood with the Turks. Mustafa Kemal warned of degenerate individuals in Istanbul who sowed divisions between Kurds and Turks with money spent in the name of "a Kurdish entity" (*Kürdlük*).[72] Karabekir, with much experience serving eastern Anatolia, viewed religion as the strongest bond between Turks and Kurds and therefore counseled using Turkish religious officials to counter the "ignorant" tribal chiefs.[73] The Kurdish Problem remained a concern throughout the war.

Between three and four million Alevi-Bektaşis (a branch of Shiism) were distributed throughout central and eastern regions of Anatolia. The sect included both Turks and Kurds. As early as 26 June 1919, Mustafa Kemal tried to rally the Alevis in the region of Tokat, whom he claimed formed 81 per cent of the population. To accomplish this goal, he sought the support of local Alevi notables for the Societies of Defense of Rights and Anti-Annexation.[74] Mustafa Kemal readily used Alevi terminology in communicating with the heads of this order, Hacıbektaş Çelebi Cemaleddin Efendi and his assistant, Niyazi Salih Baba. He thanked them for their support for the fatherland and praised them for showing "the people the true path" in the "holy struggle" for "the liberation of our beloved fatherland."[75] Mustafa Kemal wisely demonstrated sensitivity and discretion regarding the religious differences among Muslims in Anatolia.

Mustafa Kemal regularly attempted to disseminate the Nationalist message to the people, the villagers in particular. The people needed regular reminders of the threats facing their fatherland and the nation. All national organizations, corps and division commanders, and heads of the military recruitment were to partake in this duty. They were to aggressively enlist assistance from the civil bureaucracy.[76] In this early period, Mustafa Kemal viewed the army as the best vehicle for mobilizing the people.

Women joined the Nationalist cause as well. They had been mobilized in World War I, and they continued their involvement during the national resistance. Halide Edip came to symbolize the new female activist. In Istanbul, she gave patriotic speeches before crowds on the streets and in parks and helped establish a society devoted to bringing about an American mandate. She eventually joined Mustafa Kemal in Ankara in 1920, an event that became a noteworthy news item. Mustafa Kemal continually welcomed women's efforts for the nationalist cause. On 13 December 1919, he wrote the Anatolian Women's Society for the Defense of the Fatherland congratulating the organization on its recent founding (10 December) in Sivas. Branches sprouted across the country, in places like Konya, Niğde, Burdur, Erzincan, Kayseri, and Eskişehir. In his letter, Mustafa Kemal noted the need for several revolutions in the lives of women and suggested the future held great progress and enlightenment for "Turkish women" (*Türk kadınları*), because of their refinement and the seriousness of their ideals. Turkish women would join the freedom movement as spiritual and intellectual partners for the benefit of the fatherland and nation. An invitation had gone out to "Turkish ladies" (*Türk hanımları*), with the support of Mustafa Kemal, to show their patriotism.[77]

Building Momentum

Armed resistance to the Greek occupation of Izmir commenced on 15 May 1919, "the day of honor" in Turkish history, when the first blood was spilled in defense of the fatherland. Many people took to the mountains rather than submit to foreign rule. Local leaders emerged to help establish what came to be referred to as the National Forces (*Kuvve-yi Milliye*). Some were former Ottoman officers. The names of Çerkez Edhem, Demirci Efe, and Yörük Ali dominated this early period of armed resistance on the western front. Local army commanders and Societies for Defense of National Rights often supported local guerrilla leaders.[78]

These irregular forces fought under various names, such as guerrillas (çeteler), national detachments (milli müfrezeler), or fighters against the infidel (mücahidun). They dominated the landscape of the western, northern, and southeastern fronts, often assuming police and administrative functions in their localities. Some behaved more like brigands than patriotic militia, and it proved difficult to create a unified effort. Local leaders often resisted coming under the command of regular army officers assigned by corps commanders. Meanwhile, the effectiveness of these forces depended on the local support of secular and religious leaders, merchants and tradesmen, town dwellers and villagers. A number of local congresses had convened in an attempt to create a unity of effort, to mobilize local support, and to express publicly their opposition to foreign occupation. More would follow. Eight regional or local congresses had already taken place before the convening at Erzurum, then there were four between Erzurum and Sivas, and another fourteen followed Sivas, for a total of twenty-eight congresses.[79] By June 1919, approximately 6,500 irregular fighters were scattered around the western front.[80] Some of these forces conducted a low-grade insurgency against Greek forces in the Izmir region.

Local army commanders generally aided and abetted the Defense of Rights Societies. In a report on 25 June 1919, Brigadier General Yusuf İzzet, commander of XIV Corps (Bandırma), defended to Istanbul such officers as motivated by "mature patriotism" to participate in the "national movement."[81] Cooperation between irregular forces and the regular army, however, varied from area to area. Colonel Fahreddin (Altay), the commander of XII Corps in Konya, described the difficult situation facing him. Demirci Mehmed Efe had emerged as one of the most famous of the guerrilla fighters in the War of Independence, leading his zeybeks, or local guerrillas, from the mountains around Nazilli to attack the Greek positions in Aydın. A number of regular army officers had abandoned their uniforms and joined his band. Others, however, regarded these guerrillas with disdain, viewing them as ignorant of war and driven by instinct. One day in October, Demirci Mehmed Efe suddenly assumed the impressive title of "General Commander of National Forces," catching Fahreddin off guard.[82] In December 1920, Ankara would have to use military force to rein in Demirci Efe. But throughout 1919 and almost all of 1920, Mustafa Kemal was too preoccupied with political matters to address the issue of regular army versus National Forces head-on. This would have been premature.

The National Forces provided an important service on the Western front. They kept up pressure on the occupying Greek force using hit-and-run tactics, often without clearly linking their military operations to any authority. On

7 October, the Allied Supreme Council finally agreed upon the Milne Line, which was to define the Greek zone in western Anatolia. But it placed two important restrictions on the Greeks. Greek forces could pursue Nationalist guerrillas only three kilometers across the Milne Line, and then had to return to the Greek occupation zone. Athens wanted the freedom to target guerrilla logistic bases to the operational depth, but this was denied. Western Anatolia experienced a low-grade insurgency against the Greek occupation.

At the beginning of October, with the Erzurum and Sivas Congresses giving Mustafa Kemal momentum, Sultan Vahdeddin announced the holding of elections in November and December for the convening of a new parliament. In conjunction with this move, he tried to reconcile with Mustafa Kemal and the nationalists by appointing General Ali Rıza, a military officer favorably inclined toward Mustafa Kemal and his associates, to form a "Cabinet of Reconciliation." Mustafa Kemal approved of the appointment of Mersinli Cemal Paşa as war minister. In fact, on 7 October, the Representative Committee decided to support the new cabinet and lifted the ban on direct communications with Istanbul. Mustafa Kemal appointed Mersinli Cemal Paşa as an advisory member of the Representative Committee and thus its delegate in Istanbul.

On 9 October, the new cabinet in Istanbul decided to send navy minister Salih Paşa to negotiate with Mustafa Kemal in Amasya. This decision represented an important triumph for Mustafa Kemal, for it meant *de facto* recognition by Istanbul of the Nationalist movement. Negotiations between the two men lasted from 20 to 22 October and ended in "a fragile agreement" with Salih Paşa to have the National Assembly meeting in Anatolia.[83] This major concession produced a bombshell in Istanbul, and the government refused to ratify the agreement. Any disagreement with the sultan's government, however, played into Kemal's hand in Anatolia precisely because he sought to maintain his leadership in the emerging national struggle. Undeterred by a seeming setback, Mustafa Kemal remained committed to ensuring the election of deputies supportive of the Nationalist cause. Army commanders and the Societies of the Defense of Rights were instructed to support Nationalist candidates.[84] Greeks and Armenians boycotted the parliamentary elections; but the Jewish community participated. The majority of the elected deputies overwhelmingly favored the national struggle in general terms but differed on specific issues and methods. Mustafa Kemal won a seat representing Ankara.

Mustafa Kemal viewed the upcoming elections favorably and called for a conference in Sivas to develop goals and strategies for continuing the resistance.[85] Invitations went out to all the corps commanders. The XIII Corps commander (Diyarbekir) failed to appear; Fahreddin of XII Corps (Konya) claimed illness and sent his chief of staff. Karabekir and Ali Fuad both attended the conference.

Other participants included Rauf, Alfred Rüstem, and Mazhar Müfit (Kansu). Discussions lasted from 16 to 28 November. Kara Vasıf of *Karakol* arrived late, on 27 November. Mustafa Kemal quickly discovered strong opposition to his idea of convening parliament in Anatolia. For him to go to Istanbul, however, would be tantamount to him walking into a lion's den. His colleagues, though, rightly viewed meeting in Anatolia as too radical a step. The Ottoman Parliament would therefore have to meet in Istanbul.

The participants at the November conference discussed a wide range of subjects, giving Mustafa Kemal an opportunity to hear various points of view and conflicting arguments. He identified four main aims for the national movement: defending borders, ensuring independence, receiving suitable help, and ensuring rights for minorities. Mustafa Kemal revealed his political strategy and tabled any notion of forming a political party; instead, he wanted the Society for the Defense of Rights in Anatolia and Rumeli to remain as an umbrella organization. The participants agreed to the Representative Committee carrying out its duties while the new parliament was in session.[86] But Mustafa Kemal refused to loosen his reins on the situation and to allow Istanbul to upstage his leadership. But as it was, attention was bound to shift to Istanbul. At the local level, Mustafa Kemal saw the corps commanders as the main link between the Representative Committee and the provinces, going so far as to say, "We cannot trust the civilian officials." In fact, he asserted that most governors opposed the nationalists.[87] Much of the success of the struggle thus far rested heavily on the shoulders of the army, which possessed the weapons. Army commanders were expected to function both as soldiers and civil administrators.

Financial challenges also faced the nationalists; revenues did not match expenditure, and their taxation base was limited. Mustafa Kemal reminded those present: "In Abdülhamid's time, four months would pass and we would not receive our wages, but still we lived."[88] That problem had stemmed from Hamidian corruption and inefficiency. Now, individuals had to sacrifice for the noble cause of independence. Nevertheless, the financial issue received serious discussion. The struggle, for now, would be waged on a shoestring with foreign financial and material support proving highly important throughout.

With parliament scheduled to meet in Istanbul, the Representative Committee considered moving from Sivas to Eskişehir to be closer to the parliamentary proceedings in Istanbul. But increased British control of the railway between both cities led Mustafa Kemal to opt for Ankara, a town of between 20,000 and 22,000 inhabitants. Ankara offered a safe sanctuary and sat astride a railway network. No European Power, moreover, had designs on it. Moving to Ankara came to symbolize placing faith in the people and thereby loosening the ties of the country to the Ottoman political and cultural center of Istanbul.

Mustafa Kemal and several other members of the Representative Committee piled into three automobiles and departed Sivas on 22 December, arriving in Ankara on 27 December 1919. While en route to Ankara, Mustafa Kemal went out of his way to visit the center of the Bektaşi order, drink *rakı* with the head of the order, and then made a pilgrimage to the mausoleum of its spiritual founder, Hacı Bektaş.[89] Then his arrival in Ankara became a media event. A large welcoming crowd lined his path of entry into the city. The military provided 700 infantry and 3,000 cavalrymen as guards and greeters. Local government officials joined up with members of Bektaşi, Nakşbendi, Rüfai, Sadi, Bayrami, and Mevlevi Sufi orders, as well as representatives from all the trades. Mustafa Kemal worked the crowd with an emotional speech.

After the conclusion of public festivities, Mustafa Kemal quickly established a robust center for the flow of information and propaganda. Halide Edip received an assignment to follow the British and French press, regularly receiving copies of *The Times*, *Manchester Guardian*, *Daily Herald*, and the *Daily Chronicle* for evaluation.[90] Instead of transferring *İdare-i Milliye* from Sivas to Ankara, Mustafa Kemal established a new newspaper, *Hakimiyet-i Milliye*, or *National Sovereignty*, to disseminate official information. "The leaders of the national struggle wanted by means of the press to prove to the outside world the rightness of the nation's claims and to ensure mental and psychological unity in the country at the necessary time."[91] The message was clear in the name change of newspapers: instead of expressing the national will, the offical newspaper would assert national sovereignty.

During the month of January, with the opening of Parliament scheduled for February, Mustafa Kemal gave serious attention to the development of diplomatic and military strategies. In an important memorandum of 7 January 1920 to Ali Fuad, Mustafa Kemal outlined his strategic thinking. Turkey was a besieged country, surrounded on four sides. South Caucasus constituted an important front. There, the Entente Powers were intent on creating a barrier against Turkey. The Nationalists needed to develop relations with the new Muslim states of Azerbaijan and Dağistan and to coordinate an offensive with the Bolsheviks against those nations serving Entente designs. Success depended on a government capable of making definite decisions, which Istanbul appeared incapable of doing.[92] Astute diplomacy was absolutely necessary for the success of the Nationalist struggle. Mustafa Kemal also needed Moscow's aid.

Military affairs also required attention, with the Greek front drawing special attention. On 5 January 1920, Mustafa Kemal noted that the lack of military forces required reliance on protests and on the National Forces in the Aydın region.[93] With political events moving into uncharted waters, Mustafa Kemal wisely ordered the development of contingency war plans. The plans were predicated on the assumption that serious resistance to a Greek offensive might encourage Italy to withdraw her forces from Anatolia. The Greek army had two bases for launching offensive operations—Foça and İzmir. An attack along these two axes, however, would result in a separation of their forces, preventing mutual support. The Turks, therefore, would build up their forces in Akhisar and Alaşehir. The plan called for a reserve force to be stationed in Bandırma in the event Greece move its troops now facing Bulgaria into Anatolia.[94] Battlefield events within six months would show that the National Army was far from being able to put up a resolute defense against a major Greek offensive.

The plan gave suitable attention to the placement of army divisions. The XX Corps would be deployed to Afyon and there establish a headquarters for the commander in chief. The XII Corps headquarters would be moved to Alaşehir. Regular army commanders were expected to cooperate with the National Forces, including with Demirci Efe in the Aydın region.[95] Meanwhile, in the strategic rear, III Corps would watch the Christian population in the Samsun-Sinop-Merzifon area to ensure that there would be no internal revolts and no foreign intervention. To meet a French advance northwest from Adana, the plan called for the destruction of the Taurus tunnel and bridges. In the event that the situation facing III Corps (Sivas) became serious, the 11th Division would be passed under its command, and the XV Corps (Erzurum) and XIII Corps (Diyarbekir) would support III Corps. The 10th Caucasus Division, meanwhile, would receive the mission of destroying the railway connecting the British headquarters in Istanbul to İzmit, while the 1st Division guarded the İzmit-Adapazar area.[96] The tenor of this plan revealed the complexity of the threats facing the Nationalists.

According to the above plan, Mustafa Kemal assumed the position of General Commander of Anatolia (*Umum Anadolu Kumandanı*). In the east, Karabekir commanded III, XIII, and XV Corps and reported directly to Mustafa Kemal. According to this plan, Mustafa Kemal assumed the position of commander in chief, presaging his official position in August 1921.[97]

Italy constituted the weakest link among the European Powers with imperialist designs on Turkey. Rome was upset over the Greek occupation of Izmir and the new country of Yugoslavia receiving the city of Fiume. Consequently, Italian officials became sympathetic to the Nationalist movement and ill-disposed to undertake a major venture in Anatolia. Count Carlo Sforza (1872–1952), Italy's first High Commissioner in Istanbul and then foreign minister (1920–21), was among them. Italian rule created no serious opposition. A couple more years were necessary, however, before Italy reached an agreement to pull its military forces from southern Anatolia, including Konya and Antalya. In the interim, Italy gave the Nationalists a quiet front with a benign occupation.

Mustafa Kemal also moved on the Arab-Muslim front. He offered a common cause with the Arabs of Syria, Lebanon, Iraq, and Palestine; they all faced European imperialism with the occupation of their lands. In October, Turkish propaganda increased in Aleppo and Damascus. In particular, two pamphlets written by Mustafa Kemal had gained effective circulation: one outlined the aims of the Nationalist objectives and the other called for support from the population. The majority of the Muslims in Aleppo province and a very large number in Damascus province appeared sympathetic to Turkey's aspirations.[98] In December, Syrian nationalists, led by Colonel Şakir Nimet al-Sabani, the chief of the Aleppo police, had approached Mustafa Kemal with the notion of a joint action against the French. Mustafa Kemal viewed Arab support in Syria as undermining French designs on southeastern Anatolia.[99]

In October 1919, France showed its expansionist designs in Anatolia. In December 1918, French troops landed at Adana and Mersin, with British units deployed inland as far as Maraş. The Sykes-Picot Agreement between Britain and France in 1916 had assigned southeastern Anatolia as far inland as Sivas to the French. In October and November 1919, British troops turned over the towns of Anteb, Maraş, and Urfa to the French. The hand-off went so smoothly that the Ottoman XIII Corps had no chance to prevent the transfer of power. The potential for armed conflict increased with the coming of the French. In particular, the presence of many Armenian soldiers in the French occupying force aroused great anxiety among the Muslim population.[100] Many Armenian recruits had come from the United States; others were mainly refugees.[101] Muslims were concerned about retribution for the deportations and massacres of Armenians during World War I. Under British occupation, southeastern Anatolia had remained relatively calm. The Armenian military presence and French policies, however, exacerbated relations with the local Muslim population. Another major concern surfaced among the Muslim population. During the British and French occupations of the region, approximately 170,000 Armenians settled in the region as refugees, with 70,000 of them concentrating in Adana. Local Muslims were concerned that they might be incorporated into a Greater Armenia.[102] Soon southeastern Anatolia would be engulfed in a multi-faceted war.

The transfer of power by the British to the French brought both diplomatic and military responses. Mustafa Kemal instructed Ali Fuad to move his headquarters from the western front to Kayseri to monitor developments. He also selected four junior officers from his staff to depart for southeastern Anatolia to organize and conduct limited armed resistance. Major Kemal Bey, who had landed with him in Samsun, received overall command for this group. On 1 November, the four officers departed with instructions to avoid major hostilities if possible.[103] Captain Emrullahzade Asaf was assigned to the region of Maraş, and Mustafa Kemal gave him the *nom de guerre* of Kılıç Ali (Ali the Sword). In his first circular addressed to the people of the region as General Commander of the National Forces in the Region of Maraş and Anteb, Kılıç Ali spoke for the Society for Defense of Rights of Anatolia and Rumeli. He stressed the importance of offering resistance as a signal to the world and the peace conference of the unacceptability of the French occupation. In addition, he warned of the danger posed by the French arming Armenians, appealed to patriotic and religious sentiments, and attempted to bolster confidence by claiming brothers from all over Anatolia were coming to help.[104] Violent incidents began occurring shortly thereafter.

To avoid war with Mustafa Kemal, the Paris government dispatched its diplomat François Georges-Picot to meet with Mustafa Kemal at the beginning of December 1919. Picot conferred with Mustafa Kemal for two days. According to Mustafa Kemal in his letter to Karabekir, the French diplomat suggested that France might withdraw its forces from Adana in return for assurances of French economic interests in southeastern Anatolia. But armed attacks against French troops, he demanded, must cease. Mustafa Kemal defiantly rejected any economic concessions and maintained that independence had to be absolute.[105] Despite the lack of an agreement, the meeting with a senior French diplomat represented a political gain for Mustafa Kemal. France was taking Mustafa Kemal seriously and acting independently. Southeastern Anatolia, moreover, was being recognized as a zone under Ankara's, rather than Istanbul's, influence.

Contacts between Syrian nationalists and Mustafa Kemal increased as a result of the French occupation of Southeastern Anatolia. Both wanted the French expelled. Mustafa Kemal even dangled the notion of Syria's independence followed by a confederation with Turkey.[106] It was only a question of time before a spontaneous incident or planned action would erupt into a major military event. The town of Maraş was where the big fire occurred. The French imposed martial law in the town, while the local Defense of Rights Society chafed under foreign occupation, with Kılıç Ali poised to assist at the appropriate moment. A spark to ignite a combustible situation occurred on 21 January 1920. Claiming a French provocation, Muslims in Maraş rose up in revolt against the French occupation. The town had a substantial Armenian quarter, and the Armenians cooperated with the French in defending the town. In rapid fashion, Kılıç Ali entered the fray two days later with a combination of regular and irregular forces. The fighting lasted for twenty-two days.[107]

On 25 January, Mustafa Kemal provided strategic guidance for fighting the French in two general circulars to army commands. He viewed the French forces as intent on subjugating the people in piecemeal fashion. National Forces, whether big or small in numbers, therefore should engage the French everywhere. Mustafa Kemal defined the threat as "the extinction of all the foundations of life."

Sustained military operations would demonstrate to the Peace Conference the impossibility of France annexing the Adana region. In more eastern areas, like Urfa, guerrilla actions would have to be the immediate response. Mustafa Kemal ended by requesting input from his commanders.[108] This request was unusual in the sense that Mustafa Kemal sent the appeal to all his senior commanders. From afar on the Western Front, Yusuf İzzet, commander of XIV Corps (Bandırma), offered solid advice: attack railroads and telegraph lines and wage "a serious economic battle."[109]

In his second circular, Mustafa Kemal provided the same strategic analysis but also offered specific tactical targets. In response to French moves to Maraş, Mustafa Kemal directed the National Forces there to wage a guerrilla war in the following ways: first, capture and destroy small garrisons; then target railroad bridges, tunnels, and roads to make them unusable by motor vehicles; and finally, use mobile forces to cut communications and attack and set ablaze whatever forces and equipment the French sent. If an uprising should occur in Urfa, III and XII Corps should support such operations. He stressed using small-unit operations. Twenty detachments of ten fighters each could sever communications to French soldiers east of the Tigris. Tribes also needed to be involved in the struggle. If the French sought to widen their area from Maraş, then III Corps should send weapons and forces to stop them.[110]

In both circulars, Mustafa Kemal provided sound strategic and tactical guidance for conducting a classic guerrilla strategy. He expected sustained military resistance would undermine French political will by demonstrating the need for France to make a major commitment of men and material in order to hold Southeastern Anatolia. One should not, however, make too direct a comparison to Kemal's Libyan experience of guerrilla warfare, where regular and tribal forces fought a large Italian occupying force secure in coastal areas, and where engagements took place outside of urban areas between regular formations. By contrast, Southeastern Anatolia experienced more a people's war, with the key battles occurring in towns with ethnic (Turk-Armenian) and religious (Muslim-Orthodox) conflicts dotting the human landscape. This time, as a political leader, Mustafa Kemal had to focus on politics and diplomacy and leave the fine details of military operations to the discretion of local commanders. It was because of an awareness of the differences between Libya and Southeastern Anatolia in the nature of the armed struggle and his role in it that Mustafa Kemal sought advice from his commanders.

Combat in Maraş dragged on for twenty-two days, until 11 February. A small French relief column from Anteb, only seventy-eight kilometers to the south, finally reached the town on 8 February. Faced with scarce supplies, the French defenders evacuated the town during the evening of 10–11 February. Some 5,000 Armenians joined the retreating French column, an ignoble retreat that saw the loss of many soldiers and civilians to blizzard conditions and attacking National Forces. France clearly suffered its first military defeat in Anatolia. With the loss came national embarrassment.

On 11 February, buoyed by the victory at Maraş, Mustafa Kemal adjusted his strategy for the fighting in the town of Anteb that had begun on 9 February. He directed XIII Corps to focus National Forces on the Adana-Pozantı railroad and then move toward Mersin and Tarsus. The XX Corps was to establish blocking positions on bridges and tunnels along the Adana-Islahiye line as well as prevent the entry of Armenians from the north into Southeastern Anatolia. National Forces would seek to prevent the French from reinforcing Anteb while III Corps cleared the Maraş area of French forces. Finally, he ordered Aleppo to send forces to Islahiye and Anteb.[111] A serious insurgency had emerged in Southeastern Anatolia. As the armed struggle unfolded, each side claimed atrocities perpetrated on civilians by the other side. On 25 January, for example, Mustafa Kemal proclaimed that "the massacre in Maraş of Muslims by the French and Armenians continues in a manner that degrades humanity into terror."[112] Such statements appealed to Kemal's Muslim constituency. The European press, for its part, claimed the massacre of thousands of Armenians in Maraş. Civilians bore the brunt of the war in Southeastern Anatolia, as they did throughout Anatolia.

National Pact

At the beginning of January 1920, Mustafa Kemal met in Ankara with a number of newly elected deputies en route to Istanbul; he wanted to ensure parliament's ratification of the decisions made by the Erzurum and Sivas Congresses. The Ottoman Chamber of Deputies (*Meclis-i Mebusan*) assembled on 12 January with seventy-two deputies in attendance without the sultan, who feigned illness. The gathering lacked a quorum until twenty-five deputies arrived from Ankara on 22 January. Approximately sixty deputies met secretly to support the decisions reached at Erzurum and Sivas. Moreover, they elected a nine-member Executive Committee that included Rauf and Bekir Sami, both members of the Representative Committee. They also selected a name for their group in the Assembly: *Felah-ı Vatan İttifakı* (the Alliance for the Liberation of the Fatherland). *Felah-ı Vatan* grew to include a majority of the deputies in parliament.[113]

After much debate and discussion, the last Ottoman Parliament secretly accepted a definitive text on 28 January and published it on 17 February. It became known as *Misak-ı Milli*, or National Pact. The members of parliament demanded complete independence and sovereignty within the boundaries at the time of the signing of the Armistice on 30 October 1918. These boundaries were depicted as comprising "an Ottoman Muslim majority united in religion, race and aspirations." The National Pact opposed any restrictions on political, judicial, and financial development. It demanded plebiscites for areas under foreign occupation: Western Thrace, the three regions of Kars, Ardahan, and Batum, and regions with Arab majorities. It expressed willingness to negotiate the terms for the navigation between the Black Sea and Mediterranean and linked the rights of local minorities to those of Muslim minorities in neighboring countries. The text mentioned the Ottoman sultanate and in one place identified the country referred to as "Turkey."[114] In one sense, this was a victory for Mustafa Kemal. On the other hand, the deputies refused to elect Mustafa Kemal as president *in absentia*, for they saw such a step would undermine their credibility. Moreover, they proved unable to unify as a single party.[115]

On 23 February, buoyed by events in Istanbul, Karabekir saw the acceptance of the National Pact as a victory that no longer necessitated the existence of the Representative Committee.[116] Mustafa Kemal rejected such a step and instead moved to take full advantage of the Ottoman Chamber of Deputies ratifying the National Pact. In a circular of only two long sentences dated 26 February 1920, he ordered the Defense of Rights Societies to enlighten the people. Recognizing "the sincerity (*safiyet*) of our villagers," the circular stressed the importance of "properly guiding" the people. It appealed to the "religious and national duty" of "every patriotic and enlightened individual" to communicate directly with the villagers using "appropriate language." He ordered central and administrative committees to send suitable individuals with Anatolian newspapers and memoranda to villages. The circular ended with Mustafa Kemal directing the messengers to read the newspapers in village homes at night.[117] By underscoring sincerity, Mustafa Kemal stressed the need to demonstrate respect for villagers. Appropriate language meant simple and direct communication easily understandable by the audience. Mustafa Kemal wanted to galvanize intellectuals and the educated to show respect and mobilize the people. Clearly, their actions would create light in the darkness, and some outreach did occur.

On 12 February, two days after the fall of Maraş, Allied leaders opened the London Conference to discuss, among other items, a post-war arrangement with the Ottoman Empire. Lloyd George used the battle of Maraş to play upon French sensitivities to argue for punitive action against the Istanbul government. Then word arrived of the acceptance of the National Pact by the Ottoman Parliament. The National Pact helped push the Allies into making a fateful decision. On 5 March, the Supreme Council of Allied Leaders decided to place Istanbul under martial law, close Parliament, and arrest its top deputies. The High Commissioners complied on 16 March. British troops played a leading role in the second occupation of Istanbul.

The Ottoman Parliament adjourned on 18 March, never to open again in the old capital. Allied authorities tried to arrest as many key deputies as possible. Rauf, who had signed the Armistice, was apprehended and sent to the island of Malta for internment. He and other interned deputies became heroes who had sacrificed their freedom for the national cause. Mustafa Kemal had been correct in fearing this development. Nevertheless, their sacrifice exposed Western hypocrisy concerning Turkish self-determination and instead revealed imperialist designs on Ottoman territory. Occupying Istanbul and closing the Ottoman Parliament proved a major strategic blunder that Mustafa Kemal, whose position had been temporarily weakened by the shift of the national discourse to Istanbul, fully exploited.

Conclusion

Mustafa Kemal had come a long way in his first ten months in Anatolia. His command of the Ninth Army, although brief, provided him with the authority and the platform to articulate his national goals. Rauf, Karabekir, Ali Fuad, and Refet all helped Mustafa Kemal begin his rise to center stage in Anatolia. The Erzurum and Sivas Congresses offered a modicum of legitimacy for the national movement outside the reach of the Istanbul government, allowing Mustafa Kemal to act as a free agent in the interest of the people. Mustafa Kemal adopted a strategy of recognizing and working with the ethnic and religious diversity of the Anatolian people: Sunnis, Alevis, Sufis, Turks, Kurds, Circassians, and other Muslim ethnic groups. His initial success with the Erzurum and Sivas Congresses helped nudge the sultan into calling for elections and the convening of a new parliament. An overwhelming Kemalist victory in parliamentary elections meant endorsement of what became known as the National Pact. Rather than enter into serious negotiations with a representative institution, the Allies eventually chose to close Parliament and arrest many of its deputies.

Closing Parliament strengthened Kemal's position in Ankara as the voice of national aspirations for self-determination and independence. Any serious dialogue strategically shifted from the Ottoman imperial capital to the small Anatolian town of Ankara. The Allies had made a stupendous error, providing Mustafa Kemal with an opportunity to develop strategic momentum and strengthen his base, and he possessed the time to do it. The soldier-diplomat in Libya who had negotiated with tribal chiefs over military operations was gradually assuming the role of soldier-statesman at the head of a viable national movement with an army and political organization. The new Parliament in Ankara became an important part of his war strategy.

4

The Grand National Assembly

As a total phenomenon its dominant tendencies always make war a paradoxical trinity—composed of primordial violence, hatred, and enmity, which are regarded as a blind force; of the play of chance and probability within which the creative spirit is free to roam; and of its element of subordination, as an instrument of policy, which make it subject to reason alone. The first of these three aspects mainly concerns the people; the second the commander and his army; the third the government. The passions that are to be kindled in war must already be inherent in the people; the scope which the play of courage and talent will enjoy in the realm of probability and chance depends on the particular character of the commander and the army; but the political aims are the business of government alone.

Carl von Clausewitz[1]

For me, the Assembly is not a principle; it is a reality and the greatest of realities. First the Assembly, then the army, Nadi Bey.

Mustafa Kemal, April 1920

MUSTAFA KEMAL appreciated the strategic opportunities provided by Parliament's closure. By their action, the Great Powers had given him ammunition for more than a propaganda coup. Istanbul had lost its place for negotiating an honorable peace settlement with the occupying powers. Consequently, a number of important patriots in Istanbul began abandoning the capital for Ankara. The center of gravity for the national resistance now clearly shifted to Kemal's abode. For his part, Mustafa Kemal transformed Ankara into the center of a provisional government with its own parliament and set of laws, an independent state in the making. The Representative Committee, for its part, passed from the pages of history.

Revolutionary Government

Mustafa Kemal moved quickly on the propaganda front. On 17 March 1920, in response to the closing of the Ottoman Parliament by the Great Powers, the Representative Committee called for the dissemination of its national aims to the most distance places.[2] The next day, Mustafa Kemal issued a manifesto to the entire Muslim world in which he subtly stressed that the recent action by the Entente Powers harmed the sacred Islamic caliphate more than the Ottoman sultanate. He called upon Azerbaijan, North Caucasus, Turkistan, Afghanistan, India, all of Africa, and East Asia to express their solidarity with the national cause. The manifesto depicted the resistance as comprising "Ottoman national forces" and labeled the Allied Powers "crusaders" (ehl-i salib), again developing the religious theme. Toward the end, Mustafa Kemal appealed to "the passion and duty of the conscience (vicdan) of all our Muslim brothers." Finally, military commanders in eastern Anatolia were instructed to disseminate the manifesto across the border to tribal chiefs and Muslims in Iraq, Syria, Azerbaijan, and the Caucasus, relying on horses to help spread the word.[3]

Mustafa Kemal wisely decided, for both international and domestic reasons, to convene a new parliament in Ankara. Internationally, the representative institution would continue to claim to articulate the national aspirations expressed through its elected deputies. Domestically, Mustafa Kemal would enhance his power to mobilize the people under his own leadership. So on 19 March 1920, he issued in the name of the Representative Committee a general address to the provinces, independent sub-provinces (sancak), and corps commanders. He couched the appeal in terms of saving the caliphate, sultanate, and the Ottoman state, informing the public that an assembly with extraordinary powers would convene in Ankara. Every sub-province was to elect five deputies, with every individual having the right to run as an independent candidate.[4] In reality, however, Mustafa Kemal tried to influence as much as possible the selection of candidates favorable to himself. A military action complemented Kemal's political moves. On 20 March, Ali Fuad reported that the National Forces had forced the British to bow to the "will of the Ottoman nation" and withdraw their battalion from Eskişehir.[5] The Nationalists were demonstrating their resolve both politically and militarily.

Mustafa Kemal told journalist Yunus Nadi sometime shortly after the latter's arrival in Ankara on 10 April: "For me, the Assembly is not a principle; it is a reality and the greatest of realities. First the Assembly, then the army, Nadi Bey."[6] At this juncture in the struggle, building a national government outweighed military considerations in importance and immediacy, so elections were quickly held for a new parliament scheduled to reconvene in Ankara. Five deputies represented each sancak. Ottoman electoral law provided for a two-tier election with an important modification. In the first round, 50,000 eligible voters would elect one representative, and every 500 taxpayers would select one delegate to the *sancak*. Then in the second round, these delegates would be joined by members of city assemblies, provincial assemblies, and members of the Defense of Rights Societies to elect deputies to the one-chamber legislative body. By specifically including the Defense of Rights Societies, Mustafa Kemal, still a deputy from Ankara, and Karabekir agreed to restrict voting to only Muslims.[7]

April saw a flurry of activity as Mustafa Kemal moved to strengthen his position, while the sultan's government responded in kind. Mustafa Kemal moved to ensure the loyalty of senior commanders. Colonel Fahreddin (Altay), the commander of XII Corps in Konya, was one such individual. Back in November 1919, he had offered an excuse for not attending the corps commanders' conference called by Mustafa Kemal and sent his chief of staff instead. He still regarded the war minister in Istanbul as his commander, as he stated in his memoirs.[8] And for his part, Fevzi (Çakmak), the war minister, had encouraged commanders in Anatolia to remain loyal to the sultanate. So on 3 April 1920, Refet (Bele) appeared in Konya and brought Fahreddin back to Ankara under guard. In Ankara, Fahreddin submitted his resignation to Mustafa Kemal, who accepted it. Upon returning to Konya with his designated replacement, he informed his officers of the resignation and then called upon them to swear allegiance to the Ankara government. They complied promptly. The next day, Mustafa Kemal reinstated Fahreddin as corps commander. "This time," Fahreddin wrote in his memoirs, "I belonged under the command of Mustafa Kemal."[9] He would play an important role in the war as commander of the only cavalry corps.

The sultan's government, meanwhile, tried to stem the shifting of power to Kemal's side. On 11 April, the *şeyhülislam*, the head of the Islamic religious institution, issued a *fatwa*, a religious legal ruling, against the Nationalists, identifying them as infidels. On 16 April, the *mufti* of Ankara, along with some 250 other religious officials, issued a counter-*fetva* that invalidated the *şeyhülislam*'s because it was issued under the pressure of enemy states. The Anatolian clerics depicted the sultanate and caliphate as prisoners of the Allies and the country as needing all Muslims to resist the foreign occupation. On this specific occasion, Mustafa Kemal balanced religion against religion.

Meanwhile, on 14 April, Mustafa Kemal issued a general appeal in the name of the Representative Committee for officers in Istanbul to join "the national struggle" (*mücahide-i milliye*) in Anatolia.[10] Among those officers joining the exodus to Anatolia after the closure of the Ottoman Parliament were İsmet (İnönü) and Fevzi (Çakmak), both of whom would play important roles in the war. Only a few diplomats, however, followed the example of the military officers.[11] On 17 April, Mustafa Kemal commanded government and military chiefs "in all the Ottoman provinces" to carry out their patriotic duties in defending the Representative Committee.[12] The next day, the sultan established the Disciplinary Force (*Kuva-yı İnzibatiye*), also known as the Army of the Caliphate (*Hilafet Ordusu*), to fight the Nationalists. This army began forming in Adapazarı and reached a force strength of 4,000 men organized as a division with three regiments. Nationalist forces attacked this insignificant assemblage before it could develop into an effective fighting unit, and on 25 June, the Istanbul government disbanded it.

Attention now shifted to Ankara and the convening of a new Parliament, the Grand National Assembly, or *Büyük Millet Meclisi* (BMM), on 23 April. The day began with the parliamentarians attending Friday prayers. Mustafa Kemal participated as well, and his praying made for an excellent photograph for propaganda purposes. A full recitation of the Quran also took place among other religious ceremonies that together outdid "any comparable ceremony in Ottoman history."[13] Mustafa Kemal clearly wanted to appeal to Muslim sentiments. Only 127 deputies were present for the first historic session, with 23 of these coming from the former Ottoman Chamber of Deputies. One of those among the latter category was Celaleddin Arif, the head of the old Ottoman Parliament. The final count of deputies stood around 380, favoring the middle and professional classes. Some 25 per cent of the deputies had higher educations, while 19 per

6 *Prayer before opening session of Grand National Assembly. Mustafa Kemal shown at center, front row.*

cent had graduated from a *medrese*, or religious seminary. There were at least 115 government officials or retirees, 61 teachers, 51 soldiers, 49 lawyers, 37 merchants, 26 large-scale farmers, 26 farmers, 21 doctors, 8 religious leaders, 5 large landowners, 5 tribal chiefs, and 2 engineers. Although women, Christians, factory workers, and smaller farmers lacked representation, the Assembly still represented a good cross section of society.

Mustafa Kemal delivered his initial speech on 24 April, the second day of the proceedings. He provided a general outline of the national resistance, dividing the struggle into three periods: 1) from the armistice to the Erzurum Congress, 2) from the Erzurum Congress to the closure of Parliament on 16 March, and 3) from March 16 to the present. Interestingly, this division highlighted the regional Erzurum Congress as a turning point over the national one held in Sivas. Mustafa Kemal spoke in his speech of "a national unity born of the people's conscience (*vicdan*)," whereby Societies for the Defense of National Rights had sprung up in both the eastern and western parts of the country. Sivas was described as a general congress that created a national organization. In addition, he talked of "the voice of the nation" and a national power creating a movement "born in the heart and mind (*kalb ve dimağ*) of the nation." His speech emphasized Ottoman and Islamic terms such as: "the gravest sin against Islam," "Ottoman lands" (*memalik-i osmaniye*), "Ottoman society," "the Ottoman nation," and "national independence." Mustafa Kemal defined the reach of the national struggle in the broadest terms. Thus, he included Izmir, Antakya, Mosul province, and the districts of Kirkuk and Süleymaniye in Iraq. Muslims predominated within these borders, and included "Turks, Circassians and other Muslim elements." Mustafa Kemal clearly disavowed, moreover, any ties to the CUP. He also stressed the need, above all else, to declare one more time, to the entire world, the great power and tenacity of the people in defending their rights and their existence according to international law. Mustafa Kemal spoke with confidence and clarity in a public forum for international and domestic consumption.[14] Ankara had become the *de facto* seat of the government in Turkey and the new Parliament its source of legitimacy. Mustafa Kemal had captured the national narrative.

In a secret parliamentary session held on the same day, Mustafa Kemal amplified on his strategic thought. Rejecting the irredentist notion of Turanism (pan-Turkism), he instead argued for the struggle to be conducted within the country's moral and material capabilities. Assistance from the Islamic world was desired, and relations had been established with Muslim nations in the Caucasus, the peoples of Syria and Iraq, and Emir Feisal of Arabia but now in Syria. This measured and calculated language suggested no notion of pan-Islamic aspirations, despite all the Islamic festivities centered on the opening of the Assembly that had been conducted the day before. In defining the nature of the national struggle,

Mustafa Kemal spoke in terms of "Ottoman community" (*camia-i osmaniye*) tied to the caliph and *padişah* (monarch). He underscored that despite contacts with the Bolsheviks, the nation had its own customs, religious requirements, and national concerns and thus would follow an independent course. He framed the national aim in lofty terms as the nation struggling to live with "honor" (*namus ve şeref*) as other nations and human beings.[15] In this speech, Mustafa Kemal gave the impression of being a reasonable, pragmatic, and crafty leader.

The next day, on 25 April, the deputies elected Mustafa Kemal as president (*reis*) of the BMM. In a speech to the Assembly on 26 April, Mustafa Kemal declared once again that "Sovereignty belongs unconditionally to the nation. The Grand National Assembly is the true and sole representative of the nation. Legislative authority and executive power are manifested and concentrated in the Grand National Assembly." He also assured those present that their main aim was "To liberate the caliphate and the sultanate, the fatherland and the nation, within the framework of the principles of national sovereignty."[16]

Now in Ankara, the national resistance began to take on the form of a formal state. The Law of 2 May 1920 established the Council of Ministers headed by the president of the BMM. The old Representative Committee now passed out of existence. In constituting the Cabinet, the BMM elected each minister separately and then delegated its executive power to ministers. On paper, the BMM possessed much more power and authority than the Ottoman Chamber of Deputies, but in reality, Mustafa Kemal held considerable sway over the Assembly. Yet throughout the national struggle, the BMM showed a modicum of independence and vitality. Radical, liberal, conservative, traditional, secular, and religious ideas found their representatives in the organization, and eventually parties or groups emerged in the chamber. Mustafa Kemal, for his part, regularly attended the sessions and participated in the debates, and even gave account of his actions and policies. "And the BMM was not so easy to manage as he [Mustafa Kemal] had expected it to be. It had all the pride and the exaggerated sense of responsibility of a newly constituted body ... [and] the majority of the delegates stood apart from him and took up a critical attitude."[17] But most knew when to bend to Kemal's will.

The unicameral parliament had taken on the official name of the Grand National Assembly, or *Büyük Millet Meclisi* (BMM), which in February 1921 was officially changed to the Grand National Assembly of Turkey, or *Türkiye Büyük Millet Meclisi* (TBMM). The BMM had replaced the bi-cameral Ottoman Assembly of Deputies (*Osmanlı Meclis-i Mebusan*) and the Ottoman Assembly of Notables (*Osmanlı Meclis-i Ayan*). Use of the term "Grand" was to underscore a single, all-powerful chamber vested with both executive and legislative powers based on a theory of the unity of powers. (On several occasions,

Mustafa Kemal outright rejected the concept of the separation of powers as articulated by Montesquieu.) The BMM elected a president (*reis*) of the chamber as well as a cabinet of eleven ministers. A national army replaced the former Ottoman Imperial Army (*Osmanlı Ordu-yı Humayunu*), and the provisional government now possessed the Ministry of National Defense (*Müdafaa-yı Milliye Vekaleti*) rather than a War Ministry (*Harbiye Nezareti*), stressing the war's ostensible defensive nature. Britain, France, Germany, and the United States still had war ministries but only later changed that title from "war" to "defense."

Throughout the war, Mustafa Kemal devoted much time and energy to parliamentary sessions, keeping the deputies informed of developments in the field. On 21 August 1920, for example, he provided details of minor tactical events in the Demirci and Anteb areas on the western and southeastern fronts respectively.[18] Such information provided insight into the attention to detail that Mustafa Kemal gave to battlefield developments. Military field commanders also kept Parliament appraised of developments in their area of responsibility. In some speeches, Mustafa Kemal specifically referenced official communications and proclamations for his arguments. Indeed, he did so in his first speech to the assembled body. These documents became part of the historical record of the BMM. His famous six-day *Nutuk*, or *The Speech*, of 1927 contained a volume's worth of documents. This practice of including documentation to support assertions gave the appearance of scientific objectivity and influenced his contemporaries to do the same in their memoirs. Karabekir posed the best example of this practice. His two-volume account of the war essentially followed a chronology based on published documents with commentary.

This dynamic of parliamentary debate often followed by voting was important for propaganda purposes. It projected the image of a representative institution struggling to serve the interests of the people. But in the end, Mustafa Kemal certainly wielded a good deal of power through the Council of Ministers. "Most important policy decisions were made by the Council [of Ministers] and were usually debated by the BMM *in camera*, but instances were not lacking, when the Council exceeded its authority, or by-passed the BMM, which raised pandemonium at its following meeting without hesitating to criticize, or severely admonish, the Council."[19] Parliament thus gave Mustafa Kemal a new power of legitimacy, which he underscored on 27 April in his order to the Kayseri *mutasarrıf*, the head of the sancak: "the National Assembly has opened and now it has become our duty to obey and support in every way the national aspirations as seen in legally constituted action."[20]

The National Army

The headquarters of the National Army functioned in modest circumstances. A handful of staff officers worked in small rooms carrying out operations, intelligence, logistics, personnel, and other tasks. It took new arrivals from Istanbul to augment the staff enough to "create the necessary sections . . . one by one" until a normal functioning general headquarters came into being.[21] In April, İsmet and Fevzi, both professional officers with solid reputations and senior command experience, arrived in Ankara. At the beginning of the year, İsmet had stayed a month and a half and had assisted Mustafa Kemal in preparing plans and with administration, but then returned to Istanbul. Fevzi, for his part in the Nationalist struggle, was conservative and tied to the sultanate and caliphate. Both men, for their own set of reasons, resisted moving to Ankara until after the closure of Parliament. Their reluctance underscored the tenuous relationship Mustafa Kemal had with some senior commanders, Fahreddin of XII Corps being one of them. Mustafa Kemal had no binding legal authority over them, and even Karabekir and Ali Fuad communicated independently with the war ministry in Istanbul. But the BMM helped change all of this when the National Army came under Kemal's authority.

The defense minister and the chief of the General Staff were deputies in the Assembly and also members of the Cabinet, thus blurring the distinction between politics and the military. On 16 May 1920, the BMM formally defined the duties and responsibilities of the Ministry of National Defense and the General Staff. The General Staff's responsibilities included command and control, mobilization, organization, and the selection of personnel. First Branch handled military operations and Second Branch directed intelligence, following the German model. The defense minister was essentially responsible for logistics.[22] The Chief of the General Staff was the highest military authority. Colonel İsmet assumed that position. General Fevzi became the first defense minister. As the new Chief of the General Staff, İsmet immediately placed a priority on building the regular army and establishing increased control over the National Forces. The first task was to weaken their independence by having the Treasury pay them regularly and by bringing them under an orderly administration.[23]

On 29 May, in a secret session of the Assembly, the new defense minister Fevzi painted a difficult situation confronting Ankara. He noted that there were no factories to produce weapons. Just as during the war in Libya, the resistance depended on smuggling weapons, ammunition, and medicine. It was still too early for a single army, so Fevzi recommended the formation of a mobile gendarmerie, or *seyyar jandarma*, for internal security and as an auxiliary force for the regular units. The resistance needed a regular army with better command and control in order to wage "a conventional war" (*düzenli bir muharebe*). Fevzi reminded the deputies that World War I had not yet ended.[24] It was clear from Fevzi's report that the National Forces were too independent and had to be eventually brought under control by the regular army for major campaigns.

The Ankara government needed a large army with competent officers, for the Greeks had some 100,000 soldiers in western Anatolia. Recruitment for two new divisions of 10,000 men each, one based in Ankara and one in Sivas, began in earnest. A call went out to retired officers with distinguished service. On 1 July 1920, to meet the need for more officers to command an expanding army, the army established an officer training school in Ankara. The first graduates received only four months' training and then were sent out to various fronts in October 1920.[25] This training period, however intense and focused, was insufficient for preparing individuals to lead others in combat. Mustafa Kemal was acutely aware of this harsh reality. The new National Army could draw upon many experienced Ottoman commanders from World War I, but the numbers were not enough for the expanding military. Well-trained officers at the small-unit level were in short supply.

On 6 June, in answer to the need for recruits, the Council of Ministers reinstated the conscription that had ended on 21 July 1918. The national struggle would eventually need a large regular army to defeat the Greeks. Expanding the army through recruitment required time. Desertion remained a perennial problem. To address this problem, the BMM enacted a law in September defining the behavior and relationship between officers and their soldiers. Officers were expected to eat food from the same "kettle" as their men and to treat their soldiers as a "father and brother" (*peder ve kardeş*) would. Officers who failed to follow this principle could be removed from the military and possibly face trial.[26] This language recalled *Conversation with Officer and Commander*, when Mustafa Kemal wrote of officers acting like a father, or *baba*, for their troops, thus reflecting Ottoman military culture.

Developing professionalism in the army also required time. An artillery school was founded in Konya only on 21 October 1921. Much additional training had to take place at the level of corps, divisions, and regiments. Egos were often hurt when officers learned of command assignments. A number of senior officers, for example, disliked Kemal's selection of İsmet to command the National Army as chief of the General Staff. He was only a colonel when he joined the resistance in Anatolia, and he was junior to a number of them. In addition, doctrine had to be restated for field commands. In a directive on 15 October, İsmet defined the command relationship within division headquarters. The division chief of staff was to be a General Staff officer commanding divisional headquarters and addressing operational matters. Other branches within the division, such as intelligence, would fall under the authority of a second General Staff officer.[27] One military decision had important military ramifications for future battles. On 1 September 1920, Fevzi ordered the creation of two cavalry divisions of 3,000 horses each, one stationed in Sivas and the other in Kayseri.[28] This decision to expand the cavalry branch proved operationally wise, for it gave the army a marked advantage over the Greeks in mobility that helped bring victory in the Battle of Sakarya (1921) and the Great Offensive and Pursuit (1922).

The People

War requires the mobilization of the people, and in the early sessions of the Assembly, Mustafa Kemal addressed the issue of ethnicity. The national borders comprised Edirne in the west, Iskenderun in the south, and as far as Mosul, Süleymaniye, and Kerkük in the east. Within these "national borders" lived "Islamic elements," intimately linked together as "brothers" (*kardeş*) who respected each other's "racial (*ırkı*), social, and geographic rights."[29] Kemal's words stressed Islamic unity and respect for the ethnic diversity of the various Muslim peoples.

During the years 1920 to 1922, Mustafa Kemal continued to pay special attention to the home front and the imperative for popular support. The propaganda war also received serious attention. As people flocked to Ankara to join the resistance, he continued to urge individuals to reach out, to contact the people, even in the villages, and convince them to join the cause. The popular poet Mehmed Emin (Yurdakul), for example, toured Anatolia with his patriotic messages.[30] Other intellectuals joined him in the effort. Halide Edip boldly addressed peasant crowds through parts of Anatolia.[31] But Mustafa Kemal saw value in sending the educated, deputies, and others to villages, where they were advised to use "appropriate" language that connected with the people.

Mustafa Kemal had strengthened his control over the war narrative on 23 March when he imposed a ban on a number of foreign, Ottoman, Greek, and Armenian newspapers because of their opposition to the national cause.[32] On 6 April, even before the convening of the BMM, Mustafa Kemal established the Anatolian Agency, designed to be an information service for both domestic and international audiences. The journalist Yunus Nadi, Halide Edip, and her husband Dr. Adnan initially ran the bureau. In a general circular, Mustafa Kemal outlined his thinking on the press. He wanted the dissemination of official news to go out daily to big cities, provincial towns, and villages, hopefully reaching everyone, clearly an impossible goal but certainly a vision for action. The information war would counter foreign propaganda as well as support local publications. The postal service and telegraph centers would also assist in this effort.[33]

To help ensure internal security, the BMM enacted two important pieces of legislation. Passed on 29 April 1920, the Law against Treason, or *Hiyaneti Vataniye Kanunu*, empowered the new government to treat opposition to the BMM as treasonous. On 11 September, at the request of Defense Minister Fevzi, the BMM also passed the Law of Independence Courts. Each court was to be composed of three members elected from the BMM. Although possessing extraordinary powers, these courts conducted public trials in accordance with the law. They were instituted mainly to punish rebels and deserters in the army.[34] Of 59,164 accused, by one count, 1,054 were executed.[35] Rebellions, compounded by general brigandage, undermined the efforts of Ankara's government to mobilize the population by taxation and conscription.[36]

Internal revolts plagued Turkey virtually the entire period of the War of Independence. The region of Düzce and Bolu, for example, saw revolts between 16 April and 31 May and then again between 19 July and 23 September. Intelligence estimates placed the number of involved rebels at 4,000 to 5,000 Abaza Circassians who had attacked the town of Düzce during that period. On 19 April, Mustafa Kemal responded by ordering regular troops to crush the rebellion. On 20 April, the 24th Division commander, Lieutenant Colonel Mahmud Bey, left with two battalions, an artillery battery, and a cavalry detachment en route to confront the rebels. Mahmud issued a proclamation to the population appealing to their traditional values. He depicted the padişah *and* caliph as a prisoner of the English and the Istanbul government as a British tool, and he called upon the people to help the National Forces save the ruler and the nation.[37] While nearing the town of Düzce, Mahmud fell into an ambush and was killed, and most of his force surrendered to the rebels. The defeat proved a major embarrassment, and İsmet dispatched additional troops in an attempt to crush the rebellion decisively. On 20 May, İsmet had expressed the need for "severity" (*şiddet*) in suppressing the rebels.[38] In addition to regular troops, Çerkez Edhem, a former guerrilla fighter, brought part of his National Forces, now organized as the First Mobile Force. He entered Düzce on 26 May and promptly executed three ringleaders of the revolt.[39] By the end of May, Ankara had regained control of the area. Meanwhile, a revolt erupted in the Yozgat.

The Yozgat rebellion proved a more serious threat. Like Düzce, Yozgat saw two revolts, the first lasting from 15 May to 27 August.[40] The town was only 100 kilometers east of Ankara. In response to the first revolt, Mustafa Kemal tried but failed to gain the support of Alevi and Bektaşi leadership.[41] The Çapanoğulları, the leading family in the region, led the revolt. The rebels captured Yozgat on 14 June and threatened Sivas. After failing for two months to suppress the unrest, Mustafa Kemal again turned to Çerkez Edhem for assistance. His First Mobile Force had a regular army structure organized along battalion and company lines. In mid-July, Mustafa Kemal invited the Circassian to come to Ankara.

In his memoirs, Çerkez Edhem provides an interesting insight into Kemal's leadership style. In Ankara, Mustafa Kemal held a meeting with Çerkez Edhem and other senior military figures. The discussion lasted several hours and raised the possibility of Greece taking advantage of the internal turmoil facing Ankara with a Greek offensive. Mustafa Kemal said very little, preferring to listen to the various views. Then he concluded that the rebellion in Yozgat had to be suppressed within five to ten days and charged Fevzi to give attention to the Western Front.[42] The dynamics of this meeting reflected good leadership: Kemal permitted open discussion and the free exchange of ideas and analysis before reaching his decision.

From 16 to 19 June, Çerkez Edhem brought his force by train from Eskişehir to Ankara and moved out to suppress the Yozgat rebellion. From Ankara, on 20 June, Çerkez Edhem set out with a force of 70 officers, 2,100 infantry, 1,300 cavalry, one field and four mountain artillery pieces, and eight machine guns.[43] His forces captured Yozgat on 23 June. In his memoirs, İsmet complained of the bloody suppression inflicted upon the rebels by Çerkez Edhem's men. To İsmet's embarrassment, the war spoils were brought to Ankara and sold in the city's marketplace.[44] In the long run, Mustafa Kemal could not tolerate independent-minded militia commanders like Çerkez Edhem. Militia forces were useful but flawed. In some areas, they cooperated reasonably well with local army command-ers. But elsewhere, some National Forces acted more like brigands, practicing pillaging as part of their *modus operandi*. Regular army officers often expressed concern about integrating them into regular units, as their bad habits negatively affected unit morale.[45] But other army commanders like Ali Fuad preferred to avoid using the regular army units to crush civilian unrest and instead wanted the gendarmerie or the militia to handle the problem.[46] These officers wanted to hasten the build-up of a large regular army. The exigencies of the battlefield eventually resulted in a determined move to integrate National Forces into the regular army, especially on the Western Front facing the large Greek army.

Foreign Affairs

The Foreign Office began in a small room in the agricultural school where Mustafa Kemal made his headquarters. Soon the ministry moved to a building occupied by the Ottoman Public Debt administration. Most of the diplomatic agents dispatched from Ankara in the next few years were "cultured men with education along Western lines, though not trained diplomats from Ottoman days."[47] Alfred Rüstem, among these men, was unusual in being a career diplomat, but he stayed with Mustafa Kemal for less than a year. Bekir Sami (Kundak), the first Foreign Minister, had a background in civil service, including important provincial governorships.

The establishment of the BMM strengthened Kemal's hand in developing a working relationship with the Bolsheviks to counter imperialism and in furthering cooperation in the South Caucasus. Mustafa Kemal wasted no time in seeking Bolshevik support. On 24 April, he informed the BMM of dealings with Russia. "We know the Europeans are afraid of Bolshevism, while we share unity of thought and action with them. We want nothing but to protect our existence within our borders; so we have to seek help from the outside for this purpose and use every resource."[48] On 26 April, Mustafa Kemal, as the recently elected president of the BMM, wrote the Soviets suggesting a working alliance with them for the South Caucasus. Turkey had supported the Russians in their struggle against Western imperialist governments. In return, "the government of Turkey" (*Türkiye hükumeti*) was willing to assist, militarily or by other means, Bolshevik forces in incorporating Georgia into the Bolshevik union; in conducting mutual military operations against "imperialist Armenia"; and in accepting the Azerbaijan government as part of the Soviet states. Kemal's letter requested, in return, Soviet assistance in gold, weapons, medical supplies, and other war *matériel*.[49]

Mustafa Kemal considered Soviet Russia as merely reclaiming the South Caucasus as its rightful inheritance from the tsarist era. Two days after the letter, the Azerbaijan Democratic Republic surrendered to local Bolsheviks. So Kemal's correspondence merely confirmed the fait accompli on the ground with respect to the fate of Muslim Azerbaijan. Soviet Foreign Affairs Commissar Georgi Chicherin waited thirty-seven days before responding to Kemal's letter. He then expressed satisfaction with the National Pact, or *Misak-i Milli*, proposed an exchange of diplomatic representatives, and offered mediation between Turkey, Armenia, and Persia.[50] Moscow proceeded cautiously in developing relations with the new government in Ankara, however, still uncertain as to how seriously to take Mustafa Kemal and national resistance.

On 2 May, the BMM elected Bekir Sami as its first foreign minister. With him came the first serious, direct diplomatic contact between Ankara and Moscow.[51] On 11 May 1920, Bekir Sami departed for the Russian capital, arriving there on 19 July. Talks with the Russians began on 24 July, and on 28 July the Politburo agreed to send supplies and gold to Kemal's government, a major breakthrough. On 14 August, İsmet explained to his front commanders that the current talks with Russia did not constitute an alliance but a friendship pact. The Russians did not want an alliance, whereas Ankara was seeking Soviet diplomatic recognition as well as financial and material aid.[52] A draft treaty was initialed ten days later. In it, the Soviets recognized the BMM as the sole government of Turkey and expected future relations between the two countries to be as between equals. Nothing came of this agreement, as Chicherin continued to raise the issue of a small state of Armenia that would incorporate parts of the provinces of Van and Bitlis. Although Mustafa Kemal would not countenance this loss of Muslim territory, Bekir Sami had gained the assurance that the Soviet Union would provide financial and military assistance despite the disagreement over Armenia.[53]

Soviet shipments began arriving in Trabzon and Erzurum in September 1920. Ankara also received reports of Soviet agents infiltrating Anatolia. Mustafa Kemal decided on a response designed to stifle Moscow's attempt to meddle in Turkey's internal affairs. On 18 October, he authorized the establishment of the Turkish Communist Party, forcing Communist and leftist-leaning deputies to join the organization. But Mustafa Kemal stacked the party with loyal friends. Moscow was neither fooled nor amused by this ploy, and the "real" Communist Party continued to carry out its activities clandestinely.

While seeking to develop relations with Moscow, Mustafa Kemal continued to reach out to the Arab world as well. He sent two agents to Iraq to work with Iraqi nationalists opposed to British rule there. Both men travelled to Karbala and Najaf seeking support from the Shi'a clergy and others. They also established contact with Arab tribes in the area and then moved on to Baghdad. There in a meeting on 22 May, they stressed that the national movement had renounced any claims on Arab provinces and instead supported full independence for the Arabs.[54] In July, a delegate from Emir Feisal in Damascus visited Ankara to discuss the possibility of developing a united Islamic front.[55] The strategic thinking was simple and regional: the more widespread was the resistance to Western imperialism in the Middle East, the better were the chances for Turkey's success.

War against the Greeks

Between 18 and 26 April, the prime ministers of Britain, France, and Italy, joined by representatives from Belgium, Greece, and Japan, held a conference in San Remo, Italy, to discuss peace treaty arrangements. They decided to award all of Thrace and the region around Izmir to Greece. Italy was to receive Antalya and the south-central region of Anatolia. On 11 May, the Istanbul government was presented with the decisions of San Remo. This development only strengthened the Nationalists' resolve, and on the night of 14–15 June, they directly challenged Britain by attacking a British Indian force in İzmit (Nicomedia), located on the

Sea of Marmara and some 100 kilometers from Istanbul. Lacking a sufficient number of troops, Prime Ministers David Lloyd George of Britain and Alexandre Millerand of France decided to give the green light to the Greeks for a limited attack against Turkey to better secure the Straits region. Venizelos, the Greek premier, however, opted for a larger offensive.[56]

On 22 June, therefore, the Greeks attacked Kemalist forces with two corps, comprised of six divisions, and headed northeast and east from the Izmir region along three axes. The Greek army in the Izmir region numbered 90,000 to 100,000 men. On 24 June 1920, or two days into the Greek offensive, the BMM Council of Ministers appointed Ali Fuad as General Commander of the Western Front. His command consisted of XIV Corps and XII Corps, headquartered in Bandırma (north) and Konya (south) respectively, with three divisions deployed forward across the entire front, each containing between 2,000 and 3,000 men. National Forces numbered around 10,000 or so. The XX Corps also fell under Ali Fuad's command.[57] Then the next day, 25 June, the BMM issued its first conscription call for those born between 1894 and 1899; too late, however, to help the army fighting the Greeks.

The January war plans discussed earlier had called for Mustafa Kemal to assume command of the Western Front while Karabekir commanded the Eastern Front. Now, in June, when threatened by a Greek offensive, Mustafa Kemal chose to delegate the west to Ali Fuad instead. Three factors explain the change in plans. Mustafa Kemal, no doubt, did not see the Greek offensive as serious enough to warrant his focused presence at the front. He also wanted to be in Ankara building the new government there. Politics weighed heavier in importance than military operations at this stage in the national struggle. It was also prudent for Mustafa Kemal not to risk his military reputation too early in the war.

An impossible situation confronted Ali Fuad. Outnumbered and less organized, the National Army and National Forces offered limited resistance, slowing down the Greeks but not stopping them. Mustafa Kemal offered general guidance throughout the campaign and visited the front at least once. He also deployed troops from other sectors to assist Ali Fuad, including the 11th Division and Çerkez Edhem's First Mobile Force. Ali Fuad had expected the Greek main effort in the south at Uşak, but the Greek army gained its successes in the north, capturing Balıkesir on 30 June and Bursa on 8 July.[58] General Leonidas Paraskevopoulos, commanding general of the Greek army in Asia Minor, encouraged Venizelos to continue operations and to destroy the Turks, but the Allies opposed such a move. The Greek High Command, therefore, responded by transferring a division and an infantry brigade from Anatolia to Thrace, where they helped capture Edirne on 25–26 July. All of Thrace, with the exception of Istanbul and its immediate environs, by now had fallen into Greek hands.[59] The area in western Anatolia under Greek control had doubled. Further exacerbating the Nationalist position, on 13 July a British force occupied the town of İznik (Nicaea).

Mustafa Kemal, on his part, had commanded from a distance during the Greek offensive, visiting Eskişehir on 20 June in order to coordinate operations against a rebellion in Yozgat. He returned to Ankara during the night of 22–23 June. Meanwhile, the Greek offensive had commenced on 22 June. Back in Ankara, Mustafa Kemal balanced his attention with the other fronts. On 9 July, the day after the fall of Bursa, he and İsmet travelled to Eskişehir to confer with Ali Fuad, the front commander. The next day both men returned to Ankara to discover an agitated BBM as the military setbacks in June and July had created a crisis on the home front.[60] The fall of the historic city of Bursa, the first capital of the emerging Ottoman state in the fourteenth century, was especially troublesome. Now, many deputies demanded that heads roll with court-martials as a response to failures. Some deputies charged that Mustafa Kemal had devoted too much attention to fighting internal unrest at the expense of preparations to meet the Greek threat. But Mustafa Kemal dodged the bullets of criticism effectively. Instead, a local commander became the scapegoat for Bursa's fall, and on 13 July was relieved of his command. In the spring and summer of 1920, Kemal had clearly devoted more effort to building political structures than to rebuilding the army. "First the Assembly, then the Army, Nadi Bey," Mustafa Kemal had remarked earlier. But the military events of June and July now argued for more attention to the army, for Greece would likely launch another major offensive in the not too distant future.

Mustafa Kemal confronted the crisis head-on in a secret session of the BMM held on 20 July 1920, where he admitted to pursuing a strategy that placed the crushing of the internal rebellions ahead of preparing for a Greek offensive. In his calculations, the significance of the internal front had outweighed the external one. Though he did not say so, trading space for time had made sense to him given the new political developments in Ankara, where his priority lay with establishing a strong central government with its own constitution. Furthermore, he asked the deputies how it was possible to call the entire nation to arms without adequate money and material.[61] Despite his sound political reasoning, Mustafa Kemal had not expected such a poor performance by the army. So on 27–28 July, he ordered all the branches of the Societies for the Defense of Rights of Rumeli and Anatolia under the authority of the most senior government officials in their areas and placed all militia forces under the authority of the most senior commanders in their areas.[62] This order was aimed at tightening Ankara's control over local political organizations and irregular forces.

Then on the same day, Mustafa Kemal and Fevzi together departed Ankara for a major inspection tour and to ensure implementation of the above order.[63] By now the Western Front had largely stabilized as the Greeks settled into a new defensive line. The first visit was Eskişehir and a meeting with Ali Fuad. The journey included stops in Bilecik, Pazarcık, Uşak, Afyon, Konya, Pozantı, and Eskişehir again. In Afyon, Mustafa Kemal spoke with the officers with inspiring words laced with idealism. "I feel real pleasure of conscience (*zevk-ı vicdanı*)," he said, referring to the patriotism among the officers. To those who lacked patriotic devotion, he sought to spark it by his words and presence. The threat was very serious: the British and their allies were seeking to destroy the country's independence. The army, nonetheless, drew life from the nation's "conscience-based faith" (*iman-ı vicdani*) that valued independence and the need for force. He appealed directly to their personal "honor (*şeref*) and self-respect (*izzetinefs*)," reminding them that "A known military truth is that the soul of an army is in its officers." Officers had to set an example of self-sacrifice for their troops, an important theme in Kemal's thought. "Either independence or death" was the guiding principle of war.[64] In this address, Mustafa Kemal stressed the themes of patriotism, national independence, personal honor, and human dignity, all designed to stir the soul of his officers.

Pozantı was an important visit (5 August). There, Mustafa Kemal met with members of the Society of the Defense of Rights for the Adana Front, picked the governor, approved the formation of a division, and addressed the problem of needed weapons and ammunition flowing into the region. On his return trip to Ankara, Mustafa Kemal stopped in Akşehir to visit the tomb of Nasreddin Hoca, a legendary folk hero, populist philosopher, and humorous satirist of the thirteenth century, returning to Ankara on 7 August. His itinerary omitted

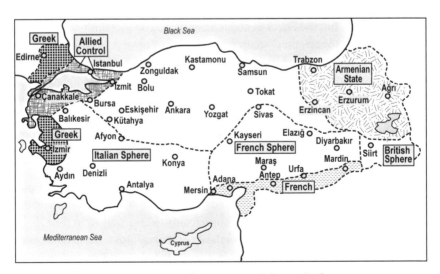

Map 4.1   *Treaty of Sèvres, 1920, Spheres of Influence*

117

Karabekir in Erzurum. Mustafa Kemal trusted this popular commander and left him to his talents and vices.

The Great Powers took advantage of the Greek victories to compel the Istanbul government to sign the Treaty of Sèvres on 10 August. According to the document, the Straits region and Istanbul fell under the control of an international commission. Moreover, the Great Powers, through this treaty, gained a stranglehold over Ottoman finances. Zones of economic influence were to be established in most of Anatolia. Greece remained in control of the Izmir region and was authorized to hold a plebiscite in five years on the issue of union. France, meanwhile, included territory as far as Sivas; the Italians administered south-central Anatolia, including Antalya, Konya, and Afyon. A Greater Armenia was promised to become a reality with the incorporation of Trabzon, Erzurum, and Van. Following a future plebiscite, the Kurds could possibly establish a small and independent Kurdistan. If implemented, Sèvres would have left a truncated Turkey centered on Ankara, arguably the harshest of terms in any of the peace settlements after World War I. At the time of the treaty, Greece occupied territory beyond its allotted zone, to include Bursa, the Çanakkale region, and as far south as just west of Afyon.

Everyone should have known that Mustafa Kemal and the Nationalists would reject the treaty outright, despite Ankara's military setbacks. Paraskevopoulos, aware of this, wanted to seize the moment and approached Venizelos, again, for permission to launch a major offensive to defeat Mustafa Kemal decisively. One thrust would capture Eskişehir and a second Afyon. Both forces would then converge on Ankara and deal a mortal blow to Kemal's forces. But Venizelos lacked Great Power support for such an adventure, so nothing came of this military scheme. But the Greek generals managed to conduct limited operations anyhow. On 29 August, they occupied Uşak in west central Anatolia. Then, on 5 September, they captured the towns of Yalova, located on the Sea of Marmara near Istanbul, and Gediz, southwest of Kütahya. The Greeks were inching their way to Ankara.

In October, Western Front commander Ali Fuad wanted to regain the initiative and recommended an attack on Gediz. İsmet opposed the idea and wanted instead to concentrate on rebuilding the army. Mustafa Kemal came to Eskişehir to resolve the disagreement and Ali Fuad got his way.[65] On 24 October, he launched an attack with the 61st and 11th Divisions along with the First Mobile Force under Çerkez Edhem, a total force of 8,000 men. The 61st Division managed to occupy the town of Gediz on 26 October, only to lose it again to the Greeks on 31 October. Yenişehir, a town northeast of Bursa, also fell to the Greeks. Recriminations followed the setbacks. Çerkez Edhem and his men blamed the front commander and regular troops, whereas the regulars complained of the poor performance and dilatory actions of the Mobile Forces.[66] The tension between conventional warfare and guerrilla warfare mindsets and traditions remained a source of friction on the Western Front.

Ali Fuad took the fall for the poor military performance, and on 8 November, Mustafa Kemal appointed him the first ambassador to Moscow. The Council of Ministers, meanwhile, divided the Western Front into two. İsmet assumed command of the Northern Front, with his headquarters at Eskişehir; the Southern Front went to Refet, located in Konya.[67] Mustafa Kemal ordered İsmet and Refet to incorporate all National Forces into their commands.

Çerkez Edhem was an independent-minded political figure with ties to the Green Army (*Yeşil Ordu*), a communist, semi-clandestine political organization with members in the Parliament. In July, Mustafa Kemal eliminated Green Army with an eye on removing his Circassian rival. On 26 December, Çerkez Edhem was virtually compelled to revolt rather than integrate his forces with the regular army. But some of his men deserted rather than fight against Ankara. İzzeddin, Kemal's former chief of staff, soundly defeated Çerkez Edhem and his forces on 5 January 1921, forcing him to flee with a much reduced force. He remained a minor nuisance and an enemy of the Ankara government for the remainder of the war.[68] The era of the National Forces on the Western Front essentially came to an end with his defeat and that of Demirci Efe by Refet in December 1920. Those who resisted pliant integration into the regular army felt Ankara's wrath. "Extreme force was used to suppress them, sometimes not only against the rebels themselves but also their families and immediate relatives. Sometimes even against their villages."[69] Magnanimity might have been a wiser policy, but intimidation became the favored route. The Western Front had essentially consolidated into a single army despite setbacks on the battlefield against the Greeks.

War in Eastern and Southeastern Anatolia

The regions of Adana and Diyarbekir, unlike the Western Front, experienced an insurgency and people's war through the year 1920 and into 1921.[70] A mixed force, including Kurdish tribesmen, surrounded an isolated 700-man French garrison at Urfa and conducted a siege that lasted from 9 February to 11 April, which ended in a Nationalist victory. The capture of Maraş on 11 February by Nationalist forces (discussed in chapter three) encouraged more resistance to the French presence. In Anteb, the local Muslim population organized and revolted against the French, and Kılıç Ali of Maraş fame brought his National Force unit to assist in the resistance. The fighting for Anteb began on 1 April and lasted ten months and nine days, until 9 February 1921.

Mustafa Kemal wanted to keep the conflict confined to the areas already occupied by the French. In April, he instructed Colonel Salaheddin, in command of III Corps at Sivas, to use "political efforts" to avoid providing an excuse for the French to expand their effort but wanted resistance to any attempt to occupy Pazarcık.[71] Meanwhile, the French appeared interested in reaching a political solution. A senior French official visited Ankara and on 28 May both sides agreed to an armistice of twenty days, which lasted from 30 May to 19 June before hostilities resumed again.

The war in southeastern Anatolia involved armed civilians, as well as National Forces and the regular army. Local Muslims and Armenians armed themselves, heightening ethnic and religious sentiments in this people's war. Stories of atrocities continued to appear from all sides in the conflict. On 1 August, the French attempted to assuage Muslim emotions and disbanded the notorious Armenian Legion. But France lacked a sufficient number of troops to pacify the region, a recipe for a French defeat, especially since Mustafa Kemal had strengthened his position in Ankara over the passage of time and he could continue the resistance from his safe haven. Mustafa Kemal, meanwhile, pressed for armed resistance. In a communiqué of 6 August 1920 to the Adana commander, he outlined his twin military strategy for the army at this point in the struggle: an increase in the presence of National Forces and their integration over time into regular army formations. The unconventional character of the war on this front enhanced the importance of National Forces, unlike the Western Front facing the Greeks. In the meantime, it was important for the National Forces to continue to harass the enemy until the formation of more regular army units.[72] Mustafa Kemal lacked sufficient forces to deal a major blow to the French.

The battle for the town of Anteb began on 1 April 1920 and continued until 9 February 1921. In recognition of the population's heroism and sacrifice, on 8 February 1921 the BMM added the title of *Gazi*, or "fighter for the Islamic faith," to the town's name, so that Anteb became Gazianteb. This award was designed to soften the blow coming the next day. On 9 February, the Council of Ministers ordered the city to surrender so that forces fighting there could be transferred to meet the emerging Greek threat on the Western Front.[73] By then, combat, disease, malnutrition, and flight had reduced the city's population from 50,000 to 13,000.

Kurdish tribal revolts in southeastern Anatolia compounded Kemal's problems. A revolt from 1 June to 15 September led by the Kurdish tribe Milli Aşireti in the region of Diyarbekir, Urfa, and Mamuretülaziz (Elağız), complicated the battle against the French. So on 26 June, Mustafa Kemal created the Elcezire Front, which encompassed the provinces of Mosul, Bitlis, Diyarbekir, Mamuretülaziz (Elağız), and the independent sub-provinces of Urfa and Hakkari, and he appointed Brigadier General Nihad (Anılmış) Paşa, an officer sympathetic to the Nationalist cause, as its commander. Nihad assumed full responsibility for external threats and internal security and reported directly to the General Staff and to the defense ministry. His headquarters absorbed that of XIII Corps in Diyarbekir.[74] Nihad experienced some difficulty suppressing the Kurdish Milli Aşireti and Karakeçi tribes, and in January 1921, Mustafa Kemal ordered the deportation of these rebellious elements and the settlement of refugees from other parts of Anatolia.[75] In addition to securing the region, the Elcezire Front served as a base for conducting small-scale military operations in support of resistance to the British occupation of northern Iraq, including Mosul, territory claimed by the National Pact.[76]

From his headquarters in Erzurum, Karabekir remained a major proponent of taking decisive action against Armenia. He frequently sent reports of massacres of Muslim civilians by the Armenian government. Some of his analysis was alarmist. On 26–27 August 1919, for example, Karabekir had described the Armenian revolutionary organization Tashnak as intent on cleansing Muslims from the regions of Revan and Aras, as well as the three sancaks of Kars, Ardahan, and Artvin, so that "not a single Muslim" would be left. According to him, Armenian regular troops were executing a deliberate policy of cleansing by perpetuating massacres, stoning those calling Muslims to prayer, and abusing Muslim women.[77]

Karabekir, nonetheless, proved an effective front commander.[78] Sometimes on his own initiative, he sent officers and small detachments to support the local Muslim population in the Caucasus. Like Mustafa Kemal, he viewed Armenia as a threat, especially because of Armenian claims on the eastern provinces of Anatolia. With the approach of summer, Karabekir became eager to attack Armenia, and on 26 April, he requested permission to make preparations for launching an attack in the second half of May. With the Bolshevik Army occupying Azerbaijan, Karabekir felt the time was right for military action against the Armenian state. Mustafa Kemal, for his part, wanted a firm agreement with Moscow, as well as assurance of material aid, before launching such an offensive. He was about to send an official delegation to Moscow. Moreover, Mustafa Kemal felt that a military operation could lead to more massacres of Armenians, and thus would only have a negative political effect in Europe and the United States. Strengthening the militia forces in the region of Kars, Ardahan, and Batum was, according to Mustafa Kemal, the best course of action for the moment.[79] Mustafa Kemal wanted Soviet cooperation so much that he had Turkish officers assisting the Bolsheviks in their occupation of Azerbaijan.[80] In the beginning of June, Karabekir received permission to order mobilization in the eastern provinces, and on 13 June, the Council of Ministers appointed him to command the Eastern Front with full civil and military authority. There would be no major offensive against Armenia in the summer months, but rather a small border war between both countries.

Moscow, meanwhile, preferred to press its aims in the South Caucasus before reaching a firm agreement with Ankara. But Soviet money and war *matériel*, none-theless, began reaching Anatolia in September. Finally, after months of negotiations in Moscow, Mustafa Kemal decided to send a military signal to Moscow, and on 20 September, the Council of Ministers gave Karabekir permission to conduct a limited offensive against the Armenians. The Eastern Army would attack in the direction of Kars, advancing to the Kağızman–Novo Selim–Merdenk Line for the first phase of operations, with the main aim being to "annihilate (*imha*) the Armenian armed forces" rather than capture terrain. Annihilation as a military term meant destroying the army's combat power, its ability to fight. The direc-tive ordered measures to prevent attacks on unarmed Armenian people. At the same time, Mustafa Kemal wanted to ensure Georgia's neutrality. Karabekir possessed the authority to enter into relations with Georgia, but he was also to avoid entering into Georgian territory. While remaining cautious of possible Georgian movements, Karabekir was to focus on Armenia as his main effort.[81] On the same day, İsmet underscored for Karabekir the need to watch develop-ments in Georgia, for a Georgian intervention could defeat the Nationalist effort. Therefore, Karabekir had to move quickly and decisively. A possibility existed that Georgia might intervene militarily and join forces with Armenia and that together they might be able to defeat the XV Corps.[82]

On 24 September, Karabekir issued his order to XV Corps, justifying the military operation as a direct response to atrocities committed by the Tashnak Armenian government. On 27 September, the 9th and 12th Divisions would lead the main attack in the direction of Sarıkamış. Tribal regiments meanwhile would occupy Kağızman. The lines of advance would not extend to Kars, how-ever. Karabekir warned his troops against the Armenians faking surrender with white flags and using the Turkish language.[83] Such words discouraged taking risks in capturing prisoners. From the above operational order, it is clear that Mustafa Kemal did not aim to defeat Armenia; instead, he wanted Karabekir to move cautiously, to capture some territory, and then to let Ankara assess the political situation before proceeding on to Kars. Policy and military operations were inexorably linked.

The attack began on 28 September at 0300. The XV Corps' records showed a force structure of 1,422 officers and 17,069 soldiers, with 5,000 to 5,500 tribal forces. The Armenian strength was estimated at 13,000, thus giving Karabekir an advantage in numbers. He also commanded a battle-hardened corps. Outnumbered, the Armenians offered little or no resistance when attacked. Problems of coordination between advancing Turkish units, however, allowed most of the Armenians to escape to fight another day. One day later, on 29 September, the 12th Division entered Sarıkamış, again without facing any serious resistance; the 9th Division, meanwhile, occupied Zivin, and the XV Corps ceased operations on 30 September, achieving all its objectives. While Mustafa Kemal analyzed the diplomatic situation, Karabekir returned to Erzurum on 1 October. The Soviets, meanwhile, disassociated themselves from Ankara's attack and publicized their friendly feelings for the Armenians.[84]

Armenia responded to Turkey's offensive by declaring war on it on 4 October, and Mustafa Kemal acted in kind. İsmet ordered XV Corps to destroy the Armenian Army quickly before Georgia intervened. On 7 October, Karabekir launched another attack, but this time his forces encountered Armenian counterattacks. Seizing an opportunity, the Soviet Politburo decided on 13 October to occupy Armenia. On 30 October, XV Corps finally captured the long-coveted city of Kars with only nine killed and forty-seven wounded. On 3 November, Karabekir advanced toward Erevan, the Armenian capital, and captured Iğdir. Armenia now requested a truce, and on 7 November, Karabekir complied but with the provision that Armenia withdraw from the Alexandropol region. Meanwhile, the Soviet Eleventh Army began its invasion of Armenia from the north.

On 8 November, Ankara's Acting Foreign Minister Ahmed Muhtar sent a new set of demands for the Armenians to Karabekir. In a second letter on the same day, he provided more specific guidance. The Council of Ministers made it known that they viewed Armenia and Greece as natural allies with the common aim "to hinder our development." Withdrawing from Armenia was thus out of the question. Ahmed Muhtar defined Turkey's long-range aim as emasculating Armenia as a viable state: "Consequently it is most necessary to destroy Armenia politically and materially." (*Binaenaleyh Ermenistanı siyaseten ve maddeten ortadan kaldırmak elzemdir.*) In conducting negotiations, Karabekir was instructed to portray an image of being "peace-loving" (*müsalemetperver*) in intent, and he should employ "vague and gentle" (*mübhem ve mülayım*) language. For now, he could accept the boundary as outlined in the Treaty of Brest-Litovsk, but he had to ensure that the fate of the Muslim population under Armenian rule was secure and served as solid leverage in future dealings with Armenia. The document ended with the caution that Karabekir should consider these instructions for his eyes only.[85] Mustafa Kemal wanted a decisive political victory, one that left Armenia severely weakened as a state in the Caucasus, thus posing no threat to Turkey in the future.

In Erevan, the Tashnak government, not surprisingly, rejected the terms offered by Karabekir, apparently hoping for last-minute foreign intervention. But no such development occurred. Karabekir, therefore, renewed military operations, forcing Erevan to capitulate on 17 November. The Treaty of Alexandropol, or Gümrü, was signed on 2 December. In it, Turkey recognized Armenian independence, and Armenia agreed to a plebiscite in the Kars region. Armenia also rejected the terms of the Sèvres Treaty and accepted a force limit on its gendarmerie of only

1,500 men, a force much smaller than a division, with no national conscription. In this case, Armenia would essentially be without a viable military, but there was no limit on the size of its gendarmerie for internal security. Turkish military units, moreover, would maintain a presence in the districts of Itur and Nahcivan, thereby securing communication routes with Azerbaijan. A plebiscite would determine the fate of both occupied districts. The Treaty of Gümrü ensured Armenia would pose no conventional military threat to Turkey, and it left the country unable to defend itself from an outside aggressor.

With this treaty, Turkey incorporated the sancak of Kars. Georgia remained in control of two sancaks of Ardahan and Batum. Meanwhile, Erevan agreed to become an "independent" Armenian Soviet Republic within the Soviet Union. This decision precluded Turkey having any influence over Armenia. A Soviet Army now occupied Armenia, in fact, ending the country's short-lived independence and its notion of a Greater Armenia. At the same time, Greece had lost its supporter in the east. The National Army, for its part, now claimed its first major military victory, and Karabekir emerged a war hero. The Treaty of Gümrü rejected the Treaty of Sèvres and sent another unmistakable message to the world of Nationalist resolve.

A New Political Covenant

Between 24 and 30 January 1921, the Allied leaders met in Paris, largely to discuss Germany. They decided to convene a third conference in London, scheduled to begin on 21 February. The Istanbul government was naturally invited, but the new French Prime Minister Aristide Briand suggested the inclusion of moderate representation from Ankara. Mustafa Kemal refused to be part of the Istanbul delegation and rejected the Treaty of Sèvres as the basis of discussions. However, he did send a separate delegation to London under Foreign Minister Bekir Sami. The Allied leaders ended up negotiating with Bekir Sami. The Third London Conference lasted from 21 February to 9 March. The Allies naturally favored the Istanbul delegation, because the Ankara delegation demanded rejection of the Sèvres Treaty and the acceptance of the National Pact. Although no serious progress was made on this front, Mustafa Kemal had gained recognition of Ankara's existence and a platform to present his view right in the heart of Europe.

Much effort went into rebuilding and expanding the National Army after its defeats at the hands of the Greeks. Toward the end of 1920, the National Army had grown significantly in an economically depressed area of Anatolia. Records show a force structure nearly doubled in size to 5,232 officers and 81,284 soldiers from the 50,000 after demobilization. Of these, the Western Front numbered 1,728 officers and 27,571 soldiers, or 33.9 per cent of the total. The Eastern

Front was second in size, with 1,425 officers and 20,181 men, or 28.4 per cent. Elcezire in southeastern Anatolia had only 700 officers and 6,066 men. The III Corps at Amasya counted 477 officers and 9,256 soldiers, with the Ankara Command registering the smallest numbers, at 399 officers and 4,471 soldiers respectively.[86] These numbers were hardly sufficient to wage a conventional war against the Greeks and drive them out of Anatolia.

In line with seeking the integration of the people into the war effort, Mustafa Kemal appreciated that final victory required the mobilization of the entire Anatolian population. And Ankara needed a provisional constitution to give greater legality to the national movement. Mustafa Kemal often spoke of "populism" (*halkçılık*) or a "people's government" (*halk hükümeti*). This theme would remain over the next couple of years. Rather than meaning the empowerment of the people in a democracy, Mustafa Kemal used the terms as a means of undermining the Istanbul government and mobilizing the people in a social contract under his leadership.

Agreeing on a provisional constitution took time and effort. Finally, on 20 January 1921, the BMM passed a new political covenant between the government and the people. Rather than naming the constitution the Fundamental Law, or *Kaunu-i Esasi*, as in 1876, it was called the Law of Fundamental Organization, or *Teşkilat-ı Esasiye Kanunu*. Article 1 placed sovereignty in the *millet*, or nation, reiterating the link to the people. Article 2 ascribed to the Grand National Assembly both executive and legislative powers, and restated that legitimacy came from the representative nature of the Parliament. Article 3 identified the political entity as the "State of Turkey," or *Türkiye Devleti*, and gave the name of the government as the Government of the Grand National Assembly, or *Büyük Millet Meclisi Hükumeti*. Article 7 granted the Assembly "basic rights such as the ratification of treaties and the declaration [of war] for the defense of the fatherland."[87] The Law for Basic Organization nudged the national movement closer toward being a republic. Most striking, it failed to mention the sultanate or the caliphate at all. It gave the Assembly the right to declare a defense of the fatherland, thereby essentially justifying only a defensive war. No mention was made of "war," or *harb*, but it was obviously implied.[88] This wording reiterated the defensive nature of the struggle, maintaining continuity with the *Defense* (*müdafaa*) of Rights Societies and the new Ministry of National *Defense* (*müdafaa*) (the italics of the English word are the author's).

The Law of Fundamental Organization identified the president of the Assembly, duly elected by its members, as the head of the government as well. Each minister in the council of ministers was directly selected by the BMM. On 24 January, Mustafa Kemal ensured the selection of Fevzi, a military man and deputy from Kozan, as the head of the council of ministers. "It was another instance of his ability to preserve the leadership, while delegating day-to-day administration to loyal lieutenants."[89] The selection also underscored that although the BMM provided the image of popular sovereignty, the army remained the backbone of the resistance, now under Kemal's firm control.

Despite all his numerous responsibilities and social life in Ankara, Mustafa Kemal continued to find time for personal study. In 1920, he read "with an intense concentration" about early Islamic history. This interest included the period of the first four caliphs who were elected to rule. According to Halide Edip, Mustafa Kemal came to appreciate Muawiyah (r. 661–680) who, through skill, shrewdness, and other personal qualities, both good and questionable, defeated Caliph Ali and founded the Umayyad Dynasty (661–750). Muawiyah had the reputation for taking advantage of the chivalry of his opponents. Halide Edip saw that with these studies Mustafa Kemal was preparing himself to impress Muslim clerics with his knowledge of Islamic history and also sharpening his own leadership skills.[90] Mustafa Kemal would later make use of Islamic history to justify his radical reforms.

Halide Edip was close to Mustafa Kemal during this period. She often attended evening meals with him, witnessed key discussions, and participated in social events. On one occasion, Mustafa Kemal fell into "one of the most violent rages." Halide had translated a newspaper piece in which a British official spoke of "The Big Stick Policy," a demeaning notion in reference to Turkey. Mustafa Kemal reacted: "They shall know that we are as good as they are. They shall treat us as equals. Never will we bow our heads to them!"[91] Personal and national pride constituted key driving ingredients in Kemal's personality. National dignity was a very important term in his vocabulary. Turkey and its people deserved the full respect of the West.

Mustafa Kemal continued to suffer from health problems. He had frequent fevers, no doubt suffering the result of malaria. Doctors often expressed concerns about his health.[92] Mustafa Kemal fit the category of those who worked hard and played hard. He had several physical disabilities, recurrent eye problems, malaria, venereal disease, and kidney ailments. Heavy drinking complicated his health problems. So did the great stress of his position as head of the BMM. His responsibilities spanned the entire spectrum of government, from politics to war fighting, diplomacy, and economics. He felt he had to stay abreast of events daily. The pressure of these responsibilities was immense, but Mustafa Kemal clearly had a strong will and ambition to continue. In mid-November 1920, Fikriye, the daughter of his stepfather Rağib, surprised everyone with her arrival in Ankara. She promptly moved in to live with Mustafa Kemal. Neither Kemal's mother nor his sister approved of Fikriye. What was a scandalous move for some, however, offered a ray of hope to others. Perhaps a steady female companion would bring some emotional stability to Kemal's personal life.

Conclusion

By 1921, the word "Kemalist" had become a foreign term to refer to the Nationalist movement. This recognition reflected positively on Kemal's effectiveness as a political leader, first as *reis*, or president, of the Representative Committee and then as the *reis* of the BMM. Many people had helped him on this journey, but he also had seized critical opportunities to his advantage. For one, he had given policy the main priority that it deserved in building the Nationalist resistance. The Erzurum and Sivas Congresses led to a national Parliament. The BMM, then, empowered Mustafa Kemal to establish a provisional government based on a representative institution embodying the national sentiment for self-determination and independence. And Mustafa Kemal slowly had gained firm control over the army and integrated the national militia. This army was not strong enough, however, to face the Greeks but was capable enough to defeat Armenia and secure the Eastern Front. In the process, the Ankara government had gained *de facto* diplomatic recognition from all the Great Powers, as evidenced in the participation of a separate delegation from Ankara at the Third London Conference. An Allied strategy using the Istanbul government to further its imperialist designs appeared increasingly a forlorn hope to astute observers. And in the conduct of the war against Greece, Armenia, and France, Mustafa Kemal had directed from a distance, choosing to remain in Ankara. Diplomacy played an important role on both fronts. While Mustafa Kemal sought Soviet assistance and cooperation on one front, in the east, he welcomed negotiations and an armistice with France over southeastern Anatolia.

The Ankara government derived its legitimacy from the BMM and the army, and Mustafa Kemal executed policies as head of state. The regular army had begun professionalizing its organization with an evolving command structure, but it still confronted monumental challenges in training, equipment, and money. The people, for their part, once again faced conscription, with segments of society arrayed in armed conflict against the Istanbul government. Kemal's emphasis on politics over military matters had borne fruit: Ankara had replaced Istanbul as the center of political power and the focus of Entente Power attention. And material and financial aid was arriving from the Soviet Union. These achievements reflected Kemal's leadership skills in balancing politics, diplomacy, and military matters while creating a new state. On the debit side, Mustafa Kemal had suffered a string of military reverses against the Greeks. Time and space, however, worked to his advantage in the long run, which he understood. But unrecognized by Mustafa Kemal, however, a major military crisis loomed on the horizon, one that would result in a significant adjustment on his part to the relationship between the government, the army, and the people.

5

A Crisis in Battle

He who knows when he can fight and when he cannot will be victorious.

Sun Tzu[1]

Against the offense launched by Greece with all its power, our basic duty, which is military, is the duty that we have followed since the beginning of the national struggle. And it is, whenever facing a Greek offensive, to resist this offensive and to stop it with suitable movements and to win time in order to bring the new army into existence. And in the face of this offensive, this main thought must not be far from our view.

Mustafa Kemal, 17 July 1921

IN 1920, Kemal's position and that of the national resistance had grown stronger. He had balanced the necessary political, diplomatic, and military requirements while slowly laying a foundation for post-war Turkey. The Assembly, at the beginning of 1921, changed its official name to the Grand National Assembly of Turkey, or *Türkiye Büyük Millet Meclisi* (TBMM). A provisional constitution had strengthened Kemal's legitimacy, and he had consolidated control over the regular army and much of the National Forces. A peace treaty with Russia and two battlefield victories against the Greeks enhanced his position. But then, suddenly, in the summer of 1921, the Greek army won a series of engagements that threatened the capture of Ankara. Rather than suffer a political setback, however, Mustafa Kemal exploited the serious military setback to his advantage and managed to strengthen his authority even further.

Diplomatic and Political Developments

The Treaty of Gümrü with Armenia failed to settle matters on the Eastern Front. Ankara still coveted the two regions of Ardahan and Batum as articulated in the

National Pact, making for an unsettled border with Georgia. Ali Fuad, the new ambassador to Moscow, departed for his assignment on 1 December 1920, one day before the signing of the Treaty of Gümrü with Armenia, with a set of clear instructions from Mustafa Kemal, who wanted full political and economic independence within the borders circumscribed by the National Pact. But Armenia had to renounce her claims on Van and Bitlis. Azerbaijan, on its part, should receive her independence along with full control over her oil and other natural resources. Mustafa Kemal also wanted Soviet assistance in stirring up Kurdish and Arab revolts against the British in Iraq and the French in Syria.[2] After stopping in Kars, Ali Fuad made additional stops in Tiflis and Baku to explore diplomatic relations there before reaching Moscow on 18 February.

While in need of Soviet diplomatic, financial, and material support, Mustafa Kemal also felt a kindred spirit with the Soviets. He appreciated the revolutionary spirit of the Bolsheviks and their ability to organize an effective stand against imperialism while re-establishing the former tsarist empire under a radically new system. *Yoldaşlar*, or literally "fellow travelers," the Turkish word popularly used in dealings with the Soviets, conveyed this notion of a common journey. Mustafa Kemal saw similarities between the two revolutions: Turkey's new political system with its TBMM resembled the Soviet revolutionary committees, and Bolshevism was compatible with Islam in some areas. In 1920 and 1921, *Hakimiyet-i Milliye* published a series of articles discussing revolutionary parallels between the two countries, which carried such titles as "Two Communisms" and "Russian Bolshevism and Turkish Communism."[3]

Some Western leaders and analysts, indeed, evaluated Mustafa Kemal as a communist. During the war, Mustafa Kemal "gave the impression of being a Muslim communist." But he was no Bolshevik, nor communist, clearly; he prevented the emergence of any socialist rivals for power in Turkey, and numbers of "true" communists found themselves in jail. Despite his Bolshevik-like rhetoric, Mustafa Kemal underscored Turkey's own unique route to liberation and revolution.[4] On 29 January 1921 in a meeting with Soviet representatives in Ankara, for example, he outlined several differences between the two countries that required Turkey to pursue its own distinct transformation. Turkey, for example, lacked a land problem to elicit an awakening of villagers against feudal landowners, or *ağalar*. Outside of Kurdistan, there were few large landowners. Moreover, Turkey did not have a working class like Russia, and capitalist oppression came not from within the country but from outside.[5] Such analysis stressed Turkey's independent road to revolution, and although one could easily challenge it, Kemal's pseudo-communist party attested to that description of Turkish society.

After the Sovietization of Armenia, Moscow set its sights on the small republic of Georgia. On 11 February, a week before Ali Fuad's arrival in Moscow, Soviet troops advanced into Georgia, reaching the outskirts of Tbilisi on 19 February. Risking a confrontation with the Soviets, Mustafa Kemal ordered the capture of Ardahan. The order from the General Staff reached Karabekir on 21 February, and his forces easily occupied the town, inching closer to Batum. The local Muslim population naturally greeted the army as liberators. Meanwhile, back in Moscow, after some initial discussions, the Soviets and the Ankara delegation officially commenced negotiations on 26 February, with Mustafa Kemal already in control of Kars and Ardahan. But Mustafa Kemal avoided pressing his luck and restrained himself from responding positively to appeals for assistance from the Menshevik government in Georgia. Then on 9 March, he gave the green light to Karabekir to occupy the port of Batum, which he did two days later.[6]

Lenin, although angered by Kemal's moves, wished to avoid a conflict. Thus, the government of the Russian Socialist Federal Soviet Republic and the government of the TBMM reached an agreement on South Caucasus. The Treaty of Moscow, or Treaty of Brotherhood, was signed on 16 March 1921. In the agreement, the Russians accepted the "expression Turkey" to mean the boundaries as defined by the National Pact in the Ottoman Parliament. Turkey, therefore, kept Kars and Ardahan and gained free transit for exports and imports through the port of Batum without customs duties and tax levies. An autonomous Nahcivan was awarded to Soviet Azerbaijan. Russia also renounced all capitulary rights and any claims on Turkish debt obligations to the tsarist regime. Moscow, on its part, promised to support Turkish sovereignty over the Straits and Istanbul. The Soviets also agreed to provide ten million gold rubles of annual aid and to send substantial shipments of weapons and ammunition.

The Treaty of Moscow represented a major diplomatic triumph for Mustafa Kemal. This was Turkey's first formal treaty with a European Power under Mustafa Kemal. Consequently, Ankara gained security on the Eastern Front. Mustafa Kemal also regained most of the territories in northeastern Anatolia that had been lost to tsarist Russia in the Russo-Turkish War of 1877–78. By making a second push to capture Batum, he had gained what proved to be a wise military move in support of diplomacy. Batum became a negotiating chip.

In signing the Treaty of Moscow, Mustafa Kemal demonstrated *Realpolitik* that balanced the use of politics and war in obtaining achievable goals. Karabekir, on the other hand, had wanted serious military action sooner and thus was frustrated with Kemal's more cautious strategy. Mustafa Kemal, though, focused on forging cooperation with Moscow. Waiting and patience produced positive results. By achieving his goals with minimal friction, Mustafa Kemal ensured that the two most important regional powers with direct stakes in South Caucasus worked together in imposing agreements on the other affected players while, at the same time, undermining Western imperialist designs. The Treaty of Moscow brought immediate, tangible results. On 30 March, feeling more secure on the Eastern Front with the agreements, the General Staff transferred the 3rd Caucasus Infantry Division to the Western Front, where it participated in the Battle of Sakarya. The 12th Division, which began its move at the beginning of August, never reached the battle but participated in the Great Offensive the following year. Moreover, April 1921 saw the arrival of four million gold rubles and a major shipment of weapons and ammunition in enough time to affect the critical Battle of Sakarya in August.

After the conclusion of the London Conference, Foreign Minister Bekir Sami stopped in Paris, where he reached a secret agreement on 11 March with France. French Prime Minister Aristide Briand agreed to evacuate French troops from southeastern Anatolia. In return, Turkey granted France major economic concessions in southeastern Anatolia as well as possession of land on both sides of the railroad in the region. On 12 March, Bekir Sami also signed a secret agreement with the Italian foreign minister that awarded Italy rights to the exploration and exploitation of Turkish natural resources, especially in the Ereğli coal basin. In return, Italy recognized Turkish rights in Izmir and Thrace. But Mustafa Kemal disliked both agreements and opted to procrastinate before putting them to public debate in the TBMM.[7] Timing was important. After a military victory at the Second Battle of İnönü (see p139 onwards), Mustafa Kemal let Bekir Sami present his two treaties, to the shock and dismay of many deputies. The economic concessions were the most troublesome, for they smacked of the much-hated Capitulations. The National Pact, with its demand for complete sovereignty and independence, should have been the basis for any peace agreement, the deputies in the TBMM believed. Consequently, on 8 May, the TBMM rejected the treaty with France and did not even consider the one with Italy. The people's representative institution voted for full self-determination and showed resolve to continue the struggle. As a result, Bekir Sami resigned as Foreign Minister on 16 May. On the positive side, both Italy and France showed willingness to break away from the Allied coalition and reach separate agreements with Ankara.

On 1 March, Mustafa Kemal expressed his frustration with the TBMM's productivity during its first year (Hijra calendar). From 23 April 1920 to 28 February 1921, the Assembly had met on 159 out of 311 days and held 407 sessions, with 51 of them secret and 356 public. The deputies had passed 104 laws and rejected 149 proposals. Furthermore, they had presented sixty-seven proposals to the Council of Ministers and left fifty-five for the following year. All totaled, the TBMM had dealt with 381 legislative proposals.[8] These figures depicted an active legislative body, not a rubber-stamp parliament. But for the ambitious Mustafa Kemal, they highlighted the inability of the deputies to settle matters in an efficient and timely manner. Mustafa Kemal had his way on major issues, however, usually obtaining a clear majority of votes. He had a pretty good idea of which battles to fight in the Assembly.

On 10 May 1921, in the aftermath of the debates over Bekir Sami's two secret treaties, Mustafa Kemal established a formal political party. In the TBMM, it was named "Group for the Defense of the Rights of Anatolia and Rumeli." The group incorporated the provincial Defense of Rights Societies into a nationwide political party. Article 4 of the group's Internal Regulations made the executive committee of the party also the administrative committee of the Society for the Defense of Rights in Anatolia and Rumeli until the convening of a general congress.[9] Mustafa Kemal was naturally elected the president (*reis*) of the Executive Committee. Initially, the group counted 133 deputies but quickly grew to 261. Establishing the foundations of a political party proved an important step for the future. The TBMM had demonstrated a diversity of opinion and some opposition to Mustafa Kemal. Now, rather than maintain the fiction of being a national leader above politics, Mustafa Kemal opted to begin building a political party to strengthen his position and to better mobilize the people. Before the end of the year, a viable opposition party emerged under the title of Second Group, as opposed to his First Group.

Nationalist writer Yakub Kadri (Karaosmanoğlu), who arrived in Ankara in 1921, noted that the most common complaint directed at Mustafa Kemal was that he spent too much time with politics and not enough on the army.[10] Historical hindsight, however, allows a better way of understanding the dynamic between Kemal's politics and war. He emphasized politics because he was laying the foundation for postwar Turkey, and he proved quite willing, when the timing was right, to assume full military responsibility. And when he finally gave greater attention to the army, it was with an eye to the future; his politics was playing first fiddle still.

Internal Front

The Pontus region in northern Anatolia remained a troubling spot for Ankara. An important supply route for the national cause traversed from the Black Sea coast into the interior. Consequently, Greek naval ships patrolling the coastal waters at times bombarded the shore, jeopardizing the flow of war *matériel*. The Greek army also provided officers and supplies to assist the Rum guerrillas in the area. Meanwhile, Rum and Greek bands in the Pontus region disrupted supply lines; general brigandage was rampant as well. The year 1920 saw approximately 1,100 Muslim villagers killed and thousands of homes destroyed.[11] On 19 October 1920, *Hakimiyet-i Milliye* issued a warning to the Rum population in an article titled "Elements in the New Anatolia" that said "whoever plays with imperialism against the Turks is our enemy."[12]

Mustafa Kemal decided that it was time to secure the home front and supply routes in the Black Sea region, as another Greek offensive appeared likely. On 9 December 1920, the Council of Ministers dissolved III Corps and created Central Army (*Merkez Ordusu*) in its stead. Central Army, meanwhile, took over corps headquarters in Amasya, its area of responsibility comprising Sivas province as well as the areas of Canik, Sinop, Amasya, Tokat, Çorum, and Yozgat. Brigadier General Nureddin Paşa was appointed Central Army commander. For matters of operations and security, he reported to the Chief of the General Staff. Other matters fell under the authority of the Ministry of Defense.[13] "The most important reason for establishing Central Army was to end Pontus movements."[14] Nureddin's Central Command quickly developed a force structure of 10,000 men comprised of two infantry divisions, a cavalry division, an independent cavalry brigade, an infantry regiment, and a National Forces detachment led by Topal (Lame) Osman Ağa. Intelligence estimated the number of guerrillas at approximately 5,000, with some 25,000 armed and sympathetic villagers.[15] Greece was supplying the local Greeks with arms, ammunition, and fighters.

Nureddin was a tough, disciplined, strict, and ruthless commander. He had chased Bulgarian bands in the Balkans (1902), fought in Yemen (1911), commanded in Iraq (1916), and organized resistance in Izmir prior to the Greek occupation. Mustafa Kemal selected him because he wanted to secure the home front efficiently and quickly. On 23 December, Nureddin arrived at his headquarters in Amasya and prepared for search and destroy operations. At the beginning of 1921, government authorities arrested members of two small opposition political parties, the Liberty and Entente Party and the People's Socialist Party, and closed their newspapers, charging them with damaging influences on the population. This action helped muzzle political opposition. With the unfoldment of military operations, Nureddin ordered the incarceration of seventy-five leading Rum figures, including two Orthodox Church leaders, Samsun Metropolitan Eftimos and Bishop Platon Matnoz. The Independence Court in Samsun, for its part, pronounced 485 death sentences between August and December 1921, nearly half of such verdicts passed in the entire war by other courts.[16] To help suppress the unrest, Nureddin was authorized to deport Greek males between fifteen and sixty years of age from the towns and villages bordering the Black Sea to camps in the interior areas of Sivas and Mameratülaziz (Elazığ). Some 20,000 to 30,000 Rums suffered this fate; Greeks with Russian passports were exempt. Untold numbers died during the forced marches. Moreover, during the course of counterguerrilla operations, government troops and militia killed civilians and burned Christian villages. Government sources recorded 11,188 "rebels" killed in military engagements.[17] Nureddin employed virulent language to rationalize this brutal activity: "The Rums in our country are a snake, and women are the poison of these snakes."[18] For him, there appeared no distinction between combatant and noncombatant, guilty or innocent. Reliable figures for deportations and deaths in the Pontus region are lacking.

In conjunction with military operations, Nureddin implemented a propaganda blitz, establishing "Right Guidance Committees" (İrşad Heyetileri) composed of teachers, ulema, and "virtuous people" (erbab-ı fazl) and using the press to reach the people, even in the villages. Samsun gained a new newspaper, The Crescent, for this purpose; so did the town of Çorum. Compliance was necessary. Nureddin closed one paper because it failed to publish one of his public declarations and allowed it to resume publication only when it complied. Officers and soldiers were ordered into mosques for prayers, obviously feigning religiosity for propaganda purposes.[19] Much of this activity was designed to address a Kurdish revolt.

Alongside dealing with the Rum unrest, from 6 March to 17 June Central Army faced a rebellion by Kurds located near Erzincan.[20] Developments in 1920 emboldened local Kurds. The Treaty of Sèvres had raised hopes among some Kurdish leaders. Article 62 offered Kurds autonomy in the area east of the Euphrates, south of the southern boundary of Armenia, and north of the border with Syria and Mesopotamia. Furthermore, Article 64 promised the Kurds the possibility of approaching the League of Nations with a request for independence. Finally, Greek military victories between June and October had weakened the Ankara government, offering the Kurds an opportunity to press for nationalist demands, and "Young Kurds" intensified their propaganda among the tribes.

Kurdish nationalist and tribal leaders now gathered at Hozat (near Dersim) to develop a course of action. On 15 November, they sent a memorandum to Ankara demanding clarification of the government's position on the status of Kurds. Then on 25 November came their demand for an independent Kurdistan. A harsh winter gave both sides time to prepare for hostilities. Mustafa Kemal, meanwhile, responded by dispatching a fact-finding mission to the Erzincan region and rallied Kurdish deputies in Parliament to stave off a rebellion. Nureddin, on his part, worked to win over Kurdish tribal chiefs as well. Then, in February 1921, Central Army struck first and eventually martial law was declared.

The Koçgiri tribe, located west of the town of Erzincan, led the revolt. Numbering some 40,000 to 45,000 members, the Koçgiris were Alevi, while the majority of Kurds identified with the Sunni branch of Islam. Haydar, a son of the tribal leader, belonged to the Society for Kurdish Assistance and Progress and lived in the town of Imranlı where he published the newspaper Jepin, which advocated Kurdish cultural rights. During the course of the uprising, Greece tried to coordinate its military operations with material and financial aid to the

Kurds and even released captured Kurdish soldiers as an expression of Greek goodwill.[21] Any serious local unrest concerned Ankara, for it dissipated its energy and resources away from defeating occupying foreign forces.

On 6 March, Kurdish tribal fighters entered the town of Imranlı and killed Major Halis, the commander of the 6th Cavalry Regiment and five other soldiers, and took a number of prisoners. The standard of revolt was raised. On 10 March, Ankara declared martial law and dispatched reinforcements to Central Army. Three days later, the Council of Ministers increased Nureddin's area of responsibility to include Mameratülaziz province along with the sub-provinces (*liva*) of Erzincan and Dersim. His task was to "eliminate" (*itfa*) the rebellious movements in the Ümraniye region, and the civil administration there was placed under his authority. Furthermore, all military and security forces in the region fell under his direct command.[22] In response, the Koçgiri rebels backed away from independence and instead in April modified their demands to include autonomy under a Kurdish governor with Kurdish officials and cultural rights for the provinces of Diyarbekir, Van, Mameratülaziz, and Bitlis.

Nureddin sought to seal off the rebellious area west of Erzincan, but the revolt spread to neighboring Dersim and Ovacık. At the beginning of April, Nureddin proposed the goal for the next phase of his military operation: "It will be necessary either to reduce the Koçgiri tribe to a state where it can't rebel anymore, or to deport it from the territory where it has been living until now. Which of these [two] courses will be undertaken will depend on the results of the suppression operations."[23] By mid-April, the army had crushed the Koçgiri rebellion, deporting part of the population. It took a few more weeks to secure the neighboring areas. Fortunately for Ankara, most Kurdish leaders in other regions of the country distanced themselves from the rebellion and therefore the rebels found themselves isolated and relatively easy targets for the army.[24] In the meantime, the Western Front against the Greeks heated up, beginning in March. Ankara requisitioned two infantry divisions and one cavalry division to the Western Front so that by June, Central Army had two new infantry divisions and a new cavalry brigade.

Greek Front in the Winter

On 25 October, King Alexander died from blood poisoning as a result of a monkey's bite. His death created a succession crisis, and elections were postponed until 14 November. Then came a political shock when Venizelos, the architect of the Asia Minor venture, was voted out of office, his party gaining only 118 out of 369 seats. The new government responded by holding a referendum on 5 December for the return of exiled King Constantine, who handily won. Meanwhile, the Royalist government exacted political retribution on Venizelists in the Orthodox Church, education system, civil service, judiciary, and armed forces.

The officer corps was especially hard hit by purges. At the same time, imprisoned Royalists were released from jails and many were promoted, creating inflation in the higher ranks. Some 1,500 officers returned to active duty and 500 Venizelists lost their jobs or were removed from operational commands and placed in support units. "Apolitical" officers, i.e., neither Royalist nor Venizelist, remained in their positions but in some cases watched returning Royalists pass them by, promoted as compensation for their three years of imprisonment. The High Command also experienced turmoil. Paraskevopoulos lost his command of the Army in Asia Minor. General Anastasios Papoulas, who had spent several years incarcerated after a show trial, was promoted to lieutenant general and given command of the Greek army in Anatolia. By spring 1921, the Greek commander in chief in Anatolia, all three corps commanders, and seven of nine division commanders had been replaced. Lost in the purges were a number of experienced and competent officers. Naturally these purges further politicized the armed forces into Venizelist and Royalist factions. Fortunately for the Greek army, the captains and lieutenants were essentially untouched, thereby ensuring continuity at the critical positions of small unit commands and staff work.[25] Also fortunately for Greece, the National Army in Turkey was recovering from losses sustained in the last Venizelos offensive, and therefore the strategic initiative still lay with the Greeks.

Papoulas, the new commander of the Greek army, pushed for a military operation to demonstrate to Britain that Greece remained committed to Asia Minor. He also saw an opportunity to exploit the situation as Nationalist units were engaged in defeating Çerkez Edhem. King Constantine, who recently had returned to Greece to assume the throne, sanctioned the Anatolian venture; he found an exit strategy more difficult to articulate and implement than that of maintaining irredentist aspirations in Anatolia. Meanwhile, rather than embark on a bold offensive, Papoulas opted for a cautious approach. He ordered "a reconnaissance in force" by Greek III Corps from Bursa toward Eskişehir.[26] In military parlance, this meant a probe designed to test enemy defenses, strong enough to capture terrain if only limited resistance was met.

On 6 January 1921, Greek III Corps launched its probe and managed to capture Nationalist forward-observation positions.[27] İsmet had positioned himself at his headquarters in the Kütahya area with only one division of 3,000 men. His two other divisions were in the Kütahya region nearby, one gainfully employed against Çerkez Edhem. Encouraged by their initial successes, the Greeks decided to push ahead and, on 9 January 1921, attacked the Turkish defensive positions

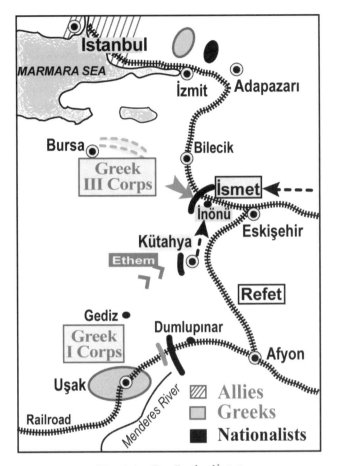

Map 5.1   *First Battle of İnönü*

before the village of İnönü, in what became known as the First Battle of İnönü, from 9 to 11 January. İsmet moved to the area under attack to take personal command, taking with him one division from Kütahya while Mustafa Kemal committed a division from Ankara to assist as well. Despite Greek superiority in numbers of troops, the weather conditions and terrain gave some advantage to the defenders. Morning fogs confused the Greek attackers. On the second day of battle, around 1310, İsmet ordered preparations for a withdrawal that evening. At 2240, Ankara approved a pullback but ordered that no artillery and machine guns be left behind. Much to the surprise of İsmet, in the early morning on 11 January, the third day, a villager reported that the Greek forces were retreating. Firm confirmation arrived at 1100. The Greeks had blinked first. İsmet quickly received approval from Ankara to organize a pursuit for 12 January.

The pursuit commenced at dawn on 12 January. Two days later, İsmet issued a circular to energize his troops to press their attacks more aggressively. In motivating them, he stressed the atrocities committed by the Greeks on the Muslim people, appealing dangerously to the emotion of revenge. The circular named devastated villages and highlighted "the forced attacks on women's honor."[28] But by then, the Greeks had returned to their original defensive positions. In the Battle of İnönü, İsmet lost 278, 95 killed and 183 wounded. Mustafa Kemal had followed these developments from a distant Ankara, where he orchestrated a propaganda effort to transform İsmet into a battle hero. On 1 March, İsmet was promoted to brigadier general, or *mirliva*, and consequently became a *paşa*.

Mustafa Kemal used the victory in the First Battle of İnönü to push his political agenda. Already on 12 January, the day after the conclusion of the battle, he claimed victory to the TBMM. On 20 January, the TBMM passed the Law of Fundamental Organization, discussed in the previous chapter. Then on 27 January, the Istanbul cabinet asked Mustafa Kemal to join its delegation going to the London Conference. Now buoyed by political and military gains, Mustafa Kemal refused the offer and instead wanted a separate invitation, and the Great Powers found it difficult not to invite the Ankara delegation.

The First Battle of İnönü had demonstrated to Mustafa Kemal and his associates that the new government in Greece had the will to expand on its Anatolian venture. So Ankara needed to give more attention to the Western Front and to expand the National Army as well. On 28 February, the TBMM broadened the ages for military service from 18 to 60. The new conscription law exempted from the draft teachers from elementary school to higher institutes. Included in the exemption were students at higher institutes, medreses, and non-Muslim religious schools, as well as scientists, doctors, and other such professionals. The law also permitted the payment of a special fee for exemptions.[29] With literacy hovering around 10 to 15 per cent, Mustafa Kemal and the TBMM thought of the future and the critical need for educated people to rebuild the country after a decade of wars. Too many talented citizens had perished in World War I. These exemptions represented a wise investment in the future.

The Ankara government continued to stress the themes of patriotism and faith. The official newspaper *Hakimiyet-i Milliye* published a poem entitled "The Turkish Soldier" by a woman named Müfide Ferid, which was addressed to the *Mehmetçiks* (the equivalent of G.I. Joes in the U.S. Army or Tommies in the British Army). "Turkish soldier! Muslim-fighting (*gazi*) soldier; blessed soldier!" Then she rattled off names of recent battlefields such as Libya, Edirne, Çanakkale, Erzurum, and Gaza, and added, "Turkish soldier, lion of Anatolia. May God be pleased with you." Müfide Ferid ended her poem with "Long live the Turkish soldier! Long live the sacred and blessed hero!"[30]

To help foster patriotism in the national psyche, months earlier the Ankara government had initiated a countrywide competition to select a national anthem. Over 700 entries were submitted to a parliamentary committee. On 12 March, the TBMM unanimously adopted the Independence March, or *İstiklal Marşı*, by the famous poet Mehmed Akıf (Ersoy). His composition ran ten stanzas with its dedication "to our heroic army." In his national anthem, Mehmed Akıf, a devoted Muslim of Albanian origin, conveyed both patriotism and Islamic faith in emotive and inspirational language and imagery without even mentioning Turkey, Turks, Ottomans, or the Ottoman sultanate and Islamic caliphate.

> *Fear not! For the crimson flag that proudly ripples in the glorious twilight shall never fade,*
> *Before the last fiery hearth that is ablaze within my nation is extinguished.*
> *That is the star of my nation, and it will forever shine:*
> *It is mine; it is solely my nation's.*

Patriotism demanded willingness for personal bravery: "Render your chest as armor and your body as trench." The anthem appealed to the human emotions of honor and shame: "You son of a martyr, take shame, hurt not your ancestor." Mehmed Akıf spoke of faith in battle thus:

> *The calls to prayer (ezan), whose martyrs are the foundations of my religion,*
> *May their noble sound last loud and wide over my eternal fatherland.*

The anthem ended with an unequivocal demand for absolute liberty:

> *For freedom is the absolute right of my ever-free flag;*
> *For independence is the absolute right of my God-worshipping nation!*

Rather than use the word *Allah* for God, Mehmed Akıf instead chose *Hakk*. On 29 May of the same year, the Ministry of Defense appreciated the value of such national sentiments so much that it decided to provide funds to the Ministry of Education as "a free gift" (*ikramiye*) to assist teachers in having their students memorize the anthem in the classroom.[31] Young schoolchildren thus became an integral part of the mobilization of society.

On 23 March, a second, much more serious battle, commenced at İnönü. This one lasted until 1 April. Athens felt increasingly isolated over the issue of

Anatolia. Britain, its best ally, still refused to provide loans to Greece; nor could the Greeks purchase British weapons. Nevertheless, on 9 March, Lloyd George gave the Greeks a green light for launching an offensive, and Athens jumped at the opportunity.[32]

The Greek general Papoulas planned for an offensive on two axes.[33] The III Corps would launch the main attack from Bursa with the aim of capturing Eskişehir. The I Corps, headquartered in Uşak, would simultaneously conduct a supportive attack in the directions of Kütahya and Afyon. Unlike the first battle, this plan called for the coordination of a two-corps offensive, one heading north to south and the other south to north. This Greek offensive confronted three separate commands. Western Command under İsmet possessed one cavalry and four infantry divisions for a combined total of 1,151 officers and 24,936 soldiers. Three divisions were deployed forward. Kocaeli Command, with 287 officers and 6,368 men, guarded the northern flank. Southern Command under Refet comprised five infantry and two cavalry divisions and a cavalry brigade with 2,287 officers and 34,044 soldiers. Two of the infantry divisions formed XII Corps; the others directly reported to Southern Command. During the two months and thirteen days between the two battles of İnönü, the General Staff and defense ministry in Ankara standardized a triangular organization for the infantry divisions. Each division comprised three infantry regiments, with each regiment composed of three battalions, along with artillery and a strike battalion. Additional division assets included a company of cavalry, of engineers, and of medical services. Division commanders were eventually supposed to have 5,000 rifles under their command.[34] In their next offensive, the Greeks would face a better organized army, but also one adjusting to its new organization.

The Greek offensive came as no surprise. From Paris on 11 March, Foreign Minister Bekir Sami, relaying intelligence information, had warned Mustafa Kemal of an upcoming main attack against Eskişehir. The next day, Mustafa Kemal passed on this information to İsmet. Then on 17 March, intelligence discovered the actual date of the attack, 23 March.[35] There was time to prepare for the Greek onslaught.

On the expected day, Greek I and III Corps began their offensives. In the north, the Second Battle of İnönü commenced on 26 March. In this battle, the Greek army committed 42,000 men, 220 artillery guns, and 24 planes; the National Army countered with 33,000 men, 103 artillery pieces, and four planes. The Greeks also possessed a small number of tanks. Heavy fighting characterized the next five days, with attacks and counterattacks by both sides, with little to show for all the effort. Ridges were lost and regained. Some commanders reported desperate situations.[36] Meanwhile, in the south, Greek I Corps at Uşak fared

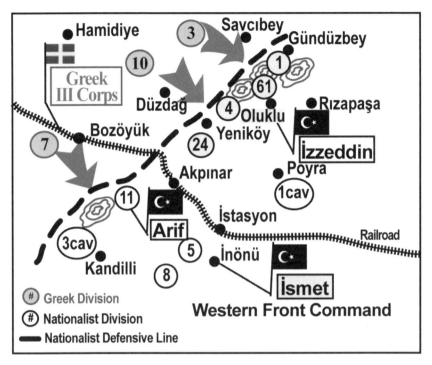

Map 5.2   *Second Battle of İnönü*

much better against Southern Command and captured Afyon on 27 March. On 28 March, Mustafa Kemal committed the TBMM's defense battalion, a force of 900 rifles and six machine guns, to the front.[37] The next day, Ankara ordered Refet to send an infantry and a cavalry division from Southern Command to help İsmet. Meanwhile, the 5th Caucasus Division from Central Army joined in the battle. On 31 March, Western Command finally broke the Greek offensive, forcing the Greeks to commence a retreat back to Bursa. This time, İsmet had defeated a corps-size attack.

When word reached Ankara of the second victory at İnönü, the city and the TBMM went into a frenzy of celebration. Mustafa Kemal proclaimed a military victory of epic proportions with inspiring words written to İsmet: "You have defeated not only the enemy but the ill fortune of our nation." Meanwhile, İsmet ordered a pursuit of the retreating Greeks. By 4 April, the battle had ended where it had started. Forty-four officers and 637 soldiers were killed, as well as losing 102 officers and 1,720 soldiers who were wounded. Total losses of killed, wounded, missing, prisoners of war, and desertions stood at 4,950. Greek figures were a little higher. Much praise was also heaped upon Fevzi, who had served as defense minister and commanded General Staff Headquarters in Ankara. For his contributions, on 3 April Fevzi was promoted to major general (*ferik*).

Fighting in the south, however, continued until 14 April. Here, Refet conducted a number of attacks to regain lost territory. The XII Corps managed to recapture Afyon during the night of 7 and 8 April. By 14 April, Greek I Corps pulled back its forces to Uşak. The Greeks had suffered a defeat that impressed upon them the emerging professionalism and combat power of the National Army. After the battles of March and April, both sides devoted more serious attention and committed more resources to this front for the next phase of the war. Meanwhile, Mustafa Kemal used the victory at the Second Battle of İnönü to present the two secret treaties with Italy and France signed by Bekir Sami to the TBMM. Strengthened by the military victory at Second İnönü, Mustafa Kemal felt confident in seeing the two agreements go down in defeat as well.

After the two İnönü battles, İnönü-Kütahya-Afyon formed the defensive line. Anticipating more fighting in the near future, the Western Front underwent a major reorganization, one of the aims of which was to establish better command and control. On 3 May, Southern Command was abolished and all forces facing the Greeks were united under Western Command. İsmet continued to hold two positions: chief of the General Staff and Western Front Commander. Fevzi remained the prime minister and defense minister. This high command structure prevented both men from focusing on one major area of responsibility, and this arrangement would disrupt the upcoming military operations.

The army overall expanded in size as the General Staff in Ankara transferred units from other fronts to the Western Command. In June, an infantry and a cavalry division reached the front from Central Army's command. In addition, another infantry division came from Ankara.[38] In July, the total army strength stood at 187,927. The Western Front had 122,131, or 64.9 per cent; the Eastern Front 16,788, or 8.9 per cent; Elcezire 12,286, or 6 per cent; Central Army 11,263, or 5.9 per cent; and the Ankara Command 9,106, or 4.8 per cent. Western Command possessed 60,103 rifles, 670 heavy and light machine guns, 162 artillery guns, and four planes.[39] Clearly, the Western Front had become the main theater of operations.

But the increase in troops required a better command and control system. During the Second Battle of İnönü, İsmet and Refet as front commanders both commanded five divisions each, and Refet also had XII Corps with two divisions. During the months of May and June, the army underwent yet another reorganization with the formation of groups or corps-sized task forces that combined two or more divisions. This reorganization streamlined the number of commands requiring direct communication from İsmet as front commander. And he had

7 *Mustafa Kemal with İsmet, early summer 1921*

an important say in choosing his commanders, thus making for better command relationships.[40] The new deployments along the front went as follows: First Group in the İnönü region; Third in Kütahya, Fourth in Çekürler south of Kütahya, and Twelfth in Afyon. The group structure functioned more as a task force without a standard organization. It needed a small staff because the responsibility for logistics fell upon the shoulders of the division commander. Each infantry division kept its triangular structure. Cavalry regiments comprised four companies and a machine gun company. The 14th Cavalry Division from Central Army became an operational reserve around Eskişehir. On 25 June 1921, to ensure internal security, the General Staff issued an order prohibiting the marriage of officers with Christian women.[41] In an interview with a *Hakimiyet-i Milliye* reporter, Mustafa Kemal expressed supreme confidence in the National Army.[42] Events would show that confidence was a bit premature. The Greek offensive caught the army still adjusting to its reorganization.[43]

Greek Summer Offensive

The military setbacks in January and March 1921 failed to deter the Greek government. Prime Minister Rallis urged the king to establish Royal Command, recalling the practice of the Balkan War, and to assume direct command as commander in chief with Dousmanis as his chief of staff. On June 12, King Constantine met with General Papoulas in Izmir, ostensibly to address the situation. All of this was done for domestic and international consumption, for Constantine functioned more as a figurehead. Meanwhile, the Athens government called up more reserves and raised the size of the army in Anatolia to 200,000, or close to twice the number of the previous year.[44] By the summer of 1921, Greece was on its own, with the army essentially facing an arms embargo imposed by the Entente Powers. Lloyd George merely offered moral support. France and Italy showed no enthusiasm for another Greek offensive. Ankara meanwhile received valuable aid from the Soviets and obtained weapons from the Italians. Greece, it appeared, was not likely to impose a military solution on Ankara in the summer of 1921.

On 10 July, Papoulas ordered the expected offensive. This time, Greece committed nine divisions organized in three army corps, and the main effort came from the south with Kütahya a key to the campaign. The aim was to capture or destroy the Turkish army by cutting off a retreat toward Ankara.[45] Western Command planned for a Greek offensive along two axes: Bursa to Eskişehir and Uşak to Kütahya.[46] However, Mustafa Kemal and İsmet expected the Greek main effort in the north, and so İsmet located his headquarters in Eskişehir. But in fact two Greek divisions from III Corps moved from Bursa to the south of Kütahya with the aim of linking up with Greek I Corps and advancing together from the south. The main effort was coming from the south, and it took time for Mustafa Kemal and İsmet to realize their error of judgment, but they never recovered to coordinate their forces and stop the Greek advances. On 13 July, the Greeks captured Afyon. On 15 July, Western Command formed the Fifth Cavalry Corps in the southern region of Yeşildağ, which consisted of three cavalry divisions under the command of Colonel Fahreddin, with the aim of gaining more concentrated mobility.[47] This cavalry corps would play an important role in subsequent battles, but it should have been formed earlier, before the July battles. On 16 July, İsmet ordered a decisive defensive battle all along the front.[48]

Despite the unfolding of a major Greek offensive, Mustafa Kemal decided to address the Congress of Male and Female Teachers' meeting in Ankara from 16 to

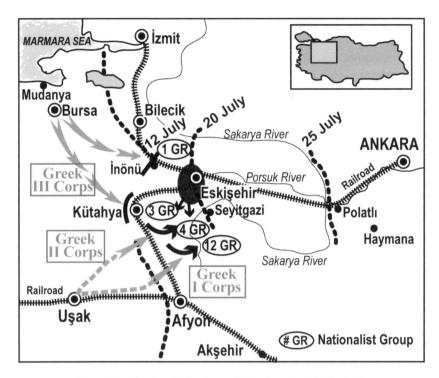

Map 5.3 *Battles of Eskişehir and Kütahya, 12–25 July 1921*

21 July. The title underscored the participation of both genders. Approximately 280 male and female teachers from all over the country attended the conference. The Ministry of Education had been established over a year earlier on 2 May 1920, and it functioned on meager funding. Dr. Rıza Nur, its first minister, underscored this harsh reality: "Naturally, we cannot do anything for now. We will work for a good administration in order to defend what we have now until the liberation of the homeland." Ankara recorded the following statistics for the year 1920. The country listed 2,345 primary schools, with 581 of them closed. There were 2,384 male and 677 female teachers, of whom only 875 had graduated from teachers' school. Ankara counted twenty-eight Imperial (*Sultani*) and fifty to sixty state (*idadi*) secondary schools, in addition to eighteen teachers' schools. Education compromised only six per cent of the overall budget. Virtually no new schools were opened in the last year; in fact, a number of school buildings were handed over for military use, such as for a hospital or medical clinic. Some teachers found their pay eight to ten months in arrears.[49]

On 16 July 1921, Mustafa Kemal delivered the opening address, referring to the gathering as "a congress of knowledge and culture of learning" (*ilim ve irfan kongresi).* Mustafa Kemal suggested that educational principles had led to the nation's decline. The goal was to establish a national program for the entire country. Turkey needed a culture of learning conducive to the development of an improved intelligence of its people. He stressed the importance of education developing civic virtues. "It is necessary to discuss a powerful love of virtue and the notion of order and discipline as qualities necessary in equipping a new generation." His message to male and female teachers carried a personal note. Although not required to fight in the army, teachers were engaged in a struggle of no less importance. He described two types of "wars" requiring two different means of fighting. One struggle employed a "weapon" (*silah*), the other the "mind" (*dimağ*). Mustafa Kemal conveyed confidence in winning both wars to the teachers.[50] On 18 July 1921, *Hakimiyet-i Milliye* reported on the education congress in an article entitled "Two Fronts," (war and education). The article described the complementary roles of the two armies. "While the army of liberation and independence is fighting the Greeks on [different] fronts, the army of teachers in Ankara is preparing a defensive program against ignorance." The article described the activities as together constituting "a cosmic event."[51]

By holding the congress, Mustafa Kemal prepared teachers for the central role that education would have in postwar Turkey. The speech was also designed to raise their morale. Teachers were a precious national asset, hence their exemption from military conscription. An abject literacy rate boded ill for the future; the country could not afford to lose any more educators. Himself an individual devoted to a pursuit of knowledge, Mustafa Kemal spoke with conviction and sincerity about the power of education. But to what end was a legitimate question to ask at the time. The timing of the conference took place in defiance of war, a situation that could not be ignored for too long. In fact, while Mustafa Kemal delivered his address to the participants, Western Command experienced a developing crisis on the battlefield that required his physical presence. So after delivering the speech, Mustafa Kemal immediately left for the front. The congress hobbled along for the next few days and ended early without achieving much. But Mustafa Kemal had delivered a clear message: waging war and preparing for peace were integral pursuits, and the wise statesmen should devote appropriate time, thought, and energy to both responsibilities and duties.

After delivering his speech to the Education Congress on 16 July, a week into the Greek offensive, Mustafa Kemal departed for Eskişehir by train, reaching the city at 0500 on 17 July. İsmet met him at the railroad station and together they went by automobile to Western Command's forward headquarters at Karacahisar, southwest of Eskişehir. After listening to intelligence reports and discussing the military situation, Mustafa Kemal realized the imperative of a pullback of forces.

Thus, he issued the following order that prepared the army for a possible general retreat. "Against the offense launched by Greece with all its power, our basic duty, which is military, is the duty that we have followed since the beginning of the national struggle. And it is, whenever facing a Greek offensive, to resist this offensive and to stop it with suitable movements and to win time in order to bring the new army into existence. And in the face of this offensive, this main thought must not be far from our view."[52] Mustafa Kemal outlined a classic strategy of giving up space for time, in this case with the aim of building the army. But this strategy was born of necessity that day, rather than a clear plan of fighting articulated by Mustafa Kemal on the eve of what became known in Turkish historiography as the Battles of Kütahya and Eskişehir. Mustafa Kemal left the front that same day, thereby distancing himself from the mushrooming battlefield crisis. İsmet spent the next week struggling to conduct an orderly retreat.

The Greeks captured Kütahya by mid-afternoon, thus threatening Eskişehir with encirclement. A major crisis was thus unfolding. At 1700 on 17 July, immediately after the loss of Kütahya, İsmet wired to the General Staff in Ankara a report of the desperate situation unfolding before him: "We have committed the greater part of the army. Not leaving the army's fate to chance, its existence depends upon pulling back to east of Seyitgazi."[53] Mustafa Kemal, meanwhile, was en route to Ankara. At 2200 on 17 July, Fevzi designated the withdrawal of all forces along the Eskişehir-Ayvacık axis, with only small covering forces left by the First and Second Groups,[54] not having formed a powerful reserve corps before the battles hurt the Turkish situation.[55] To compensate for the lack of a reserve, Mustafa Kemal assigned great importance to the Composite (*Müretteb*) Corps in the north remaining in place and thereby posing a serious threat to the Greek flank and rear, a wise move.[56] Greek forces occupied an abandoned Eskişehir on 18 July.

While pulling back forces to the Sakarya River, İsmet recommended a counterattack. On 21 July at 0230, Fevzi questioned the feasibility of such a move. According to him, both the 3rd and 14th Cavalry Divisions lacked sufficient forces for such an attack. They were also tired. Fevzi also noted that the left flank was weak and İsmet needed to strengthen it immediately with infantry from other formations.[57] Despite reservations in Ankara, İsmet launched a counterattack that day. The day ended badly for the National Army. İzzeddin, commander of First Group, attacked with two divisions toward Eskişehir only to be beaten back by the Greeks. Second Group had a similar experience.[58] By nightfall, there was no more question of anything but a rapid pull back to defensible terrain east of the Sakarya River.[59] Fourth Group commander Colonel Kemaleddin Sami confirmed this reality in his report on 22 July at 0130. Having taken heavy losses, he reported that he could not absorb another attack by the enemy.[60]

At 2110 on 21 July, even before the arrival of Kemaleddin Sami's report, Mustafa Kemal ordered İsmet to establish defenses east of the Sakarya River. Noting the lack of information on the Fourth and First Groups, Mustafa Kemal raised concern about the enemy division that had advanced to Kırk Kız Mountain, where it posed "a serious threat to the entire army." İsmet was instructed to leave a covering force to permit an orderly withdrawal. Mustafa Kemal ended his order noting that Fevzi Paşa was of the same opinion.[61] Corporate wisdom was at work. At 0100 on 22 July, Fevzi followed up on Kemal's order with detailed guidance on how to conduct the first phase of the pullback. He also raised concern about Çerkez Edhem attacking a flank.[62]

In his communiqué of 22 July 1921 to the General Staff, İsmet appeared unnerved by his defeat of the previous day. He noted difficulties in withdrawing to Sakarya in an orderly fashion. One reason was the unfavorable balance of forces. He requested guidance from the General Staff on how to fight the defensive battle.[63] In his memoirs, İsmet lay part of the blame for the defeat on the Greeks having a general mobilization after the Battle of İnönü but not the Turks.[64] But this was more of an excuse. The Greeks had surprised Ankara with their main effort and kept the National Army off balance. Over the next couple of days, Fevzi helped direct the pullback to east of the Sakarya River from General Staff headquarters in Ankara.[65] Clearly, in these battles, Mustafa Kemal and Fevzi worked closely together.

İsmet had been under great stress for a while. Halide Edip had managed to visit İsmet and had found a shaken man. Her talk of a moral victory to him failed to resonate with a man facing defeat. "He told me with bitterness that to the world it was only success that mattered. The world never considered sacrifice, however sublime and great it may be, if it was not crowned with success." Halide Edip was used to hearing such language from Mustafa Kemal, but it surprised her to hear İsmet echo the same sentiments.[66] That day, she appeared to learn something priceless about warfare and the burden of command. Losing men in battle under one's command was difficult, but losing in defeat was even more painful to bear.

Over the next couple of weeks, the National Army managed to regroup into a new defensive line east of the Sakarya River, over seventy kilometers west of Ankara. Eventually, five divisions formed the first line and two constituted the front reserve.[67] İsmet established his headquarters at Polatlı. Nationalist losses in the battles were staggering for the size of the army: 121 officers and 1,522 soldiers killed. The number of wounded stood at 267 officers and 4,714 soldiers. Adding those believed captured put the total number at 6,987. Western Command reported 30,809 men missing.[68] After the battles at Eskişehir and Kütahya, the National Army's numbers facing the Greeks had dwindled from 70,000 to 30,000 at Sakarya.[69] Many of these had deserted. These numbers added to the crisis created by the loss of the towns of Eskişehir, Kütahya, and Afyon. In addition, Ankara had lost the key railway line running north and south through these three towns. A new defensive line was very much in order. Over the next month, Mustafa Kemal rushed troops from other fronts. Much depended on the timing of their arrivals.

Confronting the Crisis

King Constantine subsequently came to Eskişehir to distribute bravery medals. Rather than being greeted with unanimous accolades, the king was surprised to hear soldiers calling for demobilization. War fatigue predominated among many soldiers, who were tired from several years of military service, a long way away from home, and were well aware of the impending sacrifice needed to reach Ankara.[70] On 24 July, Greek operations came to a temporary halt.

Two days later, a Greek war council took place in Kütahya. Political and military leaders, including Prime Minister Gounaris, joined King Constantine and Prince Andrew in the deliberations. Several courses of action were explored. One option was to await the political fallout in Ankara from the military defeats before making any decision. Others argued for resuming the offensive with the aim of occupying Ankara, destroying Ankara's infrastructure, and then withdrawing back to the Eskişehir-Kütahya line. Pressing such an attack, however, might provide Mustafa Kemal with the opportunity to rally the people around him in the face of the imminent danger to Ankara. The head of the Greek logistics branch, on his part, stressed the lack of ammunition and the danger of a possible decisive defeat.

A compromise decision was reached. The Greek army would rest for a brief period, during which time it could be replenished with more supplies. On 28 July, the plan of attack was drawn up. It called for an advance as far as the eastern section of Sakarya. If the enemy engaged and was defeated, then the advance would continue on to Ankara. If, on the other hand, the enemy set up a defensive line east of Sakarya River, then circumstances would determine the appropriate course of action. It might require withdrawing to Eskişehir but destroying the railway in the process.[71] The plan lacked a clear goal. More than that, it created confusion. Was the offensive to deliver a decisive blow or be a punitive operation?

> Papoulas allowed himself to be persuaded into launching an attack in which he only half believed, and whose objective was imprecisely formulated in the conviction that if the army ran into difficulties it could simply retire with no

harm done. The politicians, on the other hand, took the conditional hopes of the Staff memo more seriously, and had high hopes that the Kemalist army would be finally crushed.[72]

Any chance of a decisive military victory required clarity of purpose and strong will from the commander and a cooperative enemy that lacked the will for sacrifice. The Greek army found neither dynamic at work.

The meltdown of the National Army on the Western Front spawned panic and created a major crisis back in Ankara. On 22 July, Mustafa Kemal met with the Council of Ministers and decided on moving the capital from Ankara to Kayseri.[73] The next day, Fevzi had the unpleasant task of facing the TBMM in a secret session and explaining to the deputies the recent military setbacks. He emphasized the positive aspects of recent events. By fighting hard, the army had delayed the Greek advances and thus escaped encirclement. Moreover, it withdrew in an orderly fashion, preserving its cannons and machine guns. According to this reasoning, the army had suffered a tactical defeat but not a strategic one. It would live and fight again, and win the next time. Units were being rushed from all the other fronts. After providing this positive spin, Fevzi then dropped a bombshell: he informed the deputies that the Council of Ministers had decided to move the government to Kayseri. That town was in the bosom of Anatolia, well situated with respect to all the fronts.[74]

This revelation sparked a lively debate in the TBMM. Mustafa Durak, a deputy from Erzurum, asserted a well-reasoned, eloquent, and passionate argument against the decision by the Council of Ministers, forcefully labeling it "wrong" (*yanlış*). The army was not the guardian of the city, but of independence. The TBMM could not leave Ankara. Such a step would break the morale of the entire nation. Moreover, Durak expressed fear that to abandon the city would create panic in the army. If necessary, 200 deputies could take up arms and join the fight. He appealed to the employment of dispassionate reasoning: "Let us defend with our *sang-froid*, let us make judgments with logic." The nation looked up to the Assembly and followed its lead, and he called for sacrifice. His comments ignited more animated discussion. Mustafa Kemal, for his part, listened to the arguments and only interjected with a couple of minor comments.[75] The heroic passion emanating from the deputies became palpable.

A number of deputies expressed the determination to defend the capital. The TBMM decided to send a committee to the front; make military preparations to defend Ankara; to give the Council of Ministers the freedom to move to Kayseri, only if necessary; and to have the TBMM continue working without interruptions.[76] A show of defiance was necessary, but not a last-stand mentality. The deputies wanted to reassure officers and soldiers of the nation's and of their support.[77] At a critical period in the war, deputies rose to the occasion and the TBMM as an institution weathered the crisis and remained in Ankara as a symbol of the nation's mettle. A number of family members, however, did move to Kayseri over the next couple weeks.

By 26 July, all of Western Command's forces reached the east bank of Sakarya, with the exception of one division from First Group.[78] İsmet located his headquarters at Polatlı, and Mustafa Kemal and Fevzi visited him there on 26 July to help in forming a new defensive line. They returned to Ankara on 29 July.[79] On 28 July, while still at the front, Mustafa Kemal ordered the call-up of those born between the years 1889 and 1900. He selected the following areas for conscription: Bolu, Kastamonu, Çankırı, Yozgat, Çorum, Kayseri, Kırşehir, Niğde, Aksaray, Konya, Isparta, Ankara, Silifke, Burdur, Muğla, and Antalya.[80] Excluded were the eastern and southeastern regions of Anatolia, the Kurdish areas. Then on 29 July, İsmet formed a Group Reserve under the command of Brigadier General Yusuf İzzet consisting of two divisions. It was located in the Haymana and Beylik Bridge area.[81] On 1 August, back in Ankara, Mustafa Kemal reassured İsmet: "today the most important desired task is strengthening the army and people both materially and morally. The Assembly and the government will carry out this with all their power."[82]

İsmet, meanwhile, focused on preparing for the upcoming battle. On 3 August, he sent a circular addressed to heads of the bureaucracy, calling upon them to rally their officials and mobilize the people. Like Mustafa Kemal and Karabekir, he appealed to "religious duty and patriotism" (*fariza-ı diyanet ve hamiyet*) to drive the Greeks from Anatolia. He stated in unequivocal language that "We must demonstrate well to our people the greatest individual duty of Jihad or Holy War (*en büyük fariza-ı cihad*)."[83] Muslim patriotism and Muslim nationalism remained the main staples of military ethos.

On 4 August, Foreign Minister Yusuf Kemal sent a long note to his Soviet counterpart in Moscow. It began on a cosmic scale by claiming the fate of the Eastern world was being determined in these times. He recommended for the two countries to form "a common front against the imperialism and capitalism of the Western states." More than anything, Turkey wanted money and weapons, including the promised ten million gold rubles. Rather than keep matters simple, Yusuf Kemal also raised issues of the Straits, Mesopotamia, and the caliphate to underscore the threats posed to Russia. London, should Ankara go down in defeat, could use the caliphate to rally Muslims under Soviet rule.[84] Claiming financial difficulties, Chicherin promised to search for five million gold rubles. Essentially, the National Army would have to fight with what it had received to date.

Parliament's resolve to stay in Ankara raised the stakes. The upcoming battle against the Greeks loomed as a decisive one, for it involved defending the capital from occupation. Upon his return from the front, Mustafa Kemal conspired to gain extraordinary powers for him to fight and defeat the Greeks, and he relied on loyal deputies to facilitate the passage of this enabling piece of legislation. A handful of deputies submitted a bill that would confer upon Mustafa Kemal the position of commander in chief. Parliament held a secret session on 4 August to debate the proposal. On 5 August 1921, the TBMM passed Law 144, awarding Mustafa Kemal emergency powers as "commander in chief" (başkomutan) of all the armed forces. In the secret session, the measure received 169 "for" votes and 13 "against"; the public count, however, was styled "unanimous" in order to demonstrate overwhelming public support to the world.

Law 144 represented "a revolutionary step," because, according to the old Ottoman constitution, the sultan was the commander in chief.[85] The new law gave Mustafa Kemal as commander in chief the authority to make decisions in the name of Parliament on matters related to the military. Article 2 stated that "In order to develop the forces of the army materially and morally to the fullest extent, so as to secure and consolidate the leadership and the administration of these forces, the Commander in Chief will be authorized to exercise full powers of the TBMM in the name of the Assembly in these matters." Article 3 limited this authority to three months but with the possibility of renewal.[86] During World War I, Enver had commanded the armed forces as the deputy commander in chief, although in reality the sultan exerted no authority over the military. Law 144 thus reinforced how much the sultan-caliph as a person was divorced from the fight to save Anatolia from partition and how much Mustafa Kemal wanted to divorce the institution from the national struggle.

Mustafa Kemal viewed Law 144 as empowering him to give clarity of aim and unity of effort in the conduct of the war. The Greeks fell short on both scores. However, the TBMM did not relegate all authority to him as commander in chief. In addressing the deputies, Mustafa Kemal underscored that ultimate authority lay with the Assembly. Moreover, the position was limited to three months, and the Assembly could decide not to renew it. Mustafa Kemal also noted that his authority was confined to military matters only.[87] He could, of course, stretch what was meant by developing the military, but there were clear limitations to his actions. For one, Mustafa Kemal could not make treaties with other states without the Assembly's approval. Law 144 positioned Mustafa Kemal either to achieve a major success or to suffer a major setback. If he failed to defeat the Greek army in the next major battle, the Assembly could always remove him as president or assert itself more. Military success would strengthen Kemal's position. In major wars, most governments, including democracies, assume more power in order to be more effective in mobilizing the country's human and material resources to achieve victory. The Entente Powers in World War I, for example, restricted civil liberties, established censorship, and suppressed criticism to varying degrees. In Turkey's case, however, the new powers were extensive and conferred upon one man authority close to that of a full-fledged dictatorship, but not quite that far.

On the same day as the enactment of Law 144, Mustafa Kemal ordered changes in the military high command. The Greek offensive had revealed problems in the high command. Thus, in Kemal's reorganization, İsmet was to remain as Western Front commander, but relinquish his position of Chief of the General Staff. Refet was reassigned to defense minister, giving up his two positions of interior minister and commander of the Southern Front. Both İsmet and Refet, Mustafa Kemal had concluded, had carried too much responsibility by holding two positions at the same time. Now İsmet could focus his attention and energy on commanding the entire Western Front. Fevzi was elected the new Chief of the General Staff by a near unanimous vote of 183 to 1. He would serve the remainder of the war as Kemal's accessible right-hand man.

Still on the same day, 5 August, Mustafa Kemal spoke to the army and the nation in a declaration as both the president of the TBMM and the commander in chief of the army. Mustafa Kemal stressed the positive and ignored the negative: "We have created a precious Army," noting that the armies had fought with "resolve and faith," but failing to mention the recent defeat and the desertions in the army. Mustafa Kemal continued that the aim for "our national armies" remain the same: driving the enemy's army from Anatolia and liberating the country. He imparted confidence to the people by stressing that the strategic balance had tilted to the nation's side. For instance, the enemy's army was far from its base of operations. Naturally, there was no mention of contingency plans for moving the capital from Ankara to Kayseri. Toward the end of the declaration, Mustafa Kemal purposefully spoke to "every individual of the nation," reminding them of "the army that I know," one that had fought on the most important battlefield with "*civic virtues* (italics mine) and high qualities," with officer sacrifice and individual heroism. Virtue, sacrifice, and heroism were important themes for Mustafa Kemal. Such words most likely resonated better with officers than peasant soldiers.

Then Mustafa Kemal explained that the TBMM had appointed him commander in chief with the necessary authority to ensure the army's success. Achieving "liberation and independence" required the mobilization of all the country's and nation's powers. Yet, ultimately, "Success comes from divine guidance" (*Tevfik Allah'tandır*). Mustafa Kemal ended by ordering its dissemination "to the entire army down to all soldiers, all government officials, and all classes of people." His list of recipients expanded to include all provinces, all the army, the central committees of the Defense of Rights Societies, and town mayors."[88] On 7 August, *Hakimiyet-i Milliye* published the full text.

In his declaration, Mustafa Kemal had faced the nation and assumed full responsibility for the army's performance in battle. Reference to Islam as an ideological rallying cry was absent; rather, only two words called upon God's blessing. The declaration suggested that the tide had turned against the Greeks, who had overstretched their logistics lines for the upcoming battle. Yet to make this claim a reality required the National Army to break the Greek offensive with a stalwart defense.

Conclusion

Two military victories at İnönü and the Treaty of Moscow had strengthened Kemal's hand. Then, suddenly, came the unexpected major military defeat, as the Greek offensive of June and July decimated a good part of the National Army and threatened Ankara. An unanticipated crisis had compelled Mustafa Kemal to decide for the evacuation of the capital. This decision represented perhaps the lowest point in his leadership in the War of Independence. Yet a number of deputies in the TBMM never faltered but rose to the occasion and compelled Mustafa Kemal to decide on a more determined stand in defense of the capital. Seeing an opportunity for personal gain, military success, and national survival, Mustafa Kemal cleverly persuaded the TBMM to grant him extraordinary authority as commander in chief under Law 144. His immediate task was to defeat the Greeks before the gates of Ankara. He had placed his reputation and career as a leader on the line. Now, Mustafa Kemal poised the point of the spear in the sense of assuming full responsibility as a front commander. What remained was to win on the battlefield.

6

Commander in Chief

A commander in chief must also be a statesman, but he must not cease to be a general. On the one hand, he is aware of the entire political situation; on the other, he knows exactly how much he can achieve with the means at his disposal. Circumstances vary so enormously in war ... The man responsible for evaluating the whole must bring to his task the quality of intuition that perceives the truth at every point ... Truth in itself is rarely sufficient to make men act. Hence the step is always long from cognition to volition, from knowledge to ability ... that blend of brains and temperament.

Carl von Clausewitz[1]

I remind you with importance that during moments of intense combat, commanders must carefully exercise their duty and authority with mature composure and calm (*kemal-i itidal ve sükunetle*) and that they must avoid making decisions based on personal considerations and emotions that would infringe upon the general situation.

Mustafa Kemal, 1921

LAW 144 changed Kemal's position in the War of Independence. It did not create a dictatorship, but moved significantly in that direction. Mustafa Kemal put on a military uniform without rank and assumed direct command of the field army on the Western Front. In battle, he functioned as a field commander who directly observed the battlefield at key moments while, at the same time, served as the political head of the government in Ankara. Clearly, succeeding as the commander in chief would strengthen his position as president of the TBMM.

Preparations for Battle

With his new authority and facing an expected Greek offensive on Ankara, Mustafa Kemal felt the timing was right for exacting more sacrifices from his people for the defense of Ankara. On 7 and 8 August, he issued ten different commands that together became known as the National Tax Orders (*Tekalif-i Milliye Emirleri*).² Every command carried his signature as both president of the Grand National Assembly of Turkey and commander in chief. The first order created national tax commissions with branches in each district (*kaza*) to assess and collect compulsory war taxes and purchase necessary goods. Local military commanders assumed the responsibility for ensuring their proper collection. Other orders imposed specific obligations on the people. Each household, for example, was required to supply for the army a complete set of clothing that included underwear, socks, shirts, and sweaters. Shops and households were to provide 40 per cent of such items in their possession as cloth for clothes, boots, sandals, horse blankets, nails, horseshoes, and sacks for storing food and fodder. Food requisitions included sugar, rice, oil, salt, olive oil, tea, and bananas, also at the 40 per cent rate. Other orders requisitioned various weapons and animals. For most items, the tax commission issued promissory notes redeemable at some undetermined but reasonable date. With these ten orders, Mustafa Kemal sent a clear signal of the determination of the national leadership to conduct what later Turkish historiography has designated as *topyekun savaş*, or "total war." Certainly in the context of 1921, Mustafa Kemal raised the threshold of national sacrifice demanded from the people in order to attain the goals outlined in the National Pact. The TBMM, a representative institution, rallied behind Mustafa Kemal as an expression of national support and sent a message of resolve.

Approximately 30,000 troops managed to retreat in orderly fashion to the east bank of the Sakarya River. The Sakarya River was situated some seventy kilometers west of Ankara. It flowed in a great loop eastward toward Ankara, then suddenly turned northward and then westward. East of the northward turn in the river lay ridges and hills that formed a natural defensive barrier. Here is where Mustafa Kemal chose to make his stand. The advancing Greeks would have to cross the river, always a difficult maneuver, before attacking the defensive positions. Meanwhile, the Greek war council decided to launch a three-corps attack against the National Army's southern flank. From 14 to 22 August, the Greeks advanced toward Ankara with three corps composed of three infantry divisions each.

A month had elapsed since the last battle, giving Mustafa Kemal time to rush troops from the other fronts to strengthen the defenses at Sakarya. Because the eastern theater was relatively quiet, Karabekir sent all available forces and weapons to Ankara. Central Army, however, requested a month's delay, as it claimed to be engaged in fighting some 1,500 Rum, 100 Armenian, and 50 Circassian band members. These guerrilla bands served Greek military strategy by tying down some of the National troops. The Elcezire Command, when it was asked to transfer two divisions to Ankara, felt the effects of the new priority.[3] Fortunately for Mustafa Kemal, the French lacked the resources and will to launch a major offensive in support of the upcoming Greek offensive.

On the eve of the Battle of Sakarya, the Ankara government wielded authority over some 9,487,939 citizens.[4] Greece, according to its 1920 census, counted 5,536,375 inhabitants. Despite their disparity in population, the Greeks possessed a slight advantage in troop numbers, with 5,500 officers and 178,000 men, but Papoulas committed only 3,780 officers and 120,000 men for the impending battle in Anatolia. On the Nationalist side, Western Command counted 6,855 officers and 122,186 soldiers, with 5,401 officers and 96,326 soldiers at Sakarya. The National Army had 169 cannons to 286 on the Greek side; 54,572 to 75,900 rifles; 825 to 2,768 machine guns respectively.[5] The Greeks had a clear advantage overall in lethal weapons. The TBMM's army reflected the religious and ethnic diversity of Muslim Anatolia: "Sunni, Alevi, Turk, Kurd, Circassian, Abaza, Tatar, Bosnian, Laz, Pomack, [and] Arab."[6]

In the weeks before the battle, Mustafa Kemal and Fevzi closely monitored deployments in Ankara as troops kept arriving from other fronts. By 22 August, the army was in position to do battle. Starting from the south and moving northward, the groups were organized thus Fifth Cavalry Group was positioned to help protect the southern flank; it consisted of two cavalry divisions. Second Group constituted the southern flank with three infantry divisions; then came Third Group, also with three infantry divisions; Fourth Group with two; Twelfth Group with only one; and finally in the north Composite Corps with one cavalry and three infantry divisions. In the rear at Haymana, First Group with two infantry divisions formed part of the army reserve, along with three infantry and two cavalry divisions, three infantry regiments, one cavalry regiment, and one regiment of artillery.[7] This arrangement gave Mustafa Kemal a strong reserve, more troops to call forward in response to developments on the battlefield.

In his memoirs, İsmet described the simple and straightforward concept of defense: strong defenses in the center, adequate forces on both flanks, and a strong reserve. Çal Dağı formed "the pivotal point" (*istinat noktası*) in the defensive scheme; the battle-proven 57th Division was positioned there. The Fifth Cavalry Group on the southern flank had the mission of disrupting the enemy's lines of communication and its flow of supplies.[8] Fahreddin, as Fifth Cavalry Group's commander, had two cavalry divisions, the 14th with three regiments and the 4th with only two. Each division possessed Erhard batteries with four guns each and with a range of four and a half kilometers. Each regiment had four machine guns.[9] Mustafa Kemal and his command expected that the Greeks would launch their main attack on the left flank from the south where the terrain was best suited for penetration into the rear.[10]

Everything looked good on paper on the eve of battle, but the armies of the TBMM had moved into their positions with some friction and confusion. The National Army on the Western Front was battered and had recently suffered defeat. Moreover, the arrival of troops from other fronts in piecemeal fashion required regular adjustments to plans. The tribulations that faced II Corps are illustrative of the problems facing many of the units deploying from other fronts. The 9th and 5th Divisions from II Corps arrived from the Adana Front on 18 August and were renamed Second Group. Their long journey passed them through the Afyon sector. On 19 August, Second Group received its mission of anchoring defenses on the southern flank. The next day, the 5th Division was ordered to fortify the Mangal Dağı (1,414 meters high) area on the southernmost flank, a critical position if the Greeks launched their main attack there, which they did.[11] In moving into position, Second Group initially gained command of 8th and 15th Divisions, only to have the front divided and both divisions passed to the command of Third Group. This re-grouping occurred on 22 August, one day before the Greek assault.[12] First Group, which formed part of the reserve, received its final troop allocation on 21 August; it lost the 41st but gained the 24th, both infantry divisions.[13] A good deal of last-minute changes marked the final seven days before the battle, which spawned some friction and confusion, all done in an atmosphere of increasing anxiety and stress.

Mustafa Kemal at the Front

Mustafa Kemal was ready to assume full and direct responsibility for the battle. On 12 August, he and Fevzi visited the front to inspect the troops and defenses. On 15 August, while on a hilltop surveying the terrain, Mustafa Kemal experienced the serious misfortune of falling off his horse and breaking two ribs.[14] The next day saw him return to Ankara for treatment of his pre-battle wound. As noted by İsmet, throughout the battle Mustafa Kemal suffered pain and discomfort from this injury.[15] The accident accentuated the health problems that already formed an integral part of Kemal's life. But his strong will and clear mind continued to triumph over his physical ailments.

On 14 August, the Greek army began its long, nine-day march into battle, much of it over desert-type terrain where adequate water supply was of utmost importance. The Greeks were marching toward a day of reckoning. On 17 August, Mustafa Kemal hurried back to the front and remained there until the conclusion of the Battle of Sakarya. He positioned his headquarters at Alagöz, a small village ten kilometers south of the Mallıköy railroad station that afforded easy access to Ankara. Both the telegraph and telephone provided rapid communication during the battle with senior commanders in the field and with Ankara, although in the heat of battle some disruptions in the flow of information and orders occurred.

Fortunately for the historical record, Halide Edip arrived in Alagöz with direct access to Mustafa Kemal. She dined regularly with him, his aide-de-camp Colonel Arif, and İsmet and, more importantly, was present during important discussions. The house in Alagöz also served as Kemal's headquarters. Halide Edip described in heroic language her first meeting with Mustafa Kemal there on 20 August.

> The short village road is full of holes; it is muddy, and rather dark. The moon is already set. I believe it is after midnight. We cross a tiny bridge and get to the largest house in the village on the other side of the stream. . . Kemal rises from the armchair he is sitting in. His rib is evidently still very painful, for he walks with difficulty and leans against the wooden table in the middle of the room . . . At that moment I went toward Kemal Pasha with absolute reverence in my heart. In that half-built humble Anatolian room he embodied the resolve of the young to die in order that a nation might live. No palace, no title, no power will ever make him as great as he was in that room from where he was to lead the Turks to their final stand against annihilation. I went up to him and kissed his hand.[16]

Halide Edip remained at Kemal's side during most of the battle and recorded her valuable observations and interpretations.

İsmet located his headquarters in Alagöz, where he functioned more as Kemal's chief of staff than as a front commander. He held conferences with his staff and then presented proposals to Mustafa Kemal, who decided on the course of action. Still, İsmet regularly issued orders to the army as the front commander. Fevzi, for his part, moved around the battlefield, spending time at different locations. With two broken ribs, Mustafa Kemal could not easily get around the battlefield, so Fevzi provided him with eyes and ears, as can be seen from his diary showing how much he moved around.[17]

Mustafa Kemal adopted a command style appropriate for a battered and rapidly expanding army deploying along a 90-kilometer front with a depth of 25 kilometers. He kept a firm grip on minor details. In any major defensive battle, the defending army cannot hold every position; such is the nature of positional warfare, and Mustafa Kemal had to be ready to provide reinforcements at short notice for any emerging breakthroughs by the Greek army. He therefore expected group commanders to provide him with timely and honest reports. Halide Edip described Kemal's mind at work.

Kemal Pasha's knowledge of the detail, both human and material, of the army he was handling seemed to me nothing short of uncanny. He could visualize in an instant its whole ensemble, the number of every regiment down to very small units, and their position on the map. Colonel Arif supplied the exact knowledge of the lay of the land as well as knowledge of the moral qualities of many commanders.[18]

In this scenario, Mustafa Kemal relied upon Arif for valuable information on terrain and commanders to supplement his own. Victory would come, in part, from corporate expertise and experience. Mustafa Kemal brought his experience in defensive battle from Gallipoli, but the Greeks had more maneuverable space than their ANZAC counterparts. They could more easily shift troops to exploit success or to extend the front by attacking the flanks.

There in Alagöz, Mustafa Kemal faced an intellectual challenge whose roots went back to his days as a cadet. He did not want to micromanage the battle-field; nor did he seek to rob commanders of their ability to take the initiative in the fog and friction of war. Initiative, he understood, is important in war, for the battle never quite goes according to plan. *Conversation with Officer and Commander* contains some detailed discussion of this subject. At that time, Mustafa Kemal noted that it is officers at the lowest level of command who first have to confront unforeseen conditions and difficulties in battle requiring courage and initiative. How would Mustafa Kemal address this tactical issue on the eve of the battle? Two pre-battle orders stand out as his response to the timeless problems of combat.

On 19 August, Mustafa Kemal issued a Front Order (*cephe emri*) to all group commanders in which he provided general guidance on how to fight the upcoming battle. Artillery had to support the infantry. Such combined arms saved infantry lives and made for a more efficient firefight. During the battle, it was "very important" for all group commanders and their subordinate commanders to protect their lines of communication. Every subordinate commander, furthermore, had to stay in constant communication with his commander. Group commanders, on their part, had to inform army command of any important developments, whether positive or negative. Every commander was obligated to take "the initiative" (*kendiliğinden*) and immediately assist neighboring units in need of assistance.[19] In this order, Mustafa Kemal provided a clear vision of how he wanted commanders to fight the defensive battle and how they were to respond to the dynamic of combat. This guidance was designed to foster initiative vertically and horizontally among officers while providing general guidance for action.

Then on the next day, 20 August 1921, just three days before battle, Mustafa Kemal issued an order for the army, and senior commanders scrambled to disseminate the command to everyone. This order was one of his two signature commands in this war, and it provides insight into Kemal's leadership.[20] In less than a page, with only three points, Mustafa Kemal provided in succinct language a realistic vision of the upcoming defensive battle, empowering commanders with initiative but also preparing everyone, officers and men, mentally and emotionally for the unexpected in the heat of battle. First, Mustafa Kemal sought to dispel fears and raise morale by issuing words of confidence. "Our power and our duty permit us, with divine favor, to defeat the enemy." The enemy faced more difficulties than they did. In an earlier order, Mustafa Kemal had underscored that the Greek army faced peril because of long and tenuous lines of communication, and he knew that the Fifth Cavalry Group could operate in the Greek rear to make matters worse for the Greeks. Subordinate commanders, however, would have to elaborate to their troops what Mustafa Kemal meant exactly in this first part of the order.

Second, Mustafa Kemal sought to prepare each individual for the dynamic of the upcoming battle, clearly addressing the nature of combat.

> 2) Forward and reverse fluctuations at some points along a general line of battle are not unexpected events. This situation must be regarded by every unit as natural. Should a unit be forced to withdraw, neighboring units must defend their own positions with mature tenacity (*kemal-i metanetle*) and they must quickly offer artillery and infantry support to the afore-mentioned unit.

Mustafa Kemal explained to his soldiers that it was impossible for an army to hold every position, and therefore fluctuations along a long battle line were to be expected. By realistically describing the dynamic of the upcoming battle, Mustafa Kemal sought to prepare his army both intellectually and emotionally for the vicissitudes of battle while they held ground against violent Greek attacks. This part of the order empowered small-unit commanders with general guidance designed to foster initiative and courage as they carried out their duty. Mature tenacity suggested calculated resistance rather than mindless or emotional heroics.

Third, Atatürk directly addressed the intellect and emotions involved in decision-making and cautioned against letting emotions take control of sound reasoning:

> 3) I remind you with importance that during moments of intense combat, commanders must carefully exercise their duty and authority with mature composure and calm (*kemal-i itidal ve sükunetle*) and that they must avoid making decisions

based on personal considerations and emotions that would impinge upon the general situation.

Initiative had to be consistent with the mission of defending assigned positions and providing support to neighboring units. Mustafa Kemal ended by ordering that his command be read to all small units, which meant to every soldier in the army at Sakarya.

Acutely aware of the challenges in the upcoming battle, Mustafa Kemal fully appreciated that the army had just suffered defeat, and officers, soldiers, and supplies were being rushed into battle from other theaters. So the order of 20 August went out to every soldier to help them cope with the fog, friction, uncertainty, danger, fear, and chaos of war in this most critical battle to defend the government in Ankara. Rather than demand fighting to the death, Mustafa Kemal directly addressed those moments in combat when individuals might feel isolated and would have to make decisions on their own. Veterans would find some solace in knowing that their supreme commander understood the challenges facing them in the upcoming defensive battle, whereas novices had words of wisdom to guide them in the chaos of war. Moreover, this order represented intellectual continuity with the two translated German manuals and with *Conversation*, where Mustafa Kemal had emphasized the importance of preparing small-unit officers to take initiative in the face of the unexpected in combat. This notion of a mind at peace, making decisions with calm and composure, also recalls the Corps Command that Mustafa Kemal had prepared in 1916 for officers under his command in XVI Corps before heading out to the Eastern Front. The entire army at Sakarya was provided the same sheet of music with which to navigate through the combat environment. The statesman had not forgotten that he was now the commander in chief and thus playing his role of *baba*, or father of the armies of the TBMM. In essence, Mustafa Kemal demonstrated empathy for the individual officer's and soldier's plight in battle.

On 21 August 1921, Karabekir, for his part, offered advice to Mustafa Kemal on how to fight the upcoming battle: "[We must] wear out the enemy without thinking about defending this or that line or place. Hold the fronts with small forces; gather superior forces at one of the wings of the enemy and attack him there; if you are not successful try a second maneuver." Mustafa Kemal replied on the same day: "Our operational plan is along your suggestions, but a strong battle will be needed to defend Ankara."[21] In essence, though polite, Mustafa Kemal first sought a serious defensive battle to weaken the Greeks before contemplating a major counterattack. Inducing enemy attrition, then maneuvering in the attack mode was the ultimate formula, in Kemal's view. Politics certainly dictated military strategy. Deputies in the TBMM had a month earlier resisted moving to Kayseri. Thus, an initial strong defense was also necessary to avert a panic back in Ankara. Moreover, giving ground and attacking flanks requires a trained and cohesive army, which Mustafa Kemal lacked at the time. Simplicity in plans, aims, and methods was more important at this stage in the war.

Intelligence reports indicated that the Greek army had begun moving with the aim of attacking the left wing. Consequently, on 21 August, Mustafa Kemal phoned Fevzi at 1840 to assign more forces there. The 23rd and 24th Divisions and the Topal (Lame) Osman Ağa Regiment moved to Haymana to strengthen the operational reserve in the area between Toydemir and Mangal Dağı, with the expectation that the enemy might attempt to encircle from the south and then head in a northeastern direction. Mustafa Kemal also wanted to reinforce the forward positions between Toydemir and Sapanca and stationed the 57th Division as a reserve for this part of the front.[22] Then, the next day, at 1345, he asked Fevzi in writing for his opinion on moving more troops from the right to the left flanks. Fevzi's reply of 2015 came too late to affect matters.[23] But by this action, Mustafa Kemal demonstrated a willingness to seek advice and input from others. It was a fight of the collective.

Battle of Sakarya, 23 August to 13 September

The Greeks launched their offensive on 23 August. Most of the TBMM Army held its defensive positions for the first few days. However, a major problem developed on the southern flank, where the Greeks launched their main effort led by Greek I and II Corps. Six Greek divisions crossed the shallow Gök River, a tributary that flows into the Sakarya River, and moved on Kemal's southern flank. Greek II Corps, commanded by Prince Andrew, had the southernmost route, with the aim of turning the flank and breaking into the rear. Second Group, under the command of Colonel Salaheddin Adil, had the main responsibility for guarding this avenue of approach. His 9th Division defended on the right, 5th Division held the left based on Mangal Dağı, and 4th Division deployed to the rear of the 5th at Yaprakbayırı. Flat terrain stood between Mangal Dağı and Türbe Tepe. To the rear of Second Group stood First Group as part of the army reserve under Colonel İzzeddin, Kemal's chief of staff in much of World War I.

The Battle of Sakarya began on a bad foot on the southern flank. At 1845 on the first day of battle, İzzeddin received word from Salaheddin Adil that the Greeks were threatening Second Group's left wing. In response, İzzeddin decided to move with the 24th Division and the 47th Regiment to the Büyükgökgöz region, leaving the 23rd Division at Haymana. Unfortunately for the National

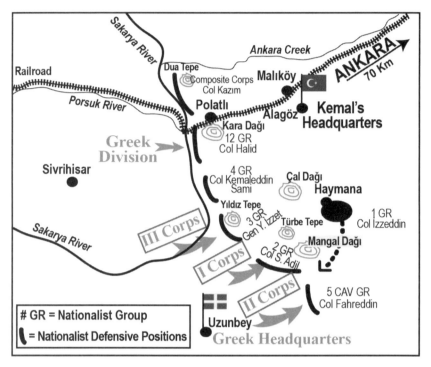

Map 6.1 *Battle of Sakarya, 23 August 1921*

Army, Mangal Dağı fell to the Greeks during the first night of battle. So the next day, front command placed the 2nd and 3rd Cavalry Divisions under İzzeddin's command to help secure the southern flank.[24] On the morning of 24 August, Mustafa Kemal ordered Fevzi to assume temporary command of the First, Second, and Third Groups with the mission of securing the southern flank. Fevzi established his command post at Haymana and stayed there until Greek advances forced him to join Mustafa Kemal at Alagöz on 1 September.[25]

Mustafa Kemal was livid when he learned that the 5th Division had abandoned Mangal Dağı. It appeared that its defenders had failed to put out a serious fight. Small units might pull back, but not an entire division, Mustafa Kemal reasoned. He immediately issued a command to Second Group and Front Commands ordering an investigation to examine the causes of what he called "inexperience" (*acemilik*). Moreover, all the commanders, officers, and soldiers in the 5th Division had to redeem their "fame and honor" (*şan ve şeref*) by throwing back the enemy. Mustafa Kemal demanded "sacrifice and zeal" (*fedakarlık ve gayret*) in the name of "religious and patriotic duty" (*bir vazife-i diyanet ve hamiyettir*). In addition to these appeals, he threatened courts-martial and executions for those committing errors. Everyone in the division had to listen to the order and understand it, and the front commander had to verify that this was done.[26] Kemal's command pushed the standard buttons: emotions of shame and honor and inner values of religious faith and patriotism, but he raised the stakes with the threat of execution. The effectiveness of his order depended on the officers and how they rallied their men under this combat duress.

The saga of the 5th Division represented a microcosm of the challenges facing the regular army. Lieutenant Colonel Mehmed Kenan (Dalbaşar), the division commander, had been in command of the Mardin sector of the Elcezire front. He had suppressed a rebellion by the Kurdish tribe of Milli Aşiret, and then in December 1920, he had been transferred to fight the French in an attempt to lift the siege of Anteb. This responsibility involved coordinating military operations with National Forces and friendly Kurdish tribes. At the end of July 1921, the 5th Division was ordered to Afyon and then moved to fight for three straight weeks a pitched battle against the Greeks at Sakarya. The 5th Division had fought in three different theaters against three different foes, which had required an adjustment in mindset, tactics, and organization.

Kenan filed a spirited report in his own defense. Both the 5th and 9th Divisions arrived in the Sakarya area on 18 August, five days before the battle. Kenan spent two days with his division before receiving the mission to defend Mangal Dağı. On 21 August, his troops commenced setting up defensive fortifications, working day and night for two straight days before the Greek onslaught. During his preparations, Kenan requested additional artillery and received a battery of three Russian mountain guns, but these kept malfunctioning during the battle. Kenan underscored, moreover, the imbalance of forces arrayed against him. According to his figures, 4,000 to 5,000 Greeks had attacked his 1,000 to 1,200 Turks. Considering that his unit was vastly outnumbered, Kenan blamed the Second Group commander and higher command for not giving him enough time and troops to face what became the Greek main effort. In addition, he emphasized that his group commander, Kemaleddin Adil, had sanctioned his pullback in order to avoid the encirclement of the division.[27]

There was merit to Kenan's defense. Responsibility for the dilatory deployment of his division also involved Mustafa Kemal, who had monitored events closely. Other problems plagued Kenan's command. The 5th Division had arrived without pickaxes with which to construct earthen fortifications, so it was, perhaps, understandable that some places lacked trenches. In addition, there were no fortifications on top of Mangal Dağı and the trenches on the slopes looked only in a southern direction, and the Greeks broke through in the valley between Mangal Dağı and Türbe Tepe. In setting up his defenses, Kenan deployed his three infantry regiments on the front line with only a reserve of one battalion and engineer company. This reserve proved inadequate to stop the Greek break-through.[28] Kenan's situation appeared extremely difficult.

Unable to regain Mangal Dağı, Kenan lost his command and suffered great embarrassment. The firing, however, did not irrevocably damage Kenan's military career, as he eventually retired from the army during the Republic era with the rank of major general after having served as a corps commander. Given Kenan's difficult situation, Mustafa Kemal let his emotions get the better of him and over-reacted. On a related note, the 5th and 9th Divisions had arrived together in enough time to slow down the Greek flank attack. If the Greeks had managed to launch their offensive a week earlier, they might have seriously imperiled the army at Sakarya. Thus, Kemal's decision on 22 July to abandon Ankara for Kayseri made some military sense, given his depleted forces at the time. Chance smiled upon him when the Greeks delayed their offensive for a month.

In his memoirs, İsmet described the basic rhythm of the Battle of Sakarya thus: "We were always writing short and definite sentences to our units . . . There was always the demand to have a decisive defense in place. When we lost a hill in a particular place, the order went out immediately for a counterattack to take back the hill."[29] In one sense, there was little art to this positional warfare on a constricted battlefield. The tactical attacks were frontal assaults. Planes dropped bombs, some on Ankara, and artillery duels took place as well. But much of the combat was at relatively close range involving rifle fire; some engagements even required bayonet fighting. Here was a repeat of some features of the Gallipoli campaign, but without the naval gunfire. The Greeks, for their part, selected dif-ferent sectors to find weak spots, sometimes to no effect and a couple of times with significant results.

Continued Greek attacks along the front created a second crisis. The Greeks captured terrain, inflicted heavy casualties, and threatened to turn the southern flank. There, the four Nationalist divisions were forced to pull back from their front lines, joined by Third Group. They formed a new front line that faced directly south. In response to what appeared to be a collapsing front, sometime in the evening of 26/27 August Mustafa Kemal produced a new operational–strategic concept for waging war against the Greeks:

> There is no line of defense. There is a plain of defense. That plain is the whole country. Not an inch of the country should be abandoned until it is drenched with the blood of citizens. Every unit, large or small, can be dislodged from its position, but every unit, large or small, will re-establish its front in the face of the enemy at the first spot where it can hold its ground, and will continue fighting. Units which observe the neighboring ones forced to retire must not link their own fate to these; they must hold their positions to the end.[30]

Mustafa Kemal described this strategic concept in the presence of Fevzi, İsmet, Western Command's chief of staff Asım, and the front's operations chief Tevfik (Bıyıklıoğlu).[31] That same evening, Mustafa Kemal also ordered defense minister Refet to move Parliament and the Council of Ministers to Kayseri. He described the move as a prudent measure and expected the process to be completed by the evening of 29 August.[32]

Mustafa Kemal was prepared to employ a new military strategy. Tactically, the army would continue to resist, and, if necessary, conduct an orderly retreat, making the Greeks pay in blood and treasure for every inch of territory. Operationally, Mustafa Kemal would pull the Greeks deeper into Turkey, while abandoning Ankara in order to save the army, rather than allow it to be destroyed by fighting in place. By retreating, the army could ultimately launch a major counterattack on an overextended invading army. Strategically, the people would refuse to accept defeat and fight until they achieved ultimate victory. There, during the night of 26–27 October, Mustafa Kemal was articulating his mindset and commitment to total war.

While prepared for a worst-case scenario, Mustafa Kemal was not yet ready to order a general pullback of the army. Rather, from his forward position at Haymana, he sent out orders throughout 27 August for the army to keep fighting in place, and he eventually rescinded his command to move the government

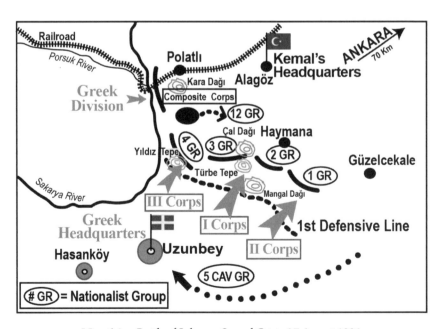

Map 6.2 *Battle of Sakarya, Second Crisis, 27 August 1921*

from Ankara to Kayseri. At 1040, for example, First Group's commander was advised to commit all his reserves so that the enemy did not become accustomed to winning battles in echelon.[33] Mustafa Kemal ordered Twelfth Group to redeploy from its position in the north facing west to the south, a move that helped prevent a breakthrough by the Greeks. Then at 2200, Mustafa Kemal ordered all group commanders to "defend to the last man." The enemy had not yet gained "a serious success," and Mustafa Kemal believed that there should be no doubt about the enemy's defeat in the very near future. If the enemy continued with night attacks, these should be repulsed with bayonet charges if necessary.[34] On 27 August, while the battle was progressing with intensity, a cavalry unit from Fahreddin's Fifth Cavalry Group unknowingly wandered into the Greek rear and came close to capturing none other than Papoulas, the Greek commander.

This was an intense period for Mustafa Kemal. A Greek breakthrough would drastically change the complexion of the battle. For Mustafa Kemal, there never seemed enough men, artillery, or ammunition, as reports from field commanders spoke of ammunition shortages, heavy losses of officers, or the lack of reserves. Mustafa Kemal, consequently, labored to economize his assets as best as possible. Halide Edip noted: "He often spoke longingly of the days in the Dardanelles when he could send eleven thousand (sic) to death in one battle. However, he was very careful this time. Every evening the diagram with the detailed list of men and arms

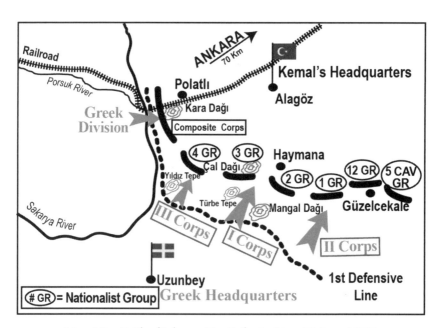

Map 6.3   *Battle of Sakarya, New Defensive Lines, 30 August 1921*

had to be presented to him."[35] The loss of human life in large numbers brought out flashes of Kemal's cynicism: "You will always find enough men in this country to send to death with or without reason. No one ever asks questions about the waste of human life."[36] But now men were desperately needed to save Ankara.

On 29 August, Papoulas renewed his efforts to force a breakthrough, this time in the center. Two fresh Greek infantry divisions and two other fresh regiments joined in the fight. The Greeks managed to break into the second line of defenses. Here, Mustafa Kemal regarded Çal Dağı as the key to his defenses. With its commanding view of the countryside, Çal Dağı formed a natural defensive position. On 31 August, Greek forces captured the western side of Çal Dağı. İsmet responded by issuing Order 31, commanding all forces to hold their positions.[37] Meanwhile, Mustafa Kemal created the Çal Front Command under Colonel Şükrü Nail (Gökberk). In addition to his own 15th Division, Şükrü Nail received the 24th Division. He was to report directly to Mustafa Kemal, who continued to function as a tactical commander.[38] Nationalist units held the eastern side of the mountain, and both sides attacked and counterattacked until Çal Dağı finally fell to Greek forces on 2 September. Kemal's direct intervention had failed to avert this loss. In addition to the fall of Çal Dağı, the Greek army cut the Haymana-Polatlı road running northeast and southwest, thereby threatening to split the National Army in half. Greek troops were within several kilometers or so of Polatlı. The darkest period in the war had arrived in Alagöz.

What proved to be twenty-two days and nights of battle placed great stress on Mustafa Kemal. İsmet described a cool, calm, and collected Mustafa Kemal during the battle.[39] Yet Halide Edip, for her part, painted a different picture. "There was something in Mustafa Kemal Pasha during Sakarya which he never had before or after. He was less cynical; he was not quite sure that this would lead to victory, and he saw that he had to die with the rest if the disaster took place. He was feeling almost as a condemned man would feel toward his comrades who will die with him."[40] At other times, Mustafa Kemal appeared beside himself. "He fumed, swore, walked up and down, talked loudly, summed up the situation with [the] rare lucidity of a delirium, and tormented himself with indecision as to whether he should order the retreat or not."[41] Reality is closer to İsmet's description. But to have been a completely cool, calm, and collected commander through it all would have been inhuman. The stress of battle took its emotional toll, and momentous decisions did not come easily. So Halide Edip does provide a glimpse into those tense periods.

Despite the pain from his broken ribs, Mustafa Kemal ventured out of Alagöz on several occasions to visit commands and observe battles with either Fevzi or İsmet.[42] At Sakarya, Mustafa Kemal, Fevzi, and İsmet worked well as a team, providing a collective effort, each with his area of responsibility. Together they sustained each other during this most critical period on the battlefield. Fevzi had outranked Mustafa Kemal in the Ottoman army, and he was a devout, practicing Muslim who found solace and strength in his faith. He came from a traditional, religious family. His education included learning Arabic and Persian and studying Islamic philosophy. During battles, he was known to read the Qur'an for extended periods or pray his beads.[43] His service record indicated knowledge of French, German, and English, as well as Albanian, Serbian, and Bulgarian. The latter languages stemmed from fifteen years of service in the Balkans. He exuded confidence and optimism based on a good sense of the battlefield. Fevzi would remain in command of the army throughout Kemal's presidency in the Republic, retiring in 1944.

İsmet had language competence in German, French, and English, also. Unlike Fevzi, İsmet had collaborated before with Mustafa Kemal. He had supported Mustafa Kemal at the 1909 CUP Congress in advocating the army's separation from politics and had served under him as chief of staff and then corps commander in World War I. Both men had long talks during that global conflict and in Istanbul before Kemal's departure for Anatolia in May 1919. İsmet possessed a mild personality; he worked to build harmony and soothe hurt feelings or bruised egos. "So he stood like a buffer state between Mustafa Kemal Pasha and those who he might easily have offended to the disadvantage of their cause."[44] İsmet served as prime minister through much of the Kemalist period, falling out of favor in 1937.

Fevzi left an important mark on the Battle of Sakarya. On 3 September, he went out to inspect the battlefield and telephoned back with encouraging words. The Greeks had spent themselves, he believed, and were not ready to continue serious offensive operations. Haymana, the last defensive position before Ankara, was a bridge too far for them.[45] Fevzi's assessment helped Mustafa Kemal to stay the course and continue to defend in place. In fact, late on 2 September, Papoulas had ordered a day of rest. Both armies needed rest after eleven days of battle. Shortages of supplies of food and ammunition added to the Greek woes and helped drive them into a tactical pause. Interdiction by the Nationalist cavalry in the Greek rear, in addition, had degraded the flow of logistics to the front.[46] The period between 4 and 7 September saw continued engagements.

On 8 September, a day of quiet along the front, Mustafa Kemal ordered Fevzi to go to the north and confer with Kazım (Özalp), the commander of Composite Corps. There, Fevzi and Kazım observed some Greek troops pulling back toward the west and concluded that the time seemed ripe for launching an offensive from the north, spearheaded by Composite Corps. Mustafa Kemal decided to see for himself and took İsmet with him. Both men arrived on 9 September around 1500 to observe Greek dispositions from atop what became known as Zafer Tepe, or Victory Hill. Fevzi presented his case for an attack, and Mustafa Kemal agreed. Plans were drawn up immediately. Kazım would lead the assault with one cavalry and four infantry divisions, with the goal of capturing Dua Tepe and Üç Pınar. İsmet also brought the 57th Infantry Division as a reserve, with the aim of launching an attack all along the front. South of Kazım, Brigadier General Yusuf İzzet Paşa would command the attack by combining the First, Second, and Third Groups. Meanwhile, Fifth Cavalry Group would continue its harassment operations in the Greek rear.[47]

On 10 September, Composite Corps launched its main effort on the Greek left flank with the aim of outflanking the Greeks. Throughout the day, Mustafa Kemal, Fevzi and İsmet observed the attack from atop Zafer Tepe, while fierce fighting took place below them. The next day, Papoulas ordered a general retreat

8 *Mustafa Kemal with binoculars directing operations, 10 September 1921*

to the west of Sakarya, and Mangal Dağı fell into Nationalist hands. On 12 September, Mustafa Kemal returned to Zafer Tepe to observe Kazım launch his attack again with the reinforced Composite Corps.[48] Çal Dağı was occupied on that day. The tide had turned for the Nationalist side. That day, Mustafa Kemal issued Front Order No. 43 calling upon the army to defeat the Greeks before they completed crossing the Sakarya.[49] The Greek army managed to use the night of 12–13 September to cross over to the west side of the Sakarya River. On 13 September, the last Greek division completed its crossing. No Greek forces were left on the east side of the Sakarya.

The National Army had won the Battle of Sakarya. Its losses amounted to 5,713 killed and 18,480 wounded. Officers accounted for 1,500 of these casualties; Greek losses were comparable. A British intelligence analysis explained the Greek defeat as stemming from overconfidence, poor intelligence, a too-complicated plan, faulty ammunition supply, and poor staff work.[50] The National Army, on its part, had fought with tenacity, with commanders and staff adjusting troop dispositions to prevent a major Greek breakthrough. The Greeks, consequently, were forced to fight for every inch of ground. The battle of attrition eventually broke their will. Mustafa Kemal, Fevzi, and İsmet had worked well together as a team to provide effective leadership. Mustafa Kemal made all the important final decisions, but Fevzi deserved special recognition for his intuition, or *coup d' œil*, at a key point during the battle. İsmet provided good staff work.

On 13 September, İsmet issued Order Number 45 calling for the pursuit of the retreating Greek army and gave each of the five groups its marching orders.[51] The Greek retreat proved orderly enough. Moreover, on the Nationalist side, the huge losses of officers, as high as 80 per cent in some units, left a less agile army. It took time to put together a pursuit. Meanwhile, in their general retreat to Eskişehir and Afyon, the Greeks burned a large swath of the countryside, in large measure to slow down any pursuing troops. The pursuit phase lasted until 10 October, when both armies settled into new defensive positions. The initiative in the war now passed to the Ankara government. A year would pass before the next and final round in the war.

A Military and Political Victory

Mustafa Kemal moved quickly and deliberately to take full advantage of the military victory. On 13 September, he ordered a general mobilization, but not solely for a military purpose. Refet Paşa, the minister of national defense, learned from him that "The declared general mobilization is designed simply for political effect externally."[52] This step sent a political signal to the world of the country's determination to continue its struggle for full independence. But more troops would be needed as well.

Meanwhile, on the same day, Mustafa Kemal changed the army's organizational structure. Groups became corps and kept their commanders. Each of the four regular corps would gain a standard organization of three infantry divisions of three infantry regiments each.[53] The only cavalry corps also received three cavalry divisions, but each division possessed four regiments. Three infantry divisions were disbanded and merged with other formations. Among the three was the 5th Division, of Mangal Dağı fame. Of the five corps commanders, only Colonel Kazım was promoted to brigadier general.[54] Mustafa Kemal, Fevzi, and İsmet sent a special note of appreciation to Fahreddin for his corps' service and sacrifice.[55] Fahreddin and his Fifth Cavalry Group played an important role in defeating the Greeks. Their military operations in the Greek army's operational rear provided valuable intelligence, disrupted the flow of supplies, and forced the Greeks to place more attention on security.

Then, as commander in chief, Mustafa Kemal broadened his authority over the army and the government in a new order issued that same day to the presidency of the TBMM and the ministers and the armies. To simplify matters, the Secretariat (*Kalem*) of the commander in chief was abolished. Henceforth, the commander in chief assumed direct control over the Ministry of the National Defense and the General Staff. In addition to the defense ministry and the General Staff Directorate, other ministries would be expected to provide officials from their particular ministry when called upon by the commander in chief.[56] This order was designed to help Mustafa Kemal mobilize more effectively both the military and civilian sectors.

On 14 September, Mustafa Kemal delivered "A Declaration to the Nation (*Millet*)", in which he revealed his Turkist sentiments with the frequent use of the word *Türk*. Credit for the victory at Sakarya went first of all to "the bayonets of the courageous Turkish soldier." The declaration spoke of "the Turkish government" and "the Turkish nation." The enemy had attacked into Anatolia without thinking of "the love of the fatherland in the chests of Turks;" he had not considered "the legitimate right of the Turkish nation." The people had placed their faith in "our struggle for independence" and made sacrifices in money, people, weapons, animals, vehicles, and other necessary items. The declaration called upon "the legitimate right of the Turkish nation whose goal was none other than to live free like every other civilized nation inside its national borders free of foreign meddling and be accepted by the world of humanity and civilization."[57] By his frequent use of the word "Turk," Mustafa Kemal placed the Turkish people in a prominent position in the national struggle, at least in this important address.

On 16 September, Mustafa Kemal returned to Ankara, leaving to his commanders the mission of conducting a pursuit.[58] Three days later, he delivered his victory speech to the TBMM, basking in the glow of victory. The deputies first heard a summary of the battle through its various phases. Mustafa Kemal stated that the enemy had sought "to annihilate (*imha*) our army," reach Ankara and scatter the government and the TBMM, and gain control of all of Anatolia; he referred to the Greeks as "Crusaders" (*ehl-i salib*). But who was worthy of praise? Mustafa Kemal first singled out two commanders for special recognition: Fevzi and İsmet. Fevzi appeared as a man of strong character, a virtuous and valuable person always ready to work tirelessly, always projecting joy and raising morale. İsmet possessed "a profound intelligence" (*derin bir zeka*) with a talent for minute detail. Always tireless, he showed ability to command and control a battlefield. Given İsmet's shaky performance earlier, the truth was stretched a bit. More to the point, Mustafa Kemal discovered that he could work well with both men, and his judgment and intuition proved accurate. During the entire period of Kemal's presidency of the Republic (1923–1938), Fevzi kept the army loyal. Meanwhile, İsmet served faithfully as prime minister from 1925 to 1937 until a rift with Mustafa Kemal resulted in his firing.

Mustafa Kemal also recognized the bravery, courage, and sacrifice of officers in general. Some 80 per cent of the officer corps suffered casualties. Consequently, Mustafa Kemal designated Sakarya as the "the officers' battle" (*zabit muharebesi*), a designation that remains today in Turkish historiography. He also praised "the courage of the Turkish soldier." Linking military outcome to diplomacy, Mustafa Kemal highlighted the friendship with Russia as important, "because Russia before anyone recognized our national rights" and provided invaluable material assistance. The struggle would end only when there were no enemy soldiers left in Anatolia.[59] True independence required removing every foreign soldier from Anatolian soil. Immediately after this rousing speech, the Assembly passed the proposal conferring on Mustafa Kemal the rank of field marshal, or *müşir*, and the title of *gazi*, or hero and holy warrior fighting for the Islamic faith, a title used by sultans. From the front, on 14–15 September, İsmet and Fevzi, as deputies from Edirne and Kozan respectively, had sent their proposal and sixty-three deputies had prepared the ground for this award.[60]

On 20 September, in the midst of the pursuit, Mustafa Kemal issued a declaration to the Army filled with praise for having achieved a victory. It was a battle waged over twenty-one days and twenty-one nights for the entire country, for its existence and independence. He described the victory as based on ideas and faith. Then he singled out three groups for their specific contributions. Commanders had shown resolve and "deep and sensitive intelligence" in developing plans in the face of increasing danger. They had also demonstrated great skill in the command and control of their troops. Officers, for their part, exhibited boundless courage and zeal out of love for their nation in the face of "a new death hovering over their young and noble heads." Soldiers fought with "conviction, faith, and obedience:" like iron, they were without fear. "The greatest part of every victory is yours," Mustafa Kemal claimed. The declaration labeled the battle as "the noblest and greatest holy war" (*en şerefli ve an ulu bir gaza*) and gave thanks to God.[61] In this address, Mustafa Kemal remained faithful to *Conversation with Officer and Commander*, where he discussed the need to treat an army not as a "herd" but as human beings. In this sense, Mustafa Kemal avoided speaking to the army as one mass or herd of people, but instead highlighted the specific contributions made by each of the three separate and distinct groups in the army: commanders, officers, and soldiers. He also idealized the motivations behind the soldiers' fighting. For many, though, it was mainly their job and their fate to follow orders and fight with their brothers in arms.

The Turkish pursuit of the Greeks ended on 8 October. On 3 October, before the new front stabilized, İsmet approved an east to west frontal attack by II and V Corps into the Greek positions in the region of Afyon, while the 6th Infantry Division attacked southwest of Afyon from Kocatepe in a northerly direction. The attack was put together hastily and lacked a main effort. Moreover, Greek I Corps had raced from Eskişehir to the Afyon region in enough time to defeat this Turkish effort. The Battle of Afyon, which lasted from 3 to 8 October, took place with İsmet at Polatlı and Mustafa Kemal in Ankara, far from this effort.[62] During the bulk of the pursuit phase, Mustafa Kemal was busy in Ankara on the political and diplomatic fronts. His presence at the battle would not have changed the outcome at Afyon. The Greeks had occupied defensible positions atop hills, and the Nationalist Army needed time to organize its forces. After twenty-two days and nights of fighting, coupled with heavy losses in the officer ranks, it was too battered a force to mount a major offensive with the aim of delivering a decisive blow to the Greek army.

In the second week of October, both armies had settled into their defensive positions. Greek III Corps deployed in the north centered on Eskişehir, while I and II Corps located in the southern half, including Afyon. On the Nationalist side, I, III, and IV Corps and Kocaeli Group deployed in the north to defend Ankara and face Eskişehir and Kütahya; II and V Corps faced Afyon in the south. The headquarters for the commander in chief and the front commanders were both located in Polatlı. The Greek army's defeat at Sakarya, meanwhile, created a political crisis in Greece. The Athens government now hid behind a defensive line impossible to defend everywhere. Fortunately for Greece, Ankara lacked the means to launch a major offensive. But the strategic initiative, nonetheless, had passed to the Nationalists. It was for Mustafa Kemal to choose the time, the place, and the manner of the next major offensive.

Although Italy failed to reach an agreement ending its occupation of Anatolia until the end of the war, France followed a different route. While the National Army was still engaged in a pursuit of the retreating Greek army, French politician Henry Franklin-Bouillon arrived in Ankara on 20 September with the authority to negotiate for France. Negotiations with Foreign Minister Yusuf Kemal (Tengirşenk) dragged on for a month before both sides signed the Ankara Agreement on 20 October. France wanted to avoid appearing to have sold out its ally Britain. So Turkey and France concluded an "agreement" (*itilafname*) rather than a formal treaty. The accord ended the state of war between the two countries. France agreed to abandon southeastern Anatolia. However, the province of Hatay with its town of İskenderun remained under French control but with a special administration. There, the Turks could fly their Turkish flag, develop cultural institutions, and use Turkish as an official language. The French failed in their effort to keep Capitulations (extraterritorial rights for French subjects) in place, and Mustafa Kemal agreed to protect the rights of minorities on the basis of the National Pact. Turkey, furthermore, recognized the French mandate over Syria. Overall the Ankara Agreement represented a major diplomatic victory, following upon the heels of a military triumph at Sakarya. In negotiations, Mustafa Kemal compromised on Hatay, which the National Pact had included within its borders.

In the parliamentary discussions, some deputies seriously opposed the agreement because it fell short of the National Pact, mainly over the issue of İskendurun. Mustafa Kemal brushed aside their objections in an interesting manner, saying "The National Pact has no definite or established line. The line that we establish with force and power will be the boundary."[63] For Mustafa Kemal, it was prudent to seek a realistic and achievable peace.[64] His speech of 24 April 1920 to a secret session of Parliament spoke of goals within material and spiritual capabilities. Compromise with France was necessary. Now in a secret session of the Assembly on 18 September 1921, Mustafa Kemal spoke of not abandoning İskendurun and Antakya. Rather, both areas would have Turkish officials, Turkish schools, Turkish as an official language, and fly the Turkish flag. The aim was eventually to have a Turkish government there.[65]

The TBMM accepted the agreement on 12 October, which was officially signed on 20 October 1921. Both countries exchanged correspondence that granted France some economic concessions. A French group could exploit iron, chrome, and silver mines in the Harchite valley in the Adana region with a ninety-nine-year lease subject to Turkish law and with 50 per cent investment and control by Turkish capital. The French, for their part, agreed to leave their war supplies in Cilicia and even provide more war *matériel*. By this accord, France formally recognized the Ankara government, which undermined the Treaty of Sèvres.[66] With Southeastern Anatolia now secure, Ankara shifted more troops to the main front against the Greeks. The Ankara Accord dealt a major blow to the pro-Greek policy of the Lloyd George government. France and Turkey had reached a negotiated settlement, with Mustafa Kemal wisely agreeing to some concessions in the interests of peace.

Relations with Russia kept bringing benefits to Ankara. In September, Mustafa Kemal sent shipments of corn and other grains to help the Soviets address their famine. Then Karabekir signed the Treaty of Kars on 23 October with the governments of Russia, Azerbaijan, Armenia, and Georgia, securing Turkey's eastern boundary. This agreement confirmed the Treaty of Moscow, but the Soviet Republics of Georgia, Armenia, and Azerbaijan also affixed their signatures. It took an important military victory against the Greeks in September, followed by an agreement between Turkey and France, to help bring about the Treaty of Kars. On 13 December, Mikhail Frunze, a successful Russian military commander and a member of the Central Committee of the Bolshevik Party, arrived in Ankara at the head of a mission with the aim of improving relations and signing a Turkish-Ukraine treaty. Mustafa Kemal permitted him to visit the troops and observe a maneuver. Frunze also addressed the TBMM. On 22 December, Frunze filed a report to Chicherin stressing the Turkish army's shortages and recommending extensive material and financial support, including the outstanding promissory note of 3.5 million gold rubles.[67] On 2 January 1922, Frunze and Yusuf Kemal (Tengirşenk) signed a Treaty of Friendship between Turkey and Ukraine. Mustafa Kemal, for his part, continued to stroke Moscow for badly needed assistance.

On 5 January, Frunze departed for Moscow. En route, he met the new incoming Soviet ambassador to Turkey, Semen Aralov, in Samsun and provided him with an assessment of Mustafa Kemal and the national struggle. The Turkish regular army, he told Aralov, was still in the process of building, and the Ankara government faced frequent rebellions and uprisings. Frunze underscored the lack of political unity in Turkey during their national struggle: "Things are hard for Mustafa Kemal. There is no single united party. There are many pashas who will do anything to sate their craving for power. Mustafa Kemal says he relies on the nation, but he himself knows that the nation is not united." In other words, Mustafa Kemal understood that "national will" did not mean unity of effort and purpose by the people, but rather the concept claimed to represent, at best, a majority position. Frunze went on to describe Mustafa Kemal as "a subtle diplomat, and not only with foreigners but with his own entourage as well. People often lie to him, but he understands that ... He told me that he had constantly to keep an eye on the moral standards and *conscience* (italics are the author's) of the people elevated by the nation."[68] Frunze also left Aralov with

177

a favorable assessment of the abilities of both Fevzi and İsmet as assistants to Mustafa Kemal.

Frunze had arrived in Ankara in the midst of the Nureddin controversy over military operations in Central Army. On 3 October, the TBMM raised the issue of Nureddin's actions as commander of Central Army, especially with regard to suppressing the Koçgiri and Ümraniye rebellions, where his methods led to the loss of civilian lives and property. Parliamentary discussions dragged into January, during which time Mustafa Kemal, Interior Minister Fethi, and Defense Minister Refet all made appearances in Parliament to answer questions. His defenders emphasized that Nureddin had faced a "brigand war (*çete harbi*) against an organized enemy" that had killed Muslim women and children. They maintained that his deportations were justified within the context of the military crisis on the Western Front, especially during the Battle of Sakarya.[69] On 8 November, Nureddin was relieved of command to face a trial. On the same day, the Council of Ministers, responding to parliamentary pressure, removed all the extraordinary powers granted to the commanders of Central Army and the Elcezire Front and limited their authority to only military matters.[70] The latter command had been suppressing Kurdish unrest.

On 22 November, Nureddin submitted two letters in his defense to Mustafa Kemal, one addressed to the commander in chief and the other to the president of the TBMM. He emphasized that his actions were always well-known by the commander in chief, the chief of the General Staff, and the defense minister, which was true. Nureddin also hid behind his sacrifice for the religion, the fatherland, and the nation, claiming to have sent six divisions and various cavalry units for service on the Western Front, an argument that stressed his efficiency as a commander but which had no direct bearing on his treatment of civilians.[71] Unconvinced by such arguments, the TBMM sent an investigative committee to Koçgiri. More parliamentary discussions took place on 16 and 17 January 1922.[72] In the end, Mustafa Kemal managed to ensure that no trial took place and Nureddin was thus able to assume a senior command later in the year.[73] However, Central Army was dissolved on 8 February 1922. Not in Nureddin's defense, but certainly the other side of the coin, Athens willingly exploited the Rum population by supplying Pontian fighters with arms, ammunition, and money, even in 1922, knowing full well such a policy had little chance of benefiting the locals but jeopardized all Christians in the Pontus; but this was war.

By protecting Nureddin from prosecution and later calling upon him again for senior command, Mustafa Kemal demonstrated that he accepted war on civilians—including the old, women, and children—taking place under his watch. Deportations, massacres, and death marches of innocent civilians had become routine in the last hundred years of Ottoman history, with Muslims bearing their share of atrocities inflicted upon them.[74] The Turkish military archives for the War of Independence contain numerous reports from all the various fronts of massacres of Muslim civilians. While not ordering the killing of civilians, Mustafa Kemal clearly accepted their occurrence under certain conditions as part of the norms of warfare. The threat from the Pontus guerrillas, however, was just not serious enough on purely military terms, not to mention moral ones, to warrant mass deportations.[75] Back on 29 May 1919, as Ninth Army commander, Mustafa Kemal had assessed that the situation in the Black Sea region was manageable (see pp. 72–73), and in 1921 Nureddin had the military forces to ensure the flow of supplies through the region.

Mustafa Kemal used the victory at Sakarya to strengthen his political position. On 5 November 1921 and again on 5 February, the TBMM extended his tenure as commander in chief, each time for another three months. Between these two renewals, Mustafa Kemal raised the issue of ministerial appointments. The TBMM voted on each appointment individually and could put forth its own candidates. Mustafa Kemal wanted more control over the process, and a compromise was reached. He would submit three names and the Assembly elect one of them. Then on 22 January, a War Council, with Mustafa Kemal chairing, was established with the aim of facilitating quick decisions on army matters. Membership comprised the chief of the General Staff, the defense minister, the vice president of the TBMM, and the finance minister.[76] In a secret session on 9 January 1922, Mustafa Kemal had explained his command philosophy. The commander in chief commanded on the battlefield, not away from it. The chief of the General Staff, on his part, was responsible for directing military operations and developing plans, but he had to be in the same place as the commander in chief.[77] This description reflected what had happened during the Battle of Sakarya.

Throughout the war, the TBMM served as an excellent platform for policy debate and ministerial reports. Mustafa Kemal often attended the sessions and presented his thoughts. In one session held on 1 December 1921 to discuss creating a War Council, Mustafa Kemal revealed some of his political thinking. In his view, each government in the world was unique. Governments in Europe differed from those in the Americas. Even the United States had states, each with its own unique form of government. Turkey finally had achieved its own, at long last. Mustafa Kemal rejected the principle of the separation of powers and instead championed a government based on national will, echoing Rousseau's notion of a "Social Contract," even though he ridiculed the French political philosopher in the same speech without providing any explanation. He went so far as to label the 1921 Law on Basic Organization as "divine (*ilahi*) law" because it came forth from "the nation's conscience (*vicdan*) and conviction (*kanaat*)."[78]

Despite his enhanced prestige after the Battle of Sakarya, Mustafa Kemal made a telling decision, the aim of which was to tighten his hold on Ankara. He appointed Topal Osman Ağa to command the presidential guard. During World War I, Osman had been involved in deportation and murder of Armenians, profiting monetarily from confiscated properties. Other former Unionists with similar involvement in the Armenian massacres also found a haven and acceptance in the national movement. One Şükrü Kaya, for example, served as Kemal's interior minister from 1927 to 1938. Described as "a sadistic ethnic cleanser of Armenians and Greeks, and the hammer of Kemal's Muslim opponents,"[79] Osman had helped Nureddin ruthlessly suppress the Christians and then the Kurds. His militia band fought in the Battle of Sakarya as the 47th Regiment in First Group under the command of İzzeddin who, upon his first inspection of the unit, noted opaquely in his war diary the unit's uniqueness: "The 47th Regiment of Osman Ağa was very different from our regular regiments. The regimental commander and most of the others were from the militia. As for the soldiers, Osman had collected them for special aims."[80]

After the Battle of Sakarya, Mustafa Kemal brought what was left of the 47th Regiment to Ankara to serve as his presidential guard under the command of Topal Osman. This appointment caused anxiety among many deputies as it suggested Kemal's willingness to resort to ruthless methods in dealing with opponents. Mustafa Kemal had once remarked, rather cynically, to Halide Edip: "Rest, what rest? After the Greeks we will fight each other, and we will eat each other."[81] Topal Osman represented the need to have the ability to apply intimidation and strong-arm tactics for the present and in the future. Matters came to a head at the end of March 1923 when Osman, apparently on his own initiative, ordered the murder of a deputy and critic of Mustafa Kemal named Ali Şükrü. Suspicion immediately fell on Osman, and Mustafa Kemal responded to pressures and ordered his arrest.[82] Refusing to surrender, Topal Osman died from wounds sustained in a firefight.

Mustafa Kemal continued to cultivate the image of a leader. On 24 December 1921, for example, he granted an interview to Ahmed Emin (Yalman) from the newspaper *Vakit*. Conducted at the presidential residence in Çankaya, Ahmed Emin later provided general information about Kemal's life. He also described Kemal's office, an account which sent a clear message to readers. The room contained a number of gifts from foreign countries, among them a sword from Şeyh Ahmad al-Sanusi, the head of the Sanusi Sufi order in Libya. A small table was furnished with two Qurans, also gifts from the Şeyh. Several French books given to Mustafa Kemal by Berthe Georges-Gaulis, a French newspaperwoman supportive of the Nationalist cause, sat prominently on the writing table. Book shelves contained French books on Turkey as well as works on politics in French and Ottoman Turkish. Mustafa Kemal entered the room punctually at 1100.[83] The setting portrayed an international figure, a soldier-statesman, a leader devoted to personal study, and a person of faith.

Conclusion

The Battle of Sakarya became a turning point in the war against Greece. Though commanding an army fresh from defeat, Mustafa Kemal was fortunate to be on the defensive in suitable terrain, while the attacking Greeks were long on communication lines and stretched on supplies. His orders of 19 and 20 August reflected the instinct and temperament of a commander sensitive to the type of guidance a reconstituting army needed on the eve of a critical battle. He provided guidance to senior commanders down to the small unit commanders and soldiers that was practical but also showed an understanding of the effects of combat on the human being. In his pronouncements, theory blended with concrete action. The defensive battle, however, differed from that at Gallipoli in that the National Army at Sakarya had vulnerable flanks to protect. The Greek army had operational depth that allowed Mustafa Kemal to exploit to his advantage with cavalry.

Kemal's presence on the battlefield helped sustain the defenses, while the the corporate–professional wisdom and experience of his colleagues provided valuable assistance. In addition to İsmet's competent staff work, Fevzi played an important role in helping the army to stay the military course. Moreover, officers and soldiers exhibited heroism, courage, and sacrifice, so much so that Mustafa Kemal labeled the Battle of Sakarya as "the battle of the officers." In its own way, the TBMM contributed as well, when a handful of courageous and resolute deputies led by Mustafa Durak helped anchor Mustafa Kemal into defending Ankara, despite pressures to abandon the city.

While basking in the glory of battle triumph at Sakarya, Mustafa Kemal never lost sight of the interconnectedness of military operations, politics, and diplomacy, and he took advantage of this evolving dynamic in his war fighting. He translated the military victory into concrete political and diplomatic gains. The first order of business was to strengthen his own position, which he did. On the diplomatic front, Mustafa Kemal embraced a compromising attitude and reached a negotiated agreement with France, giving the French the ability to embark on a face-saving exit while he faced criticism at home for deviating from the National Pact. One major battle remained to be fought, and it took a year to prepare for it.

7

From Lightning Campaign to Peace

If you concentrate on victory, with no thought for the after effect, you may be too exhausted to profit by the peace, while it is almost certain that the peace will be a bad one, containing the germs of another war.

B. H. Liddell Hart[1]

Victory is never the aim. Victory is only the most definite means of achieving a goal. Victory carries value to the extent that it serves for the realization of an idea.

Mustafa Kemal[2]

HEADING INTO 1922, both the National and Greek armies had settled into defensive positions, with the main front stretching from the Sea of Marmara in the north to Afyon in the south. Greece would most probably not abandon Anatolia without a fight. But it was impossible for the Greeks to defend everywhere. So the questions facing Mustafa Kemal were when, where, and how to launch the offensive. Militarily, there were essentially two courses of action for driving the Greek army from Anatolia. It could be done in phases, a series of battles waged over an extended period of months, or in a single, decisive campaign. The latter option would represent a military feat of operational skill that the Ottoman army had not seen in over a century. But failure of a major offensive would produce major negative repercussions. Mustafa Kemal eventually chose the knockout blow, and the TBMM's Army would leave history with its own particular version of a lightning (*yıldırım*) campaign. While preparing the army for such an offensive, Mustafa Kemal further developed the home and diplomatic fronts.

Preparing the Army

After all the dust settled from a failed pursuit, Mustafa Kemal, Fevzi (Çakmak) and the General Staff, and İsmet and Western Front Command explored the idea of launching an offensive in late October or November before the onset of winter. The main concern was that the Greeks would use the time to "wipe off the effects of the defeat at Sakarya" and rebuild their forces. Attention focused on developing the main attack in the Afyon region. On 15 October 1921, the General Staff sent a directive to Western Front Command requesting a plan on how to deal a decisive blow to the Greeks before winter. İsmet responded on 17 October. The main attack would come from south of the city of Afyon with the aim of defeating the Greek army in fifteen to twenty days.[3] Thus began the planning for Operation *Sad*, a plan that evolved until its execution in August 1922. Operation *Sad* initially looked good on paper, but the Army was unprepared for such a bold and daring offensive designed to inflict a decisive strike. The Greek army had been defeated but not annihilated, whereas the National Army needed more men, equipment, and training for a major offensive.

Western Front Command underwent significant growth and organizational changes over the next ten months. First Army was created in mid-October, with headquarters at Bolvadin, directly east of Afyon. It consisted of I, II, and IV Corps, V Cavalry Corps, and the 6th and 8th Infantry Divisions. The III Corps and Koceli Group were deployed north of First Army and both reported directly to Western Command. On 19 November, the Second Army was created with headquarters at Bolvadin, requiring First Army to relocate south to Çay. First Army now commanded I and IV Corps and the V Cavalry Corps. Second Army took over II and III Corps, and then later gained VI Corps, a new organization. The Western Front Command established its headquarters at Akşehir. This command structure remained largely intact until final changes were made for the Great Offensive in August 1922. At the end of January 1922, both field army commanders stressed the army's unpreparedness for battle in their reports: deficiencies in ammunition, vehicles, and equipment, as well as a shortage in officers.[4]

Morale problems plagued the army as well. Pay was often in arrears. Desertion rates came down but remained an overall concern. They numbered 30,000 in July, 13,000 during the tough days of Sakarya, 6,000 in October, 3,400 in November, and 3,400 in December. The lack of serious fighting and the onset of winter explained the downturn, and the Independence Courts were judged unable to affect the problem appreciably.[5] İsmet tried to ensure regular pay as one means of addressing the problem, but this depended on a regular flow of money from Ankara.[6] Sanitation conditions and food rations were also a concern. In December 1921, hospitals recorded 16,953 soldiers in residence for illness. This figure grew to 29,193 in March 1922 and stood at 27,834 in April, four months before the Great Offensive.[7] On 23 January 1922, a group of officers had the courage to petition the senior command and complain about their pay in arrears. They warned that the government could not contemplate waging war in such conditions and saw themselves as sacrificial lambs for their commanders.[8]

Despite the numerous problems and challenges, the National Army on the Western Front pressed on with its preparations. Western Command conducted a major exercise spanning three days, 9–11 February, which included the commanders of III Corps, Second Army, First Army, and Western Command. Fevzi attended the sessions, raised several questions, and made comments throughout. "What will you do if the enemy attacks? What must we do if we want to attack?" Fevzi expressed concern about how to address the expected wanton destruction inflicted by a retreating Greek army. No one offered an answer to this query. One conclusion from the exercise was the need for better defensive positions in the event the Greeks launched offensive operations.[9] Such exercises were very important in preparing the senior command and the army as a whole for the upcoming battle. Then suddenly a glitch occurred in offensive planning and preparations. On 20 February 1922, Mustafa Kemal had information that the Greeks might launch an offensive toward Ankara and therefore ordered the army to focus on dealing with such a possibility.[10] Nothing came of the intelligence.

Then on 6 March in a special secret session in the TBMM, Mustafa Kemal reported on the general military situation in stark terms. The National Army, although able to defend, was not yet ready for an offensive. Mustafa Kemal identified a known advantage: the cavalry. The enemy did not have five cavalry divisions, only one. "In the field battles, we will defend, God willing, with our superiority in cavalry."[11] But the army needed time before launching an offensive. After his report, Mustafa Kemal spent much of the month of March inspecting troops.

9 *Mustafa Kemal inspecting troops*

Kemal's March tour brought to light his character and leadership. The extensive nature of his visits in terms of time and geography indicated his professionalism and dedication. Mustafa Kemal suffered from illness, causing much discomfort and requiring naps and medical attention, yet he persevered in his self-designated duties and responsibilities, as his will triumphed over his weakened body. Despite the travel and sickness, however, Mustafa Kemal found time to read a book. True to form, Mustafa Kemal inspected troops, meeting with senior commanders and going down to lower commands. Junior officers and soldiers, those at the point of the spear, continued to require attention. One recorded speech to troops stressed the theme of the army's virtues as its strength. And finally, several occasions found Mustafa Kemal participating in readings from the Quran in order to keep up the public image of a man of faith. The March tour gave Mustafa Kemal an intuitive feel of the overall state of the army: it was not yet ready for a major offensive.[12] On 14 March 1922, in the midst of this tour, Karabekir recommended holding election for a new Assembly, but Mustafa Kemal rejected the suggestion.[13] An election would require effort to ensure that his leadership would not be seriously challenged.

Political-Diplomatic Developments

On 2 February 1922, the TBMM responded to a European tour by the Greek Prime Minister Gounaris with the decision to send its own foreign minister to Paris and London. Yusuf Kemal understood this mission involved meeting with the press to ensure a media blitz. He convinced Mustafa Kemal to let him go through Istanbul in the hope of gaining approval from the sultan to represent the Istanbul government as well. Yusuf Kemal's audience with the monarch failed to gain any support. Rather, Vahdeddin dispatched his own mission to London.[14] After failing to make any significant progress in London, Yusuf Kemal left for Paris on 21 March where French, British, and Italian foreign ministers met from 22 to 26 March. They proposed a modification to the Treaty of Sèvres favoring the Turks, an immediate armistice, and Greek evacuation of Anatolia upon the conclusion of a treaty. On 5 April, Mustafa Kemal accepted a four-month armistice provided the Greeks began an immediate withdrawal from Anatolia. The Greeks and the Great Powers rejected this proposal, and then Mustafa Kemal proposed a conference in Izmir again predicated on the commencement of an immediate Greek withdrawal. The Allies nixed this offer as well. The British wanted to reach an agreement with Ankara without preconditions.[15] Yusuf Kemal left Paris without achieving any significant diplomatic progress. On the positive side, he purchased badly needed military supplies in France, such as machine guns, trucks, and planes, which reached the Western Front in time for the Great Offensive. These purchases enhanced the possibility of an earlier offensive.

While conducting diplomacy with the West, Mustafa Kemal continued to place a high importance on good and proper relations with Russia. On 10 April, he sent a personal letter to Lenin, saying "Russia's friendship will always be a political foundation of the TBMM's government." The letter contained politically correct language designed to have a pleasant ring to a communist ear. Mustafa Kemal expressed faith in the need to form a bloc to resist the methods of "imperialism and capitalism." He assigned a "special importance" to the numerous times Russia had provided assistance to Turkey,[16] and Soviet aid continued to flow. Overall, Russia would provide 11 million gold rubles, 45,000 rifles, 1,400 light and heavy machine guns, and 96 artillery pieces.[17]

The Kurds remained an abiding concern. On 18 January, the Council of Ministers, for example, ensured that tribal chiefs who had rendered support to the government against the French in Elcazire received salaries for their services.[18] On 25 February, the TBMM, for its part, compensated the Koçgiri Kurds for losses by the actions of the Central Army. A parliamentary fact-finding commission to the Dersim region had reported some 2,000 homes had been destroyed and people left without food, livestock, and other necessities for six months. The compensation figure amounted to 40,000 Turkish pounds.[19] On 1 May, Karabekir moved to enroll young children of tribal chiefs in boarding schools and worked to create jobs. He also dispatched enlightened religious leaders for propaganda purposes.[20] A major conference was held in Van in the middle of June 1922 with local Kurdish leaders. Mustafa Kemal sent a delegation of deputies from Van, Bitlis, Muş, and Siirt with the intent of garnering support in the east. Fevzi filed a short report on 28 June 1922. "Tribal chiefs, ulema, local notables and people" held a meeting with the deputies at Van. They expressed concerns of a regional rather than a national nature. According to Fevzi, local interests had resisted foreign intrigue and traitors. Government support was offered and the meeting ended with music, dancing, and the distribution of tea and sugar to the people.[21] All these actions were designed to garner Kurdish support and avoid rebellion. The Kurdish people overall contributed to the success of the War of Independence, in some cases by simply not rebelling.

On 6 May, the TBMM met in a secret session to discuss extending Kemal's tenure as commander in chief for another three months. To gain renewal, Mustafa Kemal stressed that only a military victory would force the Greeks out of Anatolia. A deputy named Salaheddin asserted that "Our greatest duty is to make policy," to which Mustafa Kemal replied:

Our greatest duty is not to make policy; our greatest duty is to throw out the enemy who is on our lands . . . Gentlemen, today they are saying war will not create the nation. Gentlemen, today only war will create the nation; there is no other means. Unfortunately, we must give all our power, all our resources, [and] all our existence to the army and we will force the world to recognize that we have the ability to make war. Only then will it be possible for the nation to live like a human being.[22]

Mustafa Kemal expressed determination to push even further the limits of national sacrifice when he said that one cannot begrudge the army anything "even if the needs of our army necessitate slave labor for it."[23] Only a military victory would give the nation the respect it deserved in the international community. Only a military defeat of the Greeks would push diplomacy, now in a seeming logjam, to the next level of negotiations conducted from a position of strength.

Mustafa Kemal then argued that extending the position of commander in chief for another three months would not create a dictatorship because Parliament still held the reins of government. Unlike in other countries, the position of commander in chief would disappear with the war's conclusion. Fevzi, for his part, threatened to resign if Kemal's position was not renewed.[24] His support reflected confidence in Kemal's leadership based on direct experience. In the end, the TBMM renewed Kemal's mandate, with 177 votes for, 11 against, and 15 abstentions.

Although the TBMM fell in line with Mustafa Kemal on major issues, an informal opposition group developed over time. After being freed by the Allied Powers from incarceration on the island of Malta, Rauf (Orbay), who had worked closely with Mustafa Kemal on the Representative Committee, was surprised to discover the degree of opposition when he arrived in Ankara in November 1921. Mustafa Kemal welcomed his friend with open arms. There was a good deal of catching up to do, and Mustafa Kemal frequently dined with Rauf and introduced him to various important officials in Ankara. A career naval officer, Rauf had seen more of the world than Mustafa Kemal, even visiting the White House in Washington. Concerned about Kemal's growing power, however, Rauf became loosely affiliated with Second Group, an opposition group of deputies.

Now in July 1922, Mustafa Kemal decided to placate opposition deputies formed in Second Group. Back on 4 November 1921, the procedure had changed whereby Mustafa Kemal as president of the TBMM submitted to the Assembly for a vote a list of three candidates for each ministerial position. Now in July, Mustafa Kemal agreed to a more open system whereby the TBMM could elect any of its members. He also agreed to support the election of Rauf to the position of prime minister, thereby replacing Fevzi, who now could concentrate on military matters in his position as chief of the General Staff. Dr. Adnan (Adıvar) would become the new vice president of the TBMM.[25] Mustafa Kemal adopted a conciliatory approach to the opposition in order to gain a unity of effort for the upcoming offensive. On 12 July, Rauf was elected with 197 of 208 votes. With Rauf's election, Mustafa Kemal gained an internationally known figure to head the Council of Ministers as he moved toward launching the military offensive. Rauf, now a civilian, meant that the country no longer had a military man as prime minister. His election placated the opposition deputies at an important juncture in the struggle.

On 16 July, Mustafa Kemal strengthened his position within his own party with a new charter of the Society for the Defense of Rights of Anatolia and Rumeli. He also pressed the TBMM for a new law on his position as commander in chief. On 20 July, the TBMM renewed his appointment, but this time for an unlimited period. *Hakimiyet-i Milliye* reported on the event in an article entitled "A Victory of Conscience (*Vicdan*)," a moral victory. The official newspaper depicted the extension of authority as the TBMM recognizing Kemal's "character" (*kılınç*), "genius" (*deha*), and "conscience" (*vicdan*) and described Mustafa Kemal as "the great son of Turkishness" (*Türklügün büyük evladı*) in the struggle for independence and liberty of the nation. The article's last sentence clearly went beyond the pale with its accolades: "We acclaim Gazi and Field Marshal Mustafa Kemal Paşa, as the greatest personality of history who obtained the victory of conscience."[26] Anatolia had a new hero.

Strategic Setting

On the eve of the final offensive, both Greece and Turkey had issues with senior military leadership. Their armies each had a politicized military, but to different degrees and for different reasons. In Turkey, army officers constituted approximately 14 per cent of the deputies in the TBMM, among them Fevzi and İsmet. In particular, Fevzi served as prime minister from 24 January 1921 to 9 July 1922. The involvement perhaps surpassed the level envisioned by Mustafa Kemal when, as a senior captain in his speech to the 1909 CUP Congress, he had called for the separation of the military from politics. But this was war and state-building at the same time.

In his memoirs, İsmet discussed the problem from his vantage point. He recalled that "my army commanders are human beings who possess a personality, have great self-confidence, and have contacts with everyone."[27] İsmet had passed over a number of senior ranking officers when Mustafa Kemal appointed him chief of the General Staff, and some had chafed at his selection over them.

After his questionable performance during the battles of Eskişehir and Kütahya, Mustafa Kemal kept İsmet as the Western Front Commander but appointed Fevzi to replace him as chief of the General Staff. To bolster his staff functions, Asım (Gündüz) became İsmet's chief of staff. But Brigadier General Ali İhsan (Sabis) proved a thorn in İsmet's side.

Ali İhsan and Asım were Kemal's classmates. Asım had been first in his class for three years, but then Ali İhsan graduated top in his class after final exams. Mustafa Kemal was fifth. After his release from imprisonment on the island of Malta, Ali İhsan arrived in Ankara, and Mustafa Kemal appointed him to command the Afyon region and what became the First Army. The appointment essentially began the process for fleshing out the plan for the Great Offensive. Ali İhsan did not, however, take to being under the command of İsmet, who was his junior in rank and seniority, and he complained of İsmet influencing Mustafa Kemal to appoint his own man as First Army's chief of staff.[28] Ali İhsan eventually forced the officer's resignation and then found that it took five weeks to receive a replacement.[29] On 17 June, frustrated at working with Ali İhsan, İsmet formally requested Fevzi to remove him.[30] Mustafa Kemal complied on the next day, but he experienced difficulty finding a replacement. First Ali Fuad and then Refet refused command of First Army; apparently neither one wanted to serve under İsmet.[31] Finally, Nureddin, the third candidate, accepted on 30 June. He brought his own set of personality issues, including controversy over his performance as commander of Central Army.

Brigadier General Yakub Şevki (Şübaşı), the commander of Second Army, presented a different kind of problem. His style of leadership and personal beliefs caused some friction. Conservative by nature, he never drank and prayed five times a day. In keeping with his personal beliefs, he forced the replacement of the commanders for II and III Corps, arguing that both men were spent and self-indulgent. Yakub Şevki was a hard worker and dedicated professional who read reports carefully. But it was his cautious and methodical approach to war that caused some concern among his superiors. They would need speed and aggressiveness to seize opportunities.[32] During the Greek Offensive, his style of leadership created command friction, and Mustafa Kemal would have to intervene to remedy the situation.

The Greek army had more pronounced senior command problems than its counterpart.[33] On 12 May, the Gounaris cabinet fell to a coalition government, and on 25 May, Papoulas resigned as commander of the Army in Asia Minor. The new government replaced him with Lieutenant General Georgios Hatzianestis, a highly controversial selection. Hatzianestis had a reputation for eccentricity, if not unbalanced, behavior; but he possessed clear devotion to the king. The *Schisma*, or conflict, between Royalists and Venizelists remained a factor in officer promotions and appointments. Only eight of twenty-eight officers promoted to major general had seen service in the recent campaign. Loyalty outweighed performance in some cases. Such favoritism angered many veteran officers. In Turkey, political stability made for a more professional army.

Hatzianestis made several decisions that inadvertently helped Mustafa Kemal. After a tour of his new command, he wrongly concluded that the Greek defenses were secure, and so he withdrew three infantry regiments and two battalions to Thrace. The plan was to force the hand of the British by threatening a move on Istanbul. The Allies assured the Greeks that they would meet any Greek move with armed force. Tensions peaked at the end of July and the beginning of August. Greece backed down but the newly transferred troops stayed in Europe, where they faced no threat. Then Hatzianestis disbanded the Southern Army into two separate commands—I and II Corps—directly responsible to his headquarters in faraway Izmir. In the event of a breakdown of communications, the commander of I Corps, headquartered in Afyon, would assume command of the reserve II Corps. When the National Army did cut communications, much valuable time was lost in embracing the new reality and sorting out the command adjustments. Hatzianestis compounded the problem by remaining in Izmir during the entire campaign, too far away to influence the battle, while Mustafa Kemal, who did possess the advantage of possessing the initiative in the campaign, followed engagements with his binoculars.

Morale problems plagued the Greek army. Politics within the army adversely affected combat assignments. Morale also suffered from the "no war, no peace" limbo, as many Greek soldiers saw no end to their deployments and no purpose to their military service. The senior command decided not to grant standard leaves because too many soldiers failed to return to their units. Pay was often in arrears.[34] Increasing numbers of Rum (Ottoman Greeks) dodged conscription. In this general state of military strategic inertia, there also emerged an unsettling sense among numbers of officers that eventually the Greek army would have to leave Anatolia or pull back to more defensible positions. Fulfilling the *Megale Idea* of a Greek empire in Anatolia had lost some of its appeal, especially given the lack of support from the European community for the venture.

Meanwhile, the General Staff in Ankara closely monitored developments and regularly filed reports on Greek politics and the army. Fevzi organized a group of Greek-speaking officers to conduct intelligence-gathering. Reports, for example, identified tensions between king and cabinet, as well as disagreements between the monarch and the patriarch.[35] The appointment of Hatzianestis, it was noted, led to resignations of some officers.[36] One report claimed that Hatzianestis wanted to remove 398 officers.[37] On 21 August, Mustafa Kemal noted the importance of the transfer of Greek troops to Thrace as providing an opportunity for launching an offensive.[38]

Finally, on 2 July, Mustafa Kemal ordered Western Command to prepare for an offense, underscoring the need to move away from "a mentality that prefers to remain on the defense."[39] This statement indicated Kemal's awareness of the imperative of the army removing its defensive mindset and consciously taking on an offensive one. The same day, İsmet submitted Operation *Sad* to Mustafa Kemal: I and IV Corps would launch the main attack from south of Afyon with the Cavalry Corps heading toward Sincanlı Plain into the Greek rear; III Corps would move toward Seyitgazi in the direction of Eskişehir, while VI Corps would attack Afyon from the east; II Corps would attack north of Afyon in an easterly direction.[40] On 3 July, Mustafa Kemal gave his approval with one significant change: he moved II Corps to be the reserve corps for the main attack in the south with the aim of enhancing a decisive result.[41] Plan *Sad* had positioned II Corps on the Greek southern flank as a reserve for First Army but İsmet wanted to keep the corps with Second Army. Mustafa Kemal overruled him.[42] It made sense to strengthen the main effort.

Mustafa Kemal wanted all available units for the general attack. Guerrilla activity in the Pontus tied down numbers of troops. So on 14 July, Mustafa Kemal ordered the General Staff to avoid half measures or delays and apply "severe" (*şiddet*) force so that the 10th Division could be released to the front. A complete battery did move immediately to Western Front Command.[43] On 20 July, Mustafa Kemal reiterated to the chief of the General Staff, the Western Front commander, and the Eastern Front Commander the need for material, morale, and political preparations and a close monitoring of the enemy's situation. He said that he would visit the front in a few days.[44] From all appearances, Mustafa Kemal had decided on the offensive.

On 23 July, Mustafa Kemal left for the front using the pretext of meeting British General Sir Charles Townshend in Konya to discuss prospects for more negotiations. Then he used a football (soccer) match scheduled for 28 July at Akşehir as an opportunity to meet discreetly with his senior commanders to settle on some final details. Fevzi, İsmet, the two army commanders, and the commanders of I, IV and V (Cavalry) Corps, who together constituted the main effort, joined Mustafa Kemal. The meetings spanned three days and nights. The essence of the plan had Second Army fix the Greek corps and cut the Eskişehir-Afyon rail line, with First Army attaining decisive results in the Akarçay-Toklu region and V Cavalry Corps passing to the west through the Ahır Mountains to cut communications in the Greek rear. Kocaeli Group would cautiously attack the Greek northernmost corps in a manner to prevent the Greeks from sending forces to the south. All these attacks were intended to confuse the Greeks as to the location of the main Turkish effort as well as fix as many forces as possible away from the southern flank. All preparations should be complete by 15 August. Before returning to Ankara, Mustafa Kemal made it known that he would personally command the offensive.[45]

Operation *Sad* required a major redeployment by the army. On 1 August, Second Army commanded four corps: III and VI stationed forward, and II and IV in the second line behind them. First Army possessed I Corps and several independent divisions to the south and southwest of Afyon. V Cavalry Corps was stationed to the southeast of Afyon. In order to launch the main attack from the south at the underbelly of Greek forces, I, II, IV, and V Corps had to deploy stealthily to the southwest of the city of Afyon. In this redeployment, II and IV Corps passed to the command of First Army. Mustafa Kemal added a personal touch to this part of the plan. He ensured that Colonel Kemaleddin Sami and his IV Corps formed the critical part of the main attack.[46] A graduate of the Land Forces Engineering School and the Staff College, Kemaleddin Sami, who knew French and German, was placed first in a written exam competition, winning him the right to be sent to Germany for a few months. During World War I, he worked as a staff officer for various commands and served for a brief period as a liaison officer with the Bulgarian army. Kemaleddin Sami had distinguished himself in the eyes of Mustafa Kemal. He was wounded at the Second Battle of İnönü and performed well at Sakarya as commander of Fourth Group. Mustafa

Map 7.1   *Strategic Situation, 1 August 1922*

Kemal valued his bravery and aggressiveness, important qualities for a key commander in the main attack. İzzeddin, Kemal's competent chief of staff in the Great War, commanded I Corps, which deployed on IV Corps's left for the main attack.

In a conference on 20 August at İsmet's headquarters in Akşehir with all the senior commanders, Mustafa Kemal ordered the attack for 26 August. Since 6 August, İsmet had been planning for Second Army to attack one day before First Army.[47] Now Mustafa Kemal vetoed the idea in favor of a simultaneous attack all along the front to begin on 26 August.[48] Some commanders expressed reservations about the plan and going on the offensive.[49] But Mustafa Kemal could not delay any longer for political and economic reasons. The country could not continue on a war footing too much longer. Orders went out to the army to be in its attack positions by the night of 25 August for the offensive the next day. Units used the night to hide their forward movements from Greek reconnaissance planes. Mustafa Kemal moved to Şuhut on 24 August. He was atop Kocatepe by the morning of 26 August. Kocatepe, a hill 1,874 meters high southwest of Afyon, would be his observation post with a commanding view of the main attack. The Greeks had erred in not fortifying this position.

Both opposing armies entered battle with internal problems. The National Army had greater cohesion, unity of purpose, and higher morale. However, human and material numbers gave the advantage to the Greeks, offset however by the fact that they defended a 250-kilometer front.

	TURKEY	GREECE
OFFICERS	8,658	6,569
MEN	199,283	218,432
TOTAL	207,942	225,001
RIFLES	100,352	90,000
MACHINE GUNS	2,025	3,139
HEAVY MACHINE GUNS	839	1,280
ARTILLERY	323	418
SWORDS	5,282	1,280
PLANES	19	50
TRUCKS	298	4,036

The National Army planned for a substantial numerical advantage at the point of the main attack, but only if it achieved surprise, which it did. Moreover, the Greek army had been lulled into a modicum of complacency and lethargy from almost eleven months of inactivity and occupation, whereas Nationalist soldiers benefited from a few days to prepare emotionally and mentally for the general offensive as they quietly moved into their assigned positions.

On 25 August, İsmet issued Front Command No. 93, the final version of Operation *Sad*. The general attack all along the front was scheduled to commence at dawn on 26 August. First Army would attack from the south and west of Afyon, while its V Cavalry Corps moved into the rear of the enemy forces in order to conduct reconnaissance and block any enemy reserves coming from Uşak. The 6th Division would secure the left flank of First Army, while a cavalry division would attack in the direction of Uşak. II Corps, First Army's reserve, would be ready to enter the battle with its three divisions. Second Army would attack east to west with the aim of attracting the enemy's attention and occupying its reserve. In the north, Kocaeli Group would launch its attack on the left flank of Greek III Corps. The First and Second Armies received their final orders in the early afternoon.[50]

On the evening of 25 August, Mustafa Kemal moved to Kocatepe to have a commanding view of the battle. The "center of gravity" (*sıklet merkezi*) of the main attack involved I and IV Corps attacking on a forty- to forty-five kilometer front between Kaleciksivrisi in the east and Çiğiltepe in the west. Each attacking corps was reinforced with a fourth infantry division. Operation *Sad* aimed at "capturing and strangling the Greek army."[51] Mustafa Kemal went for the jugular to achieve a decisive military victory over the Greeks in a single campaign.

To enhance the probability of a decisive victory, Mustafa Kemal had added several important final touches to the plan. Deciding to attack simultaneously all along the front helped fix and confuse the Greeks. The transfer of II Corps to the main attack provided a sufficient number of troops concentrated south and west of Afyon to deal a mortal blow. The center of gravity for the main attack, however, could have been placed a little farther west where Greek forces were thinned out. This would have resulted in a more powerful and quicker thrust deeper into the Greek rear and prevented some of the wanton destruction inflicted by the retreating Greeks. The V Cavalry Corps with 6th Division lacked sufficient combat power to prevent many Greek divisions from fleeing past it. Finally, Mustafa Kemal ensured that the centerpiece of the main attack fell upon the shoulders of Kemaleddin Sami in command of IV Corps.

Only on 25 August did the Greeks learn that the Turks had sent troops to the south, but Greek intelligence estimated a force of 30,000 men. Though the Greeks wisely reinforced their southern flank, Mustafa Kemal still achieved the desired surprise and superiority of forces at the main point of attack. Thus, on the morning of 26 August, the main deployments arrayed as follows along a 350-kilometer front. On the Greek side, III Corps under Major General Petros Soumilas deployed four divisions along a line stretching from Gemlik on the Sea of Marmara to Seyitgazi, south of Eskişehir. Major General Nikolaos Trikoupis commanded I Corps with its four divisions and had the responsibility of defending the city of Afyon and the Greek army's southern flank. Greek II Corps under Major General Kimon Digenis with his headquarters at Gazlıgöl formed the front reserve with its three divisions. The bulk of the Greek forces, i.e., I and II Corps, were thus positioned in the southern half of the front where the Greeks expected the Turkish main attack. A string of hills running north and south gave the Greeks a good defensible position from Eskişehir to Afyon. On the Nationalist side, the 12,000 strong Kocaeli Group under Colonel Deli (Mad) Halid (Karsıalan) was located north of the Eskişehir-Ankara railway. Second Army comprised 50,000 men in one cavalry and five infantry divisions on a 120-kilometer front facing 120,000 Greeks. On a forty-kilometer frontage of the Greek underbelly, First Army positioned 110,000 men in twelve infantry and four cavalry divisions against 40,000 Greeks in two divisions and a regiment from I Corps.[52] Mustafa Kemal had thus gained close to a three-to-one superiority at the main attack. The hilly terrain, however, favored the defense.

In addition to clear superiority at the point of the main attack, the TBMM Army possessed a marked advantage in cavalry, both in terms of number and quality. The V Cavalry Corps carried on the centuries-old tradition of the Ottoman imperial and provincial cavalries. After the Battle of Sakarya, the General Staff placed even greater emphasis on developing this advantage. The V Cavalry Corps was blessed with a competent and aggressive commander, Colonel Fahreddin. By the time of the Great Offensive, the corps comprised three divisions with a total of 550 officers, 9,900 soldiers, 9,480 animals, 6,460 rifles, 48 machine guns (16 per division), 4,800 swords, 620 bombs, and 16 artillery pieces (four per division and headquarters). Much time and effort went into preparing the horsemen for their various missions. Fahreddin established a school for horsemanship under the command of his chief of staff. Then on 1 April, Mustafa Kemal brought the Russian and Azerbaijani ambassadors to observe the corps conducting a three-division exercise.[53] This exercise had culminated in Mustafa Kemal's March tour of the army on the Western Front. Operation *Sad* called for V Cavalry Corps to penetrate into the enemy's operational depth on the first day of the campaign and thus play an important role in the decisive defeat of the Greek army.

Aware of the organic relationship between diplomacy and war, Mustafa Kemal prepared the diplomatic ground for the military offensive. In July, he dispatched his trusted friend and interior minister Fethi (Okyar) to Paris and London with the aim of "pinning down responsibility for the war on the British government and winning over world opinion to Turkey's side." Fethi met with the British Permanent Undersecretary at the Foreign Office, one day before the Great Offensive. They agreed to a meeting with Lord Curzon in the first week

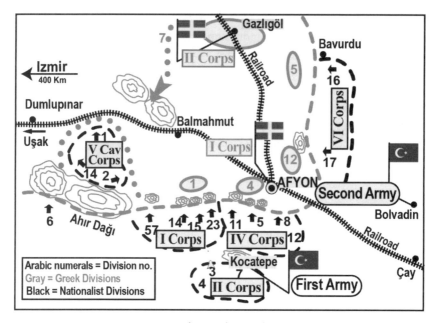

Map 7.2   *Great Offensive, the Attack, 26 August 1922*

of September.[54] On 17 August, *The Times* reported that despite Prime Minister Lloyd George's recent negative comments on Turkey, the Ankara government appeared willing to accept an invitation to attend an international conference in Venice on the Near East scheduled for September.[55] Deceptive diplomacy went down to the wire before the commencement of military operations.

The Great Offensive, 26–31 August

During the night of 25/26 August, Fahreddin moved out with his cavalry corps in the direction of Sincanlı Plain. No major breakthrough occurred on the first day of the Battle of Afyon. Attacking infantry, supported by artillery fire, had to traverse open terrain and attack into prepared Greek positions centered on hills, much like Sakarya. Not every unit advanced according to plan, forcing command adjustments throughout the hierarchy. Nationalist forces did, however, secure a number of forward positions and hills on 26 August. For example, I Corps captured Belen Tepe. Its 57th Division, however, made no progress on the first day. At 1515, First Army reinforced I Corps with the 3rd Caucasus Division, which managed to capture the western slopes of Tınaztepe.[56] The IV Corps experienced problems. Kemaleddin Sami planned for the 8th Division to attack on a broader

10 *Mustafa Kemal atop Kocatepe, 26 August 1922*

front directly north toward Afyon, while he concentrated the 5th Caucasus and
11th Divisions on narrower fronts forming the corps's left wing. Only one Greek
division faced IV Corps. Rather than attacking in kamikaze fashion, the latter
two divisions moved deliberately and cautiously, seizing a few Greek forward
positions but then experiencing some coordination difficulty. The Greeks managed to reinforce their defensive positions; so in the late afternoon Kemaleddin
Sami committed his reserve, the 12th Division, to help in the attacks. Now all
four divisions were in the assault. Tough Greek resistance, however, prevented
the capture of the important Hill No. 1310. With the arrival of darkness, division
commanders requested a period of rest for their tired troops, and Kemaleddin
Sami reluctantly complied.[57]

Fahreddin achieved the greatest success on the first day. Pushing through Ahır
Dağı into Sincanlı Plain at Çayhisar, V Cavalry Corps caused havoc in the Greek
operational depth. Mounted units destroyed the railroad at three locations and cut
communication lines between Izmir and the front at a loss of only four killed and
fifteen wounded. Blocking positions prevented the movement of Greek troops
from Uşak to the front.[58] By the end of the first day, Greek II Corps committed
a division to deal with Fahreddin's cavalry corps operating as a maneuver group
in the Greeks' operational depth. At 2340, Mustafa Kemal decided to have both

197

armies continue executing Order No. 93, but Fifth Cavalry Corps had to increase its tempo of operations, and Kocaeli Group in the north was ordered to continue its attack but to proceed with caution in the face of a superior enemy.[59] Its mission was to help pin down as much of Greek III Corps as possible.

Despite no major breakthrough by Nationalist forces on the first day, August 27 saw the commencement of a general Greek pullback and the liberation of Afyon. The main attack achieved its first significant success. In the early morning, Kemaleddin Sami took personal command of the 5th Caucasus and 11th Divisions to ensure proper coordination, and he achieved success also. Kemal's selection of him for this important attack brought results. After offering some resistance, the Greeks abandoned their defensive positions. The IV Corps now advanced toward Afyon and west of the city to cut the road to Izmir. Later in the day, Trikoupis ordered a general retreat.[60] The retreating Greeks from Afyon were joined by scores of fleeing Greek and Armenian civilians, adding to the friction and confusion. Some units had begun withdrawing even before being ordered to do so. At 1420, Western Front Command informed Second Army that the Greeks were withdrawing from the city. At 1530, Yakub Şevki claimed that he had no indication of a wholesale abandonment of Afyon and instead requested IV Corps to advance faster.[61] Mustafa Kemal and İsmet concluded that Yakub Şevki was too meticulous and cautious.[62] Friction between Second Army Command and Western Front Command continued through much of the campaign.

Informed of Greek units pulling back, Mustafa Kemal approved the commitment of II Corps, the reserve corps of First Army. Western Front Command ordered II Corps with its two divisions to advance behind IV Corps and secure Afyon. At this juncture, it would have been better to have comitted II Corps to move between I and IV Corps, rather than have fresh troops engaged in a mopping-up operation in the wake of IV Corps' success.[63] To assist II Corps, İsmet even ordered the TBMM's Defense Battalion to move to Afyon.[64] The II Corps spent time securing Afyon and putting out city fires, but without encountering any serious engagement with the Greeks on the third day of the campaign.[65] This was poor use of II Corps.

Word of a general Greek withdrawal raised the possibility of a battle of annihilation and thus required appropriate adjustments to the general plan for the next day, 28 August. First Army now had to turn I and IV Corps toward the west and northwest respectively and pursue the Greeks. Second Army was given the mission of securing the Afyon–Kütahya road to prevent Greek forces from withdrawing in the northwest direction. Rapid executions of the above missions might lead to a possible encirclement of the Greek army in the south. Meanwhile, on the Greek side, the Frangou Group, consisting of two infantry

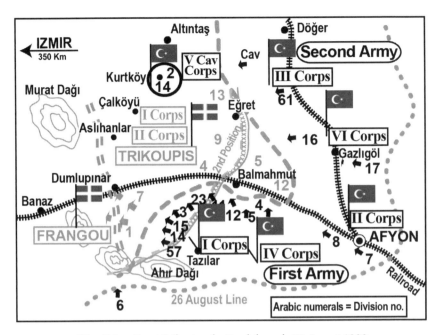

Map 7.3   *Great Offensive, the Breakthrough, 28 August 1922*

divisions, commenced a withdrawal while Trikoupis headed westward north of the railway with the bulk of I and II Corps. Meanwhile, Soumilas of Greek III Corps sent a division south to assist Trikoupis.

On 28 August, Yakub Şevki managed to cut the Afyon-Kütahya road with his cavalry. His III Corps headed toward Kütahya, while VI Corps led the advance past Afyon in a westerly direction. Meanwhile, First Army had its three corps moving in westward and northwestward directions. The I Corps took Balmahmut with its intact supply depot and then continued along the railroad toward Dumlupınar.[66] Greek I and II Corps were in full retreat, with some problems in communication and coordination, in part because of rear operations by the Turkish cavalry. In the evening, Mustafa Kemal called a conference in Afyon with Fevzi, İsmet, and Nureddin. Despite the estimate of seven badly mauled Greek divisions, Mustafa Kemal expressed concern that the Greeks might form a new line of defense. A plan of action was worked out to prevent this occurrence. At 2315, İsmet issued Order No. 96. First Army was to make haste and capture Dumlupınar. The V Cavalry Corps was to stop the retreat in the Murat Dağı area and on the Kütahya—Gediz road. Second Army was to cover the right flank of First Army as well as send a reinforced cavalry division to assist Kocaeli Group in the north.[67] On the same day, Mustafa Kemal also informed the TBMM that the army "will

199

pursue without delay the retreating enemy and will battle the covering forces."[68] There would be no let-up.

August 29 found the Greeks continuing their withdrawal, with the Turks in a determined pursuit. Trikoupis commanded some 25,000 to 30,000 troops in five battered divisions with shaken morale and shortages in ammunition and food. That night, Mustafa Kemal met with Fevzi and İsmet in Afyon. They all saw an opportunity for encircling a part of the two Greek corps. A double envelopment is a difficult task in any war. Coordinating the operations of two field armies presented more of a challenge than normal, given the friction between the Western Front and Second Army Commands. Mustafa Kemal, Fevzi, and İsmet together hatched a plan for the encirclement of the Greek army. To raise the chances for success, Mustafa Kemal made an important decision. He ordered Fevzi assume command of the advancing forces of VI Corps as well as the 61st Infantry Division from III Corps. Fevzi would attack the Greeks from the north. Meanwhile, Mustafa Kemal would join Nureddin and First Army while İsmet stayed behind in Afyon to help coordinate operations from the rear.[69] Fahreddin with his V Cavalry Corps would attempt to prevent a Greek escape westward. Mustafa Kemal headed for First Army, arriving at its headquarters in Akçaşar at 0900.

The plan had Kemaleddin Sami's IV Corps attacking from the east and the south while Fevzi with VI Corps and the 61st Division from III Corps descended from the northeast in a southwest direction.[70] Meanwhile, Fahreddin launched his cavalry units in support of Fevzi's attack. The I Corps, for its part, attacked Frangou Group in the region of Dumlupınar. The presence of Frangou Group proved an important distraction. Rather than attack northward on the left flank of IV Corps, I Corps had to fix and push back Frangou Group. Otherwise, the Greeks could have launched an attack into the flanks and the rear of Nationalist forces attacking northward. To the Greek detriment, Trikoupis had failed to link up his forces with the Frangou Group earlier, which would have helped strengthen his position.

The Battle of Dumlupınar, the second and last important engagement of the Great Offensive, began at 1400. It later became known as the Battle of the Commander in Chief. Kemaleddin Sami launched IV Corps, and advance units from Second Army under the command of Fevzi joined the battle at 1430. Mustafa Kemal observed and commanded from a low hill, later named Zafer (Victory) Tepe. During the battle, noticing that the 11th Division's artillery was not supporting its infantry in the attack, he summoned the division commander and ordered him to move forward and establish communication to ensure coordination between both combat arms.[71] This intervention recalled the order that Mustafa Kemal gave to the army on the eve of the Battle of Sakarya, which required artillery always to be in support of the infantry. The strategist continued to pay attention to tactical details. Meanwhile, Hatzianestis sat in Izmir, impotent in shaping the battle.

The armies of the TBMM failed to close the encirclement, however. Second Army had to travel some thirty kilometers, and IV Corps had two tired divisions that had fought through the night. And the Greeks fought back. Indeed, elements of V Cavalry Corps were beaten back. A three-kilometer gap permitted Trikoupis to escape during the night with 7,000 to 8,000 men.[72] Still, many Greek soldiers had been killed or captured that day.

Mustafa Kemal wanted to keep the pressure on his adversary, so in the late evening of 30 August, İsmet ordered his forces to continue pressing the Greeks. After securing prisoners of war, First Army would head toward Uşak, a town situated on the railroad, southwest of Dumlupınar. The V Cavalry Corps would stop retreating Greeks. The III Corps headquarters with the Composite Cavalry and 1st Division would head toward Kütahya to engage a Greek division. İsmet informed the army commanders that he would remain in Afyon but expected to be in Dumlupınar the next day.[73] İsmet was issuing orders from the rear while his two superiors, Mustafa Kemal and Fevzi, were commanding the main part of his forces on the front.

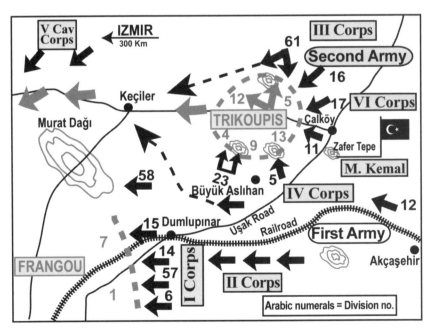

Map 7.4   *Great Offensive, the Battle of Dumlupınar, 30 August 1922*

The Greek army was still combat-effective, though badly beaten. In the north, Greek III Corps, 50,000 strong, remained largely intact in the Eskişehir region. In addition, some 35,000 to 40,000 Greek forces were combat-effective in the south, and 7,500 men had pulled out of Kütahya for Gediz. The Greeks could establish defenses in the Izmir region with a sizable force.[74] Mustafa Kemal wanted to avoid another major battle. Aggressive pursuit was the only answer.

On 31 August, Mustafa Kemal reported to Rauf in Ankara that units had occupied Kütahya and that more than 150 artillery pieces had been captured.[75] Day Six saw limited operations as most forces were in need of rest. The IV Corps spent a good part of the day policing up the battlefield, while I Corps, for its part, managed to capture Kaplangı Dağları and stop east of Uşak, where it requested the commitment of II Corps with its two divisions, but was denied and an opportunity was lost.[76] The V Cavalry Corps tried its best to stop the Greek retreat toward Izmir, but had limited success given its weak combat power.

To motivate the army to make that final, determined push to victory, Mustafa Kemal decided to reward his senior commanders by promoting them in the midst of the campaign. So on 31 August, Fevzi became a field marshal, while İsmet, Nureddin, and Yakub Şevki were promoted to major general, or *ferik*. Those rising from colonel to brigadier general were the chiefs of staff for the Front Command and First Army, as well as four corps commanders, including İzzeddin and Kemaleddin Sami and six division commanders. Ten division commanders were promoted from lieutenant colonel to full colonel. Mustafa Kemal took this step without Parliament's approval. The TBMM approved the promotions on 3 September, with a number of deputies expressing their displeasure over what they viewed as the usurpation of the Assembly's authority. Mustafa Kemal did not have the time to wait, as he wanted to seize the moment.

The Pursuit, 1–9 September

İsmet reached Dumlupınar late on 31 August and then met with Mustafa Kemal and Fevzi in Çal Köyü between 0500 and 0600, and together the three men planned a full and continuous pursuit of the Greeks. The period from 1 to 9 September witnessed Nationalist units pursuing retreating Greek forces, with intermittent engagements throughout the period. New orders had gone out to the various commands on 1 September. In the morning, V Cavalry Corps took the lead for Second Army with the mission of moving from Gediz toward Salihli with VI Corps of Second Army trailing it. Both I and II Corps led the pursuit for First Army, with IV Corps trailing them. Meanwhile, III Corps, with one cavalry and two infantry divisions, headed towards İnönü west of Eskişehir. Kocaeli

Group thus received badly needed assistance in attacking Greek III Corps. That same day, I Corps occupied Uşak in the south. Its commander İzzeddin felt a personal gratification upon entering the town on 1 September, as he had abandoned Uşak to the Greeks as a division commander two years earlier. Yet it was a sad achievement, as the Greeks had set the town aflame.[77]

From Dumlupınar on 1 September, Mustafa Kemal crafted his second signature order of the war, this one addressed to the "Armies of the TBMM," ending it with the now immortalized final line: "Armies! Your first goal is the Mediterranean. Forward." Yet what preceded this statement is worthy of analysis. Mustafa Kemal began by lauding his military audience for its historic accomplishment in battle. The great Battles of Afyonkarahisar and Dumlupınar had led to the destruction of the enemy in a short time. In this, "Our great and noble nation (*büyük ve necip milletimiz*) has proven its ability to sacrifice" and has "ensured the future of the great Turkish nation." He expressed admiration for the army's "skill and sacrifice." Then, in one declarative sentence preceding his famous final line, Mustafa Kemal offered words designed to inspire bold and audacious action: "I want everyone to continue competing in demonstrating their mental powers (*kuvayı aklıyya*) and their sources of courage (*celadet*) and patriotism (*hamiyet*).[78] *Hamiyet* could also mean zeal, and many soldiers would interpret the word as a reference to Islam.

As in his order on the eve of the Battle of Sakarya, Mustafa Kemal appealed directly to intellect and emotion. Now, however, the army needed boldness and audacity in the execution of an unrelenting pursuit, a much more complicated military operation than holding defensive positions. So in addressing the mind and emotion of his soldiers, as he did the year before, Mustafa Kemal adapted his order to inspire offensive action, delegating to his army to work out the fine details of pursuit. Commanders were to use their reason as well as look inward to whatever values inspired personal courage and patriotism. This one sentence encouraged initiative and recognized the uniqueness of all soldiers as the sources of personal courage and patriotism. The general order of 1 September came on the heels of the promotions the day before. Mustafa Kemal expected those senior officers just promoted to live up to their new ranks.

The order was also meant for domestic and international consumption and for the historical record. Mustafa Kemal went public with the order, confidently claiming a decisive military victory over the Greek army while still in the midst of the campaign. There was still the possibility that the Greeks would decide to defend Izmir if Greek III Corps at Eskişehir managed to reach the city largely intact. *Hakimiyet-i Milliye* published the order verbatim the next day, 2 September.[79] The order carried a "cosmic" significance. Rather than identifying İzmir as the final destination, to where retreating Greeks soliders were definitely heading, Mustafa Kemal spoke of the Mediterranean Sea with its link to the West. The Armies of the TBMM were in the process of making a statement to the world of Turkey's right to independence and freedom and linking the nation's fate to the larger world. Mustafa Kemal signed the historic document as both "commander in chief" and "president of the Grand National Assembly of Turkey."

On 1 September, Mustafa Kemal also addressed "The Great [and] Noble Turkish Nation" (*Büyük Asil Türk Milleti*) directly. He spoke of "the valor of the Armies of the TBMM" and of "the oppressive and haughty enemy army" being annihilated decisively, bringing "fear and awe to the mind." The address recognized the nation's sacrifice for the army and characterized the three-year struggle as one of "strength and ideals" (*kudret ve mefkure*) based on national "opinion and will" (*rey ve irade*). The future of the nation was now secure because of the army's accomplishments.[80] Mustafa Kemal confidently delivered a victory proclamation in an unfolding campaign, framing his analysis in terms of a war of intellects, ideals, and wills. *Hakimiyet-i Milliye* also published this address on the next day, 2 September.[81] In both the order to the army and the address to the nation, Mustafa Kemal awarded a position of prominence to the Turkish nation, as he did on 14 September 1921 immediately after the Battle of Sakarya.

On 2 September 1922, the 5th Caucasus Division captured both Greek corps commanders, Trikoupis and Digenis. This was the same day that *Hakimiyet-i Milliye* published both Kemal's pursuit order and his address to the nation. Battlefield developments thus confirmed Kemal's strategic *coup d'œil*. Greek I and II Corps were now left leaderless, although on paper Hatzianestis still functioned as overall commander in his war ship anchored in Izmir's harbor. Meanwhile, pursuing Nationalist forces prevented the Greeks from establishing defensive positions around Izmir and thereby forced a siege of the city.

Mustafa Kemal met with the captured Trikoupis and Digenis, showing the professional respect and courtesy due competing commanders in war. He warmly shook the defeated generals' hands and offered them coffee and cigarettes from his own case. While sitting down together at a table, Mustafa Kemal chose the occasion to engage in an analytical conversation about the campaign. It carried the trappings of Mustafa Kemal prying from Trikoupis and Digenis an after-action review. Mustafa Kemal appeared interested in understanding the decisions of his opponents as well as bragging about the victory. For example, Mustafa Kemal asked why Trikoupis failed to commit his reserves in a timely manner. Trikoupis blamed Digenis for refusing to listen to him. Digenis, on the other hand, responded that Hatzianestis had not given the order. To the inquisitive mind, such questioning provided a better understanding of what had transpired and why. Mustafa Kemal could not pass up this golden opportunity for personal enlightenment and a display of his own military prowess.

According to Halide Edip, toward the end of the discussion, Mustafa Kemal offered words of comfort to Trikoupis. "War is a game of chance, General. The very best sometimes becomes the worst. You have done your best as a soldier and an honorable man; the responsibility rests with chance. Do not be distressed."[82] Salih (Bozok), a staff officer, recorded Mustafa Kemal telling Trikoupis: "If you are convinced that you carried out your duty in accordance to your conscience (*vicdan*), then you can be at peace [with yourself]. History has recorded even the greatest commanders falling prisoner. I can, for example, show you Napoleon."[83] His consoling words showed empathy toward his defeated adversaries. That empathy also extended toward the Greek soldiers. On one occasion, as he watched a long procession of Greek prisoners of war file past him, Mustafa Kemal remarked to those around him: "The fortunes of war, gentlemen . . . and if you look carefully you will see the centuries on their faces, the progress made by man, that wonderful animal, God help him."[84] That day, Mustafa Kemal felt the human tragedy evident on the faces of captured Greeks, a sentiment laced with cynicism.

Meanwhile, operations in the north marched to a different tempo, but were clearly connected to events in the south. On 30 August, Second Army sent the headquarters of III Corps and the 1st Infantry and Composite Cavalry Divisions toward Eskişehir. These forces began arriving southwest of İnönü only on 2 September, the day that the Greeks abandoned Eskişehir. The III Corps engaged Greek forces in the İznik area on 3 September, while Greek III Corps continued withdrawing in an orderly manner, but leaving a swath of destruction in its wake. The 1st Infantry Division liberated Bursa on 10 September. With Izmir falling to First Army on 9 September, Greek III Corps retreated toward the Sea of Marmara, where the last Greek soldiers boarded ships at the port of Bandırma on 18 September. The military victory in Anatolia was now complete.

On 9 September, the Turkish army entered Izmir, a city that had been evacuated by the Greek army. Mustafa Kemal followed on 10 September. Figures vary as to the exact losses suffered by both sides. Turkish casualties stood around 2,524 killed (146 officers and 2,378 soldiers), 1,865 missing or captured, and 9,855 wounded (378 officers and 9,477 soldiers) for a total of 14,263. The Greeks suffered much greater losses. Among the prisoners of war were six Greek generals. The TBMM's Army had annihilated the enemy's army and covered 400 kilometers to reach Izmir in fourteen days. This military feat constituted a premeditated decisive military defeat of the Greek army in Anatolia.

Turkish national sentiment now gained prominence in the public arena. In one address, Mustafa Kemal identified himself as "the Turkish commander in chief" (*Türk başkomundanı*).[85] Upon the liberation of Izmir, *Hakimiyet-i Milliye* wrote of "the glorious Turkish army" (*şanlı Türk ordusu*) inspired by "Turkist spirit" (*Türklük ruhu*).[86] On September 12, for its part, the Council of Ministers praised Mustafa Kemal for his decisive leadership, clearly assigning to him a Turkish identity. It acknowledged his "genius" (*dahiyane*) of command in leading the Armies of TBMM to bring new and great honor to "Turkishness" (*Türklük*) and to "Turkish and Islamic history" (*Türk ve İslam tarihi*). The "decisive victory" (*kati zafer*) had come with "lightning speed" (*yıldırım süratiyle*), freeing Anatolia of the enemy so the nation could live free and independent. The Council of Ministers ended by giving credit to God for favoring "our national armies."[87] The officer corps was Turkish-speaking, and Turks formed a large majority of the soldiers, though many would think of themselves as Muslims first. Kemalist historiography in the Republic would later depict the army and war as Turkish.

The Road to a New Peace

Although Mustafa Kemal had defeated the Greeks decisively, the military victory was incomplete. The Allies still controlled the Straits and small parts of Anatolia, while Greek forces occupied Thrace. This strategic situation meant that Mustafa Kemal could not dictate peace but had to negotiate for it; a military option was not in his calculations. Winning the peace now required smart diplomacy calling forth skill, perseverance, and patience.

On 10 September, Mustafa Kemal arrived in Izmir and established his headquarters in the city. A dark side of war, however, surfaced, tarnishing for history the luster of an impressive military triumph. In their flight from Anatolia, Greek troops had left a scorched trail of destruction in their wake. In Manisa, for example, over 10,000 buildings—90 per cent of the town—lay in charred ruins. As they pursued the Greeks, Nationalist troops found dead bodies and passed through areas still smoldering, which inflamed their passions. Looting and killing broke out in the Greek and Armenian quarters of Izmir, fueled by the emotions of nationalist soldiers and civilians alike. An actual fire, beginning on 13 September, engulfed much of the city, which burned for five straight days. The Armenian, Greek, and European quarters were destroyed, but the Muslim and the Jewish quarters escaped destruction.[88] Mustafa Kemal appeared unfazed by the conflagration, describing it to a French admiral as a "disagreeable incident" of secondary importance when compared to other pressing questions.[89] The burning of Izmir represented yet another human tragedy in a series of like events in the War of Independence. Such was the passion and enmity of the war. Responsibility for the fire remains a point of debate, and estimates for the number of Christians killed start at 10,000 and go higher. All the death and destruction occurred under Nureddin's watch, whose First Army was responsible for the city's occupation. By 22 October, over 200,000 Greeks and other non-Muslims had evacuated Izmir.

Despite driving the Greek army from Anatolia, Mustafa Kemal faced the difficult task of negotiating a favorable peace. Greece still occupied Thrace, and British, French, and Italian troops controlled the Straits and Istanbul. The National Pact demanded the inclusion of both places within the borders of Turkey. General Maurice Pelle, the third French High Commissioner in Istanbul, and Henri Franklin-Bouillon, France's liaison to Mustafa Kemal, both came to Izmir. Paris was keen on reaching a final agreement. On 18 September, Mustafa Kemal tied participation in armistice talks to Greece abandoning Thrace.[90] This was a tough first negotiating position, but he could easily soften it.

In defeating the Greeks, the National Army had pursued Greek III Corps to the Straits. On 15 September, London authorized General Charles Harington, commander of the British Army in the Black Sea, to use force, if necessary, to defend Istanbul and the Straits. The euphoria of victory, however, failed to cloud Kemal's judgment. He deployed troops in the Straits region with prudence. On 22 September, Mustafa Kemal revealed his strategic thinking to Karabekir: "Although we are very strong, we are pursuing a very calculating and moderate policy ... We are trying to isolate the British. Our troops are concentrating in the direction of Istanbul and Çanakkale, but we prefer a political solution."[91] Kemal's military movements were designed to strengthen Kemal's diplomatic position by sending signals of resolve and determination. In line with this strategy, Mustafa Kemal demanded restraint and caution from his commanders. They were told that "those who needed [to know] would from now on [receive] instructions and commands so as not to leave an opportunity for a bad misunderstanding between our soldiers and the English units."[92] Careful, calculated brinkmanship was required to avoid hostilities with the British; a tactical mishap might have unwanted strategic consequences. In İsmet's own words, "walking on the shores of the Bosporus with the army ... was a very dangerous decision."[93] By the first half of October, Mustafa Kemal had cautiously militarized the southern Straits region with some 48,000 troops.

Although initially adopting a maximalist position by demanding Greece's immediate withdrawal from Thrace before armistice discussions, Mustafa Kemal agreed on 29 September to talks in Mudanya, a small town on the southern shore of the Sea of Marmara near Bursa. He selected İsmet to represent Turkey and instructed him to demand Thrace as far as Meriç River but left Western Thrace as a negotiable item.[94] The armistice talks began on 3 October, and Turkey and Britain reached an agreement on 10 October. On 11 October, Turkey, Italy, France, and Great Britain formally signed the Armistice of Mudanya. Greece reluctantly gave its consent on 14 October, relinquishing Eastern Thrace from the River Meriç, along with the town of Edirne. The final status of the Straits and Istanbul was left for the peace conference. The Greek pullout began on 15 October, and on 19 October, Lloyd George resigned, never to return as prime minister, leaving behind a failed Greek project. The Greek government had already succumbed back in September to a military coup, which resulted in the king's abdication, public trials, and the quick execution of five former ministers for high treason, including Prime Minister Dimitrios Gounaris and Lieutenant General Giorgios Hatzianestis. Failed Anatolian ventures helped bring down two governments.

On 11 October, the same day as the signing of the Armistice of Mudanya, Mustafa Kemal personally submitted to the TBMM a list of "commanders and officers" to be read for "their sacrificial service under fire during the battles of Afyonkarahisar and Dumlupınar and the pursuit of the enemy." On two other occasions, the 12th and 16th, the TBMM listened to the reading of more names for a grand total of 540 officers, ranging in rank from lieutenant to colonel.[95] Mustafa Kemal, like other commanders, often appealed to "fame and honor" in motivating troops. Now it was proper to give individual officers their deserved "fame and honor" before the representatives of the nation and for the public record. Earlier, senior commanders and officers had received their rewards with promotions in the heat of battle.

Putting diplomatic concerns briefly aside, Mustafa Kemal went to the recently liberated town of Bursa and on 27 October delivered an address to a meeting of 527 male and female teachers from Istanbul. This gathering recalled the Education Congress in Ankara that had been held in July 1921 but cut short owing to a crisis on the battlefield. At that time, Mustafa Kemal had described two kinds of wars, one waged on the external front requiring a "weapon" and the other on the internal front using the "mind." The Bursa speech revolved around the centrality of education as key to the country's future progress and development. Before launching into his subject, Mustafa Kemal first worked his audience by expressing his desire to be a child again so that he could learn from them. With "patriotism, good will, and sacrifice" as a foundation, "our guide will be knowledge (*ilim*) and science (*fenn*)." Mustafa Kemal also expressed strong Turkish sentiment. "The Turkish nation, Turkish craft, its economy, Turkish poetry and literature will develop with an all-encompassing new beauty." Mustafa Kemal clearly viewed science and the humanities together as central to national education and warned against circling the wagons and attempting to live without ties to the world. Instead, "we take knowledge and science wherever it is, and we will put it into the head of every individual of the nation." Here he referred to a *hadith* (saying) of the Prophet Muhammad that called for Muslims to seek after knowledge, even in China if necessary. The aim of educational programs and policies was to eradicate ignorance and develop "national genius." Toward the end of the speech, Mustafa Kemal returned to the two-war concept. "The victory won by our armies has merely prepared the ground for your victory and the victory of your armies."[96] By participating in an education congress in the midst of war and then right after its conclusion, Mustafa Kemal underscored the importance of education, science, and knowledge in the war against ignorance and illiteracy in the new Turkey.

On 17 October, Ottoman Grand Vezir Tevfik Paşa had sent a telegram to Ankara proposing an end to the dualism of government. The Allied Powers, for their part, invited both governments to participate in the peace conference in Lausanne, Switzerland. The Allied double invitation incensed many deputies; only Ankara had paid the price to warrant attendance at Lausanne. Fueling the emotions around him, Mustafa Kemal, true to form, seized "the psychological moment" at the end of October 1922 to move against the sultanate, while sparing the caliphate, a compromise designed to placate religious and other conservative elements.[97] The TBMM abolished the sultanate on 1 November. In his speech arguing for this radical step, Mustafa Kemal revealed again his Turkish sentiments and thoughts. For the last three years, the people of Turkey had held in their hands national sovereignty. Mustafa Kemal placed personal blame on Vahdeddin for nearly bringing the Turkish nation into enslavement. In its struggle, the Turkish nation had exercised its sovereignty through the Grand National Assembly of Turkey. After expressing proper deference to *Tanrı*, or God in Turkish, to Muhammad as the last of the prophets, and to the Book (Quran) as perfect, Mustafa Kemal used Islamic history to argue for popular sovereignty, underscoring that after the death of the Prophet Muhammad, the first four caliphs were elected and that they relied on consultation for matters dealing with leadership, the state, and the nation. He stressed the important place of Turks in history and their unique contribution to Islamic government. The origins of the Turkish nation went back to an individual named Turk who was the grandson of Noah, a preposterous claim. Turks had established great states in Central Asia, starting fifteen centuries ago before they first came into the Middle East as soldiers. The great Turkish nation brought to Islam the sultanate that divested the caliphate of its temporal powers. In this, Turkish rulers had established the sovereignty of the Turkish state.[98] Kemal's Turkish pride came forth clearly through the speech.

The abolishment of the Ottoman sultanate strengthened Kemal's hand both internationally and domestically. The abolishment of the Ottoman sultanate ensured that Ankara represented Turkey when the peace conference opened in Lausanne on 20 November. Unlike other treaties that ended World War I, the Treaty of Lausanne was a negotiated rather than an imposed settlement. The conference lasted eight months, divided into two sessions with a two-and-a-half-month break (5 February to 22 April) in between. On 30 January 1923, in the midst of peace negotiations, Turkey and Greece reached an important agreement with far-reaching implications for both societies. The two countries agreed to a compulsory exchange of populations set to begin on 1 May. Only Greeks in Istanbul and Muslims in Western Thrace were spared forced deportation. Over one million Ottoman Greeks moved to Greece while close to half a million Muslims relocated to Turkey. It was a preventive measure designed to create conditions for a more stable peace by each country having a more religiously homogeneous society. The ethno-religious character of past conflicts in the Balkans had undermined the empire from within. Between 1912 and 1923, Anatolia's Muslim population rose from 80 to 98 per cent. In expelling the Rum population, Turkey lost a good segment of its business and professional classes, thus setting back economic recovery. Major religious and ethnic diversity still remained within the Muslim community, however: between Sunnis and Alevis, and between Turks and Kurds. Communal tensions and conflicts thus did not go away.

On 24 July, Turkey, the British Empire, France, Italy, Japan, Greece, Rumania, and the Serb-Croat-Slovene State finally signed the Treaty of Lausanne, recognizing the independence of Turkey, whose boundaries included Istanbul and the eastern provinces with Kars. No mention was made of Kurdistan; Mosul was left for future resolution. The Treaty abolished all foreign and mixed courts in Turkey, thus subjecting foreign subjects to Turkish courts. Non-Muslim nationals lost their special privileges but theoretically gained full equality before the law and the same rights and freedoms as other Turkish nationals. Turkey was obligated to pay back a portion of the Ottoman debt to European creditors, with the remainder divided among the empire's former Arab provinces. A clean financial slate was not in the offing; economic independence had to be earned. The Straits were demilitarized with the exception of a 12,000-man garrison in Istanbul and placed under the supervision of an international commission chaired by a Turk to ensure freedom of navigation to all in peacetime. This arrangement failed to grant full sovereignty to Turkey. Nevertheless, the TBMM ratified the document on 23 August by a large margin, 213 of 227 deputies. The last of the British troops departed Istanbul on 2 October 1923.

Turkey was free at last. The country, unlike most of the Middle East, escaped foreign occupation and gained control of her destiny through war and diplomacy. Over 10,000 soldiers were killed in battle, a very small number compared to losses in World War I. But civilian deaths, physical damage, and war expenditures extracted a heavy toll. The War of Independence emerged as the first successful national liberation movement in the twentieth century and became a source of inspiration to peoples around the world during the inter-war period. Japan's defeat of Russia in the Russo-Japanese War of 1904–1905 had had a similar effect in the non-Western world prior to World War I, when an Asian country had defeated a European power decisively on land and at sea.

The Kemalist Revolution

During the no war, no peace period, Mustafa Kemal thought not just of a treaty to end the war. He also wanted to prepare the people for revolutionary changes designed to create a new Turkey. Defeating the Greeks gave him political capital on the home front, and he immediately set out to recalibrate society by introducing a peacetime narrative even as the negotiations were underway for a peace treaty. On 14 January 1923, Mustafa Kemal departed Ankara, filled with energy, on a major tour of western and southern Anatolia that included public speeches and press interviews with foreign and national journalists. The aim was to disseminate a new, post-war narrative. Until 1923, Mustafa Kemal had made only eighteen public addresses, but now in 1923, over a period of several months, he delivered thirty-four talks.[99] Among the visits were Eskişehir, Arifiye, İzmit, Bursa, Alaşehir, Salihli, Kasaba, Manisa, Izmir, Akhisar, Balıkesir, Adana, Mersin, Tarsus, Konya, Afyon, and Kütahya. His audiences included crowds in general, as well as specific groups such as women, youth, city officials, tradesmen, and farmers. Sandwiched between stops was an economic congress held in Izmir from 17 February to 4 March, with over 1,100 delegates from all over Turkey. The decisions reached at the Izmir Economic Congress shaped economic policy until the advent of the worldwide depression.

This extensive tour served three purposes. One was to consolidate power by visiting local officials and ensuring the anticipated parliamentary election would be won by his political party, as back in December 1922, Mustafa Kemal had formly established the People's Party from the Society for the Defense of Rights of Anatolia and Rumeli. He also wanted to see for himself the state of the country and to talk to people. He barraged government officials and individuals from all walks of life with questions. His inquiries pertained to matters such as schools and education, the status of women and villagers, the size of families, the state of the forests and livestock, and the care of war veterans. Mustafa Kemal also sought to educate the population about the new Turkey that would unfold over time before their very eyes. On 21 March, at Konya Sultanic School, Mustafa Kemal delineated three targets for transformation: "the nation's soul (*ruh*), conscience (*vicdan*), and thought (*fikir*)."[100] Now as leader of post-war Turkey, he applied his triad to the collective, the nation.

In his speeches and press interviews, Mustafa Kemal made frequent use of terms such as intellect, conscience, heart, and feelings. "Will means the propensities, the desires of conscience. That is to say it is a moral (*manevi*) matter."[101] On another occasion, Mustafa Kemal spoke of will as "the propensities of the heart and conscience."[102] When queried about freedom of conscience, he cautioned that laws were necessary in order to place restrictions on freedom of conscience for the common good.[103] In other words, national unity and collective conscience trumped individual rights. Mustafa Kemal also described effective foreign policy as based on "strong domestic policy, administration, and organizations ... Foreign policy is inexorably linked to domestic policy."[104] This stated the obvious, but Mustafa Kemal had effectively put words into deed. He foiled the aims of his adversaries while setting the internal foundations for the new Turkey.

In İzmit on 19 January, Mustafa Kemal delivered what might be considered a "State of the Union" address in which he analyzed the weaknesses of the Ottoman Empire and offered a vision for future development. Turkey's military policy had to be based on defense; the mentality that sought expansion and conquest had to be suppressed; and the country needed to focus its energies on internal development and the increase of its population. Economic development depended on infrastructure, roads, railroads, and ports. Farmers and herdsmen needed agricultural banks and schools. Big industrial complexes and factories were also vital for economic development. Private capital and enterprise were most welcome, as Mustafa Kemal envisioned the future creating millionaires and billionaires who made their wealth from banking, railroads, factories, businesses, and industrial establishments. The speech called for a curriculum in elementary and middle schools that taught the knowledge and science produced by civilization and humanity, for the country lacked scientists, doctors, engineers, and other professions for rapid economic development. "We need human beings who possess *serious sentiment* (italics mine)." Mustafa Kemal promised to send young people to Europe, America, and other places for education.[105] This speech revealed a comprehensive approach toward the future, one formulated over time.

During his tour, however, Mustafa Kemal did address specific topics. He suggested that the Kurdish people could expect some local autonomy, but also cautioned that drawing boundaries based on *Kürtlük*, or a Kurdish entity, would destroy Turkism and Turkey.[106] In Taurus on 18 March, a gathering of youth in a heavily Turkish area of Anatolia heard that the new State of Turkey would mobilize "the moral qualities of Turkishness."[107] In another instance, he rejected pursuing expansionist goals, such as the unity of Islam or Turanism, and instead indicated that the state's policies would focus on living within national boundaries.[108] Mustafa Kemal also indicated a general commitment to female emancipation, with the aim of both sexes eventually acquiring the same level of education. "Women will become scholars and scientists, and they will achieve the same levels of learning as men." Then Mustafa Kemal slightly altered a saying, or *hadith*, of the Prophet Muhammad that God wanted *both men and women* (italics mine) to seek after knowledge together where it may be found.[109]

When it came to the subject of Islam, Mustafa Kemal called for expanded enlightenment. There would be little need for learning Arabic if the important religious books were translated into Turkish. Such translations would permit Muslims to access the sources of their faith directly. Moreover, serious religious studies required knowing French, English, and German.[110] Reason and critical scholarship were to drive studies of faith. Islam appeared as a rational religion that completely supported "reason, logic, and truth." Mustafa Kemal envisioned a "true learned" (*hakki ulema*) class with "enlightened intellects" like the Ibn Rushds, the Ibn Sinas, the Imam Ghazalis, and the Farabis, who would bring the country out of a difficult state.[111] These medieval Muslim scholars and scientists were, with the exception of Ghazali, also controversial Islamic philosophers who accorded primacy to reason in the pursuit of knowledge. Mustafa Kemal was already contemplating their contemporary relevance in 1916 while on the Eastern Front in World War I. The Friday sermon, or *hutbe*, would serve to enlighten the people about contemporary matters. As Mustafa Kemal noted, in the time of the Prophet and his four successors, "The *minbers* were springs of spiritual power and sources of light for the minds (*dimağ*) and consciences (*vicdan*) of the people."[112] Such language suggested a desire to create an enlightened Islam supportive of modern science and thought.

The themes of his speeches were not hatched overnight; rather they represented sentiments and ideas developed over time, at least during World War I. As a whole, the speeches reflected a broad approach toward transformation, seeing many issues and various segments of society all tied together in the reconstruction. Mustafa Kemal sought to connect emotionally with his audiences in order to inculcate new aspirations and expectations in them, to form mature national sentiment. In this Anatolian tour in the first half of 1923, Mustafa Kemal acted out the role of the nation's *baba* (father) as political leader and national educator, transitioning from the father commanding military units to the father leading the nation and from the educator of soldiers to the educator of the nation.[113]

Kemal's personal life changed dramatically during the no war and no peace period. Back in Izmir in September 1922, he met a young, bright woman named Latife who came from a wealthy Muslim business family in Izmir. She had studied law in Paris and spoke French fluently. The couple married on 29 January 1923 in the midst of Kemal's tour of Anatolia. In his eyes, Latife fit the image of the modern woman for the modernization of Turkey, and she became a regular fixture at public events, accompanying him on his tours of Anatolia. "She rode with the Ghazi, walked with him, drove with him to all official ceremonies, [and] went with him to manoeuvers and to the opening of Parliament. She was unveiled and rode astride."[114] Unfortunately, the couple proved incompatible, and on 23 August 1925, Mustafa Kemal divorced her.

To embark on his reforms, Mustafa Kemal ensured that his People's Party won the national elections, establishing a one-party system. On 13 October, Ankara became the country's new capital. Then on 29 October 1923, Turkey became a Republic, with Mustafa Kemal as its president. On 3 March 1924, the TBMM approved three new bills. The first abolished the Ministry of Islamic Law and Religious Foundations and removed the Chief of General Staff from the Cabinet; the second established a single system of public education; and the third deposed the caliph and abolished the caliphate. Mustafa Kemal had spoken of educational reform in Ankara during war, then in Bursa during the period of no war and no peace, and finally achieved that vision through legislation in peacetime. In subsequent years, the Republic underwent major reforms: the closure of religious courts and Sufi mystical orders; the implementation of Western law codes; the adoption of a Latin alphabet to replace the Arabic script; the Turkification of the language; the pursuance of women's rights including the right to vote, hold elected office, attend a university with mixed classes, enter professions, and even serve as judges; the requirement for all citizens to adopt family names; and the acceptance of a Gregorian calendar, the metric system, and Sunday as a day of

11   *Mustafa Kemal listening to a farmer, Kayseri, 19 December 1930*

rest. Mustafa Kemal kept the army out of politics and gave prominence to his political party. During the Republic as president, he continued in his eclectic studies and assumed the national role of educator, explaining his reforms to his people. Then, in 1934, he took on the surname of Atatürk, or Father Turk. The prefix "*Ata* was grandeur, signifying not only a father, [but] the progenitor of a line," i.e., the Turkish Revolution.[115]

Taken together, these reforms were clearly radical and substantive. In implementing all these changes, Mustafa Kemal thought in terms of "inculcating in individuals the traditions and memories of common national thought (*fikir*), morals (*ahlak*), feeling (*his*) and emotion (*heyecan*)."[116] *Dimağ*, or the mind, stressed the cognitive based on developing science, reason, and knowledge as the motive forces for progress.[117] *Vicdan*, or conscience, meant the indoctrination of secular, civic, and national values into a new morality. *His*, or emotion, was intended to develop a mature sentiment, especially that of being a Turk and a human being: "the Turkish nation [and] national sentiment (*milli his*) . . . [and] with human sentiment (*insani his*), not with religious sentiment . . . [both] lodged within *vicdan*."[118] Mustafa Kemal thus drove his revolution, as he did his own life, along the dynamic interaction of the mind, conscience, and sentiment with the aim of firmly grounding Turkey in the twentieth century, fully integrated into the one human, albeit Western, civilization. He thus led by example. The Kemalist triad emphasized an endless process of growth and development, hence Kemal's harsh aversion to dogma. Ideally, all three were mutually supportive. Turkish national sentiment was linked, for example, to national values and Nationalist ideology.

To society's detriment, however, authoritarian, one-party rule meant the suppression in the public space of the mind, conscience, and sentiment of political opponents, pious Muslims, feminists, ethnic Kurds, and other minorities, among others. Democracy and the growth of civil society would unleash these elements, but this would take place gradually after his death in 1938. Moreover, Mustafa Kemal abandoned his war strategy with its broad appeal to a pluralist Anatolian society for a narrowly based secular, Turkish nation-state. Official ideology eventually spoke of only the Turkish *millet*, or nation, and an iron fist was used to crush opposition and unrest. In implementing all the reforms, the Kemalist Revolution thus inflicted wounds on society, in particular upon religious and ethnic minorities, as unity came to suppress diversity. And the Republic experienced its own version of militarism within the larger European context.[119] Post-Kemalist Turkey would have to recalibrate Kemal's revolutionary policies.

During the period of imposing major changes in a relatively short period, Mustafa Kemal left some thoughts and sentiments on war. He appreciated the power of history, once stating that "To write history is as important as making history." So he took upon himself the task of giving his version of the War of

Independence in a *Speech*, or *Nutuk*, to the Republican People's Party, an address that spanned six days, from 15 to 20 Oct 1927, and lasted over thirty-six hours. *Nutuk*, which became the official version of the War of Independence, unfortunately exaggerated Kemal's role and denigrated that of his compatriots. In it, however, Mustafa Kemal revealed the influence of Clausewitz's trinity when he spoke of "three means" (*üç vasıta*) in preparing for the decisive campaign to defeat the Greek army: the nation, the Assembly as the government, and the army.[120] On other occasions, he expressed thoughts and sentiments contrary to the militarism of his age, such as that only defensive wars were legitimate. Moreover, the 1930s saw the dissemination of his famous principle "Peace at home, peace abroad," a phrase not synchronous with the currents of militaristic adventurism emerging in parts of Europe. Then, for the commemoration of ANZAC Day on 25 April 1934, Mustafa Kemal sent a brief speech to Gallipoli:

> Those heroes who shed their blood and lost their lives. You are now lying in the soil of a friendly country, therefore rest in peace. There is no difference between the Johnnies and the Mehmets to us where they lay side by side here in the country of ours. You, the mothers who sent their sons from far away countries; wipe away your tears, your sons are now lying in our bosom and are in peace. After having lost their lives on this land, they have become our sons as well.

These words of reconciliation contrasted sharply with the then-current Fascist and Nazi rhetoric.

Conclusion

Kemal's leadership played an important role in the final military victory over the Greeks. Rather than proceed piecemeal, Mustafa Kemal accepted risk and aimed for a battle of annihilation, destroying the adversary in a single campaign. Failure would certainly have weakened his position, but most likely would not have led to his downfall. Mustafa Kemal spent a year of military preparation before deciding that diplomatic avenues had been exhausted, the people's patience had been strained enough, and the army had been trained and reorganized sufficiently to launch the Great Offensive. Compared to the Battle of Sakarya, the army was much better trained and equipped, with greater stability in command positions and organization. Operation *Sad* had many authors who contributed to its evolution, and it ultimately represented a mature plan based on corporate wisdom and experience. It did, however, bear Kemal's contributions and his seal of responsibility. For one, adding an entire corps to the main attack against the

Greek underbelly enhanced exploitation capabilities and options. Admittedly, the plan was not as audacious as it could have been, but the army was inexperienced at major offensive operations. Nevertheless, Mustafa Kemal and the armies of the TBMM earn a deserved place in the modern annals of lightning campaigns waged with a specially configured cavalry force designed to conduct sustained combat in the depth of the enemy's army, thereby linking forward tactical battle with rear operations. Military victory resulted, in good measure, from Kemal's leadership before and during the offensive.

Military victory also gave Mustafa Kemal political capital to embark on an offensive in the non-military arena. While engaged in achieving a peace treaty to end the War of Independence, he commenced building "the new Turkey" or *Yeni Türkiye*. The first half of 1923 revealed Kemal's energy and thought for transforming Turkey as he conducted his fact-finding and promotional tour of western and southern Anatolia. The War of Independence, if understood in a broad sense and not a narrowly defined military history, ended not with the defeat of the Greek army but with the signing of the Treaty of Lausanne and the establishment of the Republic. The latter set the foundation for a new Turkey. Mustafa Kemal knew in broad terms where he was going after the end of armed conflict, unlike those who continued to tie the country's fate to the Ottoman dynasty. Kemal's amassing of power served a higher end than personal aggrandizement. From around the time of the Battle of Sakarya, the words Turk, Turkish nation, and Turkishness gained more prominence as Mustafa Kemal laid the seeds for building a Turkish nation-state. Unlike many great men who achieved their place in recent history mainly by winning a major war, Mustafa Kemal confronted the momentous task of rebuilding his country out of the ashes resulting from a series of devastating wars, and he embraced the challenge with forethought, conviction, and passion. After fifteen years as president, he bequeathed to future generations a society shaken at its roots and driven to a major transformation. His successors would have to respond to the Kemalist Revolution with a dynamism that has pulsated into the twenty-first century.

Conclusion

If we then ask what sort of mind is likeliest to display the qualities of military genius, experience and observation will both tell us that it is the inquiring rather than a creative mind, the comprehensive rather than the specialized approach, the calm rather than the excitable head to which in war we would choose to entrust our brothers and children, and the safety and honor of our country.

Carl von Clausewitz[1]

Perhaps more than the mind, logic, or judgment, what makes history is feelings/sentiments.

Mustafa Kemal Atatürk, Adana, 15 March 1923

BY THE END OF WORLD WAR I, Mustafa Kemal Atatürk had become very much his own man, a successful military commander, broadly read, and determined to carve for himself a place of leadership in the struggle for his country's freedom. In the War of Independence, he effectively transitioned from military command to political leadership, doing both successfully. After first trying to work in Istanbul within the Ottoman imperial system as a political general, Atatürk engineered an assignment to Anatolia that allowed him to embark upon a path unshackled by the Istanbul government. Critical assets were available to him: the remnants of an imperial army, an Ottoman provincial administration, a loose underground organization of former Unionists, and a population familiar with mass politics. Success at the helm, however, did not prove to be a simple task. It required establishing an effective provisional government, rebuilding a defeated army while integrating or suppressing irregular forces, and mobilizing the people of Anatolia. In an ever-changing strategic environment, Atatürk had to develop wise policies based on reason and intuition; to weigh possibilities and take chances in the execution of diplomatic and military strategies; and, finally, to harness the passions and will of the army and the people. The army provided him with the strongest support, whereas the Grand National Assembly offered legitimacy and a means to claim to represent the people's aspirations. At his core, Atatürk was very much an ambitious pragmatist, with an instinct for timing.

From his conduct of the war, Atatürk clearly appreciated Clausewitz's understanding that "war is not merely an act of policy but a true political instrument, a continuation of political intercourse, carried on with other means."[2] To be effective as a national leader required more the mindset and temperament of a statesman than of a general, because now the full spectrum of waging war meant managing the interplay of policy, diplomacy, and fiscal matters, as well as military operations. Fortune, however, smiled upon him when he disembarked in Samsun on 19 May 1919. Four days earlier, the Greeks had begun landing an army in Izmir and the War of Independence commenced that day. Atatürk took advantage of this galvanizing event as he began claiming to represent the people's legitimate aspirations for independence, full sovereignty, and territorial integrity. These political aims were stated at the Erzurum and Sivas Congresses and then enshrined in the National Pact adopted by the duly elected Ottoman Parliament. This much was public knowledge. In addition to the publicly stated goals, however, Atatürk came to see the opportunity of establishing a republic to replace the six-century-old multi-ethnic, multi-religious, and multi-lingual Ottoman Empire. And in the last year and a half before the Treaty of Lausanne, he expressed more pronounced Turkish sentiments as well. What may have been more of a notion or a sentiment before the war became for Atatürk within the realm of possibility with the evolution of the national struggle: that is, the emergence of a republic.

The 1921 Law of Fundamental Organization defined governance by claiming sovereignty for the nation without mentioning either the sultanate or the caliphate, thus laying the legal groundwork for a republic. This provisional constitution complemented the National Pact, becoming two sides of the same coin. The pact addressed the issue of independence and boundaries while the constitution outlined the form of government. Yet, in the long run, Atatürk negotiated on final borders and agreed to economic concessions, but he would not restore the Ottoman sultanate–caliphate. The War of Independence thus developed as much a political struggle on the home front as a fight against foreign forces, and Atatürk continued trying to amass personal power while state-building and cautiously undermining the authority of the Ottoman sultanate–caliphate. Seeking to have the last Ottoman Parliament meet in Anatolia was but one such attempt. He could not let the sultan's government gain the initiative, which it had a chance to do when the newly elected deputies met in Istanbul. Fortune smiled upon him again when the Allied Powers closed down Parliament rather than seek an accommodation on the National Pact.

Gaining legitimacy required some demonstration of popular support. At the Erzurum Congress, Atatürk became a recognized political leader at the regional level with his election as president of the Representative Committee. The national struggle reached a watershed with the establishment of the Grand National Assembly in Ankara, which enhanced Atatürk's authority to construct a provisional government while accelerating the process for building an army and mobilizing the people. And Atatürk used the elected body to strengthen his political power while claiming to represent the national will. He devoted time and effort to attending its sessions and participating in its discussions, for Atatürk appreciated the Assembly's legitimizing role while at the same time enduring its debates. Abolishing it would have invalidated his claim to represent the people's aspirations. To his credit, Atatürk avoided attempting to transform the Assembly into a rubber-stamp institution but rather accepted a modicum of free expression and action among its deputies. This parliamentary dynamic eventually led to the formation of an organized opposition in the Assembly called Second Group. And sometimes, Atatürk made tactical compromises on policy with the opposition, such as limiting his appointment as commander in chief to three-month intervals and agreeing to the election of Rauf as prime minister. The Grand National Assembly of Turkey testified to the existence of a democratic current throughout the war, one that permitted displays of moral courage as when deputies forced Nureddin's removal, provided monetary compensation to Kurdish tribes for damages inflicted by government troops, and restricted the powers of two commands, that of Central Army and the Elcezire Front. Parliamentarians directly challenged Atatürk's conduct of the war as commander in chief.

As a statesman, Atatürk adjusted policies, diplomacy, and military operations according to the exigencies of war. At the beginning, on the diplomatic front, he emphasized developing good relations with the Soviets while closely monitoring military developments in the Caucasus. Both countries faced the same adversaries, but the strong ties did not come quickly and naturally at first. In the process, Atatürk and Karabekir coordinated diplomacy and military operations to affect the conquest and incorporation of the regions of Kars and Ardahan into the state of Turkey. And Russian aid played an important role in helping Mustafa Kemal win on the battlefield against the Greeks. The adversary of an adversary had become an ally. In southeastern Anatolia against the French, on the other hand, Atatürk took advantage of a prolonged people's resistance, coupled with military victories on other fronts, to demonstrate national resilience and eventually to negotiate an agreement with France. In dealing with foreign powers, Atatürk was keenly aware that he was negotiating and not dictating; so flexibility on less important demands was necessary to facilitate diplomatic closure. Compromises on Batum, Hatay, and the Straits attested to Atatürk's *Realpolitik*. Here, Atatürk practiced the art of tactical compromise for strategic ends.

Waging war proved a complex endeavor from a military perspective. The War of Independence comprised several different kinds of smaller wars. Atatürk placed a priority on securing the home front, both politically and militarily, until the battlefield crisis of July 1921. The home front experienced rebellions and brigandage with varying degrees of intensity throughout this period, and Atatürk relied on the regular army and National Forces for law and order. None of the uprisings seriously challenged his leadership, but a couple rebellions occurred embarrassingly close to Ankara. All drained scarce human and material resources. The Black Sea region, for its part, presented a special problem because of its relatively large Rum minority. Here Central Army used regular troops, reinforced with irregular combatants, to conduct counter-insurgency operations while also crushing Kurdish tribal unrest.

In the early stages of the national struggle, the Eastern Front proved the most pressing after the home front. Border clashes and cross-border operations against Armenia culminated in offensive operations that eventually incorporated the Kars and Ardahan regions into the new Turkey. The southwestern region, for its part, was largely quiet under Italian occupation, serving as a base of guerrilla forays into Greek-occupied territory. Southeastern Anatolia, however, experienced intense fighting with a combination of regular forces, militias, and an armed civilian population engaged in insurgency operations, sieges, and urban warfare against a small French occupying force. Kurdish tribal unrest also required attention in this complex front. France, rather than suffering a decisive military defeat, surrendered to a strategy of attrition. Finally, the Western Front against the Greeks evolved from National Forces and regular units largely engaged in guerrilla warfare to two large, regular armies pitted against each other in conventional battles.

Atatürk relied on the talents and experience of both the military and the bureaucracy. Senior army commanders especially played a crucial role in the War of Independence. At first, Kazım Karabekir and Ali Fuad (Cebesoy) protected Atatürk from arrest and helped mobilize local Defense of Rights Societies and the population. Some legitimacy thus came from the barrel of a gun. But to be successful in battle, Atatürk depended upon the corporate wisdom and experience of his commanders as well, and he delegated to his front commanders while providing general guidance. Consultation and delegation were central to his military successes. Atatürk welcomed input, even asked for it outright. From student days, he had learned about the uniqueness of events and thus had to maintain mental flexibility and rely on intuition. In terms of the decisive campaign against the Greeks, for example, Operation *Sad* specifically had a number of fathers. At the supreme command level, Fevzi and İsmet together emerged as an indispensable team in the Battle of Sakarya and the Great Offensive. Yet, in the final analysis, Atatürk was key to the army's successes in battle, and in the last year of war fighting, he took full responsibility as field commander, showing a willingness to risk losing in order to win. In the Battle of Sakarya and the Great Offensive, he oversaw planning and preparations for each battle and then became directly involved in commanding forces. The defensive battle at Sakarya required skills at positional warfare and proved a test of wills in an attrition struggle. Then in the Great Offensive and Pursuit, Atatürk demonstrated intuition, or *coup d'œil*, at maneuver warfare when he coordinated the advance of large units to achieve decisive victory in one continuous campaign.

Atatürk managed a political-military landscape that required adroit balancing of each front with larger goals always in mind. For the first two years of the struggle, 1919 to 1921, he had the luxury to devote attention to politics and the home front. Britain, France, and Italy lacked the means and the will to commit to a full-scale occupation of Anatolia, thus providing Atatürk with a safe haven (until the Greek offensive of August 1921 threatened Ankara for a brief period) within the country from which to build the resistance movement. He commanded each military front from a distance, making visits when appropriate. Time worked to his advantage as long as he showed progress.

Fedakarlık, or sacrifice, helped define Atatürk and his age. Atatürk described in eloquent language the sacrifices endured by the people prior to the War of Independence in his report of 20 September 1917. So two years later, he moved cautiously in escalating demands for more national sacrifice. Care was taken in reaching out to the various segments of society—religious leaders, tribal chiefs, Kurds, villagers—always adjusting the message depending on the target audience but at the same time underscoring the noble goals of independence and popular sovereignty. Muslim nationalism and Muslim patriotism were the key means for rallying support, but around the time of the Battle of Sakarya, the words Turk, Turkish, and Turkishness gained greater currency. The move to "total war" wisely awaited a major crisis. The defeat of the National Army on the Western Front in July 1921 and the subsequent threat to Ankara created an opportunity for Atatürk to extract from the Assembly extraordinary powers as commander in chief. Now it was also more palatable to requisition scarce supplies from the population. Final victory resulted from an orchestrated harmony of the Ankara government, the army of the Grand National Assembly of Turkey, and the people of Anatolia.

But what made Atatürk such a successful political and military leader in the War of Independence? Ambition certainly drove him; without it, opportunities would have easily passed him by. Perhaps as early as in high school, Atatürk committed to preparing himself to be a leader. He worked deliberately to develop the

Kemalist triad of mind, conscience, and sentiment in his own life and then applied his knowledge and intuitive skills in dealing with others. Mind and reason were important for successful leadership. In the words of Clausewitz quoted above, Atatürk possessed "an inquiring mind" with "the comprehensive rather than the specialized approach" toward problems. This cognitive orientation developed early in his military career as a student, when he matured as a dedicated lifelong learner, a student of life and people, a man in possession of a cosmopolitan mind, who devoted time and energy to personal study and reflection. From Clausewitz, Goltz, and military instructors, Atatürk gained an appreciation of the interplay of theory and practice, the importance of understanding the nature of a problem in a concrete manner.

To be an effective leader of men required both rational and intuitive knowledge, and Atatürk's eclectic mind embraced the study of human experience from various disciplines, such as literature, history, philosophy, political theory, and psychology. This broad range of interests and study helped prepare the soldier to transition to the statesman. Atatürk absorbed details and extracted inferences from them, gazing frequently toward the larger picture, appreciating the primacy of policy in war and the interplay of strategy, military operations, and tactics. His own military writings indicate that Atatürk saw learning as not merely the acquisition of knowledge but also its internalization. Knowing things intimately built confidence and developed intuitive abilities. But for him, knowledge ultimately had to have a practical application, for as a leader Atatürk had to make decisions and act upon them with determination.

Conscience, or *vicdan*, also played an important role in Atatürk's life, because from its depths sprang conviction, will, determination, and courage. Atatürk often used the word *vicdan* to underscore the source of his thoughts and actions and to motivate individuals and groups. For him, conscience comprised values, virtues, and a consciousness that together made for character, and character was most important in leadership. Without it, intellect was useless. Despite personal vices and a questionable private life, Atatürk nevertheless created a professional command climate, striving to embody and instill the values of excellence, professionalism, patriotism, honor, duty, courage, and sacrifice. He commanded by example and led with the force of his personality, an approach and attitude that he learned from his military instructors and literature and that he applied to his role of a political leader. He took care in developing his inner self and public image, as evidenced in his interest as a young captain in Benjamin Franklin's thirteen virtues and later his desire as a brigadier general to write a book for the army on moral education and military manners.

Yet Atatürk was capable of callousness and ruthlessness. An end justified the means when, for example, he readily gave Nureddin a free hand to squash

Ottoman Greek and Kurdish unrest, or enlisted the likes of Topal Osman, or authorized the mass deportation of the Pontian Greeks. He accepted the loss of innocent civilian lives as a common feature in warfare. There were, therefore, two sides to Atatürk's character, as poignantly noted by Grace Ellison, a British feminist journalist and frequent visitor to Turkey: "sometimes those eyes seemed to be the deepest blue, sometimes the deepest grey; at one moment kind almost to excess, at another cruel."[3] Ruthless, rather than cruel, would be a better word to describe Atatürk, who was, to some degree, a product of the horrors and cruelty of war. This quality helped define his character as he negotiated through the norms of his day. The deep blueness in his eyes represented more an ability to connect with people emotionally and intellectually.

Finally, Atatürk grasped the power of human emotions, as noted in his speech on 15 March 1923 to the people of Adana: "Perhaps more than the mind, logic, or judgment, what makes history is feelings/sentiments."[4] Acutely aware of the importance and range of human emotions, Atatürk often mentioned emotional maturity or mature sentiment as an antidote to prevent emotions running wild but rather harnessing them. War was certainly the application of brute force and required violent emotions from its participants. Through study, listening, and observing, Atatürk sought to mature in his own emotional intelligence. Though saddled with his own emotional issues, he was still capable of empathy for others, an empathy not necessarily born of sympathy or compassion, but born more from a need to understand life and people. It was critical as a leader to connect emotionally with people. His order of 20 August 1921, for example, issued several days before the Battle of Sakarya, spoke directly to each officer and soldier as individuals, as human beings, sensitive to what they would face in the heat of battle. It was important to discern the human psyche, in particular how human beings thought and what they felt. Hence, Atatürk was generally a good listener and an astute observer of his fellow human beings, in part to sharpen his skills at intuiting the mental faculties and emotional states of others. Moreover, such knowledge served the ultimate purpose of motivating and manipulating others and the nation to serve his and national ends.

Imbued with a sense of destiny, Atatürk was ultimately a man of military and political genius who emerged at an unstable period in history and through the influence of a powerful network of associates imposed his will in conceiving the vision and founding the modern republic of Turkey. He invested time and effort in developing along three axes, the mind, conscience, and emotions and in using these qualities in leading others. His life journey of maturation or perfection, i.e., *kemal* as a process, was a matter of *being* and *becoming* while grounded in the past. *Being* involved his living in the present. Atatürk was a dedicated professional and perfectionist who seriously studied and tackled his tasks at hand. *Becoming*, however, required an eye toward the future and a readiness and openness to tackle new problems and challenges. Life was a laboratory for enlightenment, and acquiring knowledge was both a source of power and of inspiration. By developing himself as an officer and as a person with a cosmopolitan mind and spirit, he more easily transitioned in war from the soldier to the soldier-statesman with a singularity of mind, will, and purpose. During the War of Independence, Atatürk committed to establishing a republic, and he transitioned with lightning speed to embark on peace while terminating the war through diplomacy. Turkey emerged from the Great War a sovereign and independent republic, a remarkable feat in the annals of twentieth-century history.

Notes

Introduction

1   *Atatürk'ün Söylev ve Demeçleri* (Ankara: Türk İnkılap Tarihi Enstitüsü Yayınları, 2006), II, 120. I would like to acknowledge Serdar Demirtaş for first showing me this quote in "Vecizeler," HTVD 20 (June 1957).

2   Falih Rıfkı Atay, *Çankaya: Atatürk'ün Doğumundan Ölümüne Kadar Bütün Hayat Hikayesi* (İstanbul: Doğan Kardeş Matbaacılık Sanayi A. Ş. Basımevi, 1969), 148.

3   Ş[emseddin] S[ami], *Kamus-i Türki,* two vols (Dersaadet: Ikdam Matbaası, 1315/1899), I, 619.

4   Ibid., II, 1486–87.

5   *A Turkish and English Lexicon,* edited by James A. Redhouse (Constantinople: Boyajian, 1890), 2128.

Chapter 1   The Making of an Ottoman Soldier

1   Sun Tzu, *The Art of War,* translated by Samuel Griffith (London: Oxford University Press, 1963), 63.

2   Ş[emseddin] S[ami], *Kamus al-A'lam,* vols, 4 (İstanbul: Mıhran Matbaası, 1311 H/1894), IV, 2591.

3   *Atatürk'ün Not Defterleri,* II: *Harp Akademisi Öğrencisi Kemal'in Not Defteri* (Ankara: Genelkurmay Basımevi, 2004), 168–69.

4   Ali Fuad Cebesoy, *Sınıf Arkadaşım Atatürk: Okul ve Genç Subaylık Hatıraları* (İstanbul: Baha Matbaası, 1967), 156.

5   Falih Rıfkı Atay, *19 Mayıs* (Ankara: Ulus Basımevi, 1944), 33.

6   Vamik Volkan and Norman Itzkowitz, *The Immortal Atatürk: a Psychobiography* (Chicago: University of Chicago Press, 1984), 12.

7   Lord Kinross, *Ataturk: A Biography of Kemal, Father of Modern Turkey* (New York: W. Morrow, 1965), 12.

8   Cemil Sönmez, *Atatürk'ün Yetişmesi ve Öğretmenleri* (Ankara: Atatürk Araştırma Merkezi, 2004), 23–43.

9   Falih Rıfkı Atay, *Çankaya: Atatürk'ün Doğumundan Ölümüne Kadar Bütün Hayat Hikayesi* (İstanbul: Doğan Kardeş Matbaacılık Sanayi A. Ş. Basımevi, 1969), 19–20.

10 Cebesoy, *Sınıf Arkadaşım Atatürk,* 6; Şevket Süreyya Aydemir, *Tek Adam: Kemal'ın Hayatı, I: 1881–1919* (İstanbul: Remzi Kitabevi, 2002), 52.

11 Ibid., 54–55.

12 Sönmez, *Atatürk'ün Yetişmesi ve Öğretmenleri,* 57–73, for quote p. 60.

13 Aydemir, *Tek Adam,* I, 60.

14   Andrew Mango, *Atatürk: The Biography of the Founder of Modern Turkey* (Woodstock, NY: Overlook Press, 2000), 37.

15   Ş[emseddin] S[ami], *Kamus al-A'lam*, VI, 4437.

16   Sönmez, *Atatürk'ün Yetişmesi ve Öğretmenleri*, 81.

17   Cebesoy, *Sınıf Arkadaşım Atatürk*, 9; quote also appears in Mango, *Atatürk*, 40.

18   Sönmez, *Atatürk'ün Yetişmesi ve Öğretmenleri*, 103–8.

19   Emre Kongar, *Atatürk: Devrim Tarihi ve Toplumbilim Açısından* (İstanbul: Ramzi Kitabevi, 1983), 161.

20   Uluğ İğdemir, *Atatürk'ün Yaşamı, I: 1881–1918* (Ankara: Türk Tarih Kurumu Basımevi, 1988), 5.

21   Rauf Orbay, *Siyasi Hatıralar* (İstanbul: Örgün, 2003), 253.

22   Kinross, *Ataturk*, 17.

23   Cebesoy, *Sınıf Arkadaşım Atatürk*, 12.

24   İsrafil Kurtcephe and Mustafa Balcıoğlu, *Kara Harp Okulu Tarihi* (Ankara: Kara Harp Okulu Matbaası, 1991), 134.

25   Jehuda L. Wallach, *Bir Askeri Yardımın Anatomısı: Türkiye'de Prusya-Alman Askeri Heyetleri, 1835–1919*, translated by Fahri Çeliker (Ankara: Genelkurmay Basımevi, 1985), 54; Kurtcephe and Balcıoğlu, *Kara Harp Okulu Tarihi*, 60, 108–9, 159.

26   *Atatürk'in Not Defterleri, V: Kemal'in 1870–1871 Alman-Fransız Savaşı Konusunda tuttuğu Notlar ile 1905–1908 Yılları Arasında Tuttuğu Günlük Notları* (Ankara: Genelkurmay Basımevi, 2005), 247 (Ottoman), 248 (transliteration).

27   Handan Nazir Akmeşe, *The Birth of Modern Turkey: the Ottoman Military and the March to World War I* (London: I.B.Tauris, 2005), 10–12, 21–25, 31–32; M. Şükrü Hanioğlu, *Atatürk: An Intellectual Biography* (Princeton, NJ: Princeton University Press, 2011), 33–38.

28   Colmar von der Goltz, *Millet-i müsellaha: asrımız üsul ve ahval-ı askeriyesi*, translated by Ahmed Tahir (Kostantiniye: Matbaa-ı Abuzzıya, 1305/1888), 6.

29   Ibid., 7.

30   Ibid., 61–63.

31   Ibid., 74–75.

32   Ibid., 78.

33   Ibid., 89.

34   Ibid., 125.

35   Ibid., 160.

36   Ibid., 161.

37   Ibid., 166.

38   Hikmet Bayur, *Atatürk: Hayatı ve Eseri, I: Doğumundan Samsun'a Çıkışına Kadar* (Ankara: Güven Basımevi, 1963), 41.

39   General Kalvzuvic, *İdare-i harbe dair kavaid-i esasiye*, translated by Ahmed Refik (Constantiye: İbrahim Hilmi, 1316/1899), 3–4.

40   Ibid., passim.

41   Carl von Clausewitz, *On War*, edited and translated by Michael Howard and Peter Paret (Princeton, NJ: Princeton University Press, 1984), cards (p. 86) and commerce (p. 149).

42   Cebesoy, *Sınıf Arkadaşım Atatürk*, 22.

43   Şerafettin Turan, *Kendine Özgü bir Yaşam ve Kişilik: Kemal Atatürk* (Ankara: Bilgi Yayınevi, 2004), 51.

44   Cebesoy, *Sınıf Arkadaşım Atatürk*, 39–41; Kazım Karabekir, *Hayatım* (İstanbul: Yapı Kredi Yayınları, 2007), 141–42, 158–60.

45 Cebesoy, *Sınıf Arkadaşım Atatürk*, 43–45.
46 Ibid., 21.
47 Sönmez, *Atatürk'ün Yetişmesi ve Öğretmenleri*, 127–38.
48 *Atatürk'in Not Defterleri*, V, 247, 249, 251 (Ottoman), 248, 250, 252 (transliteration).
49 *Atatürk'ün Not Defterleri*, VI: *Kemal'in İstihkam ve Topçuluk, Stratejik Taarruz ve Stratejik Savunma ile Subaylar için Yazılmış olan Hizmet-i Seferiye Talimnamesine ait Tuttuğu Notlar* (Ankara: Genel Kurmay Basımevi, 2005), 133 (Ottoman), 134 (transliteration).
50 *Atatürk'ün Not Defterleri*, II: 32–33 and 164–71 (copy of Ottoman text on even pages).
51 ABE, I, 31.
52 Hanioğlu, *Atatürk*, 65.
53 Robert Devereux, "Suleyman Pasha's 'The Feeling of the Revolution,'" *Middle Eastern Studies* 15 (1979), 3–10.
54 Colonel Dr. Ahmet Tetik, discussion, 30 June 2009, Ankara.
55 Michael Howard, "Men against fire: the doctrine of the Offensive in 1914," in *Makers of Modern Strategy: from Machiavelli to the Nuclear Age*, edited by Gordon A. Craig and Felix Gilbert (Princeton, N.J.: Princeton University Press, 1986), 519.
56 *Atatürk'ün Not Defterleri*, II, 26–30 and 134–50, 139 (martyrdom).
57 Kongar, *Atatürk*, 162; Atay, *Çankaya*, 22.
58 Muharrem Mazlum İskora, *Türk Ordusu Kurmaylık (Erkanıharbiye) Tarihçesi* (Ankara: Harb Akademesi Matbaası, 1944), 35.
59 Rahmi Apak, *Yetmişlik Bir Subayın Hatıraları* (Ankara: E. U. Basımevi, 1957), 14. See also Yusuf Kemal Tengirşenk, *Vatan Hizmetinde* (Ankara: Kültür Bakanlığı Yayınları, 1981), 25, 33.
60 Cebesoy, *Sınıf Arkadaşım Atatürk*, 30–31.
61 Kemal H. Karpat, *The Politicization of Islam: Reconstructing Identity, Faith, and Community in the Late Ottoman State* (New York: Oxford University Press, 2001), 334.
62 Ibid., 73–85. Flight (p. 78).
63 *Atatürk'ün Not Defterleri*, X: *Kemal'in 5'inci Ordu Karargahında Görevli İken Tuttuğu Notlar ile Trablusgarp Cephesindeki Günlük Emir Defteri* (Ankara: Genel Kurmay Basımevi, 2009), 208–9 (thought), 133–34 (army), 204–5 (understanding on people and life).
64 Ibid., 105/210 (Ottoman).
65 Ibid., 107–284, for Waterloo 211–70.
66 Ibid., 133–36.
67 *Atatürk'ün Not Defterleri*, V, 316–19.
68 *Atatürk'ün Not Defterleri*, X, 183–88.
69 Tarik Z. Tunaya, *Türkiye'de Siyasi Partiler* (İstanbul: Doğan Kardeş Matbaası, 1952), 149–51.
70 Erik Jan. Zürcher, *The Unionist Factor: The Role of the Committee of Union and Progress in the Turkish National Movement 1905–1926* (Leiden: Brill, 1984), 33–35.
71 Cebesoy, *Sınıf Arkadaşım Atatürk*, 108, 114–17.
72 Mango, *Atatürk*, 73–74.
73 For a translation, M. Şükrü Hanioğlu, "Garbcılar: their attitudes toward religion and their impact on the official ideology of the Turkish Republic," *Studia Islamica* 86 (August 1997), 133–58.
74 Hanioğlu, *Atatürk*, 48–65.
75 Zürcher, *The Unionist Factor*, 53.
76 Rachel Simon, "Prelude to reforms: Kemal in Libya." *Atatürk and the Modernization of Turkey*, edited by Jacob M. Landau (Boulder, CO: Westview Press, 1984), 17–23; Bayur, *Atatürk*, I, 31–34.
77 Halit Ziya Uşaklıgil, *Saray ve Ötesi* (İstanbul: Inkilap ve Aka, 1965), 55, 104, 110–11.

78   Bayur, *Atatürk*, I, 42–46; Aydemir, *Tek Adam*, I, 134–35.

79   Hanioğlu, *Atatürk*, 46; M. Naim Turfan, *Rise of the Young Turks, the Military, and Ottoman Collapse* (London: I.B.Tauris, 2000), xvi.

80   H.C. Armstrong, *Grey Wolf: Kemal, an Intimate Study of a Dictator* (New York: Minton, Balch and Company, 1933), 26.

81   Bayur, *Atatürk*, I, 41–42.

82   T. C. Genelkurmay Başkanlığı, *Türk Silahlı Kuvvetleri Tarihi, III ncü cilt, 6 ncı Kısım (1908–1920)* (Ankara: Genelkurmay Basımevi, 1996), 249.

83   General Litzmann, *Takımın Muharebe Talimi*, translated by Kolağası M[ustafa] Kemal (Selanik: Asır Matbaası, 1324/1909), 3–7. Quotes are on p. 4.

84   Muzaffer Erendil, *Askeri Yönüyle Atatürk* (Ankara: Genelkurmay Basımevi, 1981), 10–11.

85   Hanioğlu, *Atatürk*, 44.

86   *Atatürk'ün Okuduğu Kitaplar*, vol. 21, collected by Recep Cengiz (Ankara: Anıtkabir Derneği Yayınları, 2001), 312.

87   Ibid., 316–28.

88   Ibid., 334–42.

89   Ibid., 343.

90   Ibid., 347–51.

91   Ayşe Afetinan, *M. Kemal Atatürk'ün Karlsbad Hatıraları* (Ankara: Türk Tarih Kurumu Basımevi, 1983), 42.

92   Hamdi Ertuna, *1911–1912 Osmanlı-İtalyan Harbi ve Kolağası Kemal* (Ankara: Kültür ve Turizm Bakanlığı Yayınları, 1985); Erendil, *Askeri Yönlüyle Atatürk*, 13–18. For a discussion in English, see Mango, *Atatürk*, 101–11.

93   Ibid., 104 for first quote and 109 for the second.

94   Much of the following analysis appeared earlier in George W. Gawrych, "Siyasi ve Askeri Deha Olarak Atatürk," *İşveren* 46 (November 2007), 6–10.

95   ABE, I, 132–34.

96   Kemal [Atatürk], *Zabit ve Kumandan ile Hasbıhal* (İstanbul: Minber Matbaası, 1918), 28 in ATASE Arşivi, ATA-ZB 36/32–25.

97   Salih Bozok – Cemil S. Bozok, *Hep Atatürk'ün Yanında* (İstanbul: Çağdaş Yayınları, 1985), 164–65; Salih Bozok, *Yaveri Atatürk'ü Anlatıyor* (İstanbul: Doğan Kitab, 2001), 40–41; ABE, I, 137–38.

98   Hale Şıvgın, *Trablusgarp Savaşı ve 1911–1912 Türk-İtalyan İlişkileri* (Ankara: Türk Tarih Kurumu Basımevi, 1989), 83.

99   Austin Bay, *Ataturk: Lessons in Leadership from the Greatest General of the Ottoman Empire* (New York: Palgrave, 2011), 61–62; Ertuna, *1911–1912 Osmanlı-İtalyan Harbi ve Kolağası Kemal*, 63–65.

100 Jafar al-Askari, *A Soldier's Story, From Ottoman Rule to Independent Iraq: the Memoirs of Jafar Pasha Al-Askari (1885–1936)* (London: Arabian Publishing, 2003), 73.

101 *Atatürk'ün Not Defterleri*, X, 330–31.

102 İğdemir, *Atatürk'ün Yaşamı*, I, 25–26; ABE, I, 144.

103 Bayur, *Atatürk*, I, 52.

104 Şıvgın, *Trablusgarp Savaşı*, 150–51.

105 Ibid., 84; Mango, *Atatürk*, 106.

106 Edward J. Erickson, *Defeat in Detail: the Ottoman Army in the Balkans, 1912–1913* (Westport, CT: Praeger, 2003), 254–74.

107 İğdemir, *Atatürk'ün Yaşamı*, I, 26–30. The quote appears on p. 28.

108 Mango, *Atatürk*, 119; İğdemir, *Atatürk'ün Yaşamı*, I, 30–32.

109 A brief treatment of these events appears in Mango, *Atatürk*, 115–20.

110 Fethi Okyar, *Üç Devirde Bir Adam*, prepared by Cemal Kutay (İstanbul: Tercüman Yayınları, 1980), 203.

111 *Atatürk'ün Not Defterleri*, VI, v, 67–133.

Chapter 2   The Great War and an Imperialist Peace

1   Sun Tzu, *The Art of War*, translated by Samuel Griffith (London: Oxford University Press, 1963), 65.

2   Fethi Okyar, *Üç Devirde Bir Adam*, prepared by Cemal Kutay (İstanbul: Tercüman Yayınları, 2006), 203–7.

3   *Sofya Askeri Ataşesi Mustafa Kemal'in Raporları (Kasım 1913–Kasım 1914)*, edited by Ahmet Tetik (Ankara: Genelkurmay ATASE Yayınları, 2007).

4   Okyar, *Üç Devirde Bir Adam*: 215–6.

5   Mustafa Kemal [Atatürk], *Zabit ve Kumandan ile Hasbıhal* (İstanbul: Minber Matbaası, 1918), 24.

6   Ibid., 16.

7   Ibid., 3 and 4 for the quote.

8   Ibid., 6.

9   Ibid., 9.

10   Ibid., 25.

11   Ibid., 7.

12   Ibid., 15.

13   Ibid., 17.

14   Ibid.

15   Ibid., 14.

16   Ibid.

17   Ibid., 20.

18   Ibid., 21–22.

19   Hans Kannengiesser, *The Campaign in Gallipoli* (London: Hutchinson, 1927), 160.

20   Mustafa Kemal, *Zabit ve Kumandan ile Hasbıhal*, 30 (first quote), 32 (second quote).

21   ATASE Arşivi, ATA-ZB 36/32–21.

22   M. Şükrü Hanioğlu, *Atatürk: An Intellectual Biography* (Princeton, NJ: Princeton University Press, 2011), 38.

23   Fahrettin Altay, *10 Yıl Savaş ve Sonrası, 1912–1922* (Ankara: Evren Dağıtım, 2008), 84. Altay, the corps' chief of staff at the time, took the phone call from Kemal.

24   Ibid., 89–90.

25   Şefik Aker, "Çanakkale-Arnıburnu Savaşları ve 27. Alay," in *Çanakkale Hatıraları*, compiled by Metin Martı (İstanbul: Arma Yayınları, 2001), 179–233.

26   George W. Gawrych, "The Rock of Gallipoli," in *Studies in Battle Command* by Combat Studies Institute (Fort Leavenworth, KS: U.S. Army Command and General Staff College, 1995), 6.

27   Liman von Sanders, *Cinq ans de Turquie* (Paris: Payot, 1923), 104.

28   Mustafa Kemal, *Arnıburnu Muharebeleri Raporu*, prepared by Uluğ İğdemir (Ankara: Türk Tarih Kurumu Basımevi, 1968), 63–64; İzzettin Çalışlar, *On Yıllık Savaşı* (İstanbul: Türkiye İş Bankası Kültür Yayınları, 2010), 105–6; Andrew Mango, *Atatürk: The Biography of the Founder of Modern Turkey* (Woodstock, NY: Overlook Press, 2000), 147.

29   C. F. Spinall-Oglander, *Military Operations, Gallipoli* (London: Heinemann, 1929), I, 296, n. 4; Mango, *Atatürk*: 146–47.

30   Mustafa Kemal, *Anafartalar Muharebatı'na Ait Tairhçe*, 31.

31   Aspinall-Oglander, *Military Operations, Gallipoli*, II, 306.

32 Sanders, *Cinq ans de Turquie*, 104–5.
33 Çalışlar, *On Yıllık Savaşı*, 100–67 passim.
34 Mango, *Atatürk*: 150. For Atatürk's account: Mustafa Kemal, *Arnıburnu Muharebeleri Raporu*, 164–71.
35 Celal Erikan, *Komutan Atatürk* (Ankara: Türkiye İş Bankası Kültür Yayınları, 1972), 154.
36 *Atatürk'ün Özel Mektupları*, collected by Sadi Borak (İstanbul: Varlık Yayınları, 1961), 31–32; ABE, I, 228.
37 ABE, I, 272.
38 *Birinci Dünya Harb'inde Türk Harbi V. Cilt Çanakkale Cephesi Harekatı 1 nci, 2 nci ve 3 ncü Kitapların Özetlenmiş Tarihi (Haziran 1914 – 9 Ocak 1916)* (Ankara: Genelkurmay Basımevi, 2002), 81.
39 Altay, *10 Yıl Savaş ve Sonrası*, 95.
40 ABE, I, 218; Mango, *Atatürk*, 147–48.
41 Uluğ İğdemir, *Atatürk'ün Yaşamı*, I: 1881–1918 (Ankara: Türk Tarih Kurumu, 1980), 75.
42 Kannengiesser, *The Campaign in Gallipoli*, 126.
43 Ibid., 147.
44 Ibid., 130.
45 Salih Bozok, *Yaveri Atatürk'ü Anlatıyor* (İstanbul: Doğan Kitab, 2001), 56.
46 Kannengiesser, *The Campaign in Gallipoli*, 270.
47 M. Kemal, *Kolordu Emri: Ta'biye Meslesesinin Hali ve Emirlerin Sureti Tahririne Dair Nesayih* (Edirne: Edirne Sanayı Mektebi Matbaası, 1331/1916) in ATASE Arşivi, BDH, Klasör 3407, Eski Dosya 180, Yeni Dosya 32, Fihrist No. 6–1.
48 Ibid., 2.
49 Ibid., 2–3.
50 Ibid., 3.
51 İbid., 5–7.
52 Şükrü Tezer, *Atatürk'ün Hatıra Defteri* (Ankara: Türk Tarih Kurumu, 1972), 28 (first quote), 29 (second), 30 (third).
53 BDH, *Kafkas Cephesi*, 47.
54 Erik J. Zürcher, *Turkey: a Modern History*, 3rd ed. (London: I.B.Tauris, 2004), 115.
55 For diary entries during the first two months in theater, see Çalışlar, *On Yıllık Savaşı*, 192–213, 213 (quote), 260 (the Kurds).
56 Uğur Ümit Üngör, *The Making of Modern Turkey: Nation and State in Eastern Anatolia, 1913–1950* (Oxford: Oxford University Press, 2011), 110. During Kemal's service in the Diyarbekir region, the CUP government resettled Kurdish tribes, a subject outside the scope of this project. See ibid., 110–15.
57 BDH, *Kafkas Cephesi*, 109–53.
58 Ayşe Afetinan, *M. Kemal Atatürk'ün Karlsbad Hatıraları* (Ankara: Türk Tarih Kurum, 1983), 42.
59 W. E. D. Allen and Paul Muratoff, *Caucasian Battlefields: A History of the Wars on the Turco-Caucasian Border 1828–1921* (Cambridge: Cambridge University Press, 1953), 423.
60 Erikan, *Komutan Atatürk*, 173.
61 Ali Fuad Cebesoy, *Sınıf Arkadaşım Atatürk: Okul ve Genç Subaylık Hatıraları* (İstanbul: Baha Matbaası, 1967), 158–59.
62 Allen and Muratoff, *Caucasian Battlefields*, 429.
63 Mango, *Atatürk*, 162.
64 H. C. Armstrong, *Grey Wolf: Mustafa Kemal, an Intimate Study of a Dictator* (New York: Minton, Balch and Company, 1933), 65–67, with quotes on p. 67; Tezer, *Atatürk'ün Hatıra Defteri*, 1972), 13.

65 Çalışlar, *On Yıllık Savaşı*, 273, 275, 286; Suat Ilhan, *Atatürk ve Askerlik: Düşünce ve Uygalamaları* (Ankara: Atatürk Araştırma Merkezi, 1990), 58; Falih Rıfkı Altay, *Çankaya: Atatürk'ün Doğumundan Ölümüne Kadar Bütün Hayat Hikayesi* (İstanbul: Doğan Kardeş Matbaacılık Sanayii A. Ş. Basımevi, 1969), 95–96; Mango, *Atatürk*, 162.

66 Tezer, *Atatürk'ün Hatıra Defteri*, 54.

67 İğdemir, *Atatürk'ün Yaşamı*, I, 80–82; Mango, *Atatürk*, 163–64.

68 Çalışlar, *On Yıllık Savaşı*, 267–74.

69 Mustafa Kemal, *Arnıburnu Muharebeleri Raporu*, 187–88.

70 ABE, I, 462.

71 Tezer, *Atatürk'ün Hatıra Defteri*, 45.

72 Tezer, *Atatürk'ün Hatıra Defteri*, 75; İğdemir, *Atatürk'ün Yaşamı*, I, 84; Mango, *Atatürk*, 164.

73 Çalışlar, *On Yıllık Savaşı*, 260–61.

74 Tezer, *Atatürk'ün Hatıra Defteri*, 72–73, 75, 83, 85–86; İğdemir, *Atatürk'ün Yaşamı*, I: 80–87; *Mustafa Kemal Atatürk'ün Söyleyip Yazdıkalrı*, vol. 1, prepared by M. Sunullah Arısoy (Ankara: Atatürk Araştırma Merkezi, 1991), 261–65.

75 Tevfik Fikret, *Rübab-ı Şikeste* (İstanbul: Tanın Matbaası, 1327/1909), inside front page.

76 İğdemir, *Atatürk'ün Yaşamı*, I, 86; Tezer, *Atatürk'ün Hatıra Defteri*, 83.

77 Çalışlar, *On Yıllık Savaşı*, 259.

78 Ibid., 212–13.

79 İğdemir, *Atatürk'ün Yaşamı*, I, 84; Tezer, *Atatürk'ün Hatıra Defteri*, 75–76; Çalışlar, *On Yıllık Savaşı*, 264–265; Mango, *Atatürk*, 164.

80 Çalışlar, *On Yıllık Savaşı*, 265–73.

81 Ibid., 224 (novel) and 253 (history book). Çalışlar no doubt did not record everything that he read. Nevertheless, it is significant what he does deem worthy to mention and tackle after a long session with Kemal.

82 Ibid., 272–73.

83 Ibid., 298 ff, 304–5 (governors); Tezer, *Atatürk'ün Hatıra Defteri*: 107–11.

84 Nusret Baycan, *Atatürk ve Askerlik Sanatı*, 2nd printing (Ankara: Genelkurmay Basımevi, 1998), 124.

85 İğdemir, *Atatürk'ün Yaşamı*, I, 113–16; ABE, III, 40–42.

86 Azmi Süslü and Mustafa Balcıoğlu, *Atatürk'ün Silah Arkadaşları – Atatürk Araştırma Merkezi Şeref Üyeleri* (Ankara: Atatürk Araştırma Merkezi, 1999), 5.

87 The 1918 interview with a newspaper reporter named Rüşen Eşref appears in ABE, II, 139–67, 145 (fixing bayonets), 146 (order).

88 Afetinan, *M. Kemal Atatürk'ün Karlsbad Hatıraları*, 23.

89 Mango, *Atatürk*, 176; İğdemir, *Atatürk'ün Yaşamı*, I, 124.

90 Afetinan, *M. Kemal Atatürk'ün Karlsbad Hatıraları*, 41.

91 *Atatürk'ün Resmi Yayınlara Girmemiş Söylev, Demeç, Yazışma ve Söyleşileri*, collected by Sadi Borak, 2nd ed (İstanbul: Kaynak Yayınları, 1997), 313–14.

92 Mango, *Atatürk*, 181.

93 ABE, III, 55.

94 Erik Jan Zürcher, *The Unionist Factor: The Role of the Committee of Union and Progress in the Turkish National Movement 1905–1926* (Leiden: Brill, 1984), 80–85; Hanioğlu, *Atatürk*, 96.

95 BDFA, I, 20.

96 Erol Kaya, *Mustafa Kemal Paşa'nın İlk Gazetesi: Minber* (Ankara: Ebadil Yayıncılak, 2007); Tarık Z. Tunaya, *Türkiye'de Siyasi Partiler* (İstanbul: Doğan Kardeş Matbaası, 1952), 406–7; Rauf Orbay, *Siyasi Hatıralar* (İstanbul: Örgün, 2003), 243; Fethi Tevetoğlu, "Atatürk'le Okyar'ın Çıkardıkları Gazete: Minber," *Atatürk Araştırma Merkezi Degisi* 5/13 (Kasım 1988),

183–93; Alev Coşkun, *Samsun'dan Önce Bilinmiyen 6 Ay: İşgal, Hüzün, Hazırlık.* (İstanbul: Cumhuriyet Kitapları, 2009), 76–87.

97   "Mustafa Kemal Paşa ile Mülakat," *Minber* 16 (17 Teşrin-i Sani 1918), 1; Kaya, *Mustafa Kemal Paşa'nın İlk Gazetesi: Minber*, 331–34; Coşkun, *Samsun'dan Önce Bilinmiyen 6 Ay*, 78–79.

98   "Mustafa Kemal Paşa ile Mülakat," *Minber* 16 (17 Teşrin-i Sani 1918), 2; Kaya, *Mustafa Kemal Paşa'nın İlk Gazetesi: Minber*, 334–37.

99   Ahmed Hulki, "Nühüfte Bir Sima," *Minber* 18 (19 Teşrin-i Sani 1918), 1.

100 Coşkun, *Samsun'dan Önce Bilinmiyen 6 Ay*, 113.

101 Ali Fuad Cebesoy, *Milli Mücadele Hatıraları* (İstanbul: Vatan Neşirati, 1953), 36–37.

102 Coşkun, *Samsun'dan Önce Bilinmiyen 6 Ay*, 179–90.

103 Cebesoy, *Milli Mücadele Hatıraları*, 53–54.

104 ABE, III, 89–93.

105 *Belgelerle Mustafa Kemal Atatürk (1916–1922)*, directed by Yusuf Sarınay (Ankara: T. C. Başbakanlık Devlet Arşivleri Genel Müdürlüğü Yayınevi, 2003), 8–9, 248 (Ottoman text).

106 Stanford J. Shaw, *From Empire to Republic: The Turkish War of Independence 1919–1923, a Documentary Study*, 5 vols, (Ankara: Türk Tarih Kurum Basımevi, 2000), I, 364–65.

107 Arnold J. Toynbee, *The Western Question in Greece and Turkey* (London: Constable and Company, 1923), 74.

108 Michael Llewellyn Smith, *Ionian Vision: Greece in Asia Minor 1919–1922* (London: Hurst and Company, 1973/1998), 71–74.

109 Toynbee, *The Western Question in Greece and Turkey*, 167–69.

110 BOA, DH.ŞFR 100 / 106 (22 Haziran 335); 101 / 19–151 (24 Temmuz 335); 102 / 137 (14 Ağustos 335); 102 / 159 (17 Ağustos 335); 102 / 252 (25 Ağustos 335); 102 / 254 (25 Ağustos 335); 102 / 304 (29 Ağustos 335); 106 / 117 (24 Kanunisani 336); 108 / 33 (7 Mart 336).

111 Smith, *Ionian Vision*, 111.

112 Zekeriya Türkmen, *Milli Mücadele Yıllarında İstanbul Mitingleri, 15 Mayıs 1919: İzmir'in işgali üzerine aydınların kamuoyu oluşturma hereketi* (Ankara: Berikan Yayınları, 2007).

Chapter 3   Developing a Resistance

1   Raymond Aron, *Peace and War: A Theory of International Relations* (New York: Doubleday, 1966), 80.

2   Michael Llewellyn Smith, *Ionian Vision: Greece in Asia Minor, 1919–1922* (New York: St. Martin's Press, 1973), 72.

3   ATASE Arşivi, ATA-ZB 17/107–1.

4   ATASE Arşivi, ATA-ZB 34/2; Kazım Karabekir, *İstiklal Harbimiz* 2 vols (İstanbul: Yapı Kredi Yayınları, 1960/2008), I, 33.

5   Turgut Gürer, *Atatürk'ün Yaveri Cevat Abbas Gürer: Cepheden Meclise Büyük Önder ile 24 yıl* (İstanbul: Gürer Yayınları, 2006), 247.

6   Karabekir, *İstiklal Harbimiz*, I, 36–37.

7   ATASE Arşivi, ATA-ZB 10/77.

8   ATASE Arşivi, ATA-ZB 16/2, 31/10.

9   HTVD 19 (March 1957), belge 493.

10   Ibid., belge 494.

11   HTVD 1 (September 1952), belge 19.

12   ATASE Arşivi, ATA-ZB, 1/8–2. See also ATBD 56/120 (April 2007), 7, 127, 305–6. For a similar circular at this time, see ATASE Arşivi, ATA-ZB, 1/8–3.

13   Erik Jan Zürcher, "The vocabulary of Muslim Nationalism," *International Journal of the Sociology of Language* 137 (1999), 81–92. In this article, Zürcher takes an extreme position, arguing against any references to Turkish Nationalism or ethnicity by Kemal until after 1923.

14   Andrew Mango, *Atatürk: The Biography of the Founder of Modern Turkey* (Woodstock, NY: Overlook Press, 1999), 229. Mango makes this assessment citing an 18 June communiqué to Cafer Tayyar, commander of I Corps in Edirne. For the actual document, see ATBD 26/77 (September 1978), belge 1686.

15   Karabekir, *İstiklal Harbimiz*, I, 48–49.

16   Gazi Kemal, *Nutuk Muhteviyatına ait Vesaik* (Ankara: n.p., 1927), Vesika 26, 13–14; ABE, III, 107–8.

17   Ali Fuad Cebesoy, *Milli Mücadele Hatıraları* (İstanbul: Vatan Neşirati, 1953), 77.

18   Rauf Orbay, *Siyasi Hatıralarım* (İstanbul: Örgün, 2003), 306–13; Salahi Ramadan Sonyel, *Turkish Diplomacy 1913–1923: Kemal and the Turkish National Movement* (London: Sage Publications, 1975), 14; Falih Rıfkı Atay, *Çankaya: Atatürk'ün Doğumundan Ölümüne Kadar Bütün Hayat Hikayesi* (İstanbul: Doğan Kardeş Matbaacılık Sanayi A. Ş. Basımevi, 1969), 182.

19   BBA, OA, DH.ŞFR 100/174.

20   ATASE Arşivi, İSH 18/71.

21   ATASE Arşivi, İSH 18/81.

22   Mehmet Perinçek, *Atatürk'ün Sovyetler'le Görüşmeleri: Sovyet Arşiv Belgeleriyle* (İstanbul: Kaynak Yayınları, 2005), 35–36.

23   Karabekir, *İstiklal Harbimiz*, I, 61; ABE, III, 113–14.

24   Stefanos Yerasimos, *Türk-Sovyet İlişkileri: Ekim Devrimden Milli Mücadeleye*. İstanbul: Gözlem Yayınlar 1979), 105–15.

25   Bülent Gökay, *A Clash of Empires: Turkey between Russian Bolshevism and British Imperialism, 1918–1923* (London: I.B.Tauris, 1997), 63 ff.

26   Karabekir, *İstiklal Harbimiz*, I, 76–77; Mango, *Atatürk*: 235. Mango viewed this order as "a clear invitation to military revolt and a challenge to the validity of the armistice."

27   Orbay, *Siyasi Hatıralarım*, 319–23.

28   Vamik D. Volkan and Norman Itzkowitz, *The Immortal Ataturk: A Psychobiography* (Chicago: University of Chicago, 1984), 141.

29   Karabekir, *İstiklal Harbimiz*, I, 24.

30   TITE Arşivi, 31/226.

31   Mazhar Müfit Kansu, *Erzurum'dan Ölümüne Kadar Atatürk'le Beraber* 2 vols (Ankara: Türk Tarih Kurumu, 1997), I, 131.

32   ATBD 26/77 (September 1978), belge 1690; 31/82 (October 1982), belge 1785.

33   Stanford Shaw, *From Empire to Republic: The Turkish War of Independence 1919–1923, A Documentary Study*, 5 vols (Ankara: Türk Tarih Kurumu Basımevi, 2000), II, 689–98.

34   Karabekir, *İstiklal Harbimiz*, I, 90.

35   Kansu, *Erzurum'dan Ölümüne Kadar Atatürk'le Beraber*, I, 76–77.

36   Mahmut Goloğlu, *Erzurum Kongresi* (İstanbul: Türkiye İş Bankası Kültür Yayınları, 2008), 86–88.

37   ATASE Arşivi, İSH, 24–101.

38   ATASE Arşivi, ATA-ZB 4/102; TITE Arşivi 29/73.

39   ATASE, Arşivi, ATA-ZB 4/102; TITE Arşivi 31/227.

40   Karabekir, *İstiklal Harbimiz*, I, 149; Goloğlu, *Erzurum Kongresi*, 114–16.

41   Karabekir, *İstiklal Harbimiz*, I, 127–28.

42   Volkan and Itzkowitz, *Immortal Ataturk*, 146.

43   A. Rawlinson, *Adventures in the Near East 1918–1922* (New York: Dodd Mead and Company, 1924), 181.

44   For an account in English, see Shaw, *From Empire to Republic*, II, 705–16.
45   TITE Arşivi, 24/117; ATBD 38/87 (February 1989), belge 2081.
46   Mahmut Goloğlu, *Sivas Kongresi* (İstanbul: Türkiye İş Bankası Kültür Yayınları, 2008), 69, 78, 83.
47   Bekir Sıtkı Baykal, *Heyet-i Temsiliye Kararları* (Ankara: Türk Tarih Kurumu, 1974), 1–2; Karabekir, *İstiklal Harbimiz*, I, 379; Shaw, *From Empire to Republic*, II, 715.
48   Ali Fuad Cebesoy, *Kuva-yı Milliye İçyüzü* (İstanbul: Temel Yayınları, 2002), 174–75.
49   For texts see *Belgelerle Kemal Atatürk (1916–1922)* directed by Yusuf Sarınay (Ankara: Başbakanlık Basımevi, 2003), 83–86 with photocopy of Ottoman document on pp. 439–54.
50   Shaw, *From Empire to Republic*, II, 717–19
51   Nurettin Türsan, *Sakarya Meydan Muharebesinde Kemal Paşa'nın Askeri Dehası* (İstanbul: Harp Akedamileri Basımevi, 1994), 24–27.
52   TİH, *Sıvas*, 34–35.
53   BDFA, I: 117–22.
54   ATBD 56/120 (Nisan 2007), 10–15 (modern Turkish), 129–35 (Ottoman text), with the answer in Ottoman on p. 132.
55   ABE, IV, 295.
56   Major-General James Harbord, "Kemal Pasha and His Party," *World's Work* 40 (June 1920): 186.
57   Ibid., 188.
58   Ibid., 185.
59   Shaw, *From Empire to Republic*, II, 454–55.
60   ATBD 38/87 (February 1989), belge 2084.
61   Harbord, "Kemal Pasha and His Party," 184.
62   Kansu, *Erzurum'dan Ölümüne Kadar Atatürk'le Beraber*, I, 341, II, 502; Karabekir, *İstiklal Harbimiz*, I, 290; Goloğlu, *Sivas Kongresi*, 67–68.
63   Yücel Özkaya, *Milli Mücadelede Atatürk ve Basım*, 2 vols (İstanbul: Cumhuriyet, 2001), II, 26.
64   ABE, V: 329.
65   Denise Natali, *The Kurds and the State: Evolving National Identity in Iraq, Turkey, and Iran* (Syracuse: Syracuse University Press, 2005), 75.
66   HTVD 74 (September 1976), vesika 1596.
67   HTVD 9 (September 1954), vesika 207; HTVD 3/10 (December 1954), vesika 231.
68   Goloğlu, *Erzurum Kongresi*, 122.
69   ABE, III, 257, 265, 267–71.
70   ABE, V, 256.
71   ABE, IV, 39.
72   *Atatürk'ün Özel Arşivinden Seçmeler*, IV (Ankara: Genelkurmay Basımevi, 1996), belge 52; ABE, IV, 39.
73   Karabekir, *İstiklal Harbimiz*, I, 400.
74   ATASE Arşivi, ATA-ZB 1/19.
75   ATASE Arşivi, ATA-ZB 2/ 96, 3/2, 28/105.
76   ATASE Arşivi, ATA-ZB 6/79.
77   ABE, V, 363 with photocopy of Ottoman text on page 364.
78   Enver Behnan Şapolyo, *Kuvayı Milliye Tarihi: Gerılla* (Ankara: Ayyıldız Matbaası ve Gazetecilik, 1957), 7–14.
79   Alev Coşkun, *Samsun'dan Önce Bilinmiyen 6 Ay: Işgal, Hüzün, Hazırlık.* (İstanbul: Cumhuriyet Kitapları, 2009), 329.
80   Şapolyo, *Kuvayı Milliye Tarihi: Gerılla*, 80.
81   ATASE Arşivi, İSH 16/94.

82   Fahrettin Altay, *10 Yıl Savaş ve Sonrası, 1912–1922* (Ankara: Evren Dağıtım, 2008), 195–99.

83   For texts see *Belgelerle Kemal Atatürk*, 99–102 with photocopy of Ottoman document on 476–78; ABE, IV, 339–43. BEO, SYS, 34–64/III_9.

84   Karabekir, *İstiklal Harbimiz*, I, 414.

85   ABE, V, 182–319; Karabekir, *İstiklal Harbimiz*, I, 413–23; Cebesoy, *Milli Mücadele Hatıraları*, 248–50; Atay, *Çankaya*, 200; Lord Kinross, *Ataturk: A Biography of Kemal, Father of Modern Turkey* (New York: W. Morrow, 1965), 228–29.

86   Cebesoy, *Kuva-yı Milliye İçyüzü*, 285–87; ABE, V, 202–3.

87   ABE, V, 217.

88   Ibid., 281.

89   Kansu, *Erzurum'dan Ölümüne Kadar Atatürk'le Beraber*, II, 492–95.

90   Halide Edip Adıvar, *A Turkish Ordeal* (New York: The Century Company, 1928), 123, 131.

91   İzzet Öztoprak, *Kurtuluş Savaşında Türk Basını, Mayıs 1919-Temmuz 1921* (Ankara: Türkiye İş Bankası Kültür Yayınları, 1981), 42.

92   HTVD 55 (March 1966), vesika 1260.

93   ATBD 120 (April 2007), 32, 158, 323.

94   HTVD 20 (June 1957), vesika 519/2–4. For a transliteration, see Muzaffer Erendil, *Çok Yönlü Lider Atatürk* (Ankara: Genelkurmay Basımevi, 1986), 302–7; ABE, VI, 113–17.

95   HTVD 20 (June 1957), vesika 519/2–5.

96   Ibid., vesika 519/2–7.

97   Ibid., vesika 519/6

98   BDFA, I, 163.

99   Sonyel, *Turkish Diplomacy*, 22.

100 ATASE Arşivi, İSH 109/112.

101 Robert Zeidner, *Tricolor over the Taurus: the Franco-Turkish War for Cilicia, Crucible for the National Liberation Movement* (Ankara: Turkish Historical Society, 2005), 69–73.

102 Shaw, *From Empire to Republic*, II, 886.

103 Zeidner, *Tricolor over the Taurus*, 169–71.

104 Kılıç Ali, *Atatürk'ün Sırdaşı: Kılıç Ali'nın Anıları* (İstanbul: Türkiye İş Bankası Kültür Yayınları, 2005), 85–91 with the circular on pp. 86–87.

105 *Atatürk'ün Tamim, Telegraf ve Beyannameleri* (Ankara: Türk Tarih Kurumu Basımevi, 1991), 141–42.

106 Baykal, *Heyet-i Temsiliye Kararları*, 75; Zeidner, *Tricolor over the Taurus*, 173–74.

107 TİH, *Güney*, 87–99.

108 HTVD 15 (March 1956), belge no. 382. For the need for guerrilla operations in the Maraş, see HTVD 4/14 (January 1955), vesika 366.

109 HTVD 15 (March 1956), belge no. 385.

110 Ibid., belge 383; ABE, VI, 225–26.

111 Ibid., belge no. 401.

112 ABE, VI, 237.

113 Shaw, *From Empire to Republic*, II, 800–1.

114 ABE, VI, 167–68, 173–75 (copy of published Ottoman text on 17 February); Şevket Süreyya Aydemir, *Tek Adam: Kemal'ın Hayatı, II; 1919–1922* (İstanbul: Remzi Kitabevi, 2003), 201–2; Karabekir, *İstiklal Harbimiz*, I, 504–5; Shaw, *From Empire to Republic*, II, 803–4.

115 A. L. Macfie, *Atatürk* (London: Longman, 1994), 92.

116 Gazi Kemal, *Nutuk Muhteviyatına aid Vesaik*, 242–43, doc 238; Karabekir, *İstiklal Harbimiz*, I, 536.

117 ATASE Arşivi, ATA-ZB 2/65–3.

Chapter 4   The Grand National Assembly

1   Carl von Clausewitz, *On War*, edited and translated by Michael Howard and Peter Paret (Princeton, NJ: Princeton University Press, 1984), 89.

2   ATBD 30/79 (May 1981), belge 1743.

3   ATASE Arşivi, İSH 452/74.

4   ABE, VII, 153–54.

5   ATBD 38/87 (February 1989), belge 2111.

6   Yunus Nadi, *Ankara'nın İlk Günleri* (İstanbul: Sel Yayınları, 1955), 99–100.

7   Kazım Karabekir, *İstiklal Harbimiz*, 2 vols (İstanbul: Türkiye Yayınevi, 1969), I, 607–8.

8   Fahrettin Altay, *10 Yıl Savaş ve Sonrası, 1912–1922* (Ankara: Evren Dağıtım, 2008), 184.

9   Ibid., 224–30, quote on 230; Falih Rıfkı Atay, *Çankaya: Atatürk'ün Doğumundan Ölümüne Kadar Bütün Hayat Hikayesi* (İstanbul: Doğan Kardeş Matbaacılık Sanayi A. Ş. Basımevi, 1969), 246; Andrew Mango, *Atatürk: The Biography of the Founder of Modern Turkey* (Woodstock, NY: Overlook Press, 1999), 273.

10   ATASE Arşivi, ATA/ZB 29/98–2.

11   Salahi Ramadan Sonyel, *Turkish Diplomacy 1913–1923: Kemal and the Turkish National Movement* (London: Sage Publications, 1975), 37.

12   HTVD 23 (March 1958), vesika 580.

13   M. Şükrü Hanioğlu, *Atatürk: An Intellectual Biography* (Princeton, NJ: Princeton University Press, 2011), 102–3 (quote on p. 102).

14   TBMM, *Zabıt Ceridesi*, I, 8–32.

15   TBMM, *Gizli Celse Zabıtları*, I, 1–10.

16   Elaine Diana Smith, *Turkey: Origins of the Kemalist Movement and the Government of the Grand National Assembly* (Washington, D.C.: Judd and Detweiler, 1959), 44.

17   Halide Edip Adıvar, *A Turkish Ordeal* (New York: The Century Company, 1928), 183.

18   TBMM, *Zabıt Ceridesi*, III, 366–70.

19   Sonyel, *Turkish Diplomacy*, 37.

20   HTVD 15 (March 1956), vesika 382.

21   Adıvar, *Turkish Ordeal*, 146.

22   TİH, *İdari Faaliyetler*, 226–29.

23   İsmet İnönü, *Hatıralar*, 2 vols, compiled by Sabahettin Selek (Ankara: Bilgi Yayınevi, 1985), I, 193; HTVD 52 (June 1965), vesika 1191 and vesika 1193.

24   TİH, *İdari Faaliyetler*, 69–71.

25   Ibid., 279–80.

26   TBMM, *Zabıt Ceridesi*, XI, 48.

27   ATASE Arşivi, İSH 588/30.

28   HTVD 50 (December 1964), vesika 1161.

29   TBMM, *Zabıt Ceridesi*, I, 16–17, 165.

30   Donald Everett Webster, *The Turkey of Atatürk: Social Process in the Turkish Reformation* (Philadelphia: The American Academy of Political and Social Science, 1939), 182–83.

31   Adıvar, *Turkish Ordeal*, 147–48.

32   ABE, VII: 183.

33   ATASE Arşivi, İSH 575/163.

34   Erik Jan Zürcher, *The Unionist Factor: The Role of the Committee of Union and Progress in the Turkish National Movement 1905–1926* (Leiden: Brill, 1984), 146.

35   Ergün Aybars, *İstklal Mahkemeleri, 1920–1927*, 2 vols (İzmir: Dokuz Eylul Üniversitesi, 1988), 36–155.

36   Much of the general information is drawn from TİH, *Ayaklanmalar*, 87–167.

37   Ali Fuad Cebesoy, *Milli Mücadele Hatıraları* (İstanbul: Vatan Neşirati, 1953), 360.

38   ATASE Arşivi, İSH 575/119, 637/126 (severity), 637/140, 637/150.

39   TİH, *Ayakmalar*, 111.

40   Ibid., 140–58.

41   Ibid., 144.

42   Çerkes Ethem, *Çerkes Ethem'in Hatıraları* (İstanbul: Dünya Matbaası, 1962), 57.

43   Ibid., 151.

44   İsmet İnönü, *Hatıralar*, 2 vols, compiled by Sabahettin Selek (Ankara: Bilgi Yayınevi, 1985), I, 206–7.

45   Fahrettin Altay, *İstıklal Harbimizde Süvari Kolordusu* (Ankara: İnsel Kitabevi, 1949), 9.

46   Cebesoy, *Milli Mücadele Hatıraları*, 364, 408.

47   Roderic H. Davison, "Turkish Diplomacy from Mudros to Lausanne," in *The Diplomats 1919–1939*, edited by Gordon Craig and Felix Gilbert (Princeton: Princeton University Press, 1953), 183.

48   Stanford Shaw, *From Empire to Republic: The Turkish War of Independence 1919–1923, A Documentary Study*, 5 vols (Ankara: Türk Tarih Kurumu, 2000), III/2, 1459.

49   *Atatürk'ün Tamim, Telgraf ve Beyannameleri* (Ankara: Türk İnkılap Tarihi Enstitüsü Yayınları, 1991), 318; Bülent Gökay, *A Clash of Empires: Turkey between Russian Bolshevism and British Imperialism 1918–1923* (London: I.B.Tauris, 1997), 63.

50   Sonyel, *Turkish Diplomacy*, 39–40.

51   İnönü, *Hatıralar*, I, 195.

52   HTVD 15/55 (March 1966), vesika no. 1264.

53   Richard G. Hovannisian, *The Republic of Armenia: Vol. IV, Between Crescent and Sickle: Partition and Sovietization* (Berkeley: University of California Press, 1996), 161–63.

54   Shaw, *From Empire to Republic*, III/2: 1401–2.

55   Çakmak, *Mareşal Fevzi Çakmak ve Günlükleri*, 715–16.

56   Michael Llewellyn Smith, *Ionian Vision: Greece in Asia Minor 1919–1922* (London: Hurst and Company, 1973/1998), 123–25.

57   TİH, *Sıvas*, 183–84; Cebesoy, *Milli Mücadele Hatıraları*, 423–31; Celal Erikan, *Komutan Atatürk* (İstanbul: Türkiye İş Bankası Kültür Yayınları, 2006), 471–76.

58   Cebesoy, *Milli Mücadele Hatıraları*, 431–32.

59   TİH, *Sıvas*, 191–252; Smith, *Ionian Vision*, 126–28.

60   Fevzi Çakmak, *Mareşal Fevzi Çakmak ve Günlükleri*, 2 cilt, edited by Nilüfer Hatemi (İstanbul: Yeni Kredi Yayınları, 2002), 709–14.

61   ABE, IX: 99–100.

62   Ibid., 106–7.

63   For Kemal's travel log during this period, see Çakmak, *Mareşal Fevzi Çakmak ve Günlükleri*, 717–20.

64   İhsan Güneş, "Atatürk'ün Bilinmeyen Bir Konuşması," *Atatürk Araştırma Merkezi Dergisi*, sayı 5, cilt II (Mart 1986). Prof. Dr. İhsan Güneş sent me a modern Turkish publication of this address.

65   İnönü, *Hatıralar*, I, 213.

66   Rahmi Apak, *Yetmişlik Bir Subayın Hatıraları* (Ankara: E. U. Basımevi, 1957), 212–13.

67   HTVD 14/52 (June 1965), vesika 1197.

68   İnönü, *Hatıralar*, I: 215–42 passim.

69   Shaw, *From Empire to Republic*, II, 736.

70   For a good general treatment, see Robert Zeidner, *Tricolor over the Taurus: the Franco-Turkish War for Cilicia, Crucible for the National Liberation Movement* (Ankara: Turkish Historical Society, 2005).

71   HTVD 17 (September 1956), vesikalar 431 and 432.

72   ABE, IX, 137.
73   Shaw, *From Empire to Republic*, III/2, 1398.
74   ATASE Arşivi, İSH 578/193.
75   Uğur Ümit Üngör, *The Making of Modern Turkey: Nation and State in Eastern Anatolia, 1913–1950* (Oxford: Oxford University Press, 2011), 122.
76   TİH, *Güney Cepehesi*, 265–84.
77   ATBD 85 (October 1985), Belge No. 2044.
78   For a general treatment of this front, see Hovannisian, *The Republic of Armenia: Vol. III, From London to Sèvres, February–August 1920* (Berkeley: University of California Press, 1996), 290–325; TİH, *Doğu Cephesi*, 1–118 passim; Erikan, *Komutan Atatürk*, 490–97.
79   *Atatürk'ün Tamim, Telgraf ve Beyannameleri* (Ankara: Türk İnkılap Tarihi Enstitüsü Yayınları, 1991), 333–34, Karabekir, *İstiklal Harbimiz*, II, 791.
80   Gökay, *A Clash of Empires*, 74–75, 82.
81   ATASE Arşivi, İSH 615/58; BCA, 30.18.1.1/1.12.7.
82   ATBD 111 (June 1999), belge no. 4070, p. 3.
83   ATASE Arşivi, İSH 615/61; Karabekir, *İstiklal Harbimiz*, II, 987–88.
84   Sonyel, *Turkish Diplomacy*, 50–52.
85   Karabekir, *İstiklal Harbimiz*, II, 1000. Vahakn N. Dadrian, *The History of the Armenian Genocide: Ethnic Conflict from the Balkans to Anatolia to the Caucasus* (Oxford: Berghahn Books, 1995), 358.
86   TİH, *İdari Faaliyetler*, 278.
87   *Düstür, Üçüncü Tertip*, cilt 1, 196–99 obtained from www.anayasa.gen.tr/1921tek.htm.
88   Celal Erikan, *Komutan Atatürk*, 2 vols (İstanbul: Türkiye İş Bankası Kültür Yayınları, 1964), II, 433.
89   Mango, *Atatürk*, 302.
90   Adıvar, *Turkish Ordeal*, 168.
91   Ibid., 149.
92   Ibid., 161, 223.

Chapter 5   A Crisis in Battle

1   Sun Tzu, *The Art of War*, translated by Samuel Griffith (London: Oxford University Press, 1963), 82.
2   Stanford Shaw, *From Empire to Republic: The Turkish War of Independence 1919–1923, A Documentary Study*, 5 vols (Ankara: Türk Tarih Kurumu, 2000), III/2, 1549–51.
3   *Kurtuluş Savaşı'nin İdeolojisi: Hakimiyeti Milliye Yazıları*, prepared by Hadiye Bolluk (İstanbul: Kaynak Yayınları, 1992), 82–124 passim.
4   M. Şükrü Hanioğlu, *Atatürk: An Intellectual Biography* (Princeton, NJ: Princeton University Press, 2011), 105–8. Quote appears on p. 105.
5   Mehmet Perinçek, *Atatürk'ün Sovyetler'le Görüşmeleri: Sovyet Arşiv Belgeleriyle* (İstanbul: Kaynak Yayınları, 2005), 301.
6   Kazım Karabekir, *İstiklal Harbimiz*, 2 vols (İstanbul: Türkiye Yayınevi, 2008), II, 1023–27; TİH, *Doğu Cephesi*, 229–44.
7   Andrew Mango, *Atatürk: The Biography of the Founder of Modern Turkey* (Woodstock, NY: Overlook Press, 1999), 309.
8   TBMM, *Zabıt Ceridesi*, IX, 5–6.
9   Tarık Z. Tunaya, *Türkiye'de Siyasi Partiler* (İstanbul: Doğan Kardeş Matbaası, 1952), 535.

10 Yakup Kadri Karaosmanoğlu, *Vatan Yolunda: Milli Mücadele Hatıraları* (İstanbul: Selek Yayınevi, 1958), 115–16; Mango, *Atatürk*, 292.

11 TİH, *Ayaklanmalar*, 287–88.

12 Mustafa Balcıoğlu, *İki İsyan: Koçgiri Pontus, Bir Paşa: Nurettin Paşa* (Ankara: Nobel Yayın Dağıtım Ltd. Şti, 2000), 85.

13 ATASE Arşivi, İSH 588/48–3; BCA, 030.18.11 / 2.22.4; HTVD 14/52 (June 1965), vesika, 1203.

14 Balcıoğlu, *İki İsyan*, 88.

15 TİH, *Ayaklanmalar*, 291.

16 Mango, *Atatürk*, 331.

17 Shaw, *From Empire to Republic*, II, 596; Mango, *Atatürk*, 329–30; Justin McCarthy, *Death and Exile: the Ethnic Cleansing of Ottoman Muslims, 1821–1922* (Princeton, NJ: Darwin Press, 1995), 287–90; Balcıoğlu, *İki İsyan*, 45 ff., 86–127 (suppression operations); TİH, *Ayaklanmalar*, 292–94 (figure of 11,188 on p. 294).

18 Balcıoğlu, *İki İsyan*, 120.

19 Ibid., 227–32 (propaganda), 238 (mosque attendance).

20 TİH, *Ayaklanmalar*, 259–81.

21 David McDowall, *A Modern History of the Kurds* (London: I.B.Tauris, 1996), 138–39.

22 BCA, 030.18.1.1 / 2.38.20, Kararname 733.

23 TİH, *Ayaklanmalar*, 271.

24 Balcıoğlu, *İki İsyan*, 173–76.

25 For a discussion of these military developments, see Michael Llewellyn Smith, *Ionian Vision: Greece in Asia Minor 1919–1922* (London: Hurst and Company, 1973/1998), 172–79.

26 Smith, *Ionian Vision*, 183.

27 TİH, *İnönü*, 147–232; Celal Erikan, *Komutan Atatürk* (Ankara: Türkiye İş Bankası Kültür Yayınları, 2006), 530–41.

28 ATBD 40/91 (September 1991), belge 2305.

29 Shaw, *From Empire to Republic*, III/1, 991–92.

30 Cited in Mehmet Kaplan, *Devrin Yazarlarının Kalemiyle Milli Mücadele ve Gazi Kemal* (Ankara: Kültür Bakanlığı, 1992), 435–37.

31 BCA, 030.18.1.1 / 3.23.8.

32 Smith, *Ionian Vision*, 194–96.

33 TİH, *İnönü*, 282–512; Erikan, *Komutan Atatürk*, 551–72; Smith, *Ionian Vision*, 198–202.

34 TİH, *İnönü*, 274–76.

35 Ibid., 295.

36 For a personal account by a division commander, see İzzettin Çalışlar, *Gün, Gün, Saat, Saat: İstkilal Harbi'nde Garb Cephesi* (İstanbul: Türkiye İş Bankası Kültür Yayınları, 2009), 135–215.

37 HTVD 14/53 (September 1965), vesika 1124.

38 TİH, *Kütahya*, 604.

39 Ibid., 366.

40 İsmet İnönü, *Hatıralar*, 2 vols, compiled by Sabahettin Selek (Ankara: Bilgi Yayınevi, 1985), I, 255.

41 ATASE Arşivi, İSH 1435/40.

42 Utkan Kocatürk, *Atatürk ve Türkiye Cumhuriyeti Tarihi Kronolojisi, 1918–1938* (Ankara: Türk Tarih Kurumu Basımevi, 1988), 256.

43 Rıza Nur, *Hayat ve Hayatım*, III: *Rıza Nur-Atatürk Kavgası* (İstanbul: İşaret Yayınları, 1992), 186.

44 Smith, *Ionian Vision*, 207, 224.

45 Ibid., 224–25.

46 ATASE Arşivi, İSH 1341/139.
47 Fahreddin Altay, *İstiklal Harbimizde Süvari Kolordusu* (Ankara: İnsel Kitabevi, 1949), 13–14.
48 ATASE Arşivi, İSH 1396/91.
49 Howard E. Wilson and Ilhan Başgöz, *Türküye Cumhuriyetinde Milli Eğitim ve Atatürk* (Ankara: Dost Yayınları, 1968), 58–63, 59 (Nuri Rıza), 58 (Hamdullah Suphi).
50 "Evvelki gün maarif kongresi açıldı," *Hakimiyet-i Milliye* 237 (17 Temmuz 1337), 2.
51 "İki cebhe," *Hakimiyet-i Milliye* 238 (18 Temmuz 1921), 1.
52 TİH, *Kütahya*, 360; ABE, XI, 240.
53 HTBD 22/68 (March 1973), belge 1490.
54 Ibid., belge 1491.
55 Fahrettin Altay, *10 Yıl Savaş ve Sonrası, 1912–1922* (Ankara: Evren Dağıtım, 2008), 283; TİH, *Kütahya*, 332.
56 TİH, *Kütahya*, 365.
57 ATASE Arşivi, İSH 1138/25; *Harb Tarihi Vesikaları Dergisi* 15/56 (June 1966), vesika 1293.
58 Çalışlar, *Gün, Gün, Saat, Saat*, 226–29.
59 For a detailed treatment of the day's events from a Turkish perspective, see TİH, *Kütahya*, 441–89.
60 ATBD 42/95 (January 1993), belge 2512.
61 ATASE Arşivi, İSH 1198/88; 1138/19; HTVD 15/56 (June 1966), vesika 1295 and 42/95 (January 1993), belge 2509; Fahri Aykut, *İstiklal Savaşında Kütahya ve Eskişehir Muharebeleri* (Ankara: Generlkurmay ATASE Yayınları, 2006), 149.
62 ATBD 42/95 (January 1993), belge 2513.
63 HTVD 15/56 (June 1966), vesika 1296.
64 İnönü, *Hatıralar*, I, 259.
65 ATBD 42/95 (January 1993), belge 2515, 2524.
66 Halide Edip Adıvar, *A Turkish Ordeal* (New York: The Century Company, 1928), 271.
67 Gündüz, *Hatıralar*, 57–58.
68 TİH, *Kütahya*, 537.
69 Rahmi Apak, *Yetmişlik Bir Subayın Hatıraları* (Ankara: E. U. Basımevi, 1957), 241, 244.
70 Nikolas Trikupis and M. Papulas, *Yunan Generallerinin İtirafları* (Ankara: Berikan, 2001), 93.
71 Smith, *Ionian Vision*, 228–30.
72 Ibid., 230.
73 Çakmak, *Mareşal Fevzi Çakmak ve Günlükleri*, II, 811.
74 TBMM, *Gizli Celse Zabıtları*, II, 99–103.
75 Ibid., 103–14. For Durak's commentary, see 103–4.
76 TİH, *Kütahya*, 546–47.
77 ATBD 42/95 (January 1993), belge 2523.
78 Kazım Özalp, *Milli Mücadele, 1919–1922* (Ankara: Türk Tarih Kurumu Basımevi, 1985), 185.
79 Çakmak, *Mareşal Fevzi Çakmak ve Günlükleri*, II, 812–13.
80 ABE, XI, 259.
81 HTVD 15/57 (September 1966), vesika 1307.
82 Ibid., vesika 1310.
83 ATBD 42/96 (September 1994), belge 2529.
84 Stefanos Yerasimos, *Türk-Sovyet İlişkileri: Ekim Devrimden Milli Mücadeleye* (İstanbul: Gözlem Yayınlar 1979), 337 and 389–95 (documents), 389 (quote).
85 Mango, *Atatürk*, 317.
86 TBMM, *Gizli Celse Zabıtları*, II, 174–75; TBMM, *Zabıt Ceridesi*, XII, 18.

87   TBMM, *Gizli Celse Zabıtları*, II, 165–66.
88   ATASE Arşivi, ATA-ZB 40–6, İSH 1417/113.

Chapter 6   Commander in Chief

1   Carl von Clausewitz, *On War*, edited and translated by Michael Howard and Peter Paret (Princeton, NJ: University of Princeton Press, 1984), 112.
2   *Atatürk'ün Tamim, Telgraf ve Beyannameleri* (Ankara: Türk İnkılap Tarihi Enstitüsü Yayınları, 1991), IV, 414–24.
3   TİH, *Sakarya*, 109–12.
4   TİH, *İdari Faaliyetler*, 147.
5   TİH, *Sakarya*, 4.
6   Turgut Özakman, *Şu Çılgın Türkler* (Ankara: Bilgi Yayınevi, 2011), 448.
7   TİH, *Sakarya*, 4, chart.
8   İsmet İnönü, *Hatıralar*, 2 vols, compiled by Sabahettin Selek (Ankara: Bilgi Yayınevi, 1985), I, 260–63.
9   Fahrettin Altay, *İstiklal Harbimizde Süvari Kolordusu* (Ankara: İnsel Kitabevi, 1949), 20–21.
10   Asım Gündüz, *Hatıralar* (İstanbul: Kervan Kıtapçılık, 1973), 68–70.
11   Mümtaz Ulusoy, *İstiklal Harbi'nde 2 nci Kolordu* (Ankara: Genelkurmay ATASE Başkanlığı, 2006), 236, 258–59 TİH, *Sakarya*, 261.
12   Ulusoy, *İstiklal Harbi'nde 2 nci Kolordu*, 247.
13   İzzettin Çalışlar, *Gün, Gün, Saat, Saat: İstkilal Harbi'nde Garb Cephesi* (İstanbul: Türkiye İş Bankası Kültür Yayınları, 2009), 233–35.
14   HTVD 75 (September 1976), belge 1621.
15   İnönü, *Hatıralar*, I, 262.
16   Halide Edip Adıvar, *A Turkish Ordeal* (New York: The Century Company, 1928), 287.
17   Fevzi Çakmak, *Mareşal Fevzi Çakmak ve Günlükleri*, 2 cilt, edited by Nilüfer Hatemi (İstanbul: Yeni Kredi Yayınları, 2002), II, 820–27; İnönü, *Hatıralar*, I, 261–262; Gündüz, *Hatıralar*, 53.
18   Adıvar, *A Turkish Ordeal*, 292.
19   ATASE Arşivi, İSH 1314/ 116; 1371/62.
20   ATASE Arşivi, İSH 1207/78, 1285/32, 1348/88, 1348/140, 1358/11, 1453/18–2.
21   Kazım Karabekir, *İstiklal Harbimiz*, 2 vols (İstanbul: Türkiye Yayınevi, 2008), II, 1106. Stanford Shaw, *From Empire to Republic: The Turkish War of Independence 1919–1923, A Documentary Study*, 5 vols (Ankara: Türk Tarih Kurumu, 2000), III/1, 1346.
22   ATBD 42/96 (September 1994), belge 2531.
23   TİH, *Sakarya*, 299; Gündüz, *Hatıralar*, 76.
24   Çalışlar, *Gün, Gün, Saat, Saat*, 236–38; TİH, *Sakarya*, 17–18.
25   Çakmak, *Mareşal Fevzi Çakmak ve Günlükleri*, 820–23.
26   ATASE Arşivi, İSH, 1371/169.
27   ATASE Arşivi, İSH, 1371/130.
28   TİH, *Sakarya*, 9–10; Ulusoy, *İstiklal Harbi'nde 2 nci Kolordu*, 251–61.
29   İnönü, *Hatıralar*, I, 262.
30   Mustafa Kemal, *Nutuk*. 2 vols (Ankara: n.p., 1927), I, 449.
31   Gündüz, *Hatıralar*, 78.
32   TİH, *Sakarya*, 62–63; ABE, XI, 351.
33   ABE, XI, 355.
34   ATASE Arşivi, İSH 1288/36. İzzeddin received the order at 2300; Çalışlar, *Gün, Gün, Saat, Saat*, 263.

35   Adıvar, *A Turkish Ordeal*, 292–93.

36   Ibid., 294.

37   Sabahattin Selek, "Sakarya Meydan Muharebesi," in *Sakarya Savaşanlar Anlatıyor* (İstanbul: Örgün Yayınları, 2007), 36–37.

38   Alptekin Müdderisoğlu, *Sakarya Meydan Muharebeşş Günlüğü* (Ankara: Kastaş Yayınevi, 2004), 456.

39   İnönü, *Hatıralar*, I, 259.

40   Adıvar, *Turkish Ordeal*, 289.

41   Ibid., 297. Mango used the expression "depressive indecision." Andrew Mango, *Atatürk: the Biography of the Founder of Modern Turkey* (Woodstock, NY: Overlook Press, 1999), 320.

42   Çakmak, *Mareşal Fevzi Çakmak ve Günlükleri*, II, 822; Gündüz, *Hatıralar*, 88.

43   Gündüz, *Hatıralar*, 81–83.

44   Adıvar, *A Turkish Ordeal*, 297.

45   Ibid., 297–99.

46   Michael Llewellyn Smith, *Ionian Vision: Greece in Asia Minor 1919–1922* (London: Hurst and Company, 1973/1998), 233.

47   Kazım Özalp, *Milli Mücadele, 1919–1922*, 2 vols (Ankara: Türk Tarih Kurumu Basımevi, 1985), I, 204–5; Gündüz, *Hatıralar*, 100–5; Çalışlar, *Gün, Gün, Saat, Saat*, 291.

48   Özalp, *Milli Mücadele*, I, 210.

49   ABE, XI, 379–380.

50   Shaw, *From Empire to Republic*, III/1, 1353–57.

51   ATASE Arşivi, İSH 1212/18, 1215/51–1.

52   TİH, *Sakarya*, 275; ABE XI, 381.

53   Çalışlar, *Gün, Gün, Saat, Saat*, 305.

54   ATASE Arşivi, İSH 1215/51; TİH, *Sakarya*, 269–74.

55   *Atatürk'ün Tamim, Telgraf ve Beyannameleri*, IV, 431.

56   TİH, *Sakarya*, 275.

57   ATASE Arşivi, İSH 1456/28, 1472/8.

58   Çakmak, *Mareşal Fevzi Çakmak ve Günlükleri*, II, 827.

59   TBMM, *Zabıt Ceridesi*, XII, 255–62.

60   Taha Akyol, *Ama Hangi Atatürk* (İstanbul: Doğan Kitab, 2008), 127.

61   HTVD 75 (September 1976), belge 1629.

62   Fahri Belen, *Türk İstiklal Savaşı Askeri: Siyasi ve Sosyal Yönleriyle* (Ankara: Kültür ve Turizm Bakanlığı Yayınları, 1983), 365–67.

63   TBBM, *Gizli Celise Zabıtları*, II, 355.

64   Mustafa Budak, *Misak-ı Milli'den Lozan'a: İdealden Gerçeğe Türk Dış Politikası* (İstanbul: Küre Yayınları, 2002), 256–57.

65   TBMM, *Gizli Celise Zabıtları*, II, 364–65.

66   Shaw, *From Empire to Republic*, III/2, 1414–17.

67   Stefanos Yerasimos, *Türk-Sovyet İlişkileri: Ekim Devrimden Milli Mücadeleye* (İstanbul: Gözlem Yayınlar 1979), 343–46, 438–39 (report), 445–49 (treaty).

68   Shaw, *From Empire to Republic*, III/2, 1572–73.

69   TBMM, *Gizli Celse Zabıtları*, II, 248–56, 262–70, 403–9, 434–42, 513–19, 622–24, 627–30.

70   BCA, 030.18.1.1 / 3.25.20, Kararname 1169.

71   TBMM, *Gizli Celse Zabıtları*, II, 433–42. BCA, 030.18.1.1 4.36.8, Kararname 1177 and 030.18.1.1/4.37.1, Kararname 1190.

72   TBMM, *Gizli Celse Zabıtları*, II, 622–24, 627–30.

73   Andrew Mango, "Atatürk and the Kurds," *Middle Eastern Studies* 35 (1999), 14.

74   For the Muslim side to this issue, see Justin McCarthy, *Death and Exile: the Ethnic Cleansing*

of Ottoman Muslims, 1821–1992 (Princeton, NJ: Darwin Press, 1996) and *The Ottoman Peoples and the End of Empire* (London: Arnold, 2001).

75 McCarthy, *Death and Exile*, 289.

76 ABE, XII, 233.

77 TBMM, *Gizli Celise Zabıtları*, II, 606–10.

78 Ibid., 432–44, 436 (divine law).

79 Mango, *Atatürk*, 383.

80 Çalışlar, *Gün, Gün, Saat, Saat*, 235.

81 Adıvar, *A Turkish Ordeal*, 355.

82 Rauf Orbay, *Siyasi Hatıralar* (İstanbul: Örgün Yayınevi, 2003), 553–54.

83 ABE, XII, 159–171, 159 (setting).

Chapter 7   From Lightning Campaign to Peace

1 Basil Liddell Hart, *Strategy* (New York: Praeger, 1967), 366.

2 Şerafettin Turan, *Kendine Özgü bir Yaşam ve Kişilik: Mustafa Kemal Atatürk* (Ankara: Bilgi Yayınevi, 2008), 344.

3 TİH, *Hazırlık*, 51–53.

4 Ali İhsan Sabis, *Harb Hatıralarım*, V: *İstiklal Harbi ve Gizli Cihetleri* (İstanbul: Nehir Yayınları, 1993), 422–31.

5 ATASE Arşivi, İSH 1755/62.

6 İsmet İnönü, *Hatıralar*, 2 vols, compiled by Sabahettin Selek (Ankara: Bilgi Yayınevi, 1987), I, 279.

7 Hikmet Özdemir, *The Ottoman Army 1914–1918: Disease and Death on the Battlefield* (Salt Lake City: University of Utah Press, 2008), 101.

8 Sabis, *Harb Hatıralarım*, V, 415–16.

9 ATASE Arşivi, İSH, 1775/92.

10 HTVD 59 (March 1967), vesika 1346.

11 TBMM, *Gizli Celise Zabıtları*, III, 2–19, 7 (castle).

12 *Atatürk'ün Not Defterileri*, prepared by Ali Mithat İnan (Ankara: Gündoğan, 1996), 124–32.

13 Fahri Belen, *Türk İstiklal Savaşı: Askeri, Siyasi ve Sosyal Yönleriyle* (Ankara: Kültür ve Turizm Bakanlığı Yayınları, 1983), 389.

14 Yusuf Kemal Tengirşak, *Vatan Hizmetinde* (Ankara: Kültür Bakanlığı Yayınları, 1981), 239–43.

15 Davison, Roderic H. "Turkish Diplomacy from Mudros to Lausanne," in *The Diplomats, 1919–1939*, edited by Gordon A. Craig and Felix Gilbert (Princeton: Princeton University Press, 1953), 196; Michael Llewellyn Smith, *Ionian Vision: Greece in Asia Minor 1919–1922* (London: Hurst and Company, 1973/1998), 252–57.

16 *Atatürk'ün Tamim, Telgraf ve Beyannameleri* (Ankara: Türk İnkılap Tarihi Enstitüsü Yayınları, 1991), 456–57.

17 Stefanos Yerasimos, *Türk-Sovyet İlişkileri: Ekim Devrimden Milli Mücadeleye* (İstanbul: Gözlem Yayınları, 1979), 631–34.

18 BCA, 030.18.01.01/4.4.52.

19 TBMM, *Zabıt Ceridesi*, XVII, 129–32.

20 Stanford Shaw, *From Empire to Republic: The Turkish War of Independence 1919–1923, A Documentary Study*, 5 vols (Ankara: Türk Tarih Kurumu, 2000), III/1, 1121–25.

21 ATASE Arşivi, İSH 1719/15-3.

22 TBMM, *Gizli Celise Zabıtları*, III, 338.

23 Ibid.

24 Ibid., 339, 342 (Fevzi).

25   Rauf Orbay, *Siyasi Hatıralar* (İstanbul: Örgün Yayınevi, 2003), 492–95.

26   "Bir Vicdan Zaferi," *Hakimiyet-i Milliye*, 22 July 1922, 1.

27   İnönü, *Hatıralar*, I, 269.

28   Sabis, *Harb Hatıralarım*, V, 120–28.

29   Ibid., 372–74, 386.

30   ATASE Arşivi, İSH 1796/60.

31   Kazım Özalp, *Milli Mücadele, 1919–1922*, 2 vols (Ankara: Türk Tarih Kurumu Basımevi, 1985), I, 229; Asım Gündüz, *Hatıralar* (İstanbul: Kervan Kitapçılık, 1973), 125–28; İnönü, *Hatıralar*, I, 273–75; Falih Rıfkı Atay, *Çankaya: Atatürk'ün Doğumundan Ölümüne Kadar Bütün Hayat Hikayesi* (İstanbul: Doğan Kardeş Matbaacılık Sanayi A. Ş. Basımevi, 1969), 308.

32   Sadık Atak, *Bir Komutan'dan Anılar: Orgeneral Yakup Şevki* (Ankara: Ayyıldız Matbaası, 1977), 14–16.

33   Smith, *Ionian Vision*, 237–52, 272–86. 246 (promotions), 251 (evacuation), 261–65 (Papoulas), 266–75 (Hatzianestis), 284 (new command structure), 285 (reserves and communications), and 277–78 (troops to Thrace).

34   Nikolas Trikupis and M. Papulas, *Yunan Generallerinin İtirafları* (Ankara: Berikan, 2001), 95–97.

35   ATASE Arşivi, İSH 1747/59 (cabinet) and 1748/27 (patriarch).

36   ATASE Arşivi, İSH 1747/64.

37   ATASE Arşivi, İSH 1720/62.

38   ATASE Arşivi, İSH 1748/11; ABE, XIII, 203.

39   Gündüz, *Hatıralar*, 141.

40   TİH, *Hazırlık*, 178.

41   HTVD 75 (September 1976), vesika 1631; Gündüz, *Hatıralar*, 142–43.

42   Belen, *Türk Istiklal Savaşı*, 422–23.

43   ABE, XIII, 144.

44   CAA, 5–1/37–3.

45   Asım Gündüz, *Hatıralar* (İstanbul: Kervan Kitapçılık, 1973), 146–48.

46   Ibid., 133.

47   ATBD 43/97 (January 1994), belge 2582.

48   Gündüz, *Hatıralar*, 151; TİH, *Büyük Taarruz*, 25.

49   Gündüz, *Hatıralar*, 139–40.

50   ATBD 43/97 (January 1994), belge 2593; TSKT, *TBMM*, 489–90; TİH, *Büyük Taarruz*, 57–58.

51   Ibid., 3.

52   Celal Erikan, *Komutan Atatürk* (İstanbul: Türkiye İş Bankası Kültür Yayınları, 2006), 690–96; İsmet Görgülü, *Büyük Taarruz* (Ankara: Genelkurmay Basımevi, 1992), 16–21; Smith, *Ionian Vision*, 285.

53   Fahrettin Altay, *İstiklal Harbimizde Süvari Kolordusu* (Ankara: İnsel Kitabevi, 1949), 37–39.

54   Osman Okyar, "Turco-British Relations in the Inter-War Period: Fethi Okyar's Missions to London," in *Four Centuries of Turco-British Relations: Studies in Diplomatic, Economic and Cultural Affairs*, edited by William Hale and Ali İhsan Bağış (North Humberside: The Eothen Press, 1984), 69–73. Quote appears on p. 70.

55   "Near East Conference in Venice," *The Times*, 17 August 1922, 7.

56   TİH, *Büyük Taarruz*, 111.

57   Ibid., 97–99; Fahri Aykut, *İstiklal Savaşı'nda IV ncü Kolordu* (Ankara: Genelkurmay Basimev, 2006), 204–33.

58   TİH, *Büyük Taarruz*, 111–14, 122; Altay, *İstiklal Harbimizde Süvari Kolordusu*, 46–47.

59   ATBD 43/97 (January 1994), belge 2595.

60 Smith, *Ionian Vision*, 289–91.
61 TİH, *Büyük Taarruz*, 126–27.
62 Fahri Belen, *Büyük Türk Zaferi: Afyon'dan İzmir'e Kadar* (İstanbul: Cumhuriyet, 1999), 46–47.
63 Görgülü, *Büyük Taarruz*, 29–30.
64 HTVD 60 (June 1967), vesika 1369.
65 Erikan, *Komutan Atatürk*, 707.
66 Görgülü, *Büyük Taarruz*, 30.
67 ATBD 43/97 (January 1994), belge 2606.
68 CAA, 5–1/72.
69 TİH, *Büyük Taarruz*, 241–42; İnönü, *Hatıralar*, I, 290; Salih Bozok, *Yaveri Atatürk'ü Anlatıyor* (İstanbul: Doğan Kitab, 2001), 84.
70 TİH, *Büyük Taarruz*, 197.
71 Bozok, *Yaveri Atatürk'ü Anlatıyor*, 84.
72 Belen, *Büyük Türk Zaferi*, 77–80; Smith, *Ionian Vision*, 294.
73 TİH, *Büyük Taarruz*, 279.
74 Belen, *Türk Kurtuluş Savaşı*, 483.
75 BCA, 030.10/54.355.7, document no. 11.
76 Belen, *Büyük Türk Zaferi*, 104–5.
77 İzzettin Çalışlar, *Gün, Gün, Saat, Saat: İstkilal Harbi'nde Garb Cephesi* (İstanbul: Türkiye İş Bankası Kültür Yayınları, 2009), 415–16; Gündüz, *Hatıralar*, 167–68.
78 ATASE Arşivi, İSH 1786/159–29; 1796/71; ATBD 43/97 (January 1994), belge 2626.
79 *Hakimiyet-i Milliye*, 2 Eylul 1922, 1.
80 ATBD 43/97 (January 1994), belge 2627.
81 *Hakimiyet-i Milliye*, 2 Eylul 1922, p. 1.
82 Halide Edip Adıvar, *A Turkish Ordeal* (New York: The Century Company, 1928), 366.
83 Salih Bozok and Cemil S. Bozok, *Hep Atatürk'ün Yanında* (İstanbul: Çağdaş Yayınları, 1985), 202; Bozok, *Yaveri Atatürk'ü Anlatıyor*, 86.
84 İrfan and Margarete Orga, *Atatürk* (London: Michael Joseph, 1962), 200.
85 *Hakimiyet-i Milliye*, 10 Eylul 1922, 1.
86 *Hakimiyet-i Milliye*, 11 Eylul 1922, 1.
87 *Belgelerle Mustafa Kemal Atatürk (1916 - 1922)*, directed by Yusuf Sarınay (Ankara: Başbakanlık Basımevi, 2003), 212 and 662 for photocopy of document.
88 Smith, *Ionian Vision*, 305–11.
89 Lord Kinross, *Ataturk: A Biography of Mustafa Kemal, Father of Modern Turkey* (New York: W. Morrow, 1965), 372.
90 İnönü, *Hatıralar*, II, 19.
91 CAA, 5–1/112. English translation in Andrew Mango, *Atatürk: The Biography of the Founder of Modern Turkey* (Woodstock, NY: The Overlook Press, 1999), 352. Modern Turkish text is in *Atatürk'ün Tamim, Telgraf ve Beyannameleri* (Ankara: Türk İnkılap Tarihi Enstitüsü Yayınları, 1991), 484.
92 HTVD 66 (December 1968), vesika 1477.
93 İnönü, *Hatıralar*, II, 16.
94 Ibid., 33.
95 TBMM, *Zabıt Ceridesi*, XXIII, 336 (Kemal's words), 362–3, 427–32.
96 *Atatürk'ün Söylev ve Demeçleri* (Ankara: Türk İnkılap Tarihi Enstitüsü Yayınları, 2006), II, 46–50. 46 (feelings), 47 (patriotism, guide, and poetry), 48 (ties to the world), 48–49 (two aims), and 49 (prepare ground). Two contemporary newspapers published the reference to China.

97   Kinross, *Ataturk*, 395.
98   For a photocopy of the Ottoman text, see ATBD 120 (Nisan: 2007), 291–300. For the transliteration: TBMM, *Zabıt Ceridesi*, XXIV, 305–11.
99   Frederick P. Latimer, "The Political Philosophy of Mustapha Mustafa Kemal Ataturk as Evidenced in His Published Speeches and Interviews," (Ph.D. Dissertation, Princeton University, June 1960), 103–4.
100   *Atatürk'ün Söylev ve Demeçleri*, 3 vols (Ankara: Türk İnkılap Tarihi Enstitüsü Yayınları, 2006), II, 157.
101   Mustafa Kemal Atatürk, *Eskişehir – İzmit Konuşmaları (1923)* (İstanbul: Kaynak Yayınalrı, 1993), 60.
102   Ibid., 138.
103   Ibid., 136.
104   Ibid., 170.
105   Ibid., 173–241.
106   *Atatürk'ün Söylev ve Demeçleri*, II, 104–5.
107   Ibid., II, 137.
108   Ibid., 60.
109   Ibid., 89–91.
110   ABE, XV, 97.
111   *Atatürk'ün Söylev ve Demeçleri*, II, 159.
112   Ibid., 100.
113   Klaus Kreiser, *Atatürk: Bir Biografi*, translated by Dilek Zaptçıoğlu (İstanbul: İletişim Yayınları, 2010), 213 ff. Kreiser uses the concept of *baba* for the period of 1922 onwards, whereas Mustafa Kemal already used the term for soldiering as earlier as 1914 in his book *Conversation*.
114   Grace Ellison, *Turkey Today* (London: Hutchinson, 1928), 83.
115   Mango, *Atatürk*, 498.
116   *Medeni Bilgiler ve M. Mustafa Kemal Atatürk'ün El Yazıları*, compiled by A. Afetinan (Ankara: Türk Tarih Kurum, 1998), 23 and 378 (handwritten).
117   The notion of a cognitive revolution comes from Metin Heper, discussion with author, Ankara, 4 July 2009.
118   *Medeni Bilgiler ve M. Mustafa Kemal Atatürk'ün El Yazıları*, 369–70 (handwritten). There is a discrepancy with the printed version on page 21 that eliminates the words "not with religious sentiment."
119   Ayşe Gül Altınay, *The Myth of the Military-Nation: Militarism, Gender, and Education* (New York: Palgrave-MacMillan, 2004) for a recent study of this subject.
120   Gazi Mustafa Kemal, *Nutuk* (Ankara: no publisher, 1927), 461–62.

Conclusion

1   Carl von Clausewitz, *On War*, edited and translated by Michael Howard and Peter Paret (Princeton, NJ: Princeton University Press, 1984): 112.
2   Ibid., 87.
3   Grace Ellison, *Turkey Today* (London: Hutchinson, 1928), 20.
4   *Atatürk'ün Söylev ve Demeçleri*, (Ankara: Türk İnkılap Tarihi Enstitüsü Yayınları, 2006), II, 120.

Biographical Notes of Key Figures

Mustafa Kemal (Atatürk), 1880/81–1938

1880–81	Born in Selanik
1893–95	Military preparatory school in Selanik
1895–99	Military High School in Manastır
1899–1902	13 March, entered War College
1902	10 December, graduated as second lieutenant
1903	Entered Staff College
1905	10 December, graduated Staff College as captain and assigned to Syria
1907	20 June, promoted to senior captain, or *kolağası*
	13 September, assigned to Third Army headquarters in Selanik
1908	September, sent to Libya to garner local support for the Constitution
1909	April, operations officer for Action Army in suppressing revolt in Istanbul
1910	September, observer of French maneuvers in France
1911	27 November, promoted to major
1911–12	1 December–24 October, service in Libya
1912–13	November to July, service in Balkan Wars
1913	27 October, assigned as military attaché in Sofia
1914	1 March, promotion to lieutenant colonel
1915	Service in Gallipoli campaign
	1 June, promoted to colonel
	8 August, designated commander of Anafartalar Group
	10 December, departed Gallipoli for Istanbul
1916	27 January, appointed to command XVI Corps
	1 April, promoted to brigadier general
	7–8 August, captured Muş and Bitlis from Russians

1917	7 March, appointed to command Second Army
	14 May, recaptured Muş after abandoning the town the previous September
	1 July, appointed to command Seventh Army
	4 October, resigned command and returned to Istanbul
	20 December, accompanied Prince Vahdeddin to Germany
1918	25 May, departed on medical leave to Austria and returned 2 August
	7 August, reappointed to command Seventh Army
1919	19 May, landed in Samsun
	22 June, Amasya Protocol
	23 July–7 August, Erzurum Congress
	4–11 September, Sivas Congress
	27 December, arrival in Ankara
1920	23 April, Grand National Assembly opens in Ankara
	24 April, elected president of the Grand National Assembly
	10 August, Treaty of Sèvres
	3 December, Treaty of Gümrü
1921	9–11 January, First Battle of İnönü
	20 January, provisional constitution
	16 March, a friendship treaty with Russia signed in Moscow
	26 March–1 April, Second Battle of İnönü
	10 July, Greeks launch major offensive
	5 August, Law 144 appointed Mustafa Kemal as commander in chief
	23 August–13 September, Battle of Sakarya
	20 October, French–Turkish Accord
	31 October, reappointed for another three months as commander in chief
1922	2 February, reappointed for another three months as commander in chief
	6 May, reappointed for another three months as commander in chief
	20 July, appointed commander in chief for indefinite period
	26 August–18 September, Great Offensive and Pursuit
	3–11 October, Mudanya Conference
	1 November, abolishment of Ottoman sultanate
1923	14 January, began tour of Anatolia
	24 July, Treaty of Lausanne
	29 October, establishment of the Republic

Ali Fuad (Cebesoy), 1882–1968, was born in Istanbul, the son of a general. He studied at St. Joseph French Lycée in Istanbul and was Kemal's classmate at the War College, both graduating in 1905. Later, he served with Kemal in Syria and Macedonia. In 1911, Ali Fuad fought against rebels in northern Albania and during the Balkan Wars became a prisoner of war. In World War I, he commanded a division on the Eastern Front and later a corps on the Sinai Front. He was promoted to brigadier general in 1917 and commanded Seventh Army under Kemal's *Yıldırım* Group. He began the War of Independence as commander of XX Corps in Ankara. In September 1919, at the Sivas Congress, he was appointed commander of the Western Front National Forces and later from June to November 1920 of the Western Command. He served as first ambassador in Moscow from November 1920 to June 1922 and vice president of the TBMM from December 1922 to October 1923. Ali Fuad possessed excellent knowledge of French and German and published several memoirs. In 1924, he helped found the Progressive Republic Party in opposition to Kemal's Republican People's Party.

Carl von Clausewitz, 1787–1831, was a Prussian general, theorist, and historian. His unfinished work *Vom Krieg* (*On War*), published in 1833, is a classic on warfare. In *On War*, Clausewitz provides both a philosophical and practical treatment of war. He also wrote a number of military histories, including works on the 1812 and the 1815 campaigns in the Napoleonic era.

(İsmail) Enver, 1881–1922, was born in Istanbul to a family of humble means. Enver graduated from the Staff College in 1903. He gained fame fighting guerrillas and emerged as one of the heroes of the 1908 Revolution. He briefly served as a military attaché in Berlin and fought in Libya as a commander. The Balkan Wars enhanced his reputation as a liberator of Edirne. He then married a niece of the sultan and rose to become war minister and chief of the General Staff in January 1914. Enver played a major role in bringing the Ottoman Empire onto the side of Germany in World War I. He fled to Germany at the end of the war and then cooperated with the Bolsheviks in fighting the British. Kemal refused his return to Turkey. Enver died fighting the Bolsheviks in Tajikistan.

Fahreddin (Altay), 1880–1974, was born in İşkodra, northern Albania, his father an army colonel. He graduated from the Staff College in 1902 and gained combat experience fighting against Kurdish tribes. He subsequently commanded a tribal cavalry regiment during the Balkan Wars. Later, he served as chief of staff for III Corps during the Gallipoli campaign. Promoted to colonel in December 1915, he held division and corps commands during World War I. At the beginning of the War of Independence, he was commander of XII Corps in Konya and served with distinction as commander of the Fifth Cavalry Group in the Battle of Sakarya and commander of V Cavalry Corps in the Great Offensive. Fahreddin was promoted successively to brigadier general after Sakarya and major general after the Great Offensive. By 1926, he was a lieutenant general. Possessed of knowledge of French and German, he published several books, including his memoirs of the War of Independence.

(Ali) Fethi (Okyar), 1880–1943, was a soldier and diplomat born in Prilep, Macedonia. Kemal's schoolmate at Manastır Military High School, he served in Libya and the Balkan Wars. Briefly secretary-general of the CUP, he became ambassador to Sofia from 1913–1917. He subsequently collaborated with Kemal in publishing the newspaper *Minber*. Afterward, he was exiled to Malta by the Allies. Upon returning to Turkey, he became interior minister from 1921–22. He later published his memoirs. Ali Fethi had an excellent command of French and helped Kemal improve his knowledge of the language.

Fevzi (Çakmak), 1876–1944, was born in Istanbul into a military family. He graduated from the Staff College in 1898 and performed long service in the Albanian regions of the Balkans. Promoted to colonel in 1913 and brigadier general in 1914, he replaced Kemal as commander of Anafartalar Group in Gallipoli. He commanded Seventh Army in Sinai in 1917. Fevzi joined Kemal in Ankara in April 1920, becoming defense minister and then prime minister from January 1921 to July 1922. Promoted to major general in 1921, he became chief of the General Staff for the Great Offensive and was promoted to marshal in 1922. Fevzi claimed various levels of competence in French, German, English, Persian, Arabic, Serbian, Bulgarian, and Albanian. He commanded the Turkish Armed Forces throughout the Kemalist Republic until İsmet İnönü forced his retirement in 1944. As commander of the armed forces, he directed military studies on the Western Front in the Balkan Wars and the Eastern Front in the Great War.

Halide Edip (Adıvar), 1882–1964, was a feminist and novelist. Her father had been a secretary to Sultan Abdülhamid II. She was educated by private tutors and in Istanbul attended a Rum school and the American College. She possessed a knowledge of French, English, and Greek. Before World War I, she established an intellectual salon for women. Subsequently, she divorced her husband and remarried Dr Adnan Adıvar. During the armistice, she founded a Wilson Society to advocate an American mandate. She soon gained fame for public speeches opposing foreign occupation. Halide Edip joined Kemal and served at the front with him during the Battle of Sakarya and the Great Offensive. Opposed to Kemal's reforms, she left for the United States. Her memoir *A Turkish Ordeal*, written in English, forms an invaluable source of information and insight into Kemal and the War of Independence. She published a number of other works in English. Halide Edip returned to Turkey after Kemal's death.

İsmet (İnönü), 1884–1973, was born in Izmir. He graduated from the Staff College in 1906 at the top of his class. He possessed language proficiency in German, French, and English. He was promoted to major in 1912 for exemplary service in Yemen and became a colonel in 1915. During World War I, he became Kemal's chief of staff in Second Army and then one of his corps commanders in the last Sinai campaign. He served as chief of the General Staff and then commander of the Western Front during the War of Independence. İsmet was foreign minister during the Mudanya Armistice and the Treaty of Lausanne. He was prime minister in 1923 and from 1925 to 1937. He became president of Turkey upon Kemal's death.

İzzeddin (Çalışlar), 1882–1951, was born in Yanya, Albania. He graduated from the Staff College in 1906 and served on various staffs. He was Kemal's chief of staff at Gallipoli and then on the Eastern Front until 1917. İzzeddin served with distinction as commander of First Group at the Battles of Eskişehir and Sakarya and then of I Corps in the Great Offensive. He knew German, French, and Greek.

Kazım Karabekir, 1882–1948, was born in Istanbul and graduated from the Staff College in 1905. He first gained combat experience fighting guerrilla bands in Macedonia, and during the Balkan Wars served as chief of staff of a division in the defense of Edirne. In 1915, he assumed the position of chief of staff for a field army in Iraq and in 1917 was a corps commander on the Caucasus Front, an experience that served him well during the War of Independence. He gained fame in capturing the cities of Erzurum and Kars. He was promoted to brigadier general in 1918 and hosted the Erzurum Congress. During the War of Independence, Karabekir commanded XV Corps in Erzurum and then the Eastern Front. He possessed knowledge of Bulgarian, German, French, and Russian.

(Mehmed) Nureddin, 1873–1932, was born in Bursa, the son of a field marshal. He graduated from the War College in 1893 but did not attend the Staff College. Promoted to major in 1901, he fought against guerrilla bands in Macedonia. He was promoted to colonel in 1914 and served as governor of Basra in 1915 and Baghdad in 1916. Nureddin finished World War I commanding several different corps in Anatolia. He was promoted to brigadier general in 1918 and during the War of Independence he commanded the Central Army in the brutal suppression of the Ottoman Greeks and Kurds in northern and central Anatolia.

He commanded First Army in the Great Offensive. Nureddin spoke German, French, Russian, and Arabic.

Nuri Conker, 1881–1937, was born in Selanik, a distant relative to Kemal. He graduated from the Staff College in 1905 and served on the staff of Bingazi Forces in Libya. He was wounded in the Battle of Bolayır against the Bulgarians. Later, he commanded a regiment in Gallipoli and then a division in Kemal's XVI Corps on the Eastern Front. Nuri was Kemal's close companion until his own death. He knew German well, and authored *Zabit ve Kumandan* (*Officer and Commander*).

Rauf (Orbay), 1882–1964, was a naval officer who gained fame commanding a battleship during the Balkan Wars. He was also involved in covert operations in Afghanistan and western Iran. He was one of the participants at the Brest-Litovsk Treaty in 1918 and then signed the infamous Mudros Armistice as naval minister. Rauf was Kemal's close associate in 1919, serving on the Representative Committee. He was arrested by the British in March 1920 and exiled to Malta. Upon his release, Rauf returned to Ankara and became prime minister in July 1922. Later, he fell out of favor with Kemal and spent time in Europe before returning to Turkey in 1935.

(Main sources: Andrew Mango, *Ataturk: The Biography of the Founder of Modern Turkey* (Woodstock, NY: Overlook Press, 2000), 541–55; Azmi Süslü and Mustafa Balcıoğlu, *Atatürk'ün Silah Arkadaşları – Atatürk Araştırma Merkezi Şeref Üyeleri* (Ankara: Atatürk Araştırma Merkezi, 1999).

Bibliography

PRIMARY SOURCES

Turkish Archives

Başbakanlık Cumhuriyet Arşivi (BCA). Ankara.
Başbakanlık Osmanlı Arşivi (BOA). İstanbul.
Cumhurbaşkanlık Atatürk Arşivi (CAA). Ankara.
Genelkurmay Askeri Tarih ve Stratejik Etüt Başkanlığı (ATASE). Ankara.
    Atatürk Kolesiyonu (ATA-ZB).
    Birinci Dünya Harbi (BDH).
    İstiklal Harbi Koleksiyonu (İSH).
Türk Inkilab Tarihi Enstitüsü Arşivi (TITE). Ankara.
Türk Tarih Kurumu Arşivi (TTK). Ankara.

Newspapers and Journals with Published Documents

Askeri Tarih Belgeleri Dergisi (ATBD).
Hakimiyet-i Milliye.
Harp Tarihi Vesikaları Dergisi (HTVD).
Minber.

Published Primary Documents

Atatürk, Mustafa Kemal. *Anafartalar Muharebatı'na Ait Tarihçe*. Ankara: Türk Tarih Kurum Basımevi, 1962.
____. *Arıburnu Muharebeleri Raporu*. Ankara: Türk Tarih Kurum Basımevi, 1968.
____. *Atatürk ile İlgili Arşiv Belgeleri (1911–1921 tarihleri arasına ait 106 belge)*. Ankara, 1981.
____. *Atatürk Özel Arşivinden Seçmeler*. 4 vols. Ankara: ATASE Yayınları, 1981–96.
____. *Atatürk'ün Askerliğe Dair Eserleri*. Ankara: Doğuş Ltd. Şirketi Matbaası, 1959.
____. *Atatürk'ün Bütün Eserleri* (ABE), vols 1–15. İstanbul: Kaynak Yayınları, 1998–2005.
____. *Atatürk'ün Milli Diş Politikası: Milli Mücadele Dönemine ait 100 Belge, 1919–1923*. 2 vols. 2nd ed. Ankara, 1992.
____. *Atatürk'ün Not Defterleri*, prepared by Ali Mithat İnan. Ankara: Gündoğan, 1996.
____. *Atatürk'ün Not Defterleri, II: Harp Akademisi Öğrencisi Mustafa Kemal'in Not Defteri*. Ankara: Genelkurmay Basımevi, 2004.

____. *Atatürk'ün Not Defterleri, V: Mustafa Kemal'in 1870–71 Alman-Fransız Savaşı Konusunda Tuttuğu Notlar ile 1905–1908 Yılları Arasında Tuttuğu Günlük Notları*. Ankara: Genel Kurmay Basımevi, 2005.

____. *Atatürk'ün Not Defterleri, VI: Mustafa Kemal'in İstihkam ve Topçuluk, Stratejik Taarruz ve Stratejik Savunma ile Subaylar için Yazılmış olan Hizmet-i Seferiye Talimnamesine ait Tuttuğu Notlar*. Ankara: Genel Kurmay Basımevi, 2005.

____. *Atatürk'ün Not Defterleri, X: Mustafa Kemal'in 5'inci Ordu Karargahında Görevli İken Tuttuğu Notlar ile Trablusgarp Cephesindeki Günlük Emir Defteri*: Ankara: Genel Kurmay Basımevi, 2009.

____. *Atatürk'ün Okuduğu Kitaplar*, vol. 21, collected by Recep Cengiz. Ankara: Anıtkabir Derneği Yayınları, 2001.

____. *Atatürk'ün Özel Mektupları*, collected by Sadi Borak. İstanbul: Varlık Yayınları, 1961.

____. *Atatürk'ün Söylev ve Demeçleri*, 3 vols. Ankara: Türk İnkılap Tarihi Enstitüsü Yayınları, 2006.

____. *Atatürk'ün Resmi Yayınlara Girmemiş Söylev, Demeç, Yazışma ve Söyleşileri*, collected by Sadi Borak. 2nd ed. İstanbul: Kaynak Yayınları, 1997.

____. *Atatürk'ün Tamim, Telgraf ve Beyannameleri*. Ankara: Türk İnkılap Tarihi Enstitüsü Yayınları, 1991.

____. *Eskişehir – İzmit Konuşmaları (1923)*, edited by Doğu Perinçek. İstanbul: Kaynak Yayınalrı, 1993.

____. *Kolordu Emri: Ta'biye Meslesesinin Hali ve Emirlerin Sureti Tahririne Dair Nesayih*. Edirne: Edirne Sanayı Mektebi Matbaası, 1331/1916.

____. *Medeni Bilgiler ve M. Kemal Atatürk'ün El Yazıları*, compiled by Afet İnan. Ankara: Türk Tarih Kurum, 1998.

____. *Nutuk*. 2 vols. Ankara: no publisher, 1927.

____. *Sofya Askeri Ataşesi Mustafa Kemal'in Raporları (Kasım 1913 – Kasım 1914)*, edited by Ahmet Tetik. Ankara: Genelkurmay ATASE Yayınları, 2007.

____. *Takımın Muharebe Talimi*. Translated by Mustafa Kemal. Selanik: Asır Matbaası, 1324/1909.

____. *Zabit ve Komundan ile Hasbıhal*. İstanbul: Minber Matbaası, 1918.

Baykal, Bekir Sıtkı (ed). *Heyet-i Temsiliye Kararları*. 2nd ed. Ankara: Türk Tarih Kurumu Basımevi, 1989.

Belgelerle Mustafa Kemal Atatürk (1916–1922), directed by Yusuf Sarınay. Ankara: Başbakanlık Basımevi, 2003.

Borak, Sadi. *Atatürk'ün Resmi Yayınlara Girmemiş Söylev Demeç Yazışma ve Söyleşileri*. İstanbul: Kaynak Yayınları, 1997.

British Documents on Foreign Affairs (BDFA): Reports and Papers from the Foreign Office Confidential Print, Part II: From the First to the Second World War, Series B: Turkey, Iran, and the Middle East 1918–1939, editor Robin Bidwell. Washington, DC: University Publications of America, 1985. Volumes 1–3.

Bulut, Faik. *Belgelerle Dersim Raporlar*. İstanbul: Yön, 1991.

Gazi Mustafa Kemal Atatürk'ten Bize: Söylevleri, Konuşmaları, Söyleşileri, Anıları, Genelgeler, Yazışmaları (1903–1938), cilt 1, 1903–22/4/1920. İstanbul: Hürriyet Vakfı Yayınları, 1997.

Gökay, Bülent. *British Documents on Foreign Affairs: Reports and Papers from the Foreign Office Confidential Print*, Volume 29, Part II, *From the First to the Second World War, Series B: Turkey, Iran and the Middle East, 1918–1939, Turkey August 1922–July 1923*. Frederick, MD: 1997.

Heyet-i Temsiliye Tutanakları, edited by Uluğ İğdemir. Ankara: Atatürk Kültür, Dil ve Tarih Yüksek Kurumu Türk Tarih Kurumu Yayınları, 1989.

Kaplan, Mehmet. *Devrin Yazarlarının Kalemiyle Milli Mücadele ve Gazi Mustafa Kemal*. Ankara: Kültür Bakanlığı, 1992.

Kalvzuvic, General. *İdare-i harbe dair kavaid-i esasiye*, translated by Ahmed Refik. Constantiye: İbrahim Hilmi, 1316/1899.

Kurtuluş Savaşı'nin İdeolojisi: Hakimiyeti Milliye Yazıları, prepared by Hadiye Bolluk. İstanbul: Kaynak Yayınları, 1992.

Peker, Nurettin. *İstiklal Savaşının Vesika ve Resimleri*. İstanbul: Gür Yayınları, 1955.

Perinçek, Mehmet. *Atatürk'ün Sovyetler'le Görüşmeleri: Sovyet Arşiv Belgeleriyle*. İstanbul: Kaynak Yayınları, 2005.

Sami, Şemseddin. *Kamus al-A'lam*, 6 vols. İstanbul: Mıhran Matbaası, 1316 H/1898.

____. *Kamus-i Türki*, 2 vols. Dersaadet: Ikdam Matbaası, 1315/1899.

Sanders, Liman von. *Cinq ans de Turquie*. Paris: Payot, 1923.

Shaw, Stanford J. *From Empire to Republic: The Turkish War of Independence 1919–1923, A Documentary Study*. 5 volumes. Ankara: Türk Tarih Kurum Basımevi, 2000.

Simşir, Bilal (ed.). *Atatürkle ile Yazışmalar I (1920–1923)*. Ankara: Türk Tarih Kurum Basımevi, 1981.

____. *British Documents on Atatürk*. 4 vols. Ankara: Türk Tarih Kurum Basımevi, 1973–1984.

Spinall-Oglander, C. F. *Military Operations, Gallipoli*, vol. 1. London: Heinemann, 1929.

Türkiye Büyük Millet Meclisi. *Gizli Celse Zabıtları*. Devre 1. 3rd printing, 3 vols. Ankara: T.B.M.M. Matbaası, n.d.

____. *Zabıt Ceridesi*. Devre 1. 3rd printing, 27 vols. Ankara: T.B.M.M. Matbaası, 1959–81.

Memoirs and Other Contemporary Publications

Adıvar, Halide Edip. *A Turkish Ordeal*. New York: The Century Company, 1928.

Akçam, Taner. *A Shameful Act: the Armenian Genocide and the Question of Turkish Responsibility*. New York: Holt Paperback, 2006.

Aker, Şefik. "Çanakkale-Arnıburnu Savaşları ve 27. Alay," in *Çanakkale Hatıraları*, compiled by Metin Martı (İstanbul: Arma Yayınları, 2001) 175–292.

Altay, Fahrettin. *İstklal Harbimizde Süvari Kolordusu*. Ankara: İnsel Kitabevi, 1949.

____. *10 Yıl Savaş ve Sonrası, 1912–1922*. Ankara: Evren Dağıtım, 2008.

____. *Türkiye Muharebatında Süvari Kolordusunun Harekatı*. İstanbul: İnsel, 1925.

Apak, Rahmi. *Yetmişlik Bir Subay Hatıraları*. Ankara: E. U. Basımevi, 1957.

Artu, İbrahim. *Yeniden Doğuş: Türk Kurtuluş Savaşı*. İstanbul: Kasab Yayınları, 2001.

al-Askari, Jafar. *A Soldier's Story, From Ottoman Rule to Independent Iraq: the Memoirs of Jafar Pasha Al-Askari (1885–1936)*. London: Arabian Publishing, 2003.

Atak, Sadık. *Bir Komutan'dan Anılar: Orgeneral Yakup Şübası*. Ankara: Ayyıldız Matbaası, 1977.

Atay, Falih Rıfkı. *Çankaya: Atatürk'ün Doğumundan Ölümüne Kadar*. 2nd ed. İstanbul: Doğan, 1969.

____. *19 Mayıs*. Ankara: Ulus Basımevi, 1944.

Aybars, Ergün. *İstklal Mahkemeleri, 1920–1927*, 2 vols. İzmir: Dokuz Eylul Üniversitesi, 1988.

Aydemir, Şevket Süreyya. *Tek Adam: Atatürk*. 3 vols. İstanbul: Rezmi Kitabevi, 2003.

Bayur, Yusuf Hikmet. *Atatük Hayatı ve Eseri*. Ankara: Güven Basımevi, 1963.

Belen, Fahri. *Atatürk'ün Askeri Kişiliği*. İstanbul: Milli Eğitim Basımevi, 1963.

____. *Büyük Türk Zaferi: Afyon'dan İzmir'e Kadar*. İstanbul: Cumhuriyet, 1999.

____. *Türk Kurtuluş Savaşı: Askeri, Siyasi ve Sosyal Yönleriyle*. Ankara: Kültür ve Turizm Bakanlığı Yayınları, 1983.

Bıyıklıoğlu, Tevfik. *Atatürk Anadolu'da*. Ankara: Türk Tarih Kurumu, 1959.

Bozok, Salih. *Yaveri Atatürk'ü Anlatıyor*. İstanbul: Doğan Kitab, 2001.

Bozok, Salih and Cemil S. Bozok. *Hep Atatürk'ün Yanında*. İstanbul: Çağdaş Yayınları, 1985.

Cebesoy, Ali Fuad. *Kuva-yı Milliye İçyüzü*. İstanbul: Temel Yayınları, 2002.

____. *Milli Mücadele Hatıraları*. İstanbul: Vatican Neşriyatı, 1953.

____. *Moskova Hatıraları*. İstanbul: Vatan, 1955.

____. *Sınıf Arkadaşım Atatürk: Okul ve Genç Subaylık Hatıraları*. İstanbul: Baha Matbaası, 1967.

Çakmak, Fevzi. *Mareşal Fevzi Çakmak ve Günlükleri*, 2 cilt, edited by Nilüfer Hatemi. İstanbul: Yeni Kredi Yayınları, 2002.

Çalışlar, İzzettin. *Gün, Gün, Saat, Saat: İstkilal Harbi'nde Garb Cephesi*. İstanbul: Türkiye İş Bankası Kültür Yayınları, 2009.

____. *On Yıllık Savaşı*. İstanbul: Türkiye İş Bankası Kültür Yayınları, 2010.

Ellison, Grace. *Turkey Today*. London: Hutchinson, 1928.

Ethem, Çerkes. *Çerkes Ethem Hatıraları*. İstanbul: Dünya Matbaası, 1962.

Goltz, Colmar Freiherr von der. *Millet-i Müsellaha: Asrımız Üsul ve Ahval-ı Askeriyesi*, translated by Ahmed Tahir. Kostantiniye: Matbaa-ı Abuzzıya, 1305/1888.

Gündüz, Asım. *Hatıralarım*. İstanbul: Kervan Yayınları, 1973.

Gürer, Turgut. *Atatürk'ün Yaveri Cevat Abbas Gürer: Cepheden Meclise Büyük Önder ile 24 yıl*. İstanbul: Gürer Yayınları, 2006.

Harbord, James. "Mustapha Kemal Pasha and his Party," *World's Work* 40 (June 1920), 176–93.

İnan, Afet. *Atatürk Hakkında Hatıraları ve Belgeleri*. Ankara: Türk Tarih Kurumu Basımevi, 1954.

İnönü, İsmet. *Hatıralar*, 2 vols, compiled by Sabahettin Selek. Ankara: Bilgi Yayınevi, 1985.

Kannengiesser, Hans. *The Campaign in Gallipoli*. London: Hutchinson, 1927.

Kansu, Mazhar Müfit. *Erzurumdan Ölümüne kadar Atatürkle Beraber*. 2 vols. Ankara: Türk Tarih Kurumu Basımevi, 1966–68.

Karabekir, Kazım. *Hayatım*. İstanbul: Yapı Kredi Yayınları, 2007.

____. *İstiklal Harbimiz*. 2 vols. İstanbul: Yapı Kredi Yayınları, 2008.

Karaosmanoğlu, Kadri. *Vatan Yolunda: Milli Mücadele Hatıraları*. İstanbul: Selek Yayınevi, 1958.

Kılıç Ali, *Atatürk'ün Sırdaşı: Kılıç Ali'nın Anıları*. İstanbul: Türkiye İş Bankası Kültür Yayınları, 2005.

Nadi, Yunus. *Ankara'nın İlk Günleri*. İstanbul: Sel Yayınları, 1955.

____. *Kurtuluş Savaşı Anıları*. İstanbul: Erdini Basım ve Yayınevi, 1978.

Nur, Rıza. *Hayat ve Hayatım*, III: *Rıza Nur-Atatürk Kavgası*. İstanbul: İşaret Yayınları, 1992.

Okyar, Fethi. *Üç Devirde Bir Adam*, prepared by Cemal Kutay. İstanbul: Tercüman, 1980.

Orbay, Rauf. *Siyasi Hatırlarım*. İstanbul: Örgün Yayınevi, 2003.

Özalp, Kazım. *Milli Mücadele, 1919–1922*. 2 vols. Ankara: Türk Tarih Kurumu Basımevi, 1972–73.

Rawlinson, Anthony. *Adventures in the Near East, 1918–1922*. New York: Dodd, Mead and Company, 1924.

Sabis, Ali İhsan. *Harb Hatıralarım*, cilt 5; *İstiklal Harbi ve Gizli Cihetleri*. İstanbul: Nehir Yayınları, 1993.

Sanders, Liman von. *My Years in Turkey*. Annapolis: United States Naval Institute, 1927.

Tengirşenk, Yusuf Kemal. *Vatan Hizmetinde*. Ankara: Kültür Bakanlığı Yayınları, 1981.

Tezer, Şükrü. *Atatürk'ün Hatıra Defteri*. Ankara: Türk Tarih Kurum Basımevi, 1972.

Trikupis, Nikolas and M. Papulas. *Yunan Generallerinin İtirafları*. Ankara: Berikan, 2001.

Vandemir, Baki. *Türk İstiklal Savaşında Sakarya'dan Mudanya'ya*. Ankara: Genelkurmay Basımevi, 2006.

MODERN STUDIES

Abadan, Yavuz. *Mustafa Kemal ve Çetecilik*. İstanbul: Varlık, 1964.

Akmeşe, Handan Nezir. *The Birth of Modern Turkey: the Ottoman Military and the March to World War I*. London: I.B.Tauris, 2005.

Aksakal, Mustafa. *The Ottoman Road to War in 1914: the Ottoman Empire and the First World War*. Cambridge: Cambridge University Press, 2008.

Akyol, Taha. *Ama Hangi Atatürk*. İstanbul: Doğan Kitab, 2008.

Altınay, Ayşe Gül. *The Myth of the Military-Nation: Militarism, Gender, and Education*. New York: Palgrave-MacMillan, 2004.

Armstrong, H. C. *Grey Wolf: Mustafa Kemal, an Intimate Study of a Dictator*. New York: Minton, Balch and Company, 1933.

Aykut, Fahri. *İstiklal Savaşı'nda IV ncü Kolordu*. Ankara: Genelkurmay Basimev, 2006.

____. *İstiklal Savaşı'nda Kütahya ve Eskişehir Muharebeleri*. Ankara: Genelkurmay ATASE Başkanlığı Yayınalrı, 2006.

Balcıoğlu, Mustafa. *İki İsyan: Koçgiri, Puntus, Bir Paşa: Nurettin*. Ankara: Nobel Yayın Dağıtım Ltd. Şti, 2000.

Bay, Austin. *Ataturk: Lessons in Leadership from the Greatest General of the Ottoman Empire*. New York: Palgrave, 2011.

Baycan, Nusret. *Atatürk ve Askerlik Sanatı*. Ankara: Genelkurmay Basimev, 1998.

Belen, Fahri. *Birinci Cihan Harbinde Türk Harbi*. 5 vols. Ankara: Genelkurmay Basımevi, 1964–67.

Budak, Mustafa. *Misak-ı Milli'den Lozan'a: İdealden Gerçeğe Türk Dış Politikası*. İstanbul: Küre Yayınları, 2002.

Clausewitz, Carl von. *On War*, edited and translated by Michael Howard and Peter Paret. Princeton, NJ: Princeton University Press, 1984.

Coşkun, Alev. *Samsun'dan Önce Bilinmeyen 6 Ay: Işgal, Hüzün, Hazırlık*. İstanbul: Cumhuriyet Kitapları, 2009.

Criss, Nur Bilge. *Istanbul under Allied Occupation, 1918–1923*. London: Brill, 1999.

Dadrian, Vahakn N. *The History of the Armenian Genocide: Ethnic Conflict from the Balkans to Anatolia to the Caucasus*. Oxford: Berghahn Books, 1995.

Davison, Roderic H. "Turkish diplomacy from Mudros to Lausanne," in *The Diplomats, 1919–1939*, edited by Gordon A. Craig and Felix Gilbert. Princeton: Princeton University Press, 1953, pp. 172–209.

Demirel, Ahmet. *Birinci Meclis'te Muhalefet: İkinci Grup*. İstanbul: İşletim Yayınları, 1994.

Devereux, Robert. "Suleyman Pasha's 'The Feeling of the Revolution,'" *Middle Eastern Studies* 15 (1979), 3–35.

Erendil, Muzaffer et al. *Askeri Yönlüyle Atatürk*. Ankara: GATA Basımevi, 1981.

____. *Çok Yönlü Lider Atatürk*. Ankara: Genelkurmay Basimev, 1986.

Erickson, Edward. *Defeat in Detail: the Ottoman Army in the Balkans, 1912–1913*. Westport, CT: Praeger, 2003.

Erikan, Celal. *Komutan Atatürk*. İstanbul: Türkiye İş Bankası Kültür Yayınları, 2006.

Ertuna, Hamdi. *1911–1912 Osmanlı-İtalyan Harbi ve Kolağası Kemal*. Ankara: Kültür ve Turizm Bakanlığı Yayınları, 1985.

Finefrock, Michael. "Ataturk, Lloyd George and the Megali Idea: causes and consequences of the Greek plan to seize Constantinople from the Allies, June–August 1922." *The Journal of Modern History* 52 (March 1980): 1047–66.

Fromkin, David. *A Peace to End All Peace: the Fall of the Ottoman Empire and the Creation of the Modern Middle East*. New York: Avon Books, 1989.

Gawrych, George W. *The Crescent and the Eagle: Ottoman Rule, Islam and the Albanians, 1874–1913*. London: I.B.Tauris, 2006.

____. "İstiklal Harbi'nde Bir Askeri Önder Olasrak ATATÜRK," *Asker ve Devlet Adamı Atatürk Paneli (Doğumunun 128'inci Yıl Dönümü Anısına)*. Ankara: Genelkurmay Askeri Tarih ve Stratejik Etüt Başkanlığ Yayınları, 2009, 3–8.

____. "Kemal Ataturk's politico-military strategy in the Turkish War of Independence, 1919–22: From guerrilla warfare to the decisive battle," *The Journal of Strategic Studies* 11 (September 1988), 318–41.

____. "The Rock of Gallipoli," in *Studies in Battle Command* by the Combat Studies Institute. Fort Leavenworth, KS: U.S. Army Command and General Staff College, 1995, 87–95.

____. "Siyasi ve Askeri Deha Olarak Atatürk," *İşveren* 46 (Kasım 2007), 3–26.

Georges-Gaulis, Berthe. *Le nationalisme turc.* Paris: Libraire Plon, 2007.

Gingeras, Ryan. *Sorrowful Shores: Violence, Ethnicity, and the End of the Ottoman Empire, 1912–1923.* Oxford: Oxford University Press, 2009.

Goloğlu, Mahmut. *Erzurum Kongresi.* İstanbul: Türkiye İş Bankası Kültür Yayınları, 2008.

____. *Sivas Kongresi.* İstanbul: Türkiye İş Bankası Kültür Yayınları, 2008.

Gökay, Bülent. *A Clash of Empires: Turkey between Russian Bolshevism and British Imperialism, 1918–1923.* London: I.B.Tauris, 1997.

Görgülü, İsmet. *Büyük Taarruz.* Ankara: Genelkurmay Basımevi, 1992.

Grassi, Fabio L. *Atatürk.* İstanbul: Turkuvaz, 2009.

Hanioğlu, M. Şükrü. *Atatürk: An Intellectual Biography.* Princeton, NJ: Princeton University Press, 2011.

____. "Garbcılar: Their attitudes toward religion and their impact on the official ideology of the Turkish Republic," *Studia Islamica* 86 (August 1997), 133–158.

Heper, Metin. *The State and Kurds in Turkey: the Question of Assimilation.* New York: Palgrave, 2007.

Hovannisian, Richard G. *The Republic of Armenia: Vol. II, From Versailles to London, 1919–1920* (Berkeley: University of California Press, 1982.

____. *The Republic of Armenia: Vol. IV, Between Crescent and Sickle: Partition and Sovietization.* Berkeley: University of California Press, 1996.

Howard, Howard N. *The Partition of Turkey: A Diplomatic History, 1913–1923.* Norman: Oklahoma University Press, 1931.

Howard, Michael. "Men against fire: the doctrine of the offensive in 1914," in *Makers of Modern Strategy: from Machiavelli to the Nuclear Age,* edited by Gordon A. Craig and Felix Gilbert. Princeton: Princeton University Press, 1986, 510–26.

İlhan, Suat. *Atatürk ve Askerlik: Düşünce ve Uygalamaları.* Ankara: Atatürk Araştırma Merkezi, 1990.

İskora, Muharrem Mazlum. *Türk Ordusu Kurmaylık (Erkanıharbiye) Tarihçesi.* Ankara: Harb Akademsi Matbaası, 1944.

Jenkins, Peter Kincaid. "The Greco-Turkish War, 1920–22," *International Journal of Middle East Studies* 10 (November 1979), 553–65.

Karpat, Kemal H. *The Politicization of Islam: Reconstructing Identity, Faith, and Community in the Late Ottoman State.* New York: Oxford University Press, 2001.

Kinross, Lord. *Ataturk: A Biography of Mustafa Kemal, Father of Modern Turkey.* New York: W. Morrow, 1965.

Knudson, Erik Lance. *Great Britain, Constantinople, and the Turkish Peace Treaty 1919–1922.* New York: Garland Publishing, 1987.

Kongar, Emre. *Devrim Tarihi ve Toplumsalbilim Açısından Atatürk.* İstanbul: Remzi Kirabevi, 1983.

Köroğlu, Erol. *Ottoman Propaganda and Turkish Identity: Literature in Turkey during World War I.* London: I.B.Tauris, 2007.

Kreiser, Klaus. *Atatürk, Bir Biyografi,* translated by Dilek Zaptçioğlu. İstanbul: İletişim, 2010.

Latimer, Frederick. "The political philosophy of Mustapha Kemal Ataturk: as evidenced in his published speeches and interviews." Ph.D. dissertation, Princeton University, 1960.

Macfie, A. L. *Ataturk.* London: Longman, 1994.

Mango, Andrew. *Ataturk: The Biography of the Founder of Modern Turkey.* Woodstock, New York: Overlook Press, 2000.

____. "Ataturk and the Kurds," *Middle Eastern Studies* 35 (1999), 1–25.

____. *From Sultan to Ataturk: Turkey.* London: Haus, 2009.

McDowall, David. *A Modern History of the Kurds.* London: I.B.Tauris, 1996.

McCarthy, Justin. *Death and Exile: the Ethnic Cleansing of Ottoman Muslims, 1821–1992.* Princeton, NJ: Darwin Press, 1996.

____. *The Ottoman Peoples and the End of Empire.* London: Arnold, 2001.

Müdderisoğlu, Alptekin. *Sakarya Meydan Muharebeşş Günlüğü*. Ankara: Kastaş Yayınevi, 2004.

Natali, Denise. *The Kurds and the State: Evolving National Identity in Iraq, Turkey, and Iran*. Syracuse: Syracuse University Press, 2005.

Okyar, Osman. "Turco-British relations in the inter-war period: Fethi Okyar's missions to London," in *Four Centuries of Turco-British Relations: Studies in Diplomatic, Economic and Cultural Affairs*. Edited by William Hale and Ali İhsan Bağış. North Humberside: The Eothen Press, 1984, pp. 62–79.

Orga, İrfan and Margarete. *Atatürk*. London: Michael Joseph, 1962.

Özakman, Turgut. *Şu Çılgın Türkler*. Ankara: Bilgi Yayınevi, 2011.

Özdemir, Hikmet. *Atatürk'ün Liderlik Sırları*. İstanbul: Remzi Kitabevi, 2006.

____. *The Ottoman Army 1914–1918: Disease and Death on the Battlefield*. Salt Lake City: University of Utah Press, 2008.

Özkaya, Yücel. *Milli Mücadelede Atatürk ve Basım*. 2 vols. İstanbul: Cumhuriyet, 2001.

Öztoprak, İzzet. *Kurtuluş Savaşında Türk Basını, Mayıs 1919-Temmuz 1921*. Ankara: Türkiye İş Bankası Kültür Yayınları, 1981.

Shaw, Stanford J. and Ezel Kural Shaw, *History of the Ottoman Empire and Modern Turkey*, II: *Reform, Revolution, and Republic: the Rise of Modern Turkey 1808–1975*. Cambridge: Cambridge University Press, 1977.

Simon, Rachel. "Prelude to reforms: Mustafa Kemal in Libya," in *Atatürk and the Modernization of Turkey*, edited by Jacob M. Landau. Boulder, CO: Westview Press, 1984, pp. 17–23.

Smith, Michael Llewellyn. *Ionian Vision: Greece in Asia Minor, 1919–1922*. London: Hurst and Company, 1973

Sonyel, Salahi R. *Atatürk – The Founder of Modern Turkey*. Ankara: Türk Tarih Kurumu, 1989.

____. *Turkish Diplomacy 1913–1923: Mustafa Kemal and the Turkish National Movement*. London: Sage Publications, 1975.

Spinall-Oglander, C. F. *Military Operations, Gallipoli*, 2 vols. London: Heinemann, 1929–1931.

Süslü, Azmi and Mustafa Balcıoğlu, *Atatürk'ün Silah Arkadaşları – Atatürk Araştırma Merkezi Şeref Üyeleri*. Ankara: Atatürk Araştırma Merkezi, 1999.

Şapolyo, Enver Behnan. *Kuvayi Milliye Tarihi: Gerilla*. Ankara: Ayyıldız ve Gazetecilik, 1957.

Şıvgın, Hale. *Trablusgarp Savaşı ve 1911–1912 Türk-İtalyan İlişkileri*. Ankara: Türk Tarih Kurumu Basımevi, 1989.

Şimşir, Bilal N. *Bizim Diplomatlar*. Ankara: Bilgi Yayınevi, 19.

T. C. Genelkurmay Başkanlığı and Harp Tarihi Dairesi, *Birinci Dünya Harbi'nde Türk Harbi*, II/2: *Kafkas Cephesi, 2 nci Ordu Harekatı: 1916–1918*. Ankara: Genelkurmay Basımevi, 1978.

____. *Birinci Dünya Harbi'nde Türk Harbi V: Çanakkale Cephesi Harekatı 1 nci, 2 nci ve 3 ncü Kitapların Özetlenmiş Tarihi (Haziran 1914 – 9 Ocak 1916)*. Ankara: Genelkurmay Basım Evi, 2002.

____. *Birinci Dünya Harbi'nde Türk Harbi* (BDH): *Kafkas Cephesi, 2 nci Cilt, 2 nci Kısım Kafkas Cephesi, 2 nci Ordu Harekatı: 1916–1918*. Ankara: Genelkurmay Basımevi, 1978.

____. *Türk İstiklal Harbi* (TIH), II: *Batı Cephesi, 3: Birinci, İkinci İnönü, Aslıhanlar ve Dumlupınar Muaerebleri (9 Kasım 1920 – 15 Nisan 1921)*. Ankara: Genelkurmay Basımevi, 1966.

____. *Türk İstiklal Harbi*, II: *Batı Cephesi, 4: Kütahya, Eskişehir Muaerebleri (15 Mayıs 1921 – 25 Temmuz 1921)*. Ankara: Genelkurmay Basımevi, 1974.

____. *Türk İstiklal Harbi*, II: *Batı Cephesi, 5/1: Sakarya Meydan Muharebesinden Önceki Olaylar ve Mevzi İlerisindeki Harekat (25 Temmuz – 22 Ağustos 1921)*. Ankara: Genelkurmay Basımevi, 1972.

____. *Türk İstiklal Harbi*, II: *Batı Cephesi, 6/1: Kitap Büyüuk Taarruza Hazırlık ve Büyük Taarruz (10 Ekim 1921 – 31 Temmuz 1922)*. Ankara: Genelkurmay Basımevi, 1967.

____. *Turk İstiklal Harbi*, II: *Batı Cephesi, 6/2: Büyük Taarruz (1–31 Ağustos 1922)*. Ankara: Genel Kurmay Basımevi, 1995.

261

____. *Türk İstiklal Harbi*, II:, *Batı Cephesi*, 6/4: *İstiklal Harbinin Son Safhası (18 Eylul 1922: 1 Kasım 1923)*. Ankara: Genelkurmay Basımevi, 1969.

____. *Türk İstiklal Harbi*, III: *Doğu Cephesi (1919–1921)*. Ankara: Genelkurmay Basımevi, 1965.

____. *Türk İstiklal Harbi*, IV: *Güney Cephesi (15 Mayıs 1919–30 Ekim 1921)*. Ankara: Genelkurmay Basımevi, 1965.

____. *Türk İstiklal Harbi*, VI: *İstiklal Harbinde Ayaklanmalar (1919–1921)* Ankara: Genelkurmay Basımevi, 1974.

____. *Türk İstiklal Harbi*, VII: *İdari Faaliyetler (15 Mayıs 1919 – 2 Kasım 1923)* Ankara: Genelkurmay Basımevi, 1975.

____. *Türk Silahlı Kuvvetleri Tarihi*, *III ncü cilt, 6 ncı Kısım (1908–1920)*. Ankara: Genelkurmay Basımevi, 1996.

____. *Türk Silahlı Kuvvetleri Tarihi*, *Türkiye Büyük Millet Meclisi Hükümeti Dönemi (23 Nisan 1920–29 Ekim 1923) IV ncü cilt, 1 nci Kısım*. Ankara: Genelkurmay Basımevi, 1984.

Tevetoğlu, Fethi. "Atatürk'le Okyar'ın Çıkardıkları Gazete: Minber," *Atatürk Araştırma Merkezi Degisi* 5/13 (Kasım 1988), 183–193.

Torumtay, Necip. *Atatürk: Çağdaş Türkiye Cumhuriyeti Devleti'nin Kurucusu Lider*. İstanbul: Doğan Kitapçılık, 2001.

Toynbee, Arnold J. *The Western Question in Greece and Turkey*. London: Constable and Company, 1923.

Tunaya, Tarik Z. *Türkiye Büyük Millet Meclisi Hükumeti'nin Kuruluş ve Siyasi Karakteri*. İstanbul: İstanbul Üniversitesi, 1958.

____. *Türkiye'de Siyasi Partiler*. İstanbul: Doğan Kardeş Matbaası, 1952.

Turan, Şerafettin. *Kendine Özgü bir Yaşam ve Kişilik: Mustafa Kemal Atatürk*. Ankara: Bilgi Yayınevi, 2008.

Turfan, M. Naim. *Rise of the Young Turks, the Military, and Ottoman Collapse*. London: I.B.Tauris, 2000.

Türkmen, Zekeriyya. *Milli Mücadele Yıllarında İstanbul Mitingleri, 15 Mayıs 1919: İzmir'in işgali üzerine aydınların kamuoyu oluşturma hereketi*. Ankara: Berikan Yayınları, 2007.

____. *Mütareke Döneminde Ordunun Durumu ve Yeniden Yapılması (1918–1920)*. Ankara: Türk Tarih Kurumu, 2001.

Türsan, Nurettin. *Atatürk'ün Türk Kurtuluş Savaşı Stratejisi*. Ankara: Genelkurmay Basımevi, 1983.

Üngör, Uğur Ümit. *The Making of Modern Turkey: Nation and State in Eastern Anatolia, 1913–1950*. Oxford: Oxford University Press, 2011.

Wallach, Jehuda L. *Bir Askeri Yardımın Anatomısı: Türkiye'de Prusya-Alman Askeri Heyetleri, 1835–1919*, translated by Fahri Çeliker. Ankara: Genelkurmay Basımevi, 1985.

Webster, Donald Everett. *The Turkey of Atatürk: Social Process in the Turkish Reformation*. Philadelphia: The American Academy of Political and Social Science, 1939.

Yasamee, F. A. K. "Colmar Freiherr von der Goltz and the rebirth of the Ottoman Empire." *Diplomacy and Statecraft* 9 (2 July 1998), 91–128.

Yel, Selma. *Yakup Şevki ve Askeri Faaliyetleri*. Ankara: Atatürk Araştırma Merkezi, 2002.

Yerasimos, Stefanos. *Türk-Sovyet İlişkileri: Ekim Devrimden "Milli Mücadele"ye*. İstanbul: Gözlem Yayınları, 1979.

Zeidner, Robert. *Tricolor over the Taurus: the Franco-Turkish War for Cilicia, Crucible for the National Liberation Movement*. Ankara: Turkish Historical Society, 2005.

Zürcher, Erik Jan. *Turkey: a Modern History*, 3rd ed. London: I.B.Tauris, 2004.

____. *The Unionist Factor: The Role of the Committee of Union and Progress in the Turkish Nationalist Movement, 1905–1926*. Leiden: Brill, 1984.

____. "The vocabulary of Muslim Nationalism," *International Journal of the Sociology of Language* 137 (1999), 81–92.

____. *The Young Turk Legacy and Nation Building: From the Ottoman Empire to Atatürk's Turkey*. London: I.B.Tauris, 2010.

Index

Numbers in bold indicate illustrations